VIETNAM:
A Guide to Reference Sources

Michael Cotter

G. K. HALL & CO., 70 LINCOLN STREET, BOSTON, MASS.

Copyright © 1977 by Michael Cotter

Library of Congress Cataloging in Publication Data

Cotter, Michael.
   Vietnam, a guide to reference sources.

   Includes index.
   1. Reference books--Vietnam. 2. Vietnam--
Bibliography. I. Title.
Z3228.V5C68 [DS556.3]   011'.02   77-22448
ISBN 0-8161-8050-4

This publication is printed on permanent/durable acid-free paper
MANUFACTURED IN THE UNITED STATES OF AMERICA

Contents

CONTENTS

Contents

Introduction

A reference work is generally considered to be a publication intended for consultation for a specific purpose rather than for consecutive reading. It includes "ready-reference" works such as dictionaries, handbooks, and atlases, and works that provide access to information that may be located elsewhere, such as bibliographies. This bibliography is the first known compilation of reference works about Vietnam. It lists about 1,400 books, periodical articles, serials, government publications, and other materials in the human and natural sciences, primarily in romanized Vietnamese (quốc-ngữ), French, and English from 1651 (the date of the first dictionary using romanized Vietnamese, by Msgr. Alexandre de Rhodes) until 1976. It is intended for use by persons interested in Vietnam at a beginning level as well as at an advanced level by including standard reference works on Vietnam and modern translations of classical texts. It is based on the holdings of the Harvard University Library and has been considerably supplemented by research in many bibliographies, documentary sources, and published catalogs of other libraries.

Arrangement

The bibliography is arranged in classified order, following the arrangement of Guide to reference books, by Constance M. Winchell, 8th ed. (Chicago: American Library Association, 1967). Most chapters are divided into "major sources" and "other sources" to reflect the amount of coverage of material about Vietnam in the respective sections; also, although a user of this bibliography might not have access to any of the "major sources," the "other sources" might be sufficient to provide some basic reference information about Vietnam. Except for part A General Reference Works, the section titled "major sources" in each chapter is arranged by type of work (bibliographies, dictionaries, etc.), by historical period, or by botanical and zoological classification. The publications in each section are arranged alphabetically, beginning with the important and comprehensive bibliographies by Henri Cordier (Bibliotheca indosinica, described in entry AA23) and Paul Boudet and Rémy Bourgeois (Bibliographie de l'Indochine française, entry AA22). The exceptions to the arrangement used by Winchell are chapter CE Mythologya (which has been omitted and for which the reader should consult chapters BD Literature and

CF Folklore) and part D Area Studies (for which I have substituted History and Related Subjects).

Citations and references

Each citation is as bibliographically complete as possible, and most entries have been verified in a standard bibliography or library catalog. Works which could be verified have an abbreviation of the name of the library in which a copy was located or the bibliographic source which cited the publication; these abbreviations and sources are placed at the lower left-hand line of the annotation or in the body of the annotation, and a list of them is at the end of this Introduction. Each publication I have not examined personally is indicated with an asterisk (*) after the entry number, such as for entry *AA29. The annotations describe the arrangement, scope, and format as well as the presence of special features such as annotations, indexes, or appendices; they are not intended to be critical annotations of the contents. In instances where I have located book reviews in the course of the compilation, I have included the citations. In most cases, the inclusive pagination is given, omitting preliminary pagination; no distinction is made between works printed on one side of a page (leaves) or on both sides (pages).

Each Vietnamese-language work has been checked against A checklist of the Vietnamese holdings of the Wason Collection, Cornell University Libraries, by Giok Po Oey (AA38), and if located therein has been marked "NIC," corresponding to the abbreviation used for the Cornell University Libraries among American and Canadian libraries. The Southeast Asia catalog of the Cornell University Libraries (AA24) was published only in 1976, by which time this manuscript was substantially complete and the publisher's deadline was near; it is unlikely that a thorough search in it would have turned up many additional references, in view of the number of other bibliographies that I searched.

Each citation in the bibliography has an entry number (AA1, AA2, etc.) similar to the type of entry numbers used by Winchell; the references in the index are for these entry numbers.

Entries

In most cases, the form and choice of entry has followed the usual practices among American libraries. Names of Western authors are entered under the family name, followed by the personal name. Names of Vietnamese authors are entered under the family name, with the first letter of each element of the name capitalized and no hyphens between the elements of the name:

Nguyễn Hùng Cường
    not
Nguyễn-hùng-Cường (usually on the title page)
    nor
Nguyễn, Hùng Cường
    nor
Cường, Nguyễn Hùng (usually in indexes)

This is the form recommended by the Vietnam Studies Group--a group of American scholars--to the Library of Congress, as described in entry AB2; it is the order in which names appear on the title page and is the most convenient way for persons unfamiliar with the structure of Vietnamese names to write them.

In most instances, I have included the necessary diacritical markings with the names of personal authors; in a few cases where I could not establish the correct markings, I have omitted them.

Certain types of government publications--constitutions, laws and statutes, and treaties or other international agreements--are entered under the name of the government followed by the "form heading":

Indochina. Laws, statutes, etc.
Vietnam (Democratic Republic). Constitution, 1946.
Vietnam (Republic). Treaties, etc.

In entries where an issuing body is cited on the title page of the publication, but another heading has been chosen for the entry, an "at head of title" note is included after the bibliographic description:

DE21 Geneva. Conference, 1954. Conférence de
      Genève sur l'Indochine.... Paris:
      Impr. Nationale, 1955. 470 p. At head
      of title: Ministère des affaires
      étrangères.

In this case, some libraries might use the entry:

France. Ministère des Affaires étrangères.
    Conférence de....

The exceptions to the form of catalog entry generally used among American libraries are for official publications, in order to differentiate between various Vietnamese governments, or as in the first example below, to eliminate redundancy:

Indochina instead of Indochina, French;
Cochinchina as a French colony; and
Cochinchina (Republic) for the government from
    1946 to 1949;
Vietnam (Democratic Republic) instead of Viet-
    nam (Democratic Republic, 1946-);
Vietnam (State) from 1949 to 1955; and
Vietnam (Republic) from 1955 to 1975 instead of
    Vietnam.

Suggestions for using the bibliography

This bibliography is arranged in classified order so that most of the works on a subject will appear in the chapter most directly related to that subject. Several bibliographies and other reference works cover more than one subject, however, and have been placed in certain "broad-area" chapters such as AA Bibliography, AF Periodicals, CA Social Sciences, CI Political Science and Government, DB History--bibliographies, and EA Science. The user should therefore consult a selection of bibliographies or other reference works in the chapters most directly related to one's interest as well as look through the broad-area chapters. This will enable the user to review the range of publications in the field and to find works on subjects that have not been well-documented in this bibliography, such as education and sociology.

The level of one's research and knowledge about Vietnam will also influence the uses made of this bibliography. An undergraduate writing a term paper on political events in the Republic of Vietnam, for example, might find all of the necessary material in English or French in the Bibliography of Asian studies (AA21) without using any sources in chapter CI Political Science and Government, while a scholar writing about Vietnamese society during the 18th century might use the works under "Traditional Vietnam" in chapter CI, chapter CJ Law, and the "Classical histories" in chapter DA History--general works. Finally, the user should look at "ready-reference" works such as encyclopedias, handbooks, and general history texts for factual background information. Three useful works in these categories are the Historical and cultural dictionary of Vietnam, by Danny J. Whitfield (AD4), Connaissance du Viêt-Nam, by Pierre Huard and Maurice Durand (DF3), and Le Viêt-Nam, histoire et civilisation, by Lê Thành Khôi (DA7).

Terminology

In most instances, the annotation for a publication specifies the terminology for Vietnam as used in that publication if it is not readily apparent. For anyone studying Vietnam through Western writings, however, it is necessary to remember that the terminology has changed over the centuries, and one might find the following terms used: Annam, Cochinchina (or Cochinchine), French Indochina, Indochina (or Indochine and Indochine française), Tonkin, Tongking, Tunquin, and Vietnam.

Throughout the bibliography, the term "Vietnam" is used to refer to the territory of Vietnam without regard to political divisions. Where it is necessary to differentiate between the different political entities, I have used the official terms: Democratic Republic of Vietnam (DRVN), Republic of Vietnam (RVN), National Front for the Liberation of South Vietnam (NFLSVN), or Provisional Revolutionary Government of the Republic of South Vietnam (PRG). (I do not use the term "Việt Cộng," literally "Vietnamese Communist," which is an epithet used by the Republic of Vietnam and its allies to refer to their opponents.)

The terms "Vietnam war" and "the present war" refer to the war which intensified in 1961 and ended on April 30, 1975, with the surrender of the government of the Republic of Vietnam to the Provisional Revolutionary Government.

The terms "North," "South," and "Center" have been used to specify the traditional areas of Vietnam before French colonial rule, during which the corresponding areas were Tongking, Cochinchina, and Annam.

Limitations of the bibliography

This bibliography has several recognized limitations or omissions in coverage, some unavoidable and others intentional. The limitation I regret the most is reference works from the Democratic Republic of Vietnam, which are difficult to obtain outside of the country. Another limitation is reference works in Chinese, Japanese, and Russian languages, with a few exceptions for the bibliographies in entries AA91 to AA97, language dictionaries, and works on statistics, economics, and treaties concerning the DRVN. A third major limitation is works about the ethnic minorities in Vietnam, which was made in order to keep the bibliography within a definite focus and to avoid extending it beyond its already lengthy size. Eight publications are listed in chapter AA (references AA98 to AA105) as introduction to the literature. This brief listing is in no way intended to detract from the importance of ethnic minorities in Vietnamese history and their contribution to Vietnamese society.

The bibliography omits instructional materials for learning Vietnamese and many English-and-Vietnamese language dictionaries that were published in Saigon during the 1960's that did not seem to be of scholarly value. It also omits many grammars and dictionaries published before 1935 that were cited in the bibliographies by Henri Cordier and by Boudet and Bourgeois.

Many short bibliographies have been omitted because they did not add to the information available in more extensive bibliographies listed in this work; among English-language publications, the bibliographies in the works by Joseph Buttinger (DA6) and the American University (AA105, DF1) contain more references than did several other separately-published bibliographies that were at first considered for inclusion but finally omitted.

This bibliography does not include unpublished works such as papers prepared for conferences or for personal or classroom use and computer print-outs of data files because bibliographic access to these materials is unreliable. It also omits descriptions of data files themselves, which could be a topic for separate research, particularly in view of the number of public opinion surveys, statistical surveys concerning wartime conditions, and other research by American scholars during the 1960's and early 1970's.

Although the bibliography includes a few works of major importance published in 1975 and 1976, for the most part the coverage ends in 1974. It does not include materials on the last months of the war nor on the occupation of Saigon by the Provisional Revolutionary Government on April 30, 1975. This gap in coverage should not deter one from using this bibliography as a source of research into continuing events in Vietnam, however, for many bibliographies and other publications are serials and will continue to include publications about Vietnam or current events there.

Finally, this bibliography includes no references to the Vietnam studies newsletter, published by the Vietnam Studies Group, of the Association for Asian Studies. Although the Newsletter does not contain substantive articles on reference works, it publishes news of current research, translations, new publications, library collections, and other information about Vietnamese studies in North America. Its counterpart in France is the Institut d'Etude du Viet-Nam Contemporain, which issues a newsletter, Notes et informations, and a journal, Vietnam contemporain.

* * *

During the eight years of work on this bibliography, I received assistance from several people. I am particularly indebted to Mr. Nguyễn Hùng Cường, former Acting Director of National Archives and Libaries in Saigon, who has corresponded with me since 1970 and has sent many bibliographies published in Saigon. Since immigrating to the United States in 1975, he has continued our correspondence and read a draft of the manuscript. Without his assistance, I could not have included so many reference works from Saigon and would not have been able to verify most of the historical texts cited in the bibliography.

I am indebted in a personal way to my wife, Mary, who with our daughter Ellen has not only sustained me and put up with this disruption in our family life, but resumed her career outside the home which enabled me to continue working on this bibliography in 1976 and 1977.

I am grateful to the Vietnam Studies Group and the Committee on Research Materials on Southeast Asia (CORMOSEA) of the Association for Asian Studies for their grants for defraying the expenses of preparing the manuscript and the index. I also appreciate the contribution of the Harvard University Library, Douglas W. Bryant, Director, for released time from work while I was Chief Documents Librarian. I have based the format of this bibliography on the classified arrangement of Guide to reference books, 8th ed., by Constance M. Winchell (Chicago: American Library Association, 1967) and am using this format with the permission of the American Library Association.

Several librarians in Widener Library helped with ideas or research or read the manuscript at various stages: Vida Margaitis and David Paul (of the Government Documents Section); Sheila Hart, Heather Cole, and Marion Schoon (Reference Division); Edwin E. Williams (Associate University Librarian); Hilda Conlan, Edward Peterson, Barbara Dames, and Ruth Hoppe (Inter-Library Loan); and Marie Carden and Maria Brasil (typing correspondence while with Government Documents). Edith Kimball, Reference Librarian for Documents at the Countway Library of Medicine, explained the MEDLINE system for searching medical literature by computer. Frank E. Trout, Curator of the Justin Winsor Map Room in the Harvard College Library, explained the mapping system of the U.S. Army Map Service.

Others who read the manuscript and corrected typographical errors were Allan E. Goodman, Nguyễn Ngọc Huy, Huỳnh Sanh Thông, Trần Văn Liêm, and Tạ Văn Tài. Professor Robert Silberglied, of the Museum of Comparative Zoology at Harvard University, and Dr. J. L. Gressitt, of the Wau Ecology Institute of Papua New Guinea, read the section on insects.

Finally, I want to acknowledge the contribution of Barbara Garrey, of G. K. Hall & Co., for imposing order upon the manuscript.

Despite the suggestions and other contributions of persons mentioned above, I alone am responsible for the content of this bibliography.

Abbreviations

ACRPP: Association pour la Conservation et la
Reproduction de la Presse Photographique

AID: U.S. Agency for International Development

Ajia: Ajia Keizai Kenkyūjo [Institute of Asian Economic Affairs], Tokyo. Union catalogue of documentary materials on Southeast Asia (AA18)

Anglemyer-Gee-Koll: Editors of Selected bibliography, Lower Mekong Basin (AA50)

Anh: Nguyễn Thế Anh. Bibliographie critique sur les relations entre le Viet-Nam et l'Occident (DB13)

BAS: Bibliography of Asian studies (AA21)

BAVH: Bulletin de la Société des Amis du Vieux Hué (AF38)

BCAI: Bulletin du Comité Agricole et Industriel de la Cochinchine (AF30)

BEFEO: Bulletin de l'Ecole française d'Extrême-Orient (AF32)

BEI: Bulletin économique de l'Indochine (CG6)

BGI: Bibliographie géographique internationale (CK6)

BMC: British Museum. Dept. of Printed Books. General catalogue of printed books

BN: Bibliothèque nationale, Paris. Catalogue général des livres imprimés: Auteurs

BOIC: Bulletin officiel de l'Indochine française (CJ75)

BSEI: Bulletin de la Société des Etudes indochinoises (AF39)

BSGF: Bulletin de la Société géologique de la France

BSGI: Bulletin de la Société Géologique de l'Indochine

Berton: Berton, Peter, and Alvin Z. Rubenstein. Soviet works on Southeast Asia (AA93)

Biblo. Services: Bibliographical services throughout the world, 1965-1969, comp. by Paul Avicenne. Paris: UNESCO, 1972.

Bongert: Bongert, Yvonne. "Indochine." In Introduction bibliographique à l'histoire du droit et à l'ethnologie juridique (CJ7)

Boudet 1: Boudet, Paul, and Rémy Bourgeois. Bibliographie de l'Indochine française, 1913-1926 (AA22)

Boudet 2: ____. ____, 1927-1929

Boudet 3: ____. ____, 1930.

Boudet 4: ____. ____, 1930-1935: Matières

CBVNCH: Vietnam (Republic). Công-báo Việt-Nam Cộng-hòa (CJ95)

Châu: Phan Thiện Châu, Vietnamese communism, a research bibliography (CI48)

Connaissance du Việt-Nam: Huard, Pierre, and Maurice Durand, Connaissance du Việt-Nam (DF3)

CORDS: U.S. Military Assistance Command, Vietnam. Civil Operations for Revolutionary Development Support.

CtY: Yale University Library

CtY-L: Yale Law Library

CU: University of California Library, Berkeley

Cordier: Cordier, Henri. Bibliotheca indosinica (AA23)

Cường: Nguyễn Hùng Cường. Correspondence with the compiler

Cường, Soc sci.: Nguyễn Hùng Cường. Thư-tịch về khoa-học xã-hội tại Việt-Nam; ...a bibliography of social science materials published in Vietnam (1947-1967) (CA2)

Cương mục: Khâm định Việt-sử thông-giám cương-mục (DA3)

DAS: U.S. Dept. of Environmental Sciences Services Administration, Atmospheric Sciences Library

DDC: Dewey Decimal Classification

DLC: U.S. Library of Congress

DLC SAAL: ____. ____. Orientalia Division.
  Southern Asia accessions list (AA27)

DLC Phillips: ____. ____. Map Division. A list
  of geographic atlases in the Library of Congress,
  comp. by Philip Lee Phillips (CK12)

DNAL: U.S. National Agricultural Library

DRVN: Democratic Republic of Vietnam

DSm: Smithsonian Institution Library

Diêu: Phạm Văn Diêu. "200 năm lịch sử văn học Nhà
  Lý." (BD22)

EARI: U.S. Engineer Agency for Resources Inventories. (Copy annotated usually verified in Vietnam subject index catalog (AA25)

ECAFE: United Nations. Economic Commission for
  Asia and the Far East

EFEO: Ecole française d'Extrême-Orient

ESCAP: United Nations. Economic and Social Commission for Asia and the Pacific

FGI: Flore générale de l'Indochine (EC24)

FLPH: Foreign Languages Publishing House, Hanoi

Gélinas: André Gélinas, mail order service for
  books from Saigon (until April 1975)

GPO: United States Government Printing Office

Grandin: Grandin, A. Bibliographie générale des
  sciences juridiques, politiques, économiques et
  sociales de 1800 à 1925/26 (CJ6)

Gregory: List of the serial publications of foreign
  governments, 1815-1931, comp. by Winifred
  Gregory (AH1)

ICarbS: Southern Illinois University, Carbondale,
  Ill., Library

ICC: International Commission for Supervision and
  Control

ICRL: Center for Research Libraries, Chicago

ICSC: International Commission for Supervision and
  Control

IDC: Inter-Documentation Center, Zug, Switzerland

IDEO: Imprimerie d'Extrême-Orient

JAS: Journal of Asian studies

JOIF: Journal officiel de l'Indochine française
  (CJ76)

JORF: Journal officiel de la République française

JPRS: U.S. Joint Publications Research Service.

JSEAH: Journal of Southeast Asian history

Johnson: Johnson, Donald Clay. A guide to reference
  materials on Southeast Asia (AA6)

Jumper: Jumper, Roy L. Bibliography on the political and administrative history of Vietnam, 1802-
  1962 (DB9)

Keyes: Keyes, Jane Godfrey. A bibliography of
  Western-language publications concerning North
  Vietnam in the Cornell University Library (CI55)

Khai-trí: Nhà sách Khai-trí. Thư-mục 1968 (AA78)

Kiel: Kiel. Universität. Institut für Weltwirt-
  schaft. Bibliothek. Kataloge (CH4)

KimSa: Trần Thị KimSa. Bibliography on Vietnam,
  1954-1964 (CA7)

KimSa, "Mục-lục.": ____. "Mục-lục phân-tích tạp-chí
  Việt-ngữ" (AF18)

Kyoto: Kyoto University. Research Institute of
  Humanistic Studies. Annual bibliography of
  Oriental studies (AA19)

Lê Đình Tường: Lê Đình Tường. Thư mục về cuộc
  bành trướng quốc thổ Việt-Nam (DB10)

Lorenz: Catalogue général de la librairie française, 1840-1925

MB: Boston Public Library

MBCo: Countway Library of Medicine, Harvard
  University

MC: Monthly catalog of United States government
  publications (AH9)

mgc: Personal copy of the compiler

MH: Harvard College Library

MH-AH: Harvard University, Andover-Harvard Library

MH-B: ____, Biological Laboratories Library

MH-BH: ____, Blue Hill Meteorological Library

MH-CSCL: ____, Cabot Science Center Library

MH-E: ____, Gutman Library, Graduate School of
  Education

MH-EB: ____, Oakes Ames Library of Economic
  Botany

MH-F: ____, Farlow Reference Library of Cryptogamic Botany

MH-FA: ____, Fine Arts Library

MH-G: ____, Gray Herbarium Library

MH-Geol: ____, Geological Sciences Library

MH-H: ____, Houghton Library

MH-HS: ____, History of Science Library

MH-HY: ____, Harvard-Yenching Library

MH-L: ____, Law School Library

MH-M: ____, Gordon McKay Library

MH-Map: ____, Justin Winsor Map Room

MH-O: ____, Oakes Ames Orchid Library

MH-P: ____, Peabody Museum Library

MH-V: _____, Vietnamese library, c/o Harvard-
    Yenching Library

MH-Z: _____, Museum of Comparative Zoology Library

MiU-L: University of Michigan Law Library

MSGI: Mémoires du Service Géographique de l'Indo-
    chine

NCHC: Nghiên-cứu hành-chánh (Saigon)

NCLS: Nghiên-cứu lịch-sử (Hanoi)

NFLSVN: National Front for the Liberation of South
    Viet-Nam

NIC: Cornell University. (Vietnamese-language
    titles marked NIC have been located in A check-
    list of the Vietnamese holdings of the Wason
    collection, by Giok Po Oey (AA38)

NIC (date): Copy verified in the Southeast Asia
    accessions list, Cornell University, for that
    month

NjP: Princeton University Library

NLF: Abbreviated form of National Front for the
    Liberation of South Vietnam; see NFLSVN

NN: New York Public Library

NNC: Columbia University Library

NTIS: National Technical Information Service, U.S.
    Dept. of Commerce. Copies of publications indi-
    cated with "AD" or "PB" prefixes are available
    for purchase in printed or microfiche copy from
    NTIS

Novaiia: Novaiia literatura po Iuzhnoi, Iugo-
    Vostochnoi Azii [etc.]

PLTS: Pháp-lý tập-san (Saigon)

PRO: Gt. Brit. Public Record Office

QH: Quê-hương (Saigon)

QPVT: Quy-pháp vựng-tập (CJ91) (Saigon)

RQ: RQ (Chicago, American Library Association)

RVN: Republic of Vietnam

Smith: Smith, Ralph B. "Sino-Vietnamese sources
    for the Nguyễn period" (DB16)

SOAS: London. University. School of Oriental and
    African Studies

TTAPC: Thư-tịch về ấn-phẩm-công Việt-Nam; bibliog-
    raphy on Vietnamese official publications, 1960-
    1971 (AH4)

TTHTQGVN: Thư-tịch hồi-tố quốc-gia Việt-Nam, retro-
    spective national bibliography of Vietnam (1963-
    1967) (AA84)

TTTV, VQGTK: Tin tức thư-viện, Viện Quốc-gia Thống-
    kê (CG3)

TTQGVN: Thư-tịch quốc-gia Việt-Nam (AA82)

Thanh-long: Catalogs from Thanh-long, bookseller,
    Brussels

Thompson: Thompson, Laurence C. A Vietnamese
    grammar (BC13)

Thư-mục: Thư-mục; catalogue of books (AA81)

Toàn-thư: Đại Việt sử-ký toàn-thư (DA2)

Unesco: Vietnam (Republic). National Commission
    for UNESCO. Thư-mục chú-giải về văn-hóa Việt-
    Nam...commented bibliography on Vietnamese cul-
    ture (CA6)

USAID: U.S. Agency for International Development

VN Buddh.: Vietnam (Republic). Nha Văn-khố và
    Thư-viện Quốc-gia. Thư-tịch về Phật-giáo...a
    bibliography on Buddhism (BB6)

Williams: Williams, Llewelyn, Vegetation of South-
    east Asia... (EK31)

Woodside: Woodside, Alexander B. Vietnam and the
    Chinese model. Cambridge: Harvard University
    Press, 1971

ZR: Zoological record

Glossary

*: copy not verified personally by the compiler

1. éd.: first edition (or 2. éd., second edition)-- used for French-language titles

[ ]: printed material relating to the author, title, or publication information that does not appear on the title page

bộ mới: new series

comp.: compiler; compiled by

của: written by

dịch: translator; translated by

do: written by

éd.: éditeur; édition

ed.: editor; édition; edited by

et al: and others

enl.: enlarged [edition]

Hán: Sino-Vietnamese characters (or Chinese characters)

hiệu đính: to revise, edit

impr.: imprimerie

in lần 2 or in lần 2: second edition

n.d.: no date of publication

n.p.: no publisher; no place of publication

n.s.: new series; nouvelle série

nôm: demotic or vulgar script, as distinct from Hán script

p. or pp.: pages

phiên âm và chú thích: to transcribe phonetically and annotate

phiên âm và dịch nghĩa: to transcribe phonetically and translate

quốc-ngữ: romanized Vietnamese. Literally "national language," before the 20th century, was used to distinguish Vietnamese language from Chinese language used by scholars and mandarins

repr.: reprint

rev.: revise; revised; reviewed by

trans.: translator; translated by

từ-điển: dictionary of words and expressions

tự-điển: dictionary giving individual morphemes and corresponding Sino-Vietnamese characters

U.P.: University Press

x. b.: xuất bản [publisher]

A General Reference Works

BIBLIOGRAPHY AA

Bibliographies are important for beginning a search of the published literature on a topic, for obtaining complete bibliographic descriptions of printed materials, and for locating additional publications which may be omitted from less comprehensive subject bibliographies. This chapter consists of bibliographies on a variety of subjects too broad to include in the specific subject chapters in this Guide. It begins with bibliographies of bibliographies, among which the Bibliographic index (AA4) is useful for finding bibliographies published as part of books or periodical articles. The section "Reference works" includes bibliographies on a variety of subjects, such as are found in this Guide. The section "Historical bibliography" lists the bibliographies which have enumerated printed works during the course of Vietnamese history. Note that this section is arranged chronologically by date of publication.

In the next two sections, the major difference between the bibliographies of "primary importance" and "secondary importance" is the extent of coverage. In both cases, the scope of the works comprises all or nearly all topics; otherwise, a bibliography has been placed in a separate chapter according to its subject. The section of bibliographies published before Henri Cordier's Bibliotheca indosinica (AA23) are the French bibliographies on Vietnam covering literature from as early as Marco Polo's time.

The section "National and trade bibliography" consists of bibliographies which are compiled from publications submitted for copyright or for publishing license, acquisitions of a national library, and catalogs of publishing houses. The sections on bibliographies in Chinese, Japanese and Russian languages and on ethnic minorities are intended to provide only a selection of publications on those topics. In the final two sections, book reviews and translations are included as additional sources for bibliographical information.

BIBLIOGRAPHIES OF BIBLIOGRAPHIES

MAJOR SOURCES

AA1　Besterman, Theodore. A world bibliography of Oriental bibliographies, rev. and brought up to date by J. D. Pearson. Totowa, N.J.: Rowman and Littlefield, 1975. 727 p.

Based on Besterman's World bibliography of bibliographies, 4th ed., Geneva, 1965-66, 4 vols. Includes bibliographies in most languages, including Vietnamese, among which are several published in Saigon by the Nha Văn-Khố và Thư-Viện Quốc-Gia in the late 1960's. Bibliographic description usually includes an estimate of the number of citations in each bibliography. About 180 bibliographies are cited under "Southeast Asia" and "Indochina, Annam, Vietnam." Does not list bibliographies published in periodicals. No annotations. Author index.
MH

BIBLIOGRAPHY AA

AA2   Lê Xuân Khoa. "Vấn đề thư-tịch Việt-Nam"
[Bibliography in Vietnam]. Bách-khoa,
no. 128 (May 1962), 19-27.

    Bibliographical essay, discussing the
reasons for the sparse record of bibliographical activities for materials written
in Hán and Nôm, and listing over 20 bibliographical sources for modern Vietnamese
studies, all of which have been included
in this bibliography. Encourages the
compilation of a comprehensive bibliography for modern Vietnam to continue the
work of Boudet and Bourgeois.
MH-V

AA3   Maybon, Charles B. "Note sur les travaux
bibliographiques concernant l'Indochine
française." BEFEO, 10 (1910), 409-421.

    Bibliographic essay of 38 bibliogra-
phies published on various subjects between 1862 and 1910. Includes bibliographies which list only publications about
Indochina as well as those, such as Blair
and Robertson's The Philippine Islands,
which include some publications about
Indochina as part of a larger volume.
MH

OTHER SOURCES

AA4   Bibliographic index, a cumulative bibliography of bibliographies. New York:
Wilson, 1937- .

AA5   Centre for East Asian Cultural Studies,
Tokyo. A survey of bibliographies in
western languages concerning East and
Southeast Asian studies. [Ed. by Kazuo
Enoki, comp. by Tokihiko Tanaka], Tokyo
[1966-69], 2 vols. (Its Bibliography,
no. 4-5).

REFERENCE WORKS

MAJOR SOURCES

AA6   Johnson, Donald Clay. A guide to reference
materials on Southeast Asia, based on the
collections in the Yale and Cornell University libraries. New Haven and London:
Yale U.P., 1970. 160 p. (Yale Southeast
Asia studies, 6)

    Bibliography of "all reference books
and pamphlets in the Yale and Cornell
University libraries." Scope includes all
subjects and works in the Roman alphabet
or with a title page in the Roman alphabet. Not annotated. Does not list reference materials in periodicals. About
190 of the 1,970 works cited are about
Vietnam, most of which are included in
this Guide.
MH

AA7   U.S. Library of Congress. Orientalia Division. Southeast Asia; an annotated bibliography of selected reference sources,
comp. by Cecil Hobbs. Washington, D.C.,
1952. 163 p.

    Lists 345 publications, of which 50 are
on Indochina; see also "Southeast Asia--
general." Extensive descriptive annotations. Emphasis on French-language publications, which were readily available
at the time. "Reference sources" are defined to include bibliographies as well
as texts with background information on
history, economics, social conditions,
and cultural life.
MH

AA8 _____. _____. Southeast Asia; an annotated
bibliography of selected reference sources
in western languages. Rev. and enl.
Comp. by Cecil Hobbs. Washington, D.C.,
1964. 180 p.

Lists 535 publications, of which 85 are
on Vietnam, Laos, and Cambodia; see also
"Southeast Asia--general." Extensive descriptive annotations. Includes publications from Vietnam, studies and translations by the Human Relations Area Files,
and U.S. government publications. Updates
the 1952 bibliography (AA7), but does not
supersede it.

The 1952 edition should be consulted
for older publications; 27 titles about
Vietnam appearing in that edition are
omitted from the 1964 edition.
MH

OTHER SOURCES

AA9 Guide to reference books. [Ed.] Constance
M. Winchell. 8th ed. Chicago: American
Library Association, 1967. 741 p.

AA10 Guide to reference books, [First to third]
supplements, ed. Eugene P. Sheehy. Ibid.,
1968-1972. 3 vols.

AA11 Malclès, Louise-Noëlle. Les sources du travail bibliographique. Geneva: Droz,
1950-1958. 3 vols. in 4.

AA12 Nunn, G. Raymond. Asia, a selected and annotated guide to reference works. Cambridge: MIT Press [1971]. 223 p.

HISTORICAL BIBLIOGRAPHY

AA13 Lê Quý Đôn. "Nghệ-văn chỉ" [Literature].
In Đại Việt Thông Sử [Complete history of
Vietnam], 1749.
Annotated bibliography of 115 works in
government, classics and history, litera-

ture, and various subjects, from about
1026 to about 1786. Annotations are brief
commentaries on biographical or bibliographical information. Bibliography was
located in modern times only in 1922 (cf.
Trần Văn Giáp [AA17], p. 22) and therefore not available to Cadière and Pelliot
in 1904 (AA15).
Two major translations exist:
1) Emile Gaspardone, "Bibliographie annamite" (AA16), and 2) Trần Văn Giáp,
"Les chapitres bibliographiques de Lê-quý-
Đôn et de Phan-huy-chú" (AA17).

AA14 Phan Huy Chú. "Văn-tịch chỉ" [Bibliography].
In Lịch-triều hiến-chương loại-chỉ [Mono-
graphs of the institutions of the dynas-
ties], ca. 1821. See AD1 for description
of main work.
Annotated bibliography of chapters
42-45 in Lịch-triều. Contains 214 works
on government, classics and history, verse
and prose, and diverse subjects, from
about 1026 to about 1786, arranged chronologically within each subject. Based upon
"Nghệ-văn chỉ" by Lê Quý Đôn and adds
about 87 works to it. Annotations are
brief commentaries on biographical or
bibliographical information. A copy of
the original work was located only in
1907 (cf. BEFEO 7 (1907), p. 153) and
therefore was not available to Cadière and
Pelliot in 1904.
At least five translations of "Văn-tịch
chỉ" exist: 1) Translation of the complete text of Lịch-triều into quốc-ngữ
(Hanoi: Viện Sử Học, 1960-1961) (AD1);
2) Translation of the complete text of
Lịch-triều into quốc-ngữ and reprinting
of the Chinese characters as vol. 9 of
the edition published in Saigon (Bộ Văn
Hóa Giáo Dục và Thanh Niên, 1974; 272,
CCXIV p.) (AD1); 3) Emile Gaspardone,
"Bibliographie annamite" (AA16); 4) Trần

Văn Giáp, "Les chapitres bibliographiques
de Lê-quý-Đôn et de Phan-huy-chú" (AA17);
5) Huỳnh Khắc Dụng, Sử-liệu Việt-Nam (DB8).
Pp. 72-133 of the latter is an annotated
listing of titles in "Văn-tịch chí." Includes references to the annotations by
Gaspardone, Trần Văn Giáp, Pelliot and
Cadière, and other sources.

Of the latter three translations, the
versions by Trần Văn Giáp and Huỳnh Khắc
Dụng are arranged in order similar to the
original, while the annotations by Gaspardone are longest.

AA15   Cadière, L. M., and Paul Pelliot. "Première
étude sur les sources annamites de l'histoire d'Annam." BEFEO, 4 (1904), 617-671.
Also issued separately: Hanoi: IDEO,
1904. 55 p.

Study of historical materials in Chinese characters which are now located at
the Viện Khao Cô in Saigon (Jumper).
"Notes on five major Vietnamese works and
on the lives and work of 17 historians up
to the beginning of the nineteenth century." (Source: Trần Văn Giáp, "Chapitres
bibliographiques.") A bibliographic essay
with list of sources arranged by stroke
and list of authors by stroke. Includes
about 175 entries. Extensive footnotes,
listing various editions, including Japanese and French editions, and location of
manuscripts.

Based upon works cited in Đại Việt sử
ký (1272) and Khâm định Việt sử thông giám
cương mục (1859-1884, various editions),
neither of which were complete biblio-
graphic works. According to Trần Văn
Giáp, 1938, p. 21 (AA17), Cadière and
Pelliot listed only 40 of the 115 works in
"Nghệ-văn chí" and 133 of the 214 works in
"Văn-tịch chí."
MH

AA16   Gaspardone, Emile. "Bibliographie annamite." BEFEO, 34 (1934), 1-174.

Annotated translation of "Nghệ-văn chí"
by Lê Quý Đôn and of "Văn-tịch chí" by
Phan Huy Chú. Pp. 1-34, bibliographic essay on these and other historical writings. Pp. 35-174, bibliography of 154
publications, arranged according to one of
four subjects: government, history, literature, and myths, religions and diverse
topics. Annotations by Gaspardone are
lengthy, that for Sử-ký toàn-thư is 25
pages and includes the preface as originally written, a description of the
sources used in compiling it, and a résumé
of the Toàn-thư and its various editions.

Indexes by name (including names in
Sino-Vietnamese and in quốc-ngữ) and by
title or subject. Arrangement of the
bibliography itself does not follow the
arrangement of the original works by Lê
Quý Đôn and Phan Huy Chú, unlike the compilation by Trần Văn Giáp.
MH

AA17   Trần Văn Giáp. "Les chapitres bibliographiques de Lê-quí-Đôn et de Phan-huy-Chú."
BSEI, n.s. 13, 1 (1938), 1-217.

Annotated bibliography of the 329
titles in "Nghệ-văn chí" by Lê Quý Đôn
(AA13) and "Văn-tịch chí" by Phan Huy Chú
(AA14); an updated and revised version of
"Bibliographie annamite" by Gaspardone
(AA16). Pp. 46-98, integral translations
of titles listed by Lê Quý Đôn; pp. 99-140,
translation of titles listed by Phan Huy
Chú. Annotations by Trần Văn Giáp include
historical and bibliographical information, references to Cadière and Pelliot
(AA15), references to each title if included by Gaspardone, and references to
comments by Phan Huy Chú about titles
listed by Lê Quý Đôn. Indexes are in quốc
ngữ and Sino-Vietnamese characters.

Emphasis is on the influence of Chinese literature upon Vietnam, in order to give background information for a history of Chinese literature in Vietnam. Differs from Gaspardone's work which, in Giáp's words, was concerned especially with the history of books written by Vietnamese authors. Both works should be consulted, for annotations are different and works are complementary.

MH

BIBLIOGRAPHIES OF PRIMARY IMPORTANCE

AA18 Ajia Keizai Kenkyūjo. Union catalogue of documentary materials on Southeast Asia. Tokyo, 1964. 5 vols.

Subject listing of books in western European languages available in 31 libraries in Japan as of the end of 1961. Vol. 4, "Other countries in Asia" contains citations for publications on Indochina (pp. 58-139). Vol. 5, author index. Includes a large number of analyzed series.

MH

AA19 Annual bibliography of Oriental studies. Kyoto: Kyoto University, Research Institute of Humanistic Studies, 1935- .

Annual bibliography of books and articles in European and in Chinese, Japanese, and Korean languages. No index by country. Includes obituary articles and notices of book reviews. Unlike the Bibliography of Asian studies (AA21), includes fewer publications in English and more in Russian and Far Eastern languages. Includes very few publications in Vietnamese.

MH-HY

AA20 Association for Asian Studies. Cumulative bibliography of Asian studies, 1941-1965.

Boston: G. K. Hall, 1969. Author bibliography, 4 vols., subject bibliography, 4 vols.

_____. _____, 1966-1970. Ibid., 1972. Author bibliography, 3 vols., subject bibliography, 3 vols.

Photo-reproduction and cumulation of entries in the "Bulletin of Far Eastern Bibliography" and the "Bibliography of Asian Studies" (AA21). Important for Western-language books and periodical articles on the social sciences, with some emphasis on humanities. Scope includes publications and periodical articles from a wide variety of sources. See author bibliographies under "Vietnam" and "Vietnam (Democratic Republic)," "United States," and "United Nations" and subject bibliographies under "Indochina," "Vietnam," and "Vietnam, Cambodia, and Laos."

Title pages of 1941-1965 cumulation read "Association of Asian Studies."

MH

AA21 Bibliography of Asian studies. Ann Arbor, Mich.: Association for Asian Studies, 1941- . Title varies: 1941-1957, "Bulletin of Far Eastern bibliography," in Far Eastern quarterly. Issued as no. 5 of each volume of Journal of Asian studies, 1957-1968.

The basic annual bibliography of works on Asia in European languages. Emphasis is upon the social sciences and humanities. Includes books, pamphlets, periodical articles, dissertations, and official publications. Arranged by geographic area; references to Vietnam are usually in "Vietnam," "Indochina," and "Southeast Asia."

Issues for 1941-1970 are cumulated in the Cumulative bibliography of Asian studies, 1941-1965 and 1966-1970 (AA20).

MH

AA22   Boudet, Paul, and Rémy Bourgeois. Bibliographie de l'Indochine française. Hanoi:
IDEO; Paris: Maisonneuve, 1929-1967.
4 vols. in 5.

Contents: Vol. I, 1913-1926 (Hanoi,
1929); Vol. II, 1927-1929 (Hanoi, 1931);
Vol. III, 1930 (Hanoi, 1931); Vol. IV,
1931-1935: Ordre alphabétique (Hanoi,
1943, 496 p.); Vol. IV, 1931-1935:
Matières (Paris, 1967).

Second of two comprehensive bibliographies for Vietnamese studies in modern
times, preceded by the bibliography by
Cordier. Alphabetical arrangement by subject, with more than one listing per work
if appropriate, and author indexes in
vols. I-III. Vol. I lists some of the
works cited by Cordier, but includes periodical articles only if published after
1913. Some annotations. Vols. III and IV
include publications in vernacular languages published in 1930 or later, particularly valuable for locating Vietnamese-
language publications on Buddhism, Caodai-
ism, "Langue annamite," "Littérature annamite," and "Périodiques." Entries in
Vietnamese have titles translated into
French. Vol. IV includes publications in
Russian and some other European languages.

References in Vol. I were published serially in Revue indochinoise, n.s. 13
(1924)-14 (1925), and numbered 481-2020.
References before no. 481 were published
in RI (1921), 399-490 as Pour mieux con-
naître l'Indochine.

Vol. IV: Ordre alphabétique not at MH;
cited in La librairie française, tables
décennales, auteurs, 1946-1955, t. 1,
p. 275
MH

AA23   Cordier, Henri. Bibliotheca indosinica;
dictionnaire bibliographique des ouvrages
relatifs à la péninsule indochinoise.
Paris: Leroux, 1912-1915. 4 vols.

Index, par Mme. M.-A. Roland Cabaton.
Paris: Van Oest & Leroux, 1932. 309 p.
(Publications de l'École française d'Ex-
trême-Orient, 15-18 bis) Repr. New York:
Burt Franklin, 1967. 5 vols. in 3. (Burt
Franklin bibliographic & reference series,
no. 106.) Also repr. Taipei: Ch'eng Wen
Publishing Co., 1969. 5 vols.

First of two comprehensive bibliographies for Vietnamese studies in modern
times, followed by the bibliography by
Boudet and Bourgeois. Comprises publications in romanized languages from earliest
publications on Indochina until the early
twentieth century. Some annotations for
book reviews and additional bibliographic
information. Classified arrangement, with
references for Indochina in vols. 3 and 4.
MH

AA24   Cornell University. Libraries. Southeast
Asia catalog. [Compiled under the direction of Giok Po Oey.] Boston: G. K. Hall,
1976. 7 vols.

Catalog of books, serials, pamphlets,
newspapers, and maps on Southeast Asia in
all languages in the Wason Collection and
in other libraries at Cornell, published
in commemoration of the 25th anniversary
of the Cornell University Southeast Asia
Program.

Arranged by type of language (western,
vernacular, Russian, Chinese, Japanese,
other) and subdivided according to country and type of publication (monographs,
newspapers, serials, and maps). Entries
comprise one main entry card for each work
(no subject or cross-reference cards), although Vietnamese portion does include
cross-references from pseudonyms to actual
names.

For works on Vietnam, see vol. 3,
Western-language monographs; vol. 6, vernacular monographs; and vol. 7, serials,
newspapers, and maps; also vol. 1, general

monographs; vol. 3, monographs in Russian; vol. 6, monographs in Chinese, Japanese, and other languages, and general serials on Southeast Asia; and vol. 7, general maps on Southeast Asia. About 19,000 cards are listed in the various portions on Vietnam. Information in serials volumes includes issues received in the library.

"Introduction" to the vernacular language section on Vietnam in volume 6, by Prof. David W. P. Elliott, states that this is the best collection of Vietnamese language materials in the United States and emphasizes the balance, wide range of materials, and accessibility of the Wason Collection on Vietnam, with films of Sino-Vietnamese historical documents in the EFEO and Toyo Bunko collections; extensive runs on film or in hard copy of present-day and colonial-era serials; "a fairly complete collection of Vietnamese-language materials from both North and South in the post-1963 period...; [and] what may be the most extensive documentation on the Vietnamese side of the Vietnamese war of any single collection outside Vietnam."

The Southeast Asia catalog is in part a cumulation of listings from the Southeast Asia accessions list (monthly, 1957-) from the Wason Collection.
MH

AA25   U.S. Engineer Agency for Resources Inventories. Vietnam subject index catalog; research files of the Engineer Agency for Resources Inventories and Vietnam Research and Evaluation Information Center Bureau for Vietnam. [Eds. Gordon O. Allen and Michael J. Koll, Jr.] [Washington, D.C.] 1970. 288 p.

Subject list of the Library's holdings as of November 30, 1969. Contains over 4,500 entries--mostly in English--many listed several times under appropriate subjects. A major bibliography for publications on agriculture, aid and development, and political science, for reports prepared by consultants under contract to USAID, and for publications of U.S. government agencies in Vietnam. Library now defunct and materials dispersed.
MH

AA26   U.S. Library of Congress. Orientalia Division. Southeast Asia subject catalog. Boston: G. K. Hall, 1972. 6 vols.

Photographic reproduction of catalog cards, typed and manuscript cards, and index cards for books, periodicals and periodical articles, newspaper articles, dissertations, microfilms, pamphlets, and maps in Western languages. Not an official catalog of the Library of Congress, but a working tool to provide references to publications not usually cataloged separately. Compilation of the catalog began in 1943, but includes much retrospective indexing of journal articles published in Indochina during the colonial era. Arrangement for each country is alphabetical by subject. Coverage is wider than for Cumulative bibliography of Asian studies (AA20), particularly in the natural sciences. Unlike the Library of Congress bibliography on Indochina in 1950, this does not include publications in Vietnamese.

Vol. 5 includes South Vietnam and publications about Cochinchina and southern Annam, for the colonial era (pp. 418-795), and vol. 6 includes North Vietnam, Tongking, and northern Annam (pp. 1-212). Editing for publications from North and South Vietnam is not always consistent; several publications about South Vietnam are listed with North Vietnam and vice versa. About 13,000 cards are listed for Vietnam.
MH

AA27 _____. _____. Southern Asia accessions list. Washington, D.C., 1952-1960. 9 vols. Ceased publication.

Title varies: Jan. 1952-Jan. 1956, Southern Asia; publications in western languages, a quarterly accessions list. Beginning in April 1956, included publications in libraries other than just the Library of Congress.

Under headings "Indochina" or "Vietnam," lists books and articles published in French and English in Vietnam, Europe, and the U.S.; articles in BEFEO, BSEI, BEI, Asia, France-Asie; and embassy publications. Scope emphasizes social sciences, but includes military affairs, the arts, and physical sciences. Entries have complete bibliographical information. Beginning with June, 1958, lists publications by JPRS; beginning in May 1959, lists publications by the Michigan State University Vietnam Advisory Group. Most Vietnamese publications are in issues beginning with March 1959.
MH

AA28 _____. Reference Dept. Indochina, a bibliography of the land and people, comp. by Cecil C. Hobbs [et al.]. Washington, D.C., 1950. 367 p. Repr., Westport, Conn.: Greenwood, 1970.

Subject listing of 1,850 books, periodicals, and government publications in European and Vietnamese languages. Arranged in alphabetical order by author, within major and subordinate subject classes. Author and subject index. Some annotations--descriptive, analytical, or critical. Most entries are for works published after 1930. Entry includes LC call number or location symbol if in a library in the U.S. other than LC and complete bibliographical information. Indexes by author and subject.

Less comprehensive than the bibliographies by Cordier and Boudet, but when used in conjunction with Embree and Dotson (CD3), it fills much of the gap in bibliographies after 1935.
MH

AA29 *Vietnam (Democratic Republic). Thư Viện Khoa Học Trung Ương. Thư mục [Catalog]. Hanoi, 1958-59. 8 vols.

As described in Novaiia, 9/60, p. 83, includes books and periodicals in Hán, Nôm, quốc ngữ, European languages, and Chinese publications on Vietnamese history. As described in Lược truyện, lists Vietnamese books in quốc ngữ and is 7 vols. roneotyped.

BIBLIOGRAPHIES OF SECONDARY IMPORTANCE

AA30 Asian bibliography. Bangkok: ESCAP Library, 1952- . Semi-annually.

Accessions list of the ESCAP Library, arranged by DDC subject. Each issue lists about 10 titles from or about Vietnam, mostly Western-language books and annual reports of RVN ministries. Supersedes Supplement to the Consolidated list of publications in the ECAFE Library, Vol. 1, no. 1.
MH

AA31 Auvade, Robert. Bibliographie critique des oeuvres parues sur l'Indochine française. Paris: Maisonneuve & Larose, 1965. 153 p.

Arranged by broad subject-heading. Lengthy annotations for each item, in some cases listing the contents of books. Marred by many typographical errors and incomplete bibliographical citations. No apparent arrangement within each subject area. Indexes of personal names and of publications and authors mentioned in text.
MH

AA32 Barquissau, Raphael. <u>L'Asie française et ses
écrivains (Indochine-Inde) avec une bibliographie indochinoise</u>. Paris: Jean
Vigneau, 1947. 246 p.

A selection of writings by French ex-
plorers, administrators, and scholars.
Bibliography of about 500 titles.
MH

AA33 California. University. Center for South
and Southeast Asian Studies. <u>University
of California library holdings on Vietnam,
May 1968</u>. Berkeley, 1968. 53 p.

Author listing of about 1,000 books and
government publications. Mostly in French
and English. Entry contains author, title, publication information, and call
number. Includes about four pages each of
entries under "Vietnam (Democratic Republic)," "Vietnam," and "U.S."
CU

AA34 Chen, John H. M. <u>Viet-Nam; a comprehensive
bibliography</u>. Metuchen, N.J.: Scarecrow
Press, 1973. 314 p.

Alphabetical listing by author of
2,331 books and official publications,
mostly for the period from the establishment of the Government of Vietnam in 1949
until February 1972. Compiled from the
Library of Congress collections. Compilation is intended to include all languages,
although its coverage of Vietnamese-language books seems to be relatively few.
Includes large proportion of books on
other countries of Southeast Asia, Australia, and New Zealand "in order to show
the literature about Vietnam in perspective." Bibliographic information is
incomplete: omits series notes and pagination. Subject and title indexes.
MH

AA35 *Cochinchina. Secretariat. Bibliothèque.
<u>Catalogue méthodique des ouvrages, avec
table alphabétique des auteurs, par
L. Griffa, bibliothécaire</u>. Saigon:
Coudurier & Montégout, 1907. 747 p.

Catalogue of the general library, especially strong in law, science, literature and art in general, but also in
materials about Indochina. Does not give
complete bibliographic description.
(Source: Maybon in <u>BEFEO</u>, 10 (1910),
413-14.)

Cordier 3: 1744 also lists this as
well as <u>Catalogue par ordre alphabétique
des auteurs</u> (Saigon: Impr. Coloniale,
1901. 301 p.), issued by: République
française. Secrétariat du Gouvernement
de la Cochinchine, Saigon. Bibliothèque.
Neither work was available for
inspection.

AA36 *École française d'Extrême-Orient. Bibliothèque. <u>Inventaire alphabétique de la
bibliothèque de l'École française d'Extrême-Orient (fonds européen)</u>. Hanoi:
IDEO, 1916. 3 vol.: A-L; M-Z; Cartes et
plans. Supplément. Addenda. Table.
DLC

AA37 France. Ministère des colonies. Bibliothèque. <u>Catalogue méthodique de la bibliothèque du Ministère des colonies,
dressé par Victor Tantet</u>. Melun: Impr.
Administrative, 1905. 651 p.

Subject listing of monographs and, by
issuing agency, of periodicals. Table of
contents for Part 1 includes "Colonies
françaises," "Commerce et industrie,"
"Dialectes coloniaux," "Dictionnaires,"
"Droit," "Expositions," "Histoire coloniale," "Indo-Chine," and "Voyages" which
contain references for Vietnam and Indochina. Part 2 lists holdings of official

and non-official periodicals published in France, the colonies and in foreign countries and includes annuaires, bulletins officiels, budgets, and procès-verbaux of official bodies. Pp. 627-634 list 24 periodicals published in Indochina.
MH

AA38 Giok Po Oey. A checklist of the Vietnamese holdings of the Wason collection, Cornell University libraries, as of June 1971. Ithaca: Cornell University, Dept. of Asian Studies, Southeast Asia Program, 1971. 377 p. (Its Data Paper, 84)

Author listing of 5,707 monographs and title listings of 354 serials and 122 newspapers. Coverage is intended to be extensive, including not only scholarly but also popular works, translations into Vietnamese, sheet music, official publications, and microfilms. Scope includes all subjects. Entries are bibliographically complete, including call number of each publication in the Wason collection. Form of entry for personal names is by family name, with cross references from pseudonyms.

Indexes to monographs in history; literary history and criticism; novels, short stories, and drama; poetry; and philosophy and religion. Does not include publications about Vietnam in the Wason collection in non-Vietnamese languages.

A complementary bibliography to the Southeast Asia catalog of Cornell University Libraries and to the Bibliography of Vietnamese literature, by Marion W. Ross, listed elsewhere in this Guide.
MH

AA39 Harvard University. Library. Indochina, selected list of references, comp. by Elizabeth C. Ford. Cambridge, 1944. 108 p.

Selected holdings of Widener Library in history, economics, government, and other

social sciences, not only those in the Ind classification (See AA40).
MH

AA40 _____. _____. Southern Asia: Afghanistan, Bhutan, Burma, Cambodia, Ceylon, India, Laos, Malaya, Nepal, Pakistan, Sikkim, Singapore, Thailand, Vietnam. Cambridge: Distrib. by Harvard University Press, 1968. 543 p. (Its Widener Library shelflist, 19)

Lists, in shelflist, alphabetical, and chronological sequences, about 850 monographs and serials about Vietnamese bibliography, history, geography, and government. Includes some titles on ethnic minorities, religion, biography, and economics, although most of the books on those subjects are classified elsewhere in Widener Library. Comprises Western-language publications only. Although most publications about Vietnam are classified in Ind 9400-9998, some periodicals--BEFEO, BEI, BSEI, and others--are classified toward the beginning of the classification scheme with general periodicals.

Each entry comprises only the main entry, title, place, and date of publication.
MH

AA41 *Hội Việt-Mỹ [Vietnamese-American Association]. Catalog of books, 1966. Saigon, 1966. 369 p. (Source: Thư mục 1966.)

AA42 "Indochine annamite." BEFEO, 21 (1921), 197-278. Published as part of "L'École française d'Extrême-Orient depuis son origine jusqu'en 1920."

Bibliographic essay on European knowledge about Vietnam before 1900, and subsequent research into bibliography, geography, history, library and museum collections of the EFEO, numismatics, law,

ethnography, linguistics, and literature.
Emphasizes the research from Vietnamese
source materials performed by French
scholars. Includes lengthy quotations or
summaries of research by Cl.-E. Maitre, on
the cartography of Vietnam by Europeans
and on irrigation in North Vietnam, by
Paul Pelliot (Deux itinéraires de Chine en
Inde à la fin du VIIIe siècle), Henri Maspero (Le protectorat général d'Annam sous
les T'ang), L. Aurousseau on historical
political geography of Vietnam, and
others.
MH

AA43   "Liste des ouvrages édités par le Gouverne-
       ment général de l'Indochine, à l'occasion
       de l'Exposition coloniale internationale
       de 1931." BEFEO, 31 (1931), 503-516.

           Brief annotated list of 100 monographs.
       Annotations by Georges Cordier, Nguyễn
       Văn Tố, and J. Y. Claeys.
       MH

AA44   London. University. School of Oriental and
       African Studies. Library. Library cata-
       logue. Boston: G. K. Hall, 1963.
       28 vols. First supplement. Ibid., 1968.
       16 vols.

           1963 edition: author catalogs,
       Vols. 1-8; title catalogs, Vols. 9-13;
       subject catalogs, Vols. 14-21; manuscripts
       and microfilms, Vol. 22. Vols. 23-28,
       publications in Chinese and Japanese. Ma-
       terials on Vietnam in: subject catalogs,
       Vol. 20 under headings "Annam," "Cochin-
       china," "Indochina," "Tongking," "Viet-
       nam," and "Vietnamese." Includes works in
       Vietnamese under heading "Vietnamese lan-
       guage," and lists publications such as
       dictionaries, government budgets, folk-
       lore, and history.

           First supplement: author catalogs,
       Vols. 1-3; manuscripts and microfilms,
       Vol. 3; title catalogs, Vols. 4-6; subject

catalogs, Vols. 7-12. Vols. 13-16, publications in Chinese and Japanese. Materials on Vietnam in: subject catalogs,
Vol. 11 under headings "Cochinchina,"
"Indochina," and "Vietnam." Latter heading contains numerous citations in Vietnamese, particularly from DRVN. Publications in European languages are under
subject heading "Vietnam," while publications in Vietnamese are under heading
"Vietnamese."

    Lists books and some periodical arti-
cles in all areas of the social sciences
and humanities.
MH

AA45   Mekong Documentation Centre. Viet-Nam: a
       reading list. Bangkok: United Nations
       Economic Commission for Asia and the Far
       East, 1966. 119 p.

           Contains 1,251 books and articles in
       English and French, mostly about RVN, ar-
       ranged in decimal classification order.
       Many citations for publications by the
       governments of French Indochina, United
       States, and RVN, and by United Nations,
       International Labour Office, Banque Na-
       tionale du Vietnam, Michigan State Uni-
       versity Vietnam Advisory Group. Includes
       a list of 67 periodicals consulted.
       MH

AA46   Saigon. Học-viện Quốc-gia Hành-chánh. Thư-
       viện. Bản thống kê phân-loại sách thư-
       viện; classified catalog of books in the
       library. Saigon, 1960. 606 p.

           Lists about 7,500 books, and government
       publications, arranged in Dewey Decimal
       Classification order. By far the largest
       portion (pp. 35-399) is in the 300's
       class (social sciences). Relatively few
       works are in Vietnamese, most of the
       books being in French or English. Ex-
       cept for classes 895.92 (Vietnamese lit-
       erature) and 959.7 (Vietnamese history)

books about Vietnam are not separated from
the rest of the classification. Entries
are bibliographically complete except for
pagination. Pp. 578-596, list of newspapers (18), books on microfilm (16), and
periodicals (170). No author or title
indexes.
NIC

AA47   *Société des Etudes Indochinoises de Saigon.
Bibliothèque. Catalogue de la bibliothèque (1906). Saigon: Impr. Saigonnaise,
1906. 40 p.[1]

The library contained 2,842 volumes as
of December 1905 (Procès verbal, séance du
27 décembre 1905, BSEI, nos. 49-50 (1905),
130). The citation does not say whether
the catalog had been published.

An earlier work is cited in the BN
Catalogue générale des livres imprimés:
Péralle, [L.] Catalogue de la bibliothèque de la Société des Etudes Indochinoises. Saigon, 1897. 87 p.
[1]DLC

AA48   Southern Illinois University. Center for
Vietnamese Studies and Programs. Bibliography. Harrison Youngren, ed. Carbondale, 1969. 43 p.

"An inventory of the major publications
and research materials concerning Vietnam"
available at the Center as of July 31, 1969.
Arranged by category--books, periodical
articles, and public documents--and by subjects. Includes mostly English-language
publications, none in Vietnamese. No index. Omits series notes (all ICSC reports
omit the Command Paper designation, for
example); entries are inconsistent [both
"Vietnam (Democratic Republic)" and "North
Vietnam (DRVN)" are used, although the
latter is not a standard library heading];
and bibliography contains numerous typographical errors. Section on public
documents erroneously states that U.S.

"Congressional reports and records of
hearings which have been published for
distribution as separate documents...[are]
generally available in the Congressional
Record as well as in the form cited."
Citations omit Congressional Document or
Report number, do not distinguish between
Congressional hearings and committee
prints, and omit treaty numbers in Treaties and international acts (TIAS).
MH

AA49   _____. Library. List of Vietnam and Southeast Asian holdings. Carbondale: Morris
Library, Southern Illinois University,
1971- . Title page: Accessions list,
monographic and serial publications on
Vietnam and Southeast Asia. (Its Aces-
sions list, no. 1- , Library series,
no. 2-)

Publications in Vietnamese and Western
languages added to the Morris Library, including Vietnamese publications on areas
or subjects outside of Vietnam. About 200
to 300 publications per issue (five issues
distributed from September 1971 through
June 1974). Entries contain author, title, publisher, place of publication,
date, pagination, and call number. Includes current as well as retrospective
publications.
MH-V

AA50   U.S. Engineer Agency for Resources Inventories. Selected bibliography, Lower Mekong
basin; bibliographie choisie, bassin in-
férieur du Mékong. Eds., Mary Anglemyer,
Janet G. Gee [and] Michael J. Koll, Jr.
[n.p. Washington, D.C.?, 1969]. 2 vols.
At head of title: United Nations.

A companion volume to the Atlas of
physical, economic and social resources of
the lower Mekong basin (CK24), consisting
of references to books, articles, government publications, and pamphlets in li-

braries in the Washington, D.C. area.
References to RVN and to Indochina are in
Vol. 1, in the "Regional" section and in
Vol. 2, under "Vietnam." Subjects comprise agriculture, climate, education,
electric power, fisheries, forestry and
vegetation, geology, health, industry,
minerals, soils, telecommunications,
transportation, urban areas, and water resources. Includes a large number of publications by USAID and its contractors.
Similar in scope to Vietnam subject index
catalog (AA25).
MH

AA51   "Vietnam (et ancienne Indochine française)."
Livres actualité, no. 33 (Sept. 1971),
15 p.

"Critical and exhaustive" bibliography
of about 340 books on Vietnam that are in
print in French, from publishers in
France, Belgium, or Switzerland. Includes
works originally published in French or
translated into French. Arranged by subject. Annotations are usually one sentence in length; bibliographic descriptions are complete, but omit series titles
and prices of books.

Bibliographic essay by Jean Etienne,
pp. 5-7.
CtY

BIBLIOGRAPHIES: PRE-CORDIER

The following bibiliographies were the predecessors of Henri Cordier's Bibliotheca indosinica
(AA23). Beginning with the compilation by Bellecombe, the first collection of titles relevant to
Vietnam published in the sixteenth and seventeenth
centuries (Nguyễn Thế Anh), they provide a record of
the publications from the early years of Western
contacts with Vietnam through French intervention
and colonization. They are variously, annotated
bibliographies; reviews of periodical articles and
books; listings of publications without annotations;

biographical information on writers; and notices of
maps, manuscripts, and archival documents.

AA52   Barbié du Bocage, Victor Amédée. "Bibliographie annamite; livres, recueils, périodiques, manuscrits, plans." Revue
maritime et coloniale, fév. 1866, 360-386;
mai 1866, 140-185; août 1866, 812-831.
Also issued separately, Paris, Challamel,
1867, 107 p.

AA53   Bellecombe, André de. "Bibliographie anna-
mique." In E. Cortambert, Tableau de la
Cochinchine, pp. 337-343. Paris: A. Le
Chevalier, 1862.

AA54   "Bibliographie annamite; livres, recueils périodiques, manuscrits, cartes et plans
parus depuis 1866." Bulletin du Comité
Agricole et Industriel de la Cochinchine
3. sér., 1 (1879), 247-317.

AA55   Brébion, Antoine. Bibliographie des voyages
dans l'Indochine française du 9e au 19e
siècle. Saigon: Schneider, 1910. 299 p.
Appendice, Saigon: [Schneider?], 1911.
Pp. 301-322. Repr. New York: B. Franklin,
[1970]. (Burt Franklin bibliography and
reference series, 395. Geography and dis-
covery, 8)

AA56   _____. Livre d'or du Cambodge, de la Cochinchine et de l'Annam 1625-1910, biographie
et bibliographie. Saigon: Schneider,
1910. 79 p. Repr. New York: B. Franklin, [1971]. (Burt Franklin research and
source works series, 665. Essays in literature and criticism, 118)

AA57   Croizier, Edmé Casimir de, Marquis, et al.
Contributions à la bibliographie indochinoise pour l'année 1883. Paris:
Challamel aîné [etc.], 1884. 60 p. (Reprinted from Bulletin de la Société académique indo-chinoise de France, 2. sér.,
vol. 3 (1890), 399-540.)

BIBLIOGRAPHY AA

AA58   Finot, Louis. "Publications relatives à
       l'Indochine française." Journal asiatique,
       10. sér., vol. 17 (1911), 567-577;
       11. sér., vol. 2 (1913), 425-442.

AA59   Harmand. "Addition à la bibliographie anna-
       mite." BCAI, 4. sér., 1 (1880), 116-121.

AA60   Landes, A. and A. Folliot. "Bibliographie de
       l'Indo-Chine orientale depuis 1880."
       BSEI, 1. semestre 1889, 5-87.

AA61   Lemosoff, P. "Liste bibliographique des tra-
       vaux relatifs au Tongking publiés de 1867
       à 1883 (juillet)." Revue de géographie,
       13 (1883), 212-219.

AA62   "Liste des publications pouvant intéresser
       l'Indo-Chine parues pendant le cours de
       l'année 1882." BSEI, 1883, 105-108.

AA63   Oger, Henri. "Matériaux pour une biblio-
       graphie générale de la presqu'île indo-
       chinoise." Revue indochinoise, n.s. 9
       (1er semestre 1908), 376-387, 467-470,
       540-550, 607-614, 699-706, 783-789.

AA64   "Suite à la bibliographie annamite, publica-
       tions parues en 1880." BCAI, 122-126.

NATIONAL AND TRADE BIBLIOGRAPHIES

INDOCHINA

AA65   Indochina. Direction des Archives et des
       Bibliothèques. Liste des imprimés dé-
       posés. Hanoi: IDEO, 1922-1944; Saigon,
       1946-49. Biannual. Also issued in JOIF;
       indexed under "Dépôt légal."
          Contains the publications printed in
       Indochina and sent to the Dépôt légal.
       Includes periodical and non-periodical
       publications. Entry includes full biblio-
       graphical description. Subject and author
       indexes are in each issue. From 1923 to

1935, provided the basis for Boudet and
Bourgeois' Bibliographie de l'Indochine
française.
   Complete run of JOIF not available for
inspection; 1939 and 1945 volumes did not
include "Liste des imprimés déposés," although 1938 and 1946 did include it.
MH; MH-L

DEMOCRATIC REPUBLIC OF VIETNAM

AA66   *Mục lục giới thiệu sách mới, tháng _____
       [Bibliography, introducing new books dur-
       ing the month]. Hanoi: Sự thật. (Source:
       Novaiia, 5/61, lists issue of 7/8, 1960,
       32 p., marking the 15th anniversary of
       the DRVN.)

AA67   Mục lục sách xuất bản trong tháng _____
       [Catalog of books published during the
       month of _____]. Hanoi: Giới thiệu sách
       mới hằng tháng [Introducing new books each
       month].
          Divided into four sections: 1. Kinh
       điển [Classical works]; 2. Chính trị
       [Politics]; 3. Kinh tế [Economics];
       4. Quốc tế [International affairs].
       (Source: Novaiia, 1/61, lists issue of
       3/60: 11 p.)

AA68   *Mục lục sách "Sự thật" 1959 [Catalog of books
       published by Sự thật (Truth) in 1959].
       Hanoi: Sự thật, 1960. 23 p. (Source:
       Novaiia, 1/61.)

AA69   *Mục lục xuất bản phẩm [annual catalog of
       books published] 1957- . Hanoi: Thư
       Viện Quốc Gia, 1960- .
          Catalog of books and other materials
       deposited at the National Library in
       Hanoi. Books are listed by subject.
       Separate sections for music, posters,
       maps, gramophone records, newspapers, and
       periodicals. Indexes by author, trans-
       lator, and title. The 1963 issue listed

2,850 books and 220 newspapers. (Source:
Nunn.)

Catalog for 1972 (Hanoi, 1975, 176 p.)
cited in MLXBP, 10/75.

AA70 Mục lục xuất bản phẩm lưu chiểu hằng tháng:
bibliography of the Democratic Republic of
Vietnam; a monthly list of Vietnamese pub-
lications currently received. Hanoi: Bộ
Văn hóa, Thư viện Quốc gia, Legal Deposit
Dept.

Issues received: nos. 6-11, 1975. Arranged in classified order. About 150-200
publications in each issue. Includes
books, first issues of periodicals, maps,
and recordings. Bibliographic information
is included for each publication, as well
as number of copies printed.

MH-V

AA71 *Nhà xuất bản Công Nhân Kỹ Thuật. Giới thiệu
sách xuất bản năm 1976 [Introducing books
to be published in 1976]. Hanoi, 1975.
16 p.

Catalog from the Industrial Technology
Publishing House. (Source: MLXBP, 7/75.)

AA72 *Nhà xuất bản Lao Động. Mục lục sách 1976
[Catalog of books to be published in
1976]. Hanoi, 1975. 64 p.

Catalog of the Workers' Publishing
House. (Source: MLXBP, 9/75.)

AA73 *Nhà xuất bản Phụ Nữ. Giới thiệu sách xuất
bản năm 1976 [Introducing books to be published in 1976]. Hanoi, 1975. 52 p.

Catalog of the Women's Publishing
House. (Source: MLXBP, 10/75.)

AA74 *Nhà xuất bản Văn Hóa. Giới thiệu xuất bản
phẩm 1972-1975 [Publications of 1972-1975].
Hanoi, 1975. 56 p.

Catalog of the Culture Publishing
House. (Source: MLXBP, 7/75.)

AA75 *Nhà xuất bản Việt-Bắc. Giới thiệu sách xuất
bản năm 1976 [Introducing books to be published in 1976]. Bắc-thái, 1975. 30 p.

Catalog of publications of a publishing
house which publishes in Vietnamese, Tày,
and Nùng languages. (Source: MLXBP,
11/75.)

AA76 Sách mới Việt-Nam; livres vietnamiens. Hanoi:
XUNHASABA.

Four issues reviewed from 1960-1962 period. Entries list author, title in Vietnamese and French, publisher, pagination,
price, and short annotation. Each issue
lists between 10 and 30 books.

Titles are sold through XUNHASABA, Sở
Xuất Nhập Khẩu Sách Báo, or Book and Periodical Exporting Office.

mgc

REPUBLIC OF VIETNAM

AA77 "Bảng-kê ấn-phẩm đã nạp bản tại Nha Văn-khố
và Thư-viện Quốc-gia" [List of publications submitted for copyright at the Directorate of Archives and National Li-
brary]. Appears in CBVNCH.

Similar in format to "Liste des imprimés déposés" (AA65), although includes
number of copies printed in addition to
complete bibliographic information.

See CBVNCH, 25-3-1967, pp. 1340-1344,
for publications submitted during the
first quarter (đệ nhất tam-cá-nguyệt) of
1966; no other lists were cited for the
rest of 1966 in the CBVNCH for 1967. Indexed in CBVNCH, in quarterly indexes at
end of the chronological list or in the
alphabetical table of contents under "Ấn-
phẩm Không định kỳ," or "Văn-khố và Thư-
viện Quốc-gia."

MH-L

AA78 Nguyễn Văn. "Thư-tịch tuyển-trạch Việt-Nam
Cộng-hòa 1967-1968" [Selective bibliogra-

phy of RVN 1967-1968]. Thư-viện tập-san
(bộ mới), No. 4 (4/69), 39-66.

Lists about 300 books received in the
Ministry of Information office as compiled from the monthly list Tin tức thư-
tịch issued by that Office. Entries include author, title, publisher, pagination,
size, and price. Arranged in DDC order.
mgc

AA79   Nhà sách Khai Trí. Thư mục 1968. Saigon,
1968. 64 p.

A listing of books for sale at the Khai
Trí bookstore in 1968. Lists books in
print, not second-hand books.
TTQGVN, 2

AA80   Sách mới; nouvelles acquisitions; new acquisitions. Saigon: Nha Văn-Khố và Thư-Viện
Quốc-Gia, 1962-[1971?]. Monthly.

Accessions list of the National Library; contains Vietnamese and foreign
publications.
MH-L; NIC

AA81   Thư mục; catalogue of books; catalogue des
livres. Saigon: Nha Văn-Khố và Thư-Viện,
1965[?]-1972[?]. Annual.

An accessions list of the National Library, omitting periodicals, music, maps,
and phonograph records; includes publications in western languages published
abroad. Arranged by DDC, with index to
authors and issuing agencies. Entries include complete bibliographical information. The issue for 1965 includes accessions from June 1964 to December 1965.
Includes government publications.
mgc

AA82   Thư-tịch quốc-gia Việt-Nam; national bibliography of Vietnam. Saigon: Nha Văn-Khố
và Thư-Viện Quốc-Gia, 1968-[1972?]. Covers imprints from November 1, 1967.

DDC arrangement of monographs published in RVN and accessioned at the

Copyright Office in the National Library.
Entries include complete bibliographical
information as well as number of copies
printed and location in the National Library. Translated works include name of
translator and sometimes the title of the
original work. Indexes are by author and
title. Excludes serials, musical scores
and records, maps, and some government
publications.
mgc

AA83   Tin sách [book news]. Saigon: Hội Văn-bút
Việt-Nam [Vietnam P. E. N. Club] bộ mới
[new series], 1962-1968[?].

Monthly list of new books published
and short reviews. Emphasis is on literary works. Latest issue verified--no. 42,
12/1968.
NIC; MH-V

AA84   Vietnam (Republic). Nha Văn-Khố và Thư-Viện
Quốc-Gia. Thư-tịch hồi-tố quốc-gia Việt-
Nam; retrospective national bibliography
of Vietnam; bibliographie nationale retrospective du Vietnam (1963-1967). Saigon,
1971. 389 p.

Classified listing, corresponding to
the ten main classes of the Dewey Decimal
Classification, of 2,409 books, pamphlets,
and government publications published in
RVN. Based on publications received in
the Legal Deposit Bureau (Phòng Nạp-bản)
of the National Archives and Libraries.
Entries include author's name--with family name of author listed first--title,
publisher, year, pagination, size, number of copies printed, and location of
copy in the Library. Entries do not include series notes or indications of periodical offprints. Author and title
indexes.

The first of four projected volumes to
cover 1936-1967, the period between Bibliographie de l'Indochine française by
Boudet and Bourgeois and Thư tịch quốc-gia

Việt-Nam ⸺⸺⸺ ⸺pny of
Vietnam].
MH

TRANSLATIONS

AA85   Baruch, Jacques. Bibliographie des traduc-
        tions françaises des littératures du Việt-
        nam et du Cambodge. Brussels: Éd. Thanh-
        Long, 1968. 63 p. (Études Orientales, 3)
            Lists 256 publications translated from
        Vietnamese or published originally in
        French. Emphasis is on literary works
        (lists 11 editions of Chinh-phụ ngâm-khúc,
        12 works written by Nguyễn Du, and numer-
        ous compilations of folktales translated
        into French) but includes historical,
        scientific, and political works which are
        related to literature.
        MH

AA86   Index to Readex Microprint edition of JPRS
        Reports (Joint Publications Research Ser-
        vice). New York: Readex Microprint
        Corporation [1964?-   ]. 4 vols. as of
        1976.
            An index for converting from the JPRS
        report number to the entry number in the
        Monthly catalog of United States govern-
        ment publications, essential for libraries
        which do not subscribe to the microfilm
        edition of JPRS Reports issued by Bell and
        Howell and predecessors, but which do sub-
        scribe to the Readex Microprint edition
        (non-depository) of the Monthly catalog.
        See also AA90.
            First vol., 1958-1963, by Mary Eliza-
        beth Poole, 137 p.; second vol., 1964-
        1966, by Louise J. Hawkins, 84 p.; third
        vol., 1967-1970, by Louise J. Hawkins,
        68 p.; fourth vol., 1971-1973, by Louise J.
        Hawkins, 44 p.
        MH

AA87   Jenner, Philip N. Southeast Asian litera-
        tures in translation: a preliminary

bibliography. [Honolulu]: The University
Press of Hawaii, Asian Studies Program,
1973. 198 p. (Asian studies at Hawaii,
no. 9)
    Contains 3,690 citations of books,
chapters of books, and periodical articles,
comprised of translations, works about
literature, songs, drama, folk tales, and
myths, and works by Southeast Asians published in European languages. Pp. 142-161,
280 references to Vietnam. Bibliographic
descriptions omit pagination of books. No
author index.
MH

AA88   N. G. P. "Thư-tịch khảo về các tác-phẩm và
        truyện ngắn dịch từ Anh-Pháp ngữ sang
        Việt-ngữ (1958-1965)" [Bibliography of
        works and short stories translated from
        English and French into Vietnamese (1958-
        1965)]. Thư-viện tập-san, 5-6 (1969),
        51-91.
            Lists 448 works, arranged according to
        the 10 main classes of the DDC. Each
        entry is bibliographically complete, with
        name of work in Vietnamese, title of orig-
        inal work, publisher and date of Viet-
        namese edition, and name of translator.
        Includes works which are published in
        collections, but not in periodicals. Com-
        posed of works published in Saigon, Gia-
        định, or Hue. Largest category is litera-
        ture, with 266 works cited.
        mgc

AA89   Senny, Jacqueline. Contributions à l'appré-
        ciation des valeurs culturelles de
        l'Orient; traductions françaises de lit-
        tératures orientales. Brussels: Commis-
        sariat Belge de Bibliographie, 1958.
        299 p. (Bibliographia Belge, 37)
            Pp. 170, 176-187, translations into
        French of Vietnamese folktales and my-
        thologies, poems, stories, plays, and
        classical texts as well as works written

originally in French; is not limited to literature, but includes history and other areas. Lists 115 items. Author, title, translator, and illustrator indexes. Described by the compiler as an exhaustive bibliography of French translations of oriental literatures.

MH

AA90   Transdex; bibliography and index to United States Joint Publications Research Service translations. Wooster, Ohio: Bell and Howell Micro Photo Division, 1975- . From 1970-1975, published in New York by CCM Information, Inc.

Continuation of Catalog cards in book form for United States Joint Publications Research Service translations (1966-June 1970). See under Kyriak (CI56) for additional information.

Monthly and semi-annual cumulation of translations by JPRS, mostly from books and serials published in Communist countries. Each cumulated issue has indexes by country, subject, personal author and name of periodical indexed. Useful for translations of articles in Nhân dân, Học tập, Quân đội nhân dân, Phụ nữ Việt Nam, and other newspapers and periodicals from the DRVN or NFLSVN. Translations are not always accurate, and terminology ("North Vietnam" instead of "Democratic Republic of Vietnam," "Viet Cong" instead of "National Front for the Liberation of South Vietnam," etc.) reflects anti-Communist bias. See also AA86.

Microfiche or paper copies of translations are available from the publishers of Transdex.

MH

BIBLIOGRAPHIES IN CHINESE, JAPANESE, AND RUSSIAN LANGUAGES

AA91   Akademiia nauk SSSR. Institut narodov Azii. Bibliografiia IUgo-Vostochnoi Azii. Mos-cow: Izd-vo Vostochnoi Lit-ry, 1960. 255 p.

AA92   Berton, Peter. Bibliography of Soviet writings on Vietnam: Books and pamphlets, book reviews, and periodicals and newspapers. First quarter 1966. Los Angeles: School of International Relations, University of California at Los Angeles, 1966. 47 p.

AA93   Berton, Peter, and Alvin Z. Rubenstein. Soviet works on Southeast Asia; a bibliography of non-periodical literature, 1946-1965, with a contribution by Anna Allott. Los Angeles: University of Southern California Press, 1967. 201 p. (University of Southern California, School of Politics and International Relations. Far Eastern and Russian research series, no. 3)

AA94   Ichikawa, Kenjiro. Southeast Asia viewed from Japan; a bibliography of Japanese works on Southeast Asian societies, 1940-1963. Ithaca: Southeast Asia Program, Department of Asian Studies, Cornell University, 1965. 112 p. (Its Data Paper, 56)

AA95   Irikura, James K. Southeast Asia: Selected annotated bibliography of Japanese publications. New Haven: Southeast Asia Studies, Yale University, in association with Human Relations Area Files, 1956. 544 p. (Human Relations Area Files, Behavior science bibliographies)

AA96   McVey, Ruth T. Bibliography of Soviet publications on Southeast Asia as listed in the Library of Congress Monthly index of Russian acquisitions. Ithaca: Southeast Asia Program, Department of Far Eastern Studies, Cornell University, 1959. 109 p. (Its Data paper, 34)

AA97   Shu, Austin C. W., and William W. L. Wan.
        Twentieth-century Chinese works on South-
        east Asia: a bibliography. Honolulu,
        1968. 201 p. (Hawaii. University. East
        West Center, Institute of Advanced Proj-
        ects. Research Publications and Transla-
        tions. Occasional papers. Annotated bib-
        liography series, 3)

BIBLIOGRAPHIES OR REFERENCE WORKS ON
ETHNIC MINORITIES

AA98   Bourotte, Bernard. "Essai d'histoire des
        populations montagnardes du Sud-indochi-
        nois jusqu'à 1945." BSEI, 30 (1955),
        11-116.

AA99   Embree, John Fee, and Lillian O. Dotson.
        Bibliography of the peoples and cultures
        of mainland Southeast Asia. New Haven:
        Yale University, Southeast Asia Studies,
        1950. 821 p.

AA100   Ethnographical data, ed. Nguyễn Khắc Viện.
        (Vietnamese studies, nos. 32, 36, and 41,
        1972-1975; edition in French: Études
        vietnamiennes). Includes translation and
        summary of survey article by Lê Văn Hảo,
        "Ethnological studies and research in
        North Vietnam," originally published in
        Vietnamese in Nghiên-cứu lịch-sử, no. 133
        (July-August 1970).

AA101   Harvard University. Peabody Museum of Ar-
        chaeology and Ethnology. Library. Author
        and subject catalogues. Boston: G. K.
        Hall, 1963, 53 vols. Index to subject
        headings (Ibid., 1 vol.) Supplements one
        to three (Boston: G. K. Hall, 1970-1975,
        24 vols.).

AA102   Legay, Roger, and Trần Văn Tốt. "Essai de
        bibliographie pratique sur les populations
        montagnardes du Sud-Vietnam (1935-1966).
        BSEI, 42 (1967), 257-299.

AA103   Mountain regions and national minorities,
        ed. Nguyễn Khắc Viện. (Vietnamese stud-
        ies, no. 15, 1968, 225 p.)

AA104   Schrock, Joann L. et al. Minority groups in
        North Vietnam. Washington, D.C.: [Dept.
        of the Army], 1972. 653 p. Prepared by
        the Kensington Office of the American In-
        stitutes for Research. (Bibliography
        lists JPRS translations)

AA105   _____. Minority groups in the Republic of
        Vietnam. Ibid., 1966. 1163 p. Dept. of
        the Army pamphlet, DA Pam 550-105. Pre-
        pared by American University, Washington,
        D.C., Cultural Information Analysis Center.
        See also chapters CC Sociology and CD
        Anthropology in this Guide.

BOOK REVIEWS

The problem of locating book reviews is primarily one of locating the review in a periodical or
newspaper. Indexes to book reviews seem to cover
books published in the United States and Great Britain better than those published in France and Vietnam, and in fact the two German-language bibliographies are suggested for locating reviews of books
published in France. For reviews of books published
in Vietnam, the two best sources have been BEFEO and
BSEI.

AA106   The Index to Southeast Asian Journals, 1960-
        1974: A Guide to Journals, Book Reviews
        and Composite Works by Donald Clay Johnson
        (Boston: G. K. Hall, May, 1977) cites
        book reviews on Southeast Asia published
        from 1960 through 1974.

The following journals publish most of the
reviews of books on Vietnam: BEFEO; BSEI; Bulletin
of the School of Oriental and African Studies;
France-Asie/Asia; Journal of Asian studies; Journal
of Southeast Asian studies; Library journal; Pacific
affairs; and Southeast Asia, an international
quarterly.

BIBLIOGRAPHY AA

AA107 Bibliographie der Rezensionen, 1900-1943.
        Gautzech b. Leipzig: Dietrich, 1901-1944.
        (Internationale Bibliographie der Zeit-
        schriftenliteratur, Abt. C)

AA108 Book review digest. New York: Wilson,
        1905- .

AA109 Book review index. Detroit: Gale Research,
        1965- .

AA110 Bulletin signalétique. Paris: Centre na-
        tional de la recherche scientifique,
        1940- . Published in several sections
        according to subject.

AA111 Humanities index. New York: Wilson, 1975- .
        (Separate section at end of volume lists
        book reviews. First issue covers
        April 1974-March 1975.)

AA112 Internationale Bibliographie der Rezensionen
        wissenschaftlicher Literatur; internation-
        al bibliography of book reviews of schol-
        arly literature; bibliographie interna-
        tionale des recensions de la littérature
        savante. Osnabrück: Felix Dietrich Ver-
        lag, 1971- .

AA113 The Library Journal book review, 1967- .
        New York: Bowker, 1969- .

AA114 Social sciences index. New York: Wilson,
        1975- . (Separate section at end of vol-
        ume lists book reviews. First issue cov-
        ers April 1974-March 1975.)

LIBRARIANSHIP AB

AB1   Gardner, Richard K. Phương pháp tổng kê &
        phân loại sách với bảng phân-loại thập-
        phân Việt-Nam. Dịch giả Nguyễn Thị Cút
        [The cataloging and classification of
        books, with classification tables for

Vietnam. Trans. Nguyễn Thị Cút]. 2. ed.
rev. Saigon: Asia Foundation, 1966.
517 p.
        Adaptation of the Dewey Decimal Clas-
sification tables from the English version
of the 9th Abridged Edition of the DDC and
the 17th edition of the DDC. Pp. 11-101,
a manual of cataloging and classification;
pp. 105-517, decimal classification tables, including expansion of certain
classes for subjects related to Vietnam,
alphabetical index, and Vietnamese-English-
French glossary, with explanations in
Vietnamese. Examples of the expansion of
certain classes are of 354 "National government," with a list of classification
numbers for all ministries and departments
of the RVN government; 495 "Vietnamese language;" 895.929 "Vietnamese literature,"
with subdivisions by period; and 959.7
"Vietnamese history," with subdivisions by
period.
MH-V

AB2   Lian The Kho. "Report on the CORMOSEA Sub-
        committee on Technical Processes meeting
        on rules for Vietnamese names, held at The
        Library of Congress, 2-3 February 1973."
        CORMOSEA newsletter, 6, no. 2 (March 1973),
        11-13.
        Recommendations to The Library of Con-
gress for standardizing the cataloging
rules for Vietnamese names in three cata-
gories: family names, royal titles, and
religious titles. Recommends using family
names before personal names, similar to
present Anglo-American cataloging rules.
mgc

AB3   Newman, Lois. The catalog entry for South
        Asian names, with special reference to
        Vietnamese names. Santa Monica, Calif.:
        Rand Corporation, 1968. 6 p. ([Rand]
        P-3888)
        Comparison of different cataloging
principles, with recommendations to

follow national usage. Suggests using personal names before family names when cataloging Vietnamese names.

MH-CSCL

AB4 *Nguyễn Thị Cút. Niên-giám thư-viện tại Việt-Nam; directory of libraries in Viet-Nam. Saigon: Hội Thư-Viện Việt-Nam, 1973. 158 p. (Source: CORMOSEA newsletter, vol. 8, no. 1 (1974/75.)

List of 147 libraries in RVN (including public, school, university, government, special, and American) and their address, name of librarian, hours, year founded, size of collections, number of staff, etc. Text is in English and Vietnamese.

Previous ed. by the Hội Thư-Viện Việt-Nam in 1970 (63 p.). [Source: mgc.]

AB5 *Phạm Thị Lệ Hương. "A rationale for the entry of Vietnamese names in library catalogs." [Empire, Kan.], 1972. 75 p. "Presented to the Faculty of the Department of Library Science of Kansas State Teachers College of Emporia in partial fulfillment of the requirement for the degree of Master of Librarianship." (Source: NIC Sept. 1972.)

AB6 Thư-viện tập-san [Library journal]. Saigon: Hội Thư-Viện Việt-Nam [Vietnam Library Association], bộ mới [n.s.], no. 1- (6.68)- . quarterly.

Articles on practice and theory of librarianship, in Vietnam and abroad. Beginning with no. 4 (4/69), includes title pages in Vietnamese; English (Library bulletin; organ of the Vietnamese Library Association); and French (Bulletin d'information; organe de l'Association des Bibliothécaires vietnamiens).

mgc

AB7 Vietnam (Republic). Bộ Quốc-Gia Giáo-Dục. Organisation et fonctionnement de la Direction des archives et bibliothèques na-tionales; organization and administration of the Directorate of National Archives and Libraries. Saigon: Département de l'éducation nationale, Direction des archives et bibliothèques nationales, 1962. 32 p.

General outline of the history and organization.

MH-L

LEARNED SOCIETIES AND OTHER INSTITUTIONS   AC

AC1 Cordier, Henri. Bibliotheca indosinica. See AA23 for complete description. For citations about learned societies and other associations, see Vol. 3: 1952-1959 and 1712-1740.

Included in the references above are the École française d'Extrême-Orient (cols. 1652-1656); Comité Agricole et Industriel de la Cochinchine (with the complete contents of the Bulletin du Comité Agricole et Industriel de la Cochinchine, 1865-1881, cols. 1712-1725); and Société des Études Indochinoises (with the complete contents of the Bulletin de la Société des Études Indochinoises, 1883-1913, cols. 1726-1740).

MH

AC2 Boudet, Paul, and Rémy Bourgeois. Bibliographie de l'Indochine française. See AA22 for complete description. For publications of associations, see "Associations amicales et professionales," "Associations d'assistance," "Associations religieuses," "Associations sportives," "Sociétés de commerce et d'industrie," "Sociétés savantes," "Ecole française d'Extrême-Orient," and "Périodiques.-- Bulletins et procès-verbaux des associations" in vol. 4, and "Périodiques.-- Bulletins d'associations et groupements," in vol. 1.

MH

AC3   Asia Society. <u>American institutions and or-</u>
<u>ganizations interested in Asia, a refer-</u>
<u>ence directory</u>. Ward Morehouse, ed.
2d. ed. New York: Taplinger, 1961. 581 p.
1st edition, compiled by the Conference on
Asian Affairs, Inc., 1957.

Contains "descriptive listings, arranged alphabetically, of almost 1,000
programs of American organizations and
institutions relating to Asia..., a summary of activities...by country of activity and type of program...and appendices of
Asian government diplomatic and consular
offices in the United States and similar
installations of the U.S. government in
Asia." Includes voluntary organizations,
colleges and universities, church-spon-
sored organizations, and non-profit
organizations such as CARE, and organizations providing assistance such as schol-
arships for Asian students.

Pp. 536-581--listing, for RVN, of type
of activity by country.
MH

AC4   Bezacier, Louis. "Liste des travaux relatifs
au Viet-Nam publiés par l'École française
d'Extrême-Orient." <u>France-Asie</u>, 15 (1958),
535-58.

Lists 353 publications on ethnic Vietnamese by publication date. Author and
subject indexes. Comprises <u>BEFEO</u>, <u>CEFEO</u>,
<u>Publications de l'EFEO</u>, <u>Bulletin de</u>
<u>l'Institut Indochinois pour l'étude de</u>
<u>l'homme</u>, <u>Dân Việt-Nam</u>, and publications
<u>hors série</u>.
MH

AC5   Centre for East Asian Cultural Studies. <u>Re-</u>
<u>search institutes and researchers of Asian</u>
<u>studies in: Cambodia, Laos, Malaysia,</u>
<u>Singapore and the Republic of Vietnam</u>.
[Tokyo], 1970. 183 p. (<u>Its</u> Directories,
8)

Names of institutions at which research
is performed and names of researchers with

their biographical data and curriculum
vitae. Includes, in addition to universities, learned societies, and research libraries. Vietnam, pp. 129-177, lists 28
institutions and their researchers. Researchers of Vietnamese studies in other
countries are listed with their respective
country.

The Centre has compiled directories for
other countries in which Vietnam is studied by researchers. See: No. 1, <u>Research</u>
<u>institutes for Asian studies in Japan</u>,
1962; no. 2, <u>Japanese researchers in Asian</u>
<u>studies</u>, 1963; and no. 7, <u>Research insti-</u>
<u>tutes and researchers of Asian studies in</u>
<u>the Republic of China and in Hong Kong</u>,
1968.
MH

AC6   Durand, Maurice. "Liste des travaux publiés
par l'École française d'Extrême-Orient sur
l'histoire, l'archéologie, les moeurs et
coutumes du Viet-Nam." <u>Dân Việt-Nam</u>,
1 (1948), 71-80; also published in translation by Mộc Nghĩa: "Bản kê các tác
phẩm do Viện Đông-Phương Bắc-cổ xuất
bản..." in <u>ibid</u>., phần tiếng Việt [Viet-
namese-language portion], separately
paged, 71-80.

Alphabetical listing by author of 88
works. In the translated portion, titles
of works in non-Vietnamese languages are
translated into Vietnamese.
MH

AC7   "L'École française d'Extrême-Orient depuis
son origine jusqu'en 1920." <u>BEFEO</u>, 21
(1921), 1-420.

History of the work, studies, and publications of the École. Contains a list
of members and collaborators.
MH

AC8   Institut d'Étude du Viet Nam contemporain.
<u>Guide pratique de recherche sur le Viet</u>
<u>Nam en France</u>.

See DD16 for complete description. Includes brief descriptions of libraries and
archives in the Parisian region with collections on Vietnam.

mgc

AC9 Société des Études indochinoises de Saigon.
"Cinquantenaire de la Société des Études
indochinoises." BSEI, n.s. 8, 1 & 2
(1933), 1-215. Also published separately:
Saigon: Testelin, 1933. 215 p.

Includes indexes to Bulletin du Comité
agricole et industriel de la Cochinchine
and BSEI from 1865-1932 and "Liste des
publications de la Société des études indochinoises" from 1883 to 1932, on
pp. [61]-121. The remaining pages contain a survey of the history of the Société and its predecessor, the Comité
Agricole et Industriel de la Cochinchine;
proceedings of the committee on the Cinquantenaire and of the anniversary itself,
on February 25, 1933; and a catalog, with
illustrations, of the exhibition celebrat-
ing the anniversary.

MH

AC10 *Thái Văn Kiểm, and Trương Bá Phát. Chỉ nam
về Viện Bảo Tàng Quốc Gia Việt-Nam tại
Saigon [Handbook of the National Museum of
Vietnam in Saigon]. Saigon: Khối Văn-Hóa,
1974. 208 p.

History of the Museum and detailed description of all items in the Museum. Includes many illustrations. (Source:
Gélinas, list 033, March 15, 1975.)

AC11 *Vietnam (Democratic Republic). Ủy Ban Khoa
Học Việt-Nam. Viện Ngôn Ngữ Học. Từ
điển thuật ngữ Bảo Tàng Học Nga-Pháp-Việt
[Russian-French-Vietnamese dictionary of
museum terminology]. Hanoi: Khoa Học Xã
Hội, 1971. 63 p. (Source: NIC.)

ENCYCLOPEDIAS AD

Encyclopedias provide quick answers to questions that do not require extensive research. Unfortunately, few encyclopedias exist in the field of
Vietnamese studies, and the major encyclopedia,
Lịch-triều hiến-chương loại-chỉ, by Phan Huy Chú is
of historical interest only. For modern times, the
other encyclopedic works are not at all comparable
in scope. Standard western-language encyclopedias,
such as La grande encyclopédie (Paris, 1886-1902),
Grand dictionnaire universel du XIXe siècle, by La-
rousse (Paris, 1865-1879), Encyclopedia Britannica,
and Encyclopedia Americana are not cited here.

Another type of ready-reference work is the
handbook, some of which are cited in chapter DF
Handbooks.

AD1 Phan Huy Chú. Lịch-triều hiến-chương loại-
chỉ [Monographs of the institutions of the
dynasties]. ca. 1821. 10 volumes, 49
chapters.

Encyclopedia of Vietnamese history and
institutions from the Lý dynasty (1010-
1225) to the Lê dynasty (1428-1788). The
contents of the separate volumes are
listed below; those which have been translated are also listed in the various chapters of this Guide.

Modern translation into quốc-ngữ:
(Hanoi: Viện Sử Học, 1960-1961, 4 vols;[1]
Modern publication in quốc-ngữ and in Chinese characters (Saigon: Nha Văn-hóa,
1971-1974, 4 vols. as of 1975--see separate listing below[2] Quyển thu [Prefa-
tory chapter] and Vol. 1, Chapters 1-5,
"Địa-dư chỉ" [Geography], trans. by Nguyễn
Thọ Dực (Saigon: Nha Văn-hóa, 1972) (See
DH15); Vol. 2, chapters 6-12, "Nhân-vật
chỉ" [Biography], trans. by Nguyễn Đỗ Mục
(Hanoi?: Tân Dân, 1940) (AJ16); Vol. 2,
[1]NIC
[2]Gélinas, list 033, March 15, 1975

chapters 6-12, "Nhân-vật chí" [Biography],
also trans. by Nguyễn Thọ Dực (Saigon:
Nha Văn-hóa, 1973) (AJ16); Vol. 3, chapters 13-19, "Quan-chức chí" [Government],
trans. with vols. 6 and part of vol. 7 by
Cao Nãi Quang (Saigon: Đại-Học-Viện Saigon, 1956-1957) (CH15, CI27); Vol. 4,
chapters 20-25, "Lễ-nghi chí" [Rites and
ceremonies], trans. by Nguyễn Thọ Dực
(Saigon: Khối Văn Hóa, 1974) (CC5);
Vol. 5, chapters 26-28, "Khoa-mục chí"
[Examinations], translation in progress[2];
Vol. 6, chapters 29-32, "Quốc-dụng chí"
[Financial resources], trans. with vol. 3
and part of vol. 7 by Cao Nãi Quang (Saigon: Đại-Học-Viện Saigon, 1956-1957)
(CH15, CI27); Vol. 6, chapters 29-32,
"Quốc-dụng chí" [Financial resources],
also trans. by R. Deloustal into French in
RI, 1924-1925 (CH15); Vol. 7, chapters 33-
38, "Hình-luật chí" [Penal code], trans.
by R. Deloustal into French in BEFEO 1908
(CJ21); Vol. 7, chapter 33 of "Hình-luật
chí" trans. with vols. 3 and 6 by Cao Nãi
Quang (Saigon: Đại-Học-Viện Saigon, 1956-
1957) (CH15, CI27, CJ21); Vol. 8, chapters 39-41, "Binh-chế chí" [Military af-
fairs], translation in progress[2]; Vol. 9,
chapters 42-45, "Văn-tịch chí" [Bibliogra-
phy], trans. by Nguyễn Thọ Dực (Saigon:
Khối Văn-Hóa, 1974) (AA14); Vol. 9, chapters 42-45, "Văn-tịch chí" [Bibliography],
also trans. by Emile Gaspardone into
French in BEFEO, 1934 (AA16); Vol. 9,
chapters 42-45, "Văn-tịch chí" [Bibliog-
raphy], also trans. by Trần Văn Giáp into
French in BSEI, 1938 (AA17); Vol. 9, chapters 42-45, "Văn-tịch chí" [Bibliography],
contents listed by Huỳnh Khắc Dụng, in Sử-
liệu Việt-Nam (Saigon, 1959) (DB8);
Vol. 10, chapters 46-49, "Bang-giao chí"
[Foreign relations], no translation located
by the compiler.

[2]Gélinas, list 033, March 15, 1975

AD2   Đào Đăng Vỹ. Việt-Nam Bách-khoa tự-điển;
       dictionnaire encyclopédique viêtnamien;
       Vietnamese encyclopedic dictionary. Sai-
       gon: [the author,] 1960. 3 vols.

       General and special articles, of inter-
       est to Vietnamese or to people studying
       Vietnam. Terms are defined in Vietnamese,
       French, and English and include Chinese
       characters.
       MH-V (vol. 1); NIC (3v.)

AD3   Trịnh Văn Thành. Thành ngữ điển tích danh-
       nhân tự điển [Dictionary of literary terms
       and personnages]. Saigon: [the compiler],
       1966. 2 v.

       Includes 10,000 idioms and 5,000 liter-
       ary allusions as well as extensive bio-
       graphical information on historical
       personnages. Information for persons in-
       cludes birth and death dates, excerpts
       from writings, and political as well as
       literary accomplishments. Among the per-
       sons included are Khổng-Tử (Confucius),
       pp. 604-620; Hồ Xuân Hương, pp. 509-514;
       and Phan Bội Châu, pp. 952-963; some
       topics are Phật-giáo Hòa-Hảo (Hòa Hảo
       Buddhism), pp. 1025-1041; Phật-học (Bud-
       dhism), pp. 1042-1059; and Tam Kỳ Phổ Độ
       (Cao Đài religion), pp. 1172-1206.
       MH-V

AD4   Whitfield, Danny J. Historical and cultural
       dictionary of Vietnam. Metuchen, N.J.:
       Scarecrow Press, 1976. 369 p. (Histo-
       rical and cultural dictionaries of Asia,
       ed. by Basil C. Hedrick, no. 7)

       Dictionary of terms in all aspects of
       classical, contemporary, and French colo-
       nial history and society. Terms include
       persons (with birth and death dates and
       short biographies), places in Vietnam, and
       concepts in traditional and modern life.
       MH

LANGUAGE DICTIONARIES AE

Vietnamese-language dictionaries vary in arrangement of words, in scope, and in presentation. Although the monosyllabic nature of Vietnamese almost requires that the arrangement of each word to be defined be word-by-word (as distinct from the letter-by-letter arrangement of some dictionaries of western European languages), the arrangement can be either by etymological meaning (all compound usages of, for example, bán half, before defining compound usages of bán to sell) or alphabetical (listing bán cầu hemisphere, bán chịu to sell on credit, and bán đảo peninsula--lit. half an island--in consecutive order despite the different etymologies). Arrangement of initial letters varies: Most older Vietnamese-French dictionaries were arranged alphabetically, e. g., ca-, ch-, co-, cu-. Most present-day dictionaries are arranged with vowel combinations appearing before consonant combinations, e. g., ca-, co-, cu-, ch-. Exceptions among present-day dictionaries are orthographical dictionaries and Từ điển tiếng Việt, by Văn Tân et al (AE47). A final differentiation of arrangement is in tone marks: usually ´ ` ? ~ . or ` ´ . ? ~ with the unmarked tone appearing first.

A useful dictionary will include in its scope not only definitions of words, but of idioms, proverbs, biographical names and geographical names. Few dictionaries can be expected to include Sino-Vietnamese characters, which add to the size and cost of the work, but which are essential for understanding the etymology of Vietnamese words.

BIBLIOGRAPHIES

AE1 Cordier, Henri. Bibliotheca indosinica.

> See AA23 for complete description. For citations to language dictionaries, see 4: 2285-2294, "Lexicographie.--Dictionnaires et vocabulaires," most of which are not listed in this bibliography.
> MH

AE2 Boudet, Paul, and Rémy Bourgeois. Bibliographie de l'Indochine française.

> See AA22 for complete description. For citations to language dictionaries, see "Langue annamite" and "Dictionnaires" in each volume. Many of the shorter dictionaries are not listed in the present bibliography.
> MH

AE3 Benedict, Paul K. Select list of materials for the study of the Annamese language. New York: Southeast Asia Institute, 1947. 7 p. mimeo. (Its Language series, no. 3)

> Alphabetical listing by author of 66 books and articles, mostly in French; includes bilingual dictionaries.
> MH

AE4 Eney, R. H. A glossary of initials and acronyms encountered in Viet Nam. Washington, D.C.: USAID/Vietnam Bureau, 1969. 12 p.

> Explains about 200 initials and acronyms, mostly abbreviations of American and RVN terms used in military situations or in rural government programs. Some abbreviations are translated into English, although the original terms were in Vietnamese: APT (Armed Propaganda Team) is the abbreviation for teams of Hồi Chánh; the original Vietnamese term is not given.
> MH

AE5 Nguyễn Khắc Kham, et al. Thư-tịch tuyển-trạch về danh-từ chuyên-môn; a selected bibliography on scientific and technical terminology in Vietnamese.

> See EA11 for annotation; lists 86 dictionaries.

AE6 *Nguyễn Khắc Kham. "Lược-sử, công trình biên soạn tự-điển Việt-ngữ từ thế-kỷ thứ XVII"

[Historical survey of lexicographical
works in Vietnamese from the 17th century].
Luận-Đàm, Bộ I, 12 (11/12, 1961); Bộ II,
1 (1, 1962); 2 (2, 1962).

Divided chronologically, 1651-1884,
1884-1931, 1932-1962 (N. K. Kham, E. Asian
cultural studies).

AE7   Pencolé, P. "Dictionnaires Vietnamiens."
Bulletin de la Société des Missions Étrangères de Paris, 2. sér., no. 99 (1957),
127-140, 211-227.

Annotated bibliography of 11 major language dictionaries with chronological
chart and bibliographic description of
about 50 dictionaries from 1651 (Alexandre
de Rhodes) to 1954 (Đào Đăng Vỹ).
mgc; Ct-Y

AE8   *U.S. Operations Mission to Vietnam. Education Division. Vietnamese language instructional materials published by American agencies and Vietnamese bureaus in
Saigon. Saigon, [1961?] 36 p. (Source:
EARI)

DICTIONARIES IN NÔM, AND EARLY
CHINESE-TO-VIETNAMESE DICTIONARIES

AE9   Chen Ching-ho. "A collection of Chữ Nôm
scripts, with the pronunciation in Quốc-
ngữ." Manuscript, Keio Univ., 1970.
308 p.

Compilation of 5,700 Nôm scripts, compiled from five sources: Tự đức thánh
chế tự học giai-nghĩa-ca (Hue, 1894);
Huỳnh Tịnh Của, Đại Nam quốc-âm tự-vị
(Saigon, 1895); J. Bonet, Dictionnaire
annamite-français (Paris, 1899-1900);
A. Chéon, Recueil de cent textes annamites
(Hanoi, 1905); and Chinh phụ ngâm khúc
(18th century; modern text, 5th ed., Saigon, 1950). According to preface, author
plans to supplement the work by consulting
Taberd's Dictionarium Annamiticum-Latinum

(1838); Cung oán ngâm khúc (18th cent.);
and Kim Vân Kiều (18th cent.).

Each entry consists of the script; its
Sino-Vietnamese spelling in quốc-ngữ; and
the vernacular phoneme in quốc-ngữ, with
one or more of the sources indicated as
an authority.
MH-HY

AE10   Davidson, Jeremy H. C. S. "A new version of
the Chinese-Vietnamese vocabulary of the
Ming dynasty." Bulletin of the School of
Oriental and African Studies, 38 (1975),
296-315, 586-608.

Description of An-nan-kuo i-yü, a
Chinese/Vietnamese dictionary of about
1550 used in China, a copy of which is in
the Library of the School of Oriental and
African Studies. Vocabulary lists 669
words in Chinese characters, with translation into English and transcriptions
into romanized Vietnamese and Chinese.
MH

AE11   Gaspardone, Emile. "Le lexique annamite des
Ming." Journal asiatique, 241 (1953),
355-397.

Description of An-nan-kuo i-yü, a copy
of which was acquired by the École française d'Extrême-Orient. Lists 716 words
in Chinese characters, with translation
into French and transcription into romanized Vietnamese and Chinese.
MH

AE12   Nguyễn Quang Xỹ, and Vũ Văn Kính. Tự-điển
chữ Nôm [Nôm dictionary]. Saigon: Bộ
Giáo Dục, Trung-tâm Học-liệu [1971].
863 p.

Pp. 3-102, tables of characters, by
stroke. Includes word in quốc-ngữ.
Pp. 105-860, translation of words in nôm
into quốc-ngữ, including word in quốc-ngữ
and nôm, definition in quốc-ngữ, and etymology of nôm characters. Arranged in

alphabetical order. Bibliography of 43 dictionaries or nôm works, such as the Kim Vân Kiều by the Ban Nôm (ca. 1900). About 10,000 words are included.

MH-V

AE13 *Tạ Đức Rật. Tự điển chữ Nôm. Saigon: Đại-học Văn-khoa, 1967. 387 p.

Reviewed by Nguyễn Trần Huân in BEFEO, 56 (1969), 211. Cited by Bửu Cầm in preface to Nôm dictionary by Nguyễn Quang Xỹ and Vũ Văn Kính: work was mimeographed, printed in few copies, and not widely distributed.

AE14 Vũ Văn Kính, and Nguyễn Văn Khánh. Tự-vị Nôm [Nôm dictionary]. Saigon: Trường Đại Học Văn Khoa Saigon, 1970. 224 p.

Alphabetical list, according to quốc-ngữ order, of nôm characters. Pp. 3-19, explanation of nôm construction of words. Compared with nôm dictionary by Nguyễn Quang Xỹ and Vũ Văn Kính, this has no table of characteristics by stroke and does not break down the nôm characters to show the etymology.

MH-V

ROMANIZED VIETNAMESE-LANGUAGE DICTIONARIES (TO EARLY 20TH CENTURY)

AE15 *Aubaret, Louis Gabriel. Vocabulaire français-annamite et annamite-français, précédé d'un traité des particules annamites. Bang-Kok: Impr. de la Mission Catholique, 1861. 2 v. (Source: Cordier 4: 2287.)

AE16 Bonet, J. Dictionnaire annamite-français (langue officielle et langue vulgaire). Paris: Impr. Nationale, 1899-1900. 2 vols. (Publications de l'École des langues orientales vivantes, [1])

"Langue vulgaire" is defined as the spoken and written language, while "langue officielle" is written only, in Chinese characters. A 25-page preface contains an

outline of Vietnamese grammar and pronunciation. Each entry gives the Sino-Vietnamese character, a designation for origin--Sino-Vietnamese or original Vietnamese--the definition in French, and examples of usage in compound expressions. Alphabetical order is French. Order of tones differs from present Vietnamese arrangement. Pp. 497-519, organization of the government of pre-French Vietnam, with names transcribed into Chinese. Pp. 521-32, tables of the 214 SV radicals.

MH

AE17 [Caspar, Bp. of Hue]. Tự vị an nam-pha lang sa; dictionnaire annamite-français. Tan Dinh: Impr. de la Mission, 1877. 916 p.

Arranged by European order. Word in Vietnamese is followed by the definition in French, then by several definitions in phrases. Includes alternate spelling for some words, such as trực (trật).

MH-HY

AE18 Dronet. Lexique franco-annamite, par MM. Ravier et Dronet. Ke-so: Impr. de la Mission, 1903. 540 p. (Source: Cordier 2289.)

AE19 Genibrel, J. F. M. Dictionnaire annamite-français comprenant 1° tous les caractères de la langue annamite vulgaire...; 2° les caractères chinois nécessaires à l'étude des Tứ-thơ, ou quatre livres classiques chinois; 3° la flore et la faune de l'Indochine. Saigon: Impr. de la Mission à Tân-đinh, 1898. 987 p.

2. éd., refondue et très considerablement augmentée.[1] Repr., Saigon, 1973.[2] 3. éd. has title: Petit dictionnaire annamite-français. Saigon, n. d. 971 p.[3]

Arrangement is by quốc-ngữ word; for each entry is listed the Chinese charac-

[1] MH-HY

[2] Thanh-long cat. 32. Févr. 1975

[3] Boudet 2

ter, Vietnamese word, translation into
French, and several examples of usage.
Seems to be based upon the Saigon dialect;
abbreviations "T" and "H" indicate usage
in Tongking and Huế respectively. Separate alphabets for C, Ch; T, Th, Tr; etc.
Names of plants and animals are in the
same alphabetical sequence as other words;
Latin names of plants and animals are giv-
en. Based upon the Dictionnaire annamite-
français by Msgr. Caspar (1877).

AE20   Huỳnh Tịnh Paulus Của. Đại Nam quấc-âm tự-vị
[Dictionary of the national language].
Saigon: Rey, Curiol et Cie., 1895. 2 v.
Repr., Saigon: Khai-Tri, 1968. 2 v.

Generally considered to be a second major step in the development of romanized
Vietnamese, after the dictionary of Alexandre de Rhodes 250 years earlier. Published at a time when various elements of
Vietnamese and colonial society were interested in developing a standardized
romanized system of writing. Format consists of each word in its Chinese character, its romanized transcription, and definition and use in compound words or
phrases. Compiler's name is usually written Huỳnh Tịnh Của.
MH-V; NIC

AE21   [Morrone, Giuseppe Maria ?] "Lexicon Cochin-
sinense Latinum ad usum missionum," a
R. P. Josepho Morrone. In American
Philosophical Society, Philadelphia. His-
torical and Literary Committee. A disser-
tation on the nature and character of the
Chinese system of writing, in a letter to
John Vaughan, Esq., by Peter S. DuPonceau
.... Philadelphia, 1838. (Its Transac-
tions, vol. II) pp. 185-[376].

Dictionary of Vietnamese terms and
phrases, with translations into Latin.
Compilers have omitted tone marks and
other diacritics.
MH

AE22   Morrone, Giuseppe Maria. "Vocabulary of the
Cochinchinese language." In American
Philosophical Society, Philadelphia. Historical and Literary Committee. A dissertation on the nature and character of the
Chinese system of writing, in a letter to
John Vaughan, Esq., by Peter S. DuPonceau
.... Philadelphia, 1838. (Its Transactions, vol. II) p. 125-184 [with 10 un-
numbered pages of Chinese characters ap-
pended].

Full title on title page of first section of volume: A dissertation on the
nature and character of the Chinese system
of writing, in a letter to John Vaughan,
Esq., by Peter S. DuPonceau, to which are
subjoined, a vocabulary of the Cochinchinese language, by Father Joseph Morrone,
with references to plates, containing the
characters belonging to each word, and
with notes, showing the degree of affinity
existing between the Chinese and Cochinchinese languages, and the use they respectively make of their common system of
writing, by M. de la Palun, and a Cochinchinese and Latin dictionary, in use among
the R. C. missions in Cochinchina.

Pp. 126-138, Preface, and postscript by
Du Ponceau; pp. 139-142, Preliminary observations, by M. de la Palun. Lists 333
words, with translation into French, English, and romanized Chinese. Du Ponceau's
article discusses the relationships between Vietnamese and Chinese writing sys-
tems; see also his "Letter...to John
Vaughan..." pp. 1-123.

Morrone was an Italian missionary in
Saigon who presented this and the following vocabularies to the American Naval Lt.
John White ca. 1819. White then deposited
them in the library of the East India
Marine Society in Salem, Mass., which
later allowed Du Ponceau to reprint them
here. (White himself published an account
of his trip to Southeast Asia: History of
a voyage to the China Sea. Boston, 1823.)

Noting that the Asiatic Society of Bengal, in Calcutta, had been offered the opportunity to publish a "Cochinchinese and Latin" vocabulary by the "Vicar Apostolic of Cochinchina," or Bp. Taberd, and had decided not to publish them at that time, Du Ponceau expressed his pleasure that the United States "will have the honour of being the first to publish authentic documents respecting the language of Cochinchina, and to introduce that curious idiom to the literary world" (p. 101).

Du Ponceau also refers to Rev. William Jenks of Boston who added the Chinese words to the vocabulary; E. Jacquet of the Société Asiatique who recommended that the vocabulary be published; de la Palun, a student of Abel Rémusat, who had begun to compare the Vietnamese words with the Chinese; and to Klaproth, who refers to various "Anamitic" words in his Asia poly-glotta. The John Vaughan referred to here was librarian of the East India Marine Society; Du Ponceau presented Vaughan with the two manuscripts which he recommended be published.

MH

AE23 Nordemann, Edmond. Quảng tập viêm văn; chresthomathie annamite contenant 180 textes en dialecte tonkinois suivie d'un lexique encyclopédique français illustré de 62 fac-simile, et d'une index français concernant le lexique. Hanoi: [Schneider], 1898 [-1904]. 310 p.

Contains sample texts used in communication among government officials, in drawing up contracts, in writing personal letters, and texts of popular or classical prose and verse, proverbs, and liturgical prayers. Nordemann intended to bring out a translation in French, but did not seem to have done so. Rev. by L. M. Cadière, BEFEO, 4 (1904), 1082-87, which discusses mainly the dialects found among Vietna-

mese: terms it more correctly a dictionary of the Hanoi dialect.

MH

AE24 *Pilon, Al. Petit lexique annamite-français. Hongkong: Impr. de la Société des Missions Étrangères, 1908. 400 p. Rev. by Cordier, BEFEO 8 (1908), 568-571.

AE25 *Ravier, M. H. Dictionarium Latino-Annamiticum Completum et novo Ordine Dispositum, cui addedit Appendix praecipuas Voces proprias cum brevi Explicatione continens. Ninh Phu, 1880. (Source: Ajia.)

AE26 Rhodes, Alexandre de. Dictionarium annnamiticum, Lusitanum et Latinum ope Sacrae Congregationis de Propaganda Fide in lucem editum. Rome: Sacr. Congreg., 1651. 900 col., appendix (errata, 5 p.)

Dictionary of Vietnamese words and phrases with translations into Portuguese and Latin. The first major published Vietnamese dictionary using romanized letters.

MH-H

AE27 Taberd, Jean-Louis. Dictionarium Anamitico-Latinum, primitus inceptum ab...P. J. Pigneaux. Serampore: J. C. Marshman, 1838. 722, 128 p.

On overleaf preceding title page: Chinese characters and romanized transcription: Nam Việt Dương Hiệp Tự Vị.

The dictionary begun by Pigneau de Behaine which burned in 1778 in the fire at the missionary college in Cà-mau; Taberd reconstructed the manuscript as best as possible, then continued Pigneau's work and added a dissertation on Vietnamese grammar (pp. iii-xlvi); a section on floral specimens ("Hortus Floridus Cocincinae" in Chinese, Vietnamese, and Latin, pp. 621-66); and two indexes ("Tabula clavium, characterum Anamiticorum, in

decursu dictionarii Anamitico-Latini...",
pp. 661-719, which is a table of characters explained in the dictionary proper
and arranged in order of the radicals, and
an Appendix ad Dictionarium Anamitico-
Latinum sistens voces sinenses, 128 p.,
separately paged.)--reviewed by M. Bazin
aîné, in JA 3. sér., 9 (1840), 132-149.

Words defined are arranged in French
alphabetical order, with the Chinese
character for each morpheme placed inside
an octagon for easy identification and
compound phrases using that morpheme listed below it. Definitions include examples
of compound usage in Chinese and in Latin.
According to Bazin, use of the Tabula clavium is essential for understanding the
usage of Chinese words in the dictionary
proper.

Cordier, 2285-86, lists another printing of this work. See also the citation
for Morrone (AE22) for similarities between Taberd's and Morrone's works.
MH

AE28   _____. Dictionarium Latino-Anamiticum. Serampore: J. C. Marshman, 1838. 708,
135 p., map of Vietnam folded in back of
book: An Nam Đại Quốc Họa Đồ.

Latin words and phrases defined in
Vietnamese. Unlike his Dictionarium
Anamitico-Latinum, this does not include
Chinese words. Pp. iv-lxxxviii--Latin
grammar, in Vietnamese and in Latin; at
end of volume, the last 135 pages are an
English-French-Latin-Vietnamese vocabulary: Appendix ad Dictionarium Latino-
Anamiticum, Cochinchinese vocabulary; vocabulaire cochinchinois; index Cocin-
cinensium; tự vị An Nam. The Appendix
includes a "Dialogue between the captain
of a ship and a Cochin Chinese," pp. 77-
93; a section on Vietnamese weights,
measures, coinage, time, etc., pp. 92-109;

and a poem, "The martyrdom of Agnes,"
pp. 110-134.
MH

AE29   *Trương Vĩnh Ký. Petit dictionnaire français-
annamite. Saigon: Impr. de l'Union,
1925. 712 p.[1] Originally comp. in 1887.

[1]Boudet 1

VIETNAMESE AND CHINESE LANGUAGES

AE30   Bửu Cân. Hán-Việt thành-ngữ; lexique des
expressions sino-vietnamiennes usuelles.
In lần 2. [Saigon] Phủ Quốc Vụ Khanh
Đặc-Trách Văn Hóa, 1971. 625 p. First
ed., 1933.

Definitions of 13,000 words or phrases
of Chinese origin with transcription into
quốc-ngữ and translation into French.
MH-V; NIC

AE31   Châu Văn Cẩn. Việt-Hán Tối Tân tự-điển.
[Ultra-modern Vietnamese-Chinese dic-
tionary]. Saigon: Vi Hung, 1963.
1,189 p.

Translation of Vietnamese words into
Chinese characters. Format is compact,
double-columned size.
MH-HY

AE32   *Đào Duy Anh. Hán-Việt tự-điển giản-yếu, Hãn
Mạn Tử hiệu-đính. In lần 3. Saigon:
Trường-Thi, 1957. 605 p. (Source: NIC.)

AE33   *Đào Văn Tập. Tự-điển Hán-Việt yếu lược;
dictionnaire sino-vietnamien. Saigon:
Vĩnh Bao, 1953. 467 p. (Source: NIC.)

AE34   *Hán Việt tự điển, bản thảo [Chinese-Vietna-
mese dictionary, rough draft]. Huế:
Đắc-lập, 1925-30, fasc. 1-46; 1117 p.
(Source: Boudet 3.)

AE35 [Ho Ch'eng, et al.] Từ điển Việt Hán [Viet-
namese-Chinese dictionary]. [2d. ed.]
Peking: [The Commercial Press], 1966.
1,372 p. 1st ed., 1960.

Translates about 35,000 Vietnamese
words into Chinese. Arrangement of compound words is alphabetical. Authors'
names in Chinese characters.
MH-HY

AE36 *Hội Khai-trí Tiến-đức Khởi-thảo. Việt-Nam
tự-điển [Vietnamese dictionary]. Hanoi:
Trung-Bắc Tân-văn, 1931-1938 [?].[1] Repr.:
Hanoi: Van Mới, 1954, 663 p.[2]; Saigon:
Mặc Lâm, 1968, 663 p.[3] Saigon: Yiểm Yiểm
Thư Quán, 1968, 663 p.[4]

"Dictionnaire annamite élaboré par
l'A. F. I. M. A. (Association pour la
formation intellectuale et morale des Annamites)" (Boudet 4.) Reviewed by Nguyễn
Văn Tố in BEFEO each year as fascicles
were published and considered a "monu-
mental work."
[1]Boudet 4 [2]NIC [3]Thư-mục 1968 [4]NIC

AE37 [Huang Minh Chien]. Việt Hán từ-điển tối tân
[Ultra modern Vietnamese-Chinese diction-
ary]. Saigon: Nhã sách Chin Hoa, 1961.
947 p. Repr., 1964.

Translates 70,000 Vietnamese words and
phrases into Chinese characters. Format
is compact, double-column-sized. Compound
words arranged alphabetically. Author's
name in Chinese.
MH-HY

AE38 Lê Ngọc Trụ. Việt-ngữ chánh-tả tự-vị [Viet-
namese orthographical dictionary]. Saigon: Thanh-tân, 1959. 509, [11] p.

Lists origin of Vietnamese words, indicating whether they are of Hán or nôm
origin; their meaning and examples of
usage; alternate ways of spelling; present-
day derivations; and Chinese character
with equivalent word in quốc ngữ. Ar-

rangement is for orthographical study, so
words are not arranged alphabetically;
words beginning with, for example, "ch"
and "tr" are interspersed, as are words
ending in similar sounds such as "hoa,"
"ngoa," "oa," and "qua."

Stimulated much discussion; see re-
views listed under names of authors in
Vietnam (Republic) Nha Văn-Khố và Thư-
Viện Quốc-Gia. Sơ-thảo mục-lục thư-tịch
về ngôn-ngữ Việt-nam; reading list on
Vietnamese language (BC6).
MH-V

AE39 Lê Văn Đức. Tự-điển Việt-Nam [Vietnamese
dictionary]. Saigon: Khai Trí, 1970.
2 vols. Cover title: Việt-Nam tự-điển.

Rev. by Nguyễn Hiến Lê, "Bộ Việt-Nam
Tự-điển của ông Lê-văn-Đức," Bách-khoa,
no. 334 (1-12-70), 33-38, and compared
with Việt-nam tự-điển by the Hội Khai-trí
tiến đức; Tự-điển Việt-nam phổ-thông, by
Đào Văn Tập; and Từ-điển tiếng Việt, by
the Nhà Khoa-học Xã-hội (Hanoi). Comprises a general section, 1865 p.; 8,000
idioms; 2,000 proverbs and literary allu-
sions; and a section of 273 p. of biographical and geographical names. Arrangement is according to etymology.
MH-V; NIC

AE40 Lý Văn Hùng. Mô-phạm Việt-Hoa từ-điển
[Model Vietnamese-Chinese dictionary].
X.B. lần thứ 4. Saigon: H. V., 1956.
432 p. 1st ed., 1950.

Translates Vietnamese words into Chinese characters and gives compound words
and phrases in Vietnamese and Chinese.
MH-HY

AE41 *Nguyễn Duyên Niên. Tự điển chỉnh tả đối
chiếu tiếng Việt Nam [Comparative dictionary of Vietnamese]. [n. p., n. p.],
1950. 3 vols.

Vol. 1, S-X; vol. 2, Ch-Tr; vol. 3,
D-Gi-R. (Source: SOAS.)

AE42 Nguyễn Văn Khôn. Hán-Việt từ-điển. Saigon: Khai-trí, [1960]. 1161 p. (Location: MH-V; NIC.) Same title published in 1970 (1155 p.) (Source: TTQGVN, no. 9-10 (1970).)

Contains 40,000 words, arranged alphabetically in Vietnamese order, not in Chinese order. Each word to be defined includes the word in quốc-ngữ, its Chinese character, and a brief definition in quốc-ngữ. Order of compound words is alphabetically without regard to meaning or etymology.

AE43 Phố Căn Thâm [Fu Ken-shen]. Việt-Hán tân tự điển [Vietnamese-Chinese modern dictionary]. Cholon: Wan-Kuo, 1955. 428 p.

Translations of Vietnamese words and compound words.
MH-HY

AE44 Thanh Nghị. Việt-nam tân tự điển minh họa. Saigon, 1952.

NIC has 1968 edition: Saigon: Khai-Trí, 1968. 1,538 p.
NIC

AE45 _____. Việt-ngữ chánh-ta [Vietnamese orthographical dictionary]. Saigon: Thời-thế, 1954. 520 p.
NIC

AE46 Thiều Chiều. Hán Việt tự-điển [Chinese-Vietnamese dictionary]. Hanoi: Đuốc Tuệ, 1942. 817 p. Second edition issued with index of 92 pages: Saigon: Hưng-Long, 1966. 817, 92 p.
NIC

AE47 Từ-điển tiếng Việt [Vietnamese dictionary, ed. by] Văn Tân. Hanoi: Nhà Xuất bản Khoa-học xã hội, 1967. 1172 p.

Culmination of the work of a group organized in 1954 including Trần Văn Giáp, Ngô Thúc Lanh, and other specialists.

Words are listed in strict alphabetical order: Ca, Ch, Co; Ta, Th, Tr, Tu, etc. Orthography (chỉnh ta) is based upon Tự điển chỉnh ta phổ thông (Hanoi: Viện Văn Học, 1963). Gives Northern and Southern usages and spellings. Contains mostly definitions, although some examples of literary usage, folk sayings, and other phrases are included. Discussed by Nguyễn Hiến Lê in review of "Bộ Việt-Nam tự-điển của ông Lê-văn-Đức," Bách-Khoa, no. 334 (1-12-1970), 31-38. Reviewed by Quang Đàm in "Some thoughts about the Dictionary of the Vietnamese language," Nhân Dân, May 14, 1969, p. 3 (translated in Translations on North Vietnam, no. 557, JPRS, 48270, MC, 1969: 12875-24, and praised for expressing a spirit of independence and self government rather than relying on a Chinese or French dictionary to decide, arrange, and define words, for defining scientifically, clearly, and fully, and for emphasizing scientific and technical terms. Criticized for lack of clear-cut distinctions between normal words and idioms, proverbs, etc., for omitting certain "necessary and popular words," for inaccurate or insufficient explanations, and for using too many Chinese loan words instead of Vietnamese words.
MH-V

AE48 *Văn Tân. Từ-điển Trung-Việt. Hanoi: Sự-thật, 1956. 1,418 p. (Source: NIC, SOAS.)

AE49 *Vietnam (Democratic Republic). Ủy Ban Khoa học Nhà nước. Tự điển chỉnh ta phổ thông [Popular orthographical dictionary]. Hanoi: Viện Văn Học, 1963. 311 p. (Source: Châu.)

VIETNAMESE, CHINESE AND FRENCH LANGUAGES

AE50　Dào Duy Anh. Dictionnaire français annamite
(transcription en caractères des termes
sino-annamites.); Pháp Việt tự-điển, chú
thêm chữ Hán. Huế: Quan-hai tùng-thư,
1936. 2 vols. 2d. ed., Paris, 1950.
4th ed. Saigon: Trường-thi, [1957].
1958 p.

　　"The most scholarly lexicographic work
today."--Laurence C. Thompson. Extensive
and detailed dictionary of French words
and terms.
MH-V

AE51　*_____. Giản-yếu Hán-Việt tự-điển (dictionnaire sino-annamite) avec annotations en
français. Revu par Hãn-Mạn-Tử et Giao-
tieu. Huế: Tiếng-dân (vol. 1); Hanoi:
Lê-văn-Tân (vol. 2), 1932. 3. éd. Paris:
Minh-Tân, 1951. (Source: Boudet 4.)

　　Review of first edition by Nguyễn Văn
Tố, in BEFEO, 32 (1932), 524.

AE52　Gouin, Eugène. Dictionnaire vietnamien-
chinois-français. Saigon: IDEO, 1957.
1606 p.

　　A major work, listing words in three
languages, with numerous explanations of
words and phrases. Arranged by etymology.
MH

AE53　Hue, Gustave. Dictionnaire annamite-chinois-
français. Hanoi: Impr. Trung-hoa, 1937.
1199 p. Repr, Saigon: Khai-trí, 1971.
(Location: MH-V)

　　"Ancestor of Gouin's 1957 trilingual
dictionary," reviewed in France-Asie, 13
(1957), 649. Reviewed by Nguyễn Văn Tố,
in BEFEO, 37 (1937), 502-03.

AE54　*Savina, François Marie. Guide linguistique
de l'Indochine française.

　　See AE100 for description; includes
words in Chinese, French, and Vietnamese.

VIETNAMESE AND FRENCH LANGUAGES

AE55　Barbier, Victor. Dictionnaire annamite-
français. Hanoi: IDEO, 1922. 951 p.
3. éd., 1929, has same pagination (Location: MH).

　　Arranged in Vietnamese alphabetical
order. Includes words translated into
French and used in phrases. Does not
give parts of speech or etymology with
definitions.

AE56　_____. Dictionnaire français-annamite.
Hanoi: IDEO, 1924. 856 p. 7. éd., 1930,
has same pagination (Location: MH).

　　Contains 20,000 words and phrases.
According to Barbier, the dictionaries by
Ravier and Dronet provided a framework
for this work. Each entry lists the parts
of speech.

AE57　*Cordier, Georges. Dictionnaire annamite-
français, à l'usage des élèves des écoles
et des annamitisants. Hanoi: Impr. Tonkinoise, 1930. 1433 p. (Source:
Boudet 3.)

AE58　*_____. Dictionnaire français-annamite.
Hanoi: Impr. Tonkinoise, 1934-35.
3 vols.

　　Reviewed by Nguyễn Văn Tố, in BEFEO
34 (1934), 642, and 35 (1935), 376.
(Source: Boudet 3.)

AE59　Đào Đăng Vỹ. Pháp-Việt tự-điển (loại giản
yếu); dictionnaire français-viêtnamien.
2. éd. rev. et corr. Saigon, 1957.
1280 p. (Location: Ajia). 2. éd.
Saigon: the author, 1965. 951 p.
(Source: Thu-mục 1965); also cited as
2. éd. Saigon: Khai-trí, 1964. 2133 p.
(Source: Thu-mục 1965).

LANGUAGE DICTIONARIES AE

AE60 _____ . Việt-Pháp tân từ-điển; nouveau dictionnaire viêtnamien-français. 3. éd. Saigon, 1956. 1458 p. (Source: Ajia.)

AE61 *_____ . Việt-Pháp tiểu-từ-điển; petit dictionnaire vietnamien-français. [Saigon?] 1966. 936 p. (Source: NIC.)

AE62 *Đào Văn Tập. Từ-điển Pháp-Việt phổ thông; dictionnaire général français-viêtnamien. Saigon: Vĩnh Bao, 1953. 1242 p. (Source: Cương; NIC.)

AE63 _____ . Từ-điển Việt Pháp phổ thông; dictionnaire général viêtnamien-français. Saigon: Vĩnh Bao, 1953. 839 p. (Source: Cương; NIC.)

AE64 *Khai Anh, and Thanh Nghị. Pháp-Việt tiểu từ-điển [Small French-Vietnamese dictionary]. In lần 4. [Saigon?] Như-ý, 1968. 789 p. (Source: NIC.)

AE65 *Lê Công Đắc. Dictionnaire français-annamite. Hanoi: Impr. Thụy-ký, 1939. 912 p. An edition published in 1952 also cited as Dictionnaire français-viêtnamien (n. p., 1952). (Source: Nguyễn Khắc Kham, E. Asian cultural studies.)

AE66 *Masseron, G. Nouveau dictionnaire français-annamite. Saigon [i.e. Tân-định]: Impr. de la Mission, 1922. 1083 p. (Source: Boudet 2.)

AE67 Thanh Nghị. Từ-điển Việt-Nam. Saigon: Thời-Thế, 1958. 1515 p.
Vietnamese-Vietnamese-French. Includes examples of usage from famous quotations, folk sayings, and literature. Some biographical data.
mgc

VIETNAMESE, FRENCH, AND ENGLISH LANGUAGES

AE68 Ngô Vũ, and Thanh Nghị. Anh-Việt-Pháp tử-điển [English-Vietnamese-French dictionary]. In lần 1. [Saigon]: Thời-Thế, 1956. 650 p. In lần 2. Ibid. [1960] 650 p. NIC lists a 1968 edition by Thanh-Nghị: Saigon: Khai-trí, 1968. 650 p.
In the second edition, English words are given in Roman and in international phonetic alphabets.

AE69 *_____ . Việt-Pháp-Anh tử-điển [Vietnamese-French-English dictionary]. [Saigon] Thời-Thế, 1957. 890 p. (Source: DLC SAAL, Dec. '59.)

VIETNAMESE AND ENGLISH LANGUAGES

AE70 *Ban Tu-thư Tuấn-Tú. Anh-Việt tử điển; English-Vietnamese dictionary. Saigon: Tuấn-Tú, 1970. 1661 p. (Source: NIC.)

AE71 Emeneau, Murray B. Annamese-English dictionary, with an English-Annamese index based on work by John Sherry, by M. B. Emeneau, and Diether von der Steinen. Berkeley: Army Specialized Training Program, Univ. of Calif., 1945. 279 p.
Contains mostly definitions--no pronunciation guides, some guides to usage of terms.
MH

AE72 Lê Bá Khanh and Lê Bá Kông. Standard pronouncing Vietnamese-English and English-Vietnamese dictionary. New York: Ungar, 1955. 388, 428 p. in 1 vol.
Includes phonetic transcription of English-language words. Arrangement is alphabetical.
MH

AE73 *____. Từ điển tiêu chuẩn Việt-Anh; standard
pronouncing Vietnamese English dictionary.
Loại mới có sửa lại và thêm nhiều chữ [New
version, corrected and enlarged]. Saigon:
Ziên Hồng, 1964. 439 p. (Source: NIC.)

AE74 *Lê Bá Kông. Từ-điển tiêu chuẩn Anh-Việt;
standard pronouncing English-Vietnamese
dictionary. Saigon: Ziên-Hồng, 1968.
498 p. (Source: Thư-mục 1968.)

   NIC has rev. ed., with subtitle: "With
a guide to Vietnamese pronunciation and an
outline of Vietnamese grammar." Saigon:
Ziên Hồng, 1964. 562 p. [First ed. not
cited.]

AE75 Lê Văn Hùng, Mrs., and Dr. Lê Văn Hùng.
Vietnamese-English dictionary. Paris:
Éditions Europe-Asie, 1955. 820 p.

   Contains over 30,000 words and expressions. Arranged alphabetically. Vietnamese and English words are spelled in
standard spelling as well as phonetically.
MH

AE76 Nguyễn Đình Hòa. Vietnamese-English dictionary. Saigon: Binh Minh, 1959. 568 p.
Rev. ed. Rutland, Vt.: Tuttle, 1966.
568 p.

   A standard dictionary with clear format. Arrangement is alphabetical without
regard to etymology. Features are the use
of the letter "R" to indicate words which
must be used in a compound word, indication of the Sino-Vietnamese word corresponding to a Vietnamese word, and
indication of words which are used with
classifiers.
MH

AE77 ____. Vietnamese-English student dictionary (rev. and enl. ed.). Saigon: Vietnamese American Association, [1967].
674 p. On cover: Hoa's Vietnamese-
English student's dictionary.

A more comprehensive dictionary than
his 1966 dictionary. Arrangement is
similar, i.e. alphabetical without regard
to etymology.
MH-V

AE78 *____. Vietnamese-English vocabulary.
Washington, D.C.: Office of Training,
National Security Agency, 1955. 429 p.
(Source: DLC.)

AE79 Nguyễn Văn Khôn. English-Vietnamese dictionary; Anh-Việt từ điển. Saigon: Hồ Văn
Hoài, 1952. 1741 p. Also published in
1955.
NIC; MH

AE80 ____. Việt-Anh từ-điển, loại phổ thông;
general Vietnamese English dictionary.
Saigon: Khai Trí, 1966. 1233 p.

   Alphabetical listing, does not distinguish etymology. Omits parts of speech
from definitions. Provides numerous examples of usage.
MH-V; NIC

AE81 ____. Việt-Anh, Anh-Việt từ điển thông
dụng; usual Vietnamese-English, English-
Vietnamese dictionary. [Saigon: Khai
Trí, 1967]. 1010, [606] p.[1] Distributed
by Pacific Northwest Trading Co., Ft.
Lewis, Wash., Printed in Taiwan, Republic
of China.

   Arranged in alphabetical order without
regard to etymology. Listing of each
word, whether in Vietnamese or English,
includes its pronunciation in the International Phonetic Alphabet.

   The English-Vietnamese portion is
basically a variant edition of his Từ-điển
Anh-Việt phổ-thông; general English-Vietnamese dictionary (Saigon: Khai-Trí,
1967, 605 p.).[2]
[1]MH-V [2]NIC

LANGUAGE DICTIONARIES AE

AE82 *Nguyễn Văn Tạo. Tự-điển phổ-thông Anh-Việt; English-Vietnamese dictionary. Saigon: Tao Đàn, [1970?]. 1379 p. Cover has title: Anh-Việt tân tự điển. (Source: NIC.)

AE83 *Trần Văn Điền. Việt-Anh tự-điển, loại phổ thông; Vietnamese-English dictionary. Saigon: Sống mới, 1968. 720 p. (Source: Thư-mục, 1968.)

AE84 *Tự điển Anh-Việt. Khoảng 65.000 từ [English-to-Vietnamese dictionary. Approximately 65,000 entries]. Hanoi: Khoa học xã hội, 1975. 1,960 p.

Compiled by the Ủy ban Khoa học xã hội Việt-Nam, Viện Ngôn ngữ học [Viet-Nam Commission for the Social Sciences, Institute of Linguistics].

Cited in Vietnam studies newsletter, June 1976: "Overall quality is superior to any existing English-Viet dictionary, even though rather inadequate in terms of American idioms and colloquialisms" and obtainable from Great Eastern Book Co., Hong Kong. (Source: MLXBP, 9/75.)

AE85 U.S. Armed Forces Security Agency School. Vietnamese-English etymological glossary. Washington, D.C., 1952. 367 p.

Presents compound words and expressions in their various elements and defines each element, e.g. "Di trú" to immigrate: "di" to transfer, "trú" to reside. Emphasis on political and military terminology in order to complement the texts at the School. MH-L

VIETNAMESE AND RUSSIAN LANGUAGES

AE86 Nguyễn Năng An. Tự-điển Nga-Việt; Russko-V'etnamskij slovar' [Russian-Vietnamese dictionary], ed. P. I. Aleshima [and] Hồng-Hà. Moscow: Gosudarstvennoe izd-vo inostrannykh i natsional nykh

slovarei, 1958. 732 p.[1] [2. ed., 1961] 736 p.[2]

Contains 24,000 definitions.
[1]MH [2]Berton

AE87 *Karmannyi Russko-V'etnamskij slovar' [Pocket Russian-Vietnamese dictionary]. Ibid., 1962. 525 p. (Source: Berton.)

Contains 7,500 words.

AE88 *Russko-V'etnamskij slovar' [by] O. E. Efimova [et al, ed. by] Nguyễn Văn Thanh. Moscow: Military Publishing House, 1958. 602 p.

Defines 10,000 words. (Source: Thompson; DLC.)

AE89 *Russko-v'etnamskii uchebnyi slovar', okolo 11,200 slov. Sostavili Tolstoi I. V.; Tolstoiia R. A.; Dao Chong Tkhyong. Pod. red. Nguen van Khania. Moscow: Sovetskaia entsiklopediia, 1965. 940 p. (Source: BAS 1966.)

AE90 *Tự-điển Nga-Việt thực-dụng [by] Anh-Dao [et al, ed. by] Thanh Nguyễn. Hanoi, 1957. (Source: Thompson.)

AE91 *V'etnamsko-russkij slovar' [by] I. I. Glebova [ed. by] I. M. Osanina, Vũ Đăng Ất. Moscow: Gosudarstvennoe izdatel'stvo inostrannykh i natsional'nykh, 1961. 616 p.

Contains 36,000 definitions. (Source: Berton.)

VIETNAMESE AND POLISH LANGUAGES

AE92 *Nguyễn Trần Ba, Nguyễn Tự Thắng [et al]. Mały słownik wietnamskopolsi i polsko-wietnamski. Warszaw: Pańslwowe Wydawn Nawkowe, 1972. 423, 507 p.

Vietnamese-Polish/Polish-Vietnamese dictionary. Author's name on title page: Nguen Tran Ba. (Source: NIC Nov. 1973.)

AE93 *Osiak, J. Słownik polsko-wietnamski do
      shryptu. J. Kulaka, W. Łaciaka, I. Zelesz-
      kiewicza: Jezyk polski Dla cudzoziemcow.
      Wyd. 1. Warsaw: Pánstwow Wydawnictwo
      Naukowe, 196- . 181 p.

      Defines about 4,500 terms. (Source:
      Bibl. der Wörterbuch.)

AE94 *Thanh-Le. Rozmówki polsko-wietnamskie. Red.
      M. Jaworowski, W. Matuszyńska. Wyd. 1.
      Warsaw: Wiedza Powzechna, 1963. 235 p.

      Defines about 3,500 terms. (Source:
      Bibl. der Wörterbuch, 1962-64.)

OTHER LANGUAGES

AE95 *Ferkinghoff, Klaus. Deutsches-vietnamesisches
      wörterbuch; từ-điển Đức-Việt. Wiesbaden:
      Harrassowitz, 1962. 110 p. (Source:
      DLC.)

AE96 *Hộ Giác. Pali Việt từ điển; Pali-Vietnamese
      dictionary. Saigon: Phật-học viện Pháp
      quang, 1965. 100 p. (Source: Thư-mục
      1965.)

AE97 Karow, Otto. Vietnamesisch-Deutsches Wörter-
      buch; tự điển Việt-Đức. Wiesbaden: Har-
      rassowitz, 1972. 1086 p.

      Definitions of 40,000 words, including
      root words, Chinese equivalents in roman-
      ized Mandarin or Cantonese, and names of
      historical personnages and geographical
      locations. Hyphens between words (e.g.
      kết-luận) indicate words of Chinese ori-
      gin. Letters "SV" used to denote words of
      Sino-Vietnamese origin. Where appropriate,
      regional uses of words, vulgar words,
      obsolete words, and words used in classi-
      cal literature are indicated.

      Pp. 953-983, table of Chinese charac-
      ters. Pp. 985-1086, table of Nôm charac-
      ters and transliteration into quốc-ngữ,
      from pp. 3-102 of Từ điển chữ Nôm, by
      Nguyễn Quang Xỹ and Vũ Văn Kính (AE12).
      MH

AE98 *Lê Duy Lương. Từ-điển Việt-Lào; Ma Ha Kham
      phan Vi Lã Chít hiệu đỉnh [Vietnamese-Lao
      dictionary]. Hanoi: Văn Hóa Nghệ Thuật,
      1963. 742 p. (Source: NIC.)

AE99 *Savina, François Marie. Dictionnaire tay-
      annamite-français. Hanoi: IDEO, 1910.
      488 p. (Source: Johnson--NIC.)
      CtY

AE100 *_____. Guide linguistique de l'Indochine
      française. Hongkong: Société des Mis-
      sions Étrangères, 1939. 2 vols.

      Glossary of French words translated
      into Vietnamese and romanized Thổ, Mán,
      Mèo, Cantonese, Hoclo (romanized and
      characters), and Mandarin. Vol. 1, A-J,
      with supplement of 107 pages, numbered
      separately, of French, Vietnamese, roman-
      ized Cantonese, and Chinese characters.
      Vol. 2, K-Z. (Source: CtY; NIC.)

AE101 Văn Vi Trình, and Wakabayashi. Từ-điển Việt-
      Nhật thông thoại [Vietnamese-Japanese con-
      versational dictionary]. Saigon: Minh-
      Tâm [1970]. 487 p.

      Glossary of Vietnamese words translated
      into romanized Japanese, with numerous ex-
      amples of usage. Includes French or Eng-
      lish words or phrases with each definition.
      MH-V; NIC

AE102 *Vortaro esperatu-vjetnama; tự-điển quốc-tế-
      ngữ-Việt. Nhóm tu-thư quốc tế ngữ
      [Esperanto-Vietnamese dictionary, by the
      Esperanto publications group]. Hanoi:
      Hội Quốc tế ngữ bao vệ hòa bình tại Việt-
      Nam, 1960. 321 p. (Source: Novaiia,
      6/61.)

PERIODICALS   AF

Periodical articles are an important source
for information about Vietnam because of the number
of materials published in this form. Of the many
indexes to periodicals, only a few are listed below
which have been found to be the most comprehensive
for Vietnamese studies. In addition to the titles
listed in this chapter, bibliographies in other sections also cite periodical articles, expecially the
Bibliography of Asian studies (AA21) and Cumulative
bibliography of Asian studies, 1941-1965, 1966-1970
(AA20); Southeast Asia subject catalog (AA26); Universal reference system (CI16); and Social sciences
citation index (CA3). The Index to Southeast Asian
Journals, 1960-1974: A Guide to Journals, Book Reviews and Composite Works by Donald Clay Johnson
(Boston: G. K. Hall, May, 1977) cites periodical
articles dealing with Southeast Asia published from
1960 through 1974 (AA106).

BIBLIOGRAPHIES

MAJOR SOURCES

AF1   Cordier, Henri. Bibliotheca indosinica.

See AA23 for complete description. The
complete contents of five periodicals,
through 1913, are listed in vols. 3 and 4:
Bulletin du Comité Agricole et Industriel
de la Cochinchine (1865-1881), vol. 3:
1712-1725; Bulletin de la Société des
Études indochinoises (1883-1913), col.
1726-1740; El Correo Sino-Annamita (1866-
1910), col. 1981-2044 and (1911-1913),
vol. 4: 2939-2942; Bulletin de la Commission Archéologique de l'Indochine (1908-
1913), vol. 3: 1881-1884; and Excursions
et Reconnaissances (1879-1890), col. 1752-
1759.

Articles in other periodicals are listed individually in the appropriate subject
sections, with a virtually complete listing of periodical articles in all romanized languages. See also "Liste alphabétique des publications périodiques,"

vol. 5 (Index), p. 307-309, which also includes references to headings in the Index
des matières, pp. 224-305, for periodicals
not in the Liste, e.g. "Annales" and "Annuaires." Lists of periodicals, with
bibliographical information, are also in
vol. 3: 1661-1674 and 4: 2926-2928, in
the section "Géographique--Publications
périodiques."
MH

AF2   Boudet, Paul, and Rémy Bourgeois. Bibliographie de l'Indochine française.

See AA22 for complete description. For
names of periodicals and bibliographical
information about each periodical, see
"Périodiques" in volumes 1, 3, and 4. Includes commercial, official, trade, and
professional periodicals. Volumes 3 and 4
include periodicals in Vietnamese. In
volume 2, periodicals are listed with the
respective subjects.
MH

AF3   Association pour la Conservation et la Reproduction Photographique de la Presse. Catalogue de microfilm reproduisant des
périodiques et journaux et revues. Paris.
Annual.

The catalog for 1971 lists 12 official
gazettes published in Indochina from 1862-
1950 and 46 periodicals and newspapers
including BAVH, Nam Phong, La revue indochinoise, Trung-Bắc tân văn, and Đuốc nhà
nam.

Microfilms are made primarily from
publications in the Bibliothèque Nationale.
MH

AF4   Gélinas, André. "An exhaustive list of all
serials, journals and magazines currently
being published in Vietnam as of January 1974." CORMOSEA newsletter, 7
(1973/74), 1-17.

Annotated list of 135 serials. Annotations include frequency, languages,

pagination of average issue, publisher and
address, beginning date, and description
of contents.

mgc

AF5   Institut d'Étude du Viet Nam contemporain.
       Guide pratique de recherche sur le Viet
       Nam en France.

          See DD16 for complete description. In-
       cludes list of about 225 periodicals and
       other serial publications and the loca-
       tions in some libraries in Paris and
       Saigon.

       MH

AF6   *Masson, André. "Notes bibliographiques sur
       les débuts de la presse périodique en
       Indochine." Bulletin général de l'in-
       struction publique, 8 (N° 9, mai 1929),
       165-171, 9 (N° 1, sept. 1929), 7-12.

          "Includes data on the first publica-
       tions to appear in the French language"
       (Jumper).

AF7   Michigan. State University, East Lansing.
       Vietnam Advisory Group, Saigon. Bibliog-
       raphy of periodicals published in Vietnam.
       Saigon, 1962. 26 p.

          Part 1, reproduction of 1958 bibliog-
       raphy by Nguyễn Xuân Đào and Richard K.
       Gardner, 8 pp. Part 2, addendum, in-
       cludes only those periodicals omitted in
       the 1958 list.

       DLC

AF8   *Niên-lịch Công-đàn. Saigon: Công-đàn, 1960.
          Includes a list of Indochinese and
       Vietnamese periodicals published before
       1960.--Bibliographical services throughout
       the world, 1965-1969 (Paris: UNESCO,
       1971).

AF9   Vietnam (Republic). Nha Văn-khố và Thư-Viện
       Quốc-Gia. Mục lục báo chí Việt ngữ 1865-
       1965 [Bibliography of the Vietnamese-
       language press, 1865-1965].

          See AG1 for complete description.

AF10   _____. Thư-Viện Văn-Khố. Ấn phẩm định-kỳ
       quốc nội [Periodical publications from
       Vietnam]. Saigon: Bộ Thông Tin, 1968- .
       Annual. (Location: MH.)

          Issues for 1968 (32 p.), 1969 (44 p.)
       and 1970 (47 p.) published as of 1976.
       Lists, in alphabetical order by frequency
       of publication, about 190 newspapers,
       monthlies, quarterlies, yearbooks, and
       other periodicals published in RVN. En-
       tries include name of periodical, short
       description, publisher's or printer's
       address and telephone number, and size.
       Includes Vietnamese-language and other
       periodicals (Chinese-language periodicals
       have romanized titles only) whether pub-
       lished commercially, by the government, by
       societies, or educational institutions.

          A slightly less complete list was pub-
       lished by the librarian of the Bộ Thông
       Tin, Nguyễn Văn, as "Bảng liệt-kê báo-chí
       xuất-bản tại Việt-Nam C. H. trong năm
       1968," [List of periodicals published in
       the Republic of Vietnam during 1968] Thư-
       viện tập-san, nos. 5-6 (1969), 32-50.
       (Location: mgc.)

AF11   _____. Tổng Thư-Viện Quốc-Gia. Bảng kê tập
       san Đông Dương và Việt Nam (liste des pé-
       riodiques indochinois et vietnamiens).
       [Saigon? ca. 1962.] 44 p.

          Alphabetical listing by title of 1,003
       periodicals, with indication of the hold-
       ings of the Library. Does not list any
       periodicals from DRVN. Includes some
       newspapers. Copy examined is Xerographed
       copy of the mimeographed original, not of
       good quality, from the Library.

       MH-V; CtY; NIC

AF12   Yale University. Library. Southeast Asia
       Collection. Checklist of Southeast Asian
       serials. Boston: G. K. Hall, 1968.
       320 p.

PERIODICALS AF

Alphabetical listing by author or title
of 3,748 serials in the Yale University
Library, of which over 100 are on Vietnam.
Includes many references to government
publications, society publications, and
limited editions of materials published
before 1945 in all languages. Includes
serials on microform as well as printed
works. See "Index by country of origin,"
p. xxiv for "Vietnam, France, Great Britain, and United States; some Russian periodicals on Asia are included in the
bibliography, but are not listed in the
"Index by country of origin." Lists individual titles of monograph series and
holdings in the library of most serials.
MH

OTHER SOURCES

AF13   Annuaire de la presse et de la publicité.
        Paris, 1880- .

AF14   Bibliographie de la France, supplément A,
        Périodiques. Paris: Cercle de la
        Librairie, 1946- .

AF15   Paris. Bibliothèque Nationale. Département
        des Périodiques. Catalogue collectif des
        périodiques, du début du XVIIe siècle à
        1939. Paris, 1966- .

INDEXES TO ARTICLES IN PERIODICALS

MAJOR SOURCES

AF16   Fondation Nationale des Sciences Politiques.
        Centre de Documentation Contemporaine.
        Bibliographie courante d'articles de pé-
        riodiques postérieurs à 1944 sur les pro-
        blèmes politiques, économiques et sociaux;
        Index to post-1944 periodical articles on
        political, economic, and social problems.
        Boston: G. K. Hall, 1968. 17 vols. Sup-
        pléments 1-7, 1969-1974, Ibid., 1969-1976.

Citations and summaries for articles on
contemporary issues. Arranged alphabetically by country: See vol. 7, pp. 975-
1008 (France III); vol. 13, pp. 544-591
(Vietnam); and vol. 15, pp. 178-213 (Problèmes regionaux). Important for articles
published in European countries. Vol. 1
contains a list of periodical indexes,
classification scheme, and index to the
classification scheme. The scheme for
France is the basis upon which other countries are arranged; it is not necessary to
use the classification scheme as all entries about Vietnam are in one of three
volumes mentioned above. Publications
about "Bouddhisme" (code number 102/6),
for example are in volume 13, pp. 580-581.
Entries are inconsistent: both Nguyễn-
Quốc-Định and Định, N. Q. are used. Editing is inconsistent: p. 544-545 contains
citations for code number 10 (politique
intérieure), 211 (relations avec autres
pays), 280 (problèmes de défense) and 37
(jeunesse) interspersed.

In the suppléments, arrangement is alphabetically by country, with Vietnam in
vol. 2 of each supplément. About 80-120
references to Vietnam are in each
supplément.
MH

AF17   Lent, John A. Asian mass communications; a
        comprehensive bibliography. Philadelphia:
        School of Communications and Theater,
        Temple University, 1975. 708 p.

        References primarily in English-language
        publications. "Vietnam," pp. 518-531 and
        699-700, lists about 300 publications,
        mostly on such topics as censorship of the
        press in Saigon at various times during
        the 1960's, coverage of the war by foreign
        news reporters, and perceptions of the war
        by American journalists. Includes many
        references to the New York Times.
        MH

AF18   Trần Thị KimSa. Mục lục phân tích tạp-chí Việt-ngữ, 1954-1964; a guide to Vietnamese periodical literature, 1954-1964. Saigon: Học-viện Quốc-gia Hành-chánh, 1965. 318 p.

Also an article by the same title published in Nghiên-cứu hành-chánh, nos. 6/7 (6/7, 1961), 113-161; not available for consultation.

Index to articles in seven major social science periodicals published in Saigon and Hue. Arranged alphabetically by subject (in Vietnamese) under personal name of author; personal name index. Contains 1,976 entries, some of which are listed under more than one subject heading; cross-references to other subjects are included. MH

OTHER SOURCES

The following sources are suggested as additional indexes to periodical articles, of which the first source is particularly useful for French-language articles.

AF19   Internationale Bibliographie der Zeitschriftenliteratur aus allen Gebieten des Wissens; international bibliography of periodical literature covering all fields of knowledge; bibliographie international de la littérature périodique dans toutes les domaines de la connaissance. Osnabrück: Felix Dietrich Verlag, 1965- . Preceded by Bibliographie der Deutschen Zeitschriftenliteratur (Leipzig and Osnabrück, 1896-1964) and Bibliographie der fremdsprachigen Zeitschriftenliteratur (Ibid., 1911-1964), published as Abteilung A and B of Internationale Bibliographie der Zeitschriftenliteratur.

AF20   British humanities index. London: Library Association, 1962- . Supersedes Subject index to periodicals, 1919-1961.

AF21   Bulletin signalétique. Paris: Centre national de la recherche scientifique, 1940- . Published in several sections according to subject.

AF22   Fondation Nationale des Sciences Politiques. Bulletin analytique de documentation politique, économique et sociale contemporaine. Paris: Presses Universitaires de France, 1946- . Supersedes Bulletin bibliographique de documentation international contemporaine (Ibid., 1922-1940).

AF23   Humanities index. New York: Wilson, 1975- . Continues International index (1920-1965) and Social sciences and humanities index (1965-1974).

AF24   Public Affairs Information Service. Bulletin of the Public Affairs Information Service. New York, 1915- . (Cited as PAIS; particularly useful for locating periodical articles published in the United States on economics and politics during the 1960's.)

AF25   _____ . Public Affairs Information Service foreign language index. New York, 1972- . (Vol. 1 covers 1968-1971; subsequent volumes cover articles published in 1972 and later in French, German, Italian, and Spanish.)

AF26   Social sciences index. New York: Wilson, 1975- . Continues International index (1920-1965) and Social sciences and humanities index (1965-1974).

AF27   Soviet periodical abstracts: Asia, Africa, Latin America. New York: Slavic Languages Research Institute, 1961-1967.

AF28   Universal Reference System. Political science, government, and public policy series. Princeton, N.J.: Princeton Research Publ. Co., 1957- . (See CI16 for annotation.)

PERIODICALS AF

See also bibliographies in the subject chapters for more specific indexes to various subjects.

INDEXES OF PERIODICALS

AF29 Bulletin économique de l'Indochine. (1898-1952).

See CG3 for bibliographical description and references to indexes.

AF30 Comité Agricole et Industriel de la Cochinchine. Bulletin. (1865-1883).

INDEX: "Tables des matières traitées dans les rapports et documents du Comité Agricole et Industriel de 1865 à 1871." BCAI, 3. tome, no. 11 (2d semestre 1870, année 1871), 169-178. INDEX: "Tables... de 1872 à 1877." BCAI, 2. sér., 1. tome, no. 5 (1876), 477-483. INDEX: "Tables... de 1878 à 1881." BCAI, 4. sér., 1. tome, no. 2 (1881), I-IV. INDEX: "Tables du Bulletin du Comité Agricole et Industriel de la Cochinchine (1865-1883)." BSEI, n.s. 8, 1/2 (1933), [61-82], 113-121. Includes indexes by author, by subject, and by proper name and subject; published as part of the "Cinquantenaire de la Société des Études Indochinoises." See also Cordier 3, 1712-1725 for a list of the contents.
MH

AF31 *Đông-Dương [Indochina] (1913-1916).

INDEX: Nguyễn Hùng Cường. "Bảng tổng kê tập san Đông Dương và Việt Nam." Văn-hóa Á-châu no. 19 (1959), 94-97; no. 20 (1959), 96; no. 21 (1959), 91-97; no. 22 (1959), 86-91; nos. 23/24 (1959), 75-77. (Source: Cường.)

AF32 École française d'Extrême-Orient. Bulletin. (1900- .)

INDEX: Nguyễn Văn Tố, "Index général des tomes I-XX du Bulletin de l'École française d'Extrême-Orient." BEFEO, 21 (1921), 1-274.

Alphabetical author and subject index of articles, reviews, notices, and illustrations. Pp. 247-274, chronological list of tables of contents and author index to that listing.

_____. INDEX: "Index général des tomes XXI à XXX (années 1921 à 1930)." BEFEO, 32 (1932), 583-824.

Pp. 583-798, Index général; pp. 799-821, chronological listing of tables of contents; pp. 822-824, listing of names of authors.

Microfiche available from IDC.
MH

AF33 Excursions et Reconnaissances. (1879-1890)

Tables of contents published in Cordier 1752-1759, for the years 1879-1890; Cordier also indicates reprinted editions in Saigon (1891-1897) and in Hanoi (1899).
MH

AF34 *Học Tập [Studies]. Hanoi, 1955- .

INDEX: Tổng mục lục tạp chỉ Học Tập 10 năm, 1955-1965 [Ten-year cumulative index to the magazine Học Tập, 1955-1965]. Hanoi, 1976.

INDEX: Tổng mục lục tạp chỉ Học Tập 10 năm, 1966-1975 [Ten-year cumulative index to the magazine Học Tập, 1966-1975] Hanoi, 1976.

Học Tập is the official theoretical journal of the Vietnam Workers' Party (Đảng Lao Động). The journal itself has recently been reprinted: Tập hợp tạp chỉ Học Tập 20 năm 1955-1975 [Twenty-year cumulative reprint of Học Tập magazine, 1955-1975]. Hanoi, 1976, and Tập hợp tạp chỉ Học Tập 10 năm, 1966-1975 [Ten-year cumulative reprint of Học Tập magazine, 1966-1975]. Hanoi, 1976.

Cited in Vietnam studies newsletter, June 1976, and offered for sale through Great Eastern Book Co., Hong Kong.

AF35 Nam-Phong [Southern breeze]. (1917-1934).

INDEX: Nguyễn Khắc Xuyên. Mục-lục phân tích tạp-chỉ Nam-Phong 1917-1934 [Index to the contents of the journal Nam-Phong]. Saigon: Trung-tâm học-liệu, 1968. 461 p.

MH-V

AF36 Nghiên-cứu lịch-sử [Historical researches]. (1959-).

Contents of many issues, 1959-1963, discussed by Phan Gia Bền (DB15).

AF37 Petermanns Geographische Mitteilungen.

See CK11 for index by Sternstein and Springer.

AF38 *Société des Amis du vieux Huế. Bulletin des Amis du Vieux Huế. (1914-1941).

INDEX: L. M. Cadière, "Bulletin des Amis du Vieux Huế (1914-1923). Index analytique et résumé des matières," and "Table des matières par noms d'auteurs (1914-1923)," BAVH, 12, 2ème ptie (1925), 61-399. INDEX: L. M. Cadière, Index du Bulletin des Amis du Vieux Huế (1914-1941). Huế, 1942. 166 p.

Microfilm available from ACRPP (1914-1939).

AF39 Société des Études indochinoises, Saigon. Bulletin de la Société des Études indochinoises (1883-1975[?]).

INDEX: Métaye, Roger. "Tables du Bulletin de la Société des Études indochinoises (1883-1971)." BSEI n.s. 46 (1971), 435-604. Combined index to articles, book reviews, and notices in BSEI, with separate sections by name of author, by subject (arranged in Dewey Decimal Classification), chronologically by subject, and by name of book reviewed.

In addition to the above index, separate indexes were published from time to time: INDEX: [L. Peralle, comp.] "Table analytique des matières traitées dans les Bulletins de la Société des Études indochinoises depuis sa fondation (1883)." BSEI, no. 29 (1895), 1-39. INDEX: "Table analytique des questions traitées dans les Bulletins de la Société des Études indochinoises depuis sa fondation (1883) jusqu'en 1914." BSEI, no. 69 (1918), 133-148. (See also Cordier 3: 1726-1739 for a list of contents, 1883-1913.) INDEX: "Tables du Bulletin de la Société des Études indochinoises (1865-1932)." BSEI, n.s. 8, 1/2 (1933), 83-121. Includes an index to contents of Bulletin du Comité Agricole et Industriel de la Cochinchine (1865-1883) and a "Liste des publications de la Société des Études indochinoises de 1883 à 1932." INDEX: "Tables quinquennales du Bulletin de la Société des Etudes indochinoises (1933-1937)." BSEI, n.s. 13 (1938), 171-183. INDEX: "Tables quinquennales du Bulletin de la Société des Études indochinoises (1938-1942)." BSEI, n.s. 18 (1943), 91-103. INDEX: "Tables quinquennales du Bulletin de la Société des Études indochinoises (1943-1947), introduction par Charles Cérighelli." BSEI, n.s. 24, 1 (1949), 81-111. Comprised of summaries of selected articles, p. 81-96. INDEX: "Tables quinquennales du Bulletin de la Société des Études indochinoises, tome 23 (1948) à 27 (1952)." BSEI, n.s. 27 (1952), 483-502. INDEX: "Tables quinquennales du Bulletin de la Société des Études indochinoises, n.s. tome 28 (1953) à 32 (1957)." BSEI, n.s. 33 (1958), 371-380. INDEX: "Tables quinquennales du Bulletin de la Société des Études indochinoises, n.s. tome 33 (1958) à 37 (1962)." BSEI, n.s. 37 (1962), 473-480.

Reprinted volumes of BSEI, 1888-1923, available from Kraus Reprint, New York.

MH

AF40 Văn-hóa nguyệt-san [Culture monthly]. (1952-
1965.)

INDEX: Nguyễn Khắc Xuyên. "Mục-lục
tổng-quát Văn-hóa nguyệt-san, loại mới,
1955-1960, số 1-57" [General index to
VHNS, new series, 1955-1960, nos. 1-57].
VHNS, no. 63 (8/61), 979-1007; no. 64
(9/61), 1181-1192; no. 65 (10/61),
1367-1393; no. 66 (11/61), 1590-1622.

Arranged alphabetically by subject or
by place name in nos. 63-65; by author in
nos. 65-66; and by title of illustration
in no. 67. INDEX: Nguyễn Khắc Xuyên.
"Mục-lục...loại mới--tập X--năm 1961"
[Index...new series--volume X--1961]
VHNS, no. 76, tập XI, quyển 12 (12/62),
I-XXI, separately paged. Subject and au-
thor indexes to nos. 58-67.
MH; NIC

AF41 Văn Sử Địa [Literature, history, geography].
(1954- .)

Issues 10-20 (1955-1960) rev. by Maurice Durand in BEFEO, 50 (1962), 535-555.

Review article on the contents of Văn
Sử Địa, with extensive summaries of articles on literature, folklore, history,
modern history, and linguistics. Frequent
comments about the Marxist orientation of
the articles.

Contents of many issues, 1954-1963,
discussed by Phan Gia Bến (DB15).

NEWSPAPERS AG

The first newspaper in Vietnam published in
quốc-ngữ, Gia-định báo, began in 1865; little if
anything has been written about Sino-Vietnamese
newspapers published before then. Some of the quốc-
ngữ newspapers have been microfilmed by ACRPP, thus
preserving an early record of events under French
rule. None of the newspapers have been indexed,
however, although Le temps provided coverage of

events to readers in Europe, and its index is being
published at present (AG14).

Coverage of events in Indochina as reported
in Western newspapers seems to have begun on a regular basis during the 1930's, with daily reporting
in several Western newspapers dating from the 1950's
as political events in Vietnam came to be important
in world politics. Indexes to the major Western
newspapers have been published. They are listed at
the end of this chapter, in approximate order of the
date at which they began coverage of events in Indochina or Vietnam, and several of the newspapers
themselves have been microfilmed.

The contents of Vietnamese newspapers have
not been indexed, however, and they are seldom
available on microfilm. The U.S. Joint Publications
Research Service does index and translate the contents of some DRVN newspapers (and of Le Monde), but
the JPRS index (Transdex, AA89) does not list separately the contents of the newspapers it indexes.
Transdex indexes NFLSVN newspapers under the heading
"South Vietnam."

Newspapers published in RVN were not indexed,
although several of them were microfilmed by Bell
and Howell Co.

Although the following publications are not
newspapers as such, they provide summaries of current news and are usually inexpensive and easy to
obtain, often free from the embassies. Until
April, 1975, the embassy of the RVN in Washington,
D.C. issued Viet-Nam bulletin, Viet-Nam information
series, and Tin quê hương [News from home]; the
embassy in Kuala Lumpur issued Viet-Nam newsletter;
and embassies or consulates in other countries also
issued newsletters, usually about 10-15 pages per
issue every two weeks or monthly. The Viet-Nam
Press agency (Việt-Nam Thông Tấn Xã) in Saigon published a twice-daily edition of news summaries which
is especially useful for news of the government:
Việt-Nam Thông Tấn Xã (editions in English, Viet-Nam
Press, and in French, Viet-Nam Presse were also
published and available on subscription from Saigon). Bell and Howell Microphoto Co., Wooster,
Ohio, sells microfilms of the English-language
edition.

The embassy of the DRVN in Rangoon publishes Viet-Nam information bulletin; the Representation Commerciale de la République démocratique du Viet-Nam in Paris publishes Bulletin du Viet-Nam. Vietnam courier is a weekly newsletter from Hanoi which contains texts of speeches and documents issued by the government. It is available through subscription agents such as China Books and Periodicals in San Francisco or Chiao Liu in Hong Kong and on microfilm from Bell and Howell.

In addition to newspaper indexes listed below, a few other newspapers also publish indexes, such as the Christian Science Monitor, Minneapolis Star and Tribune, Wall Street Journal, and Texas Observer.

BIBLIOGRAPHIES AND GENERAL WORKS

AG1   Boudet, Paul, and Rémy Bourgeois. Bibliographie de l'indochine française.

     See AA22 for complete description. For lists of newspapers published in Vietnam, see "Périodiques.--Journaux" in volumes 1 and 4. The annotations in vol. 1 include birth and death dates of newspapers, dating back to the 1880's.

AG2   Association pour la Conservation et la Reproduction Photographique de la Presse. Catalogue de microfilm reproduisant des périodiques et journaux et revues.

     See AF3 for complete bibliographical description and annotation.

AG3   Bell and Howell Company. Newspapers on microfilm. Bell and Howell catalog and price list. Wooster, Ohio: The Micropublishers, Microphoto Division, Bell and Howell Co. Annual.

     The 25th anniversary catalog, for 1971, lists 3 newspapers from DRVN and 14 from RVN which are available on microfilm. The Wason Collection, Cornell University Libraries, subscribes to all of the Vietnamese newspapers listed here and coop-

erates in the compilation and preparation for microfilming. (See its Southeast Asia catalog, vol. 7 for catalog cards of the Vietnamese newspapers at Cornell.)
MH

AG4   Đoàn Thị Đỗ. "Le journalisme au Việt-Nam et les périodiques viêtnamiens de 1865 à 1944 conservés à la Bibliothèque Nationale." Bulletin d'informations de l'Association des bibliothécaires français, 25 (mars 1958), [29-36].

     Outline of publishing in Vietnam since 1865. Lists 47 titles, most of which date from the 1930's, giving location symbol in the Bibliothèque Nationale and a short description of each periodical.
MH

AG5   Huỳnh Văn Tòng. Lịch sử báo chí Việt-Nam, từ khởi thuỷ đến năm 1930 [History of newspapers in Vietnam, from the beginnings to 1930]. Saigon: Trí Đăng, 1973. 288 p.

     Describes newspapers and periodicals published in Vietnam, with descriptions of each publication, its editor and publisher, and characteristics as related to the social and historical milieu. The first chapter briefly discusses block printing before 1865, when the French began publishing Gia định báo in Saigon.

     Pp. 251-280, alphabetical and chronological list of about 100 newspapers and periodicals.

     Sources based upon extensive holdings at Bibliothèque National, Paris, and other French libraries.
MH-V

AG6   Lent, John A. Asian mass communications; a comprehensive bibliography.

     See AF18 for description.

AG7   Lim Pui Huen, P. "News resources for South-
       east Asian Research." [Proceedings] Sixth
       International Conference on Asian History,
       26-30 August 1974, Yogyakarta, Indonesia.
       36 p.

      Discusses newspapers, news releases,
       transcripts of radio broadcasts, and other
       sources for current information on events
       in Southeast Asia.
       ICRL (Ref.: INDO 74-941421)

AG8   *Mặc Thu. Tìm hiểu báo chí Việt từ 1954 đến
       1967 [Examination of the press in Vietnam
       from 1954 to 1967]. Saigon: Tủ sách
       Bách-khoa Đại-chúng, 1968. 32 p. (Source:
       Thư-mục 1968.)

AG9   *Masson, André. "Notes bibliographiques sur
       les débuts de la presse périodique en
       Indochine." Bulletin général de l'instruc-
       tion publique 8 (mai 1929), 165-171; 9
       (septembre 1929), 7-12.

      "Includes data on the first publica-
       tions to appear in the French language"
       (Jumper).

AG10   Nunn, Godfrey Raymond, and Đỗ Văn Anh.
       Vietnamese, Cambodian, and Laotian news-
       papers, an international union list. Tai-
       pei: Chinese Materials and Research Aids
       Service Center, 1972. 104 p. (Its Occa-
       sional series, 12.)

      List of 948 newspapers in 21 libraries
       --including four in Saigon--most of which
       are in Japan, France, or the United States.
       Lists 764 newspapers from Vietnam, 597 of
       which are from Saigon-Cholon and 133 of
       which are from Hanoi. List is retrospec-
       tive; therefore includes many no longer
       published. Includes official administra-
       tive newspapers as well as non-official
       publications. Does not report any hold-
       ings of libraries in Hanoi.

      Critically reviewed by P. B. Lafont in
       BEFEO, 62 (1975), 514-515 for its inac-

curacies and omissions about Vietnamese
newspapers in Cambodia from the 1930's to
the 1960's.
MH

AG11   Saigon press review of Vietnamese and Chinese
       dailies. Saigon: Joint U.S. Public Af-
       fairs Office. (Formerly Saigon press
       analysis of Vietnamese and Chinese
       dailies.)

      Translations and summaries of newspaper
       articles prepared for the U.S. mission and
       generally unavailable outside of the offi-
       cial community.
       DLC (not retained); mgc

AG12   Vietnam (Republic). Nha Văn-Khố và Thư-Viện
       Quốc-Gia. Mục lục báo chí Việt ngữ 1865-
       1965 [Bibliography of the Vietnamese-
       language press, 1865-1965]. Saigon, 1966.
       [173 p.]

      Chronological listing, by date of first
       appearance, of about 850-900 newspapers
       and periodicals. Information includes be-
       ginning and ending dates of publication,
       editor, publisher, and frequency. In-
       cludes periodicals published in Annam,
       Cochinchina, and Tongking and in RVN, most
       of the latter comprising titles from Sai-
       gon. Does not include government publica-
       tions. Index is by title.
       mgc

AG13   _____. Thư-Viện Văn-Khố. Ấn phẩm định-kỳ
       quốc-nội [Periodical publications from
       Vietnam].

      See AF10 for annotation.

INDEXES OF NEWSPAPERS

AG14   Le Temps. Tables du journal Le Temps, 1861-
       1942. Paris: Éditions du Centre National
       de la Recherche Scientifique, 1966- . At
       head of title: Institut Français de Press,
       Section d'Histoire. (In progress, vols. 1-
       6, 1886-1888, published as of 1975.)

AG15   Palmer's index to the Times newspaper, 1790-
       June 1941. London: Palmer, 1868-1943.
       Quarterly. Repr., New York: Kraus, 1965.
       Microfilm edition, Library of Congress.

AG16   The Times, London. Index to the Times,
       1906- . London: Times, 1907- . Fre-
       quency varies: 1973- , quarterly.

AG17   New York Times index. New York: Times,
       1913- . Frequency varies: 1948- ,
       semi-monthly, with annual cumulations.
       ____, prior series, September 1851-1912.
       New York: Bowker, 1966- . (In progress,
       vols. for 1851/62-1905/06 publ. as of
       1976.)

AG18   Le Monde. Index analytique, 1944/45- .
       Paris: Le Monde, 1969- . Annual. Ret-
       rospective compilation, 1944/45-1966 in
       progress: vols. for 1944/45, 1946, 1965,
       1966, 1967 published as of 1975.

AG19   Current digest of the Soviet press. New
       York: Joint Committee on Slavic Studies,
       etc., 1949- .

AG20   Survey of China mainland press. Hong Kong:
       U.S. Consulate, 1950- .

AG21   INDEX: Index to Survey of China mainland
       press, Selections from China mainland
       magazines, and Current background. Ibid.,
       1956- .
           The SCMP and its Index are also avail-
       able on microfilm from the Photoduplica-
       tion Service, The Library of Congress.

AG22   Newspaper index: Chicago Tribune, Los
       Angeles Times, The New Orleans Times-
       Picayune, The Washington Post. Wooster,
       Ohio: Newspaper Indexing Center, Micro
       Photo Division, Bell and Howell Co.,
       1972- . Monthly.

AG23   Index to The Times of India, Bombay. Bombay:
       Microfilm and Index Service, Reference
       Department, The Times of India, 1973- .
       Quarterly.

AG24   Zeitungs-Index; Verzeichnis wichtiger Auf-
       sätze aus deutschsprachingen Zeitungen.
       Pullach bei München: Verlag Dokumenta-
       tion, 1974- . Quarterly.

GOVERNMENT PUBLICATIONS AH

Government publications, also called official
publications, are basic sources, especially for research in government, history, economics, and law,
but are among the least-used of research materials
and are often difficult to obtain. In the United
States, few libraries have even a representative
collection of government publications from Indochina or the governments of Vietnam.

In addition to the works cited here, and
throughout section AA, the following references include government publications: Cordier (AA23),
Boudet and Bourgeois (AA22), Vietnam subject index
catalog (AA25), the National union catalog, especially the edition listing pre-1956 imprints,
Southeast Asia subject catalog (AA26), Liste des
imprimés déposés (AA65), Thư mục (AA81), and Thư
tịch quốc-gia Việt-Nam (AA82).

VIETNAM, FRENCH INDOCHINA, AND FRANCE

AH1   List of the serial publications of foreign
      governments, 1815-1931, ed. by Winifred
      Gregory, for the American Council of
      Learned Societies, American Library Asso-
      ciation, National Research Council. New
      York: Wilson, 1932. 720 p. (Cited as
      "Gregory.")
          Lists holdings in about 85 American
      libraries. Arranged by country, with in-
      formation about each branch of government

which has issued publications: changes in
name of issuing agency and years in which
changes occurred, titles published, and
changes in title. Publications listed
under "Annam," "Cochinchina," "France,"
"Indochina," and "Tonkin."
MH

AH2 New York (City) Public Library. Catalog of
government publications in the Research
Libraries. Boston: G. K. Hall, 1972.
40 v.

Photographic reproduction of the catalog cards of the more than one million
volumes of government publications in the
Library. Collection was begun in the
1840's and scope is world-wide. For most
publications on Vietnam, see vol. 15,
"Indochina," pp. 195-209 and vol. 37,
"Vietnam," pp. 590-600: additional entries
are found under "Annam," "Cochin-China,"
and "Tongking." The total number of references to Vietnam is about 80, mostly for
budget, yearbooks, legislative proceedings, compilations of laws, and statistical publications. Collection for French
official publications, in vol. 9, is fairly complete: see entries under "France.
Commerce, Ministère du," "France. Colonies, Ministère des," and "France. Marine, Ministère de la."
MH

AH3 Vietnam (Republic). Bộ Văn-Hóa Giáo-Dục và
Thanh-Niên. Khối Văn-Hóa. Thư-tịch về
ấn-phẩm công Việt-Nam; bibliography of
Vietnamese official publications (1960-
1971). Saigon: Ministry of Culture, Education and Youth, 1972. 170 p.

The second edition of the following title, to which has been added 164 more publications issued from 1969 and 1971. Unlike the previous edition, this edition
does not translate titles of Vietnamese-
language publications into English or
French.
mgc

AH4 ____. Nha Văn-Khố và Thư-Viện Quốc-Gia.
Thư-tịch về ấn-phẩm công Việt-Nam; bibliography on Vietnamese official publications, 1960-1969. Saigon, [n. d.]
134 p.

Lists about 800 monographs and serials
based on the documents sent by various
government bureaus to the Nha Văn-khố.
Arranged by ministry, within each ministry, by Service, and within each Service,
alphabetically by title or by family name
of author. A valuable source--although
not comprehensive--for entries contain
author, title, ministry or publisher,
place and date of publication, size of
publication, and price. Includes publications of unofficial agencies such as the
Société des Études Indochinoises, Institut
Pasteur, and Nha-trang Oceanographic
Institute.
MH; NIC

UNITED STATES

AH5 CIS/Index. Washington, D.C.: Congressional
Information Service, 1970- .

Monthly, with annual cumulation. An
index to the contents of U.S. Congressional publications; particularly important
for testimony or evidence presented in
Congressional hearings and not indexed in
the Monthly catalog of United States government publications (AH9). Examples of
testimony on Vietnam are the annual hearings on appropriations for the Department
of State, conducted by the House and Senate Committees on Appropriations, in which
the work of the Agency for International
Development is discussed, and the appropriations for the Department of Defense,
in which the conduct of the war is discussed.

A cumulative index for 1970-1974 has
been published; it lists about 500 references under "Vietnam."
MH

AH6 Government reports announcements. Springfield, Va.: U.S. National Technical Information Service, 1946- . Title varies:
1946-1949, Bibliography of scientific and
industrial reports; 1949-1954, Bibliography of technical reports; 1954-1964,
United States government research reports;
1965-1971, United States government research and development reports. Issuing
agency until 1971 varied, most recently
the Clearinghouse for Federal Scientific
and Technical Information, U.S. Dept. of
Commerce.

    Subject index and abstracts of reports
of research by scientific and technical
agencies for the U.S. government, especially the Dept. of Defense and Agency for
International Development. Reference number in Index is to the abstract in Government reports announcements. Frequency
varies, presently issued bimonthly.

    INDEXES: Cumulated indexes published
annually, by personal author, corporate
author, contract number, accession number,
and subject. Subject indexes do not always list reports by name of country.
About 20 reports are listed for each year
from 1968 through 1974, among them Land
reform in Vietnam, by the Stanford Research Institute (1970); RAND Vietnam
interviews (1972); and The effects of
herbicides in South Vietnam, by the Committee on the Effects of Herbicides in
South Vietnam of the National Research
Council and National Academy of Sciences
(1974). Other topics include counterin-
surgency, economic effects of the war,
theories of political and military developments, language structure, and zoological research.

    Reports are available for purchase from
NTIS in paper or in microform and should
be ordered by accession number (AD, PB, or
other number).

    The NTIS also offers a computer print-
out of its files according to the needs of

the users.
MH-CSCL

AH7 Government reports index. Ibid., 1965- .
Title varies: 1965-67, Government-wide
index to federal research and development
reports; 1968-1971, United States government research and development reports
index. Issuing agency until 1971:
Clearinghouse for Federal Scientific and
Technical Information, U.S. Dept. of
Commerce.

AH8 Horne, Norman P. "A guide to published
United States government documents pertaining to Southeast Asia, 1893-1941."
Unpublished dissertation, Catholic University of America, Washington, D.C., 1961.
147 p.

    "Indochina: Cambodia, Laos, and Viet-
nam," pp. 31-42. Entries consist mostly
of Hydrographic Office charts, treaties,
and consular reports on economic affairs.
See also "Southeast Asia--general,"
pp. 9-22.
MH

AH9 Monthly catalog of United States government
publications. Washington, D.C.: GPO,
1895- . Also available on microfilm
from Carrollton Press.

    The current bibliography of U.S. gov-
ernment publications. Bibliographic information is complete and catalog information may be used for buying publications
from the GPO. Comprised of publications
sent to 1,000-odd depository libraries in
the United States as well as non-depository publications often available from the
issuing agency. Index is by subject/ti-
tle, listing all publications about Vietnam or Indochina under those headings.
Important for locating Congressional hearings, reports, documents, and committee
prints, State Department publications
about U.S. involvement in Vietnam, and
translations of DRVN newspaper and

periodical articles by the Joint Publications Research Service (see also AA89).

Omits publications of the Agency for International Development and other agencies, including military units, which are issued in Vietnam. (For AID publications, see the Accessions list of the Bureau for Vietnam of the Agency for International Development (Washington, D.C., 1969?-1971?) as well as Vietnam subject index catalog by the U.S. Engineer Agency for Resources Inventories (AA25)). Most U.S. publications on Vietnam are also cited in Bibliography of Asian studies (AA21), if cited in the Monthly catalog. The Monthly catalog does not index the contents of Congressional publications (see CIS/Index (AH5)) nor of the Congressional record (CI132).

INDEX: Cumulated annually in the December issue.

INDEX: Decennial cumulative index, 1941-1950. Washington, D.C.: GPO, 1953. Contains 36 references under "Indochina."

INDEX: Decennial cumulative index, 1951-1960. Washington, D.C.: GPO, 1968. Contains 25 references under "Indochina" and about 200 under "Vietnam," most of which are for translations on DRVN by Joint Publications Research Service.

INDEX: Cumulative subject index to the Monthly catalog of United States government publications, 1900-1971. Washington, D.C.: Carrollton Press, 1973. 14 v. Entries under "Vietnam" comprise about 16 columns, or an estimated 1,000 references in addition to several hundred citations for JPRS series (not separately indexed). About 70 entries are under "Indochina."
MH

OTHER SOURCES

AH10   Bibliographie de la France; supplément F: Publications officielles. Paris: Cercle de la Librairie, 1950- .

AH11   France. Direction de la Documentation. Catalogue méthodique des publications de la "Documentation française." Paris, 1948- . (French-language texts of French and other government statements.)

AH12   _____. Ministère de l'économie et des finances. Catalogue des publications mises en vente par l'Imprimerie nationale. Paris: Impr. Nat., 1928 [?]- .

DISSERTATIONS AI

Dissertations are important sources for research because they often require extensive use of original source materials. Because few dissertations are published, however, they are not listed in most bibliographies. The researcher must consult bibliographies of dissertations, and for Vietnamese studies, the bibliographies on Southeast Asia.

An important feature of dissertations written in the United States is that they are available for purchase and that a bibliography, Dissertation abstracts international (AI3), is available as an index to most doctoral dissertations.

AI1   Bibliographie de la France; supplément D: Thèses. Paris: Cercle de la Librairie, 1932- . Issued irregularly.

Lists the dissertations in French universities. Arrangement is by university and by faculty, then alphabetically by author. Annual index by author, no index by subject or country. Useful for verification.
MH

AI2   Comprehensive dissertation index 1861-1972. Ann Arbor, Mich.: Xerox University Microfilms, 1973. 37 vols.; supplements planned.

Author and subject indexes to more than 417,000 doctoral dissertations granted in the United States. Arranged into 32 subject volumes in all fields and 4 author volumes. Arrangement in each subject volume is alphabetically by subject keyword. Information includes name of author, complete title, school, date, pagination, citation to other dissertation indexes (for finding abstracts), and order number for ordering copy of dissertation from Xerox University Microfilms. Unlike DAI, includes dissertations from Harvard University, although copies of the dissertations themselves must be obtained from the University and not from Xerox Corporation.

Vol. 27, Law and Political Science, lists about 50 dissertations in the political science section under "Vietnam," but other volumes list considerably fewer dissertations on Vietnam: Education (17 dissertations); History (9); Language and Literature (11); Business and Economics (14).

MH

AI3 Dissertation abstracts international. Ann Arbor, Michigan, 1938- . Title varies: Microfilm abstracts, 1938-1949; dissertation abstracts, 1950-1970. (Cited as DAI.)

A "monthly compilation of abstracts of doctoral dissertations submitted to University Microfilms, Inc. by more than 375 cooperating institutions in the United States and Canada." (Introduction.) Plans are eventually to enlarge the scope to include European dissertations. Copies of the complete text of dissertations may be purchased either on microfilm or Xerographic prints. Does not list most dissertations at Harvard University.

Divided into Section A, Humanities, and Section B, Sciences, then arranged by subject, with annual author and subject indexes since 1961. From 1956 to 1969, number 13 of each volume of DA was titled "Index to American doctoral dissertations"

and was arranged by broad subject, with an author index. Beginning with DAI, separate volumes titled "Keyword title index" are issued in Social Sciences, Education, Communications, and other broad subject areas; these volumes list each dissertation according to the key words in the titles.

MH

AI4 Doctoral dissertations on Asia. Comp. and ed. by Frank Joseph Shulman. [Ann Arbor, Mich.]: Xerox University Microfilms for the Association of Asian Studies, 1975- . Semiannual.

Continues the bibliographical listings by Shulman in the Newsletter of the Association for Asian Studies (vol. 14, no. 4 (May 1969) to vol. 16, no. 4 (May 1971)) and in the Asian studies professional review (Vol. 1, no. 1 (Fall 1971) through vol. 3, no. 2 (Spring 1974)).

Lists doctoral dissertations or the equivalent in the U.S., Europe, Canada, or India; includes completed dissertations as well as dissertations in progress. Information includes name and address of author, citation to Dissertation abstracts international (for those who want to purchase copies of dissertations), and translation of non-English-language titles into English. The Winter 1975 issue (vol. 1, no. 1) lists 54 references under "Indochina."

MH

AI5 Kozicki, Richard J., and Peter Ananda. South and Southeast Asia: doctoral dissertations and masters' theses completed at the University of California, Berkeley, 1906-1968. Berkeley: University of California, Center for Southeast Asian Studies, 1969. 49 p. (Its Occasional papers series, no. 1.)

"Indochina" and "Vietnam" list 11 entries for Vietnam. Appendices show tabular
data for disciplines and area.
MH

AI6   SarDesai, D. R., and Bhanu D. SarDesai.
       Theses and dissertations on Southeast
       Asia; an international bibliography in so-
       cial sciences, education, and fine arts.
       Zug, Switzerland: Inter Documentation
       Company, 1970. 176 p. (Bibliotheca
       Asiatica, 6)
          Subject listing of 2,814 doctoral dis-
       sertations presented in the U.S., U.S.S.R.,
       British Isles, Malaysia, Singapore, Aus-
       tralia, New Zealand, the Philippines, the
       Netherlands, Czechoslovakia, and Japan,
       and to a lesser extent, in France, Germany,
       Thailand, India, and Canada. Includes
       Masters' theses from American University,
       the University of Chicago, the University
       of California, and Cornell and Columbia
       universities. Includes about 284 entries
       for Vietnam or Indochina. Author index.
       Russian language dissertations are listed
       both in Russian and in English. Entries
       for Vietnamese names are inconsistent:
       Nguyen, Van-ung, but Hieu, Pham Dinh.
          According to the introductory note, the
       publisher will provide a microfiche copy
       of any dissertation listed in the
       bibliography.
       MH

AI7   Stucki, Curtis W. American doctoral disser-
       tations on Asia, 1933-June 1966, including
       appendix of master's theses at Cornell
       University, 1935-June 1968. Ithaca:
       Cornell University Southeast Asia Program,
       1968. 304 p. (Its Data paper, no. 71)
          Updates his earlier works of the same
       title for the years 1933-1958 (Data paper
       no. 37, 1959, 131 p.) and 1933-1962 (Data
       paper no. 50, 1963, 204 p.) Doctoral dis-
       sertations are listed for Vietnam on

pp. 146-148 (41 citations), with references to citations on Vietnam in other
sections; master's theses--13 citations--
are listed on p. 254. In comparison, the
1962 edition listed 20 citations on Viet-
nam-Laos-Cambodia.
MH

AI8   The, Lian, and Paul W. Van der Veur. Treas-
       ures and trivia; doctoral dissertations on
       Southeast Asia accepted by universities in
       the United States. Athens: Ohio Univer-
       sity, Center for International Studies,
       Southeast Asia Program, 1968. 141 p.
       (Its Papers in International Studies,
       Southeast Asia series, 1)
          Lists over 950 dissertations--of which
       74 are on Vietnam--arranged alphabetically
       by country, discipline, and author. In-
       cludes addenda, tables listing number of
       dissertations by discipline, by time span,
       by university, and sources.
       MH

BIOGRAPHY AJ

   Biographical sources for Vietnamese studies
include not only biographical dictionaries and collections of biographies, but also individual biographies, many of which were published in French in
BAVH, and biographical information published in
records of examinations for positions in government
(Đăng khoa lục, chapter CI, Political science and
government).

AJ1   Cordier, Henri. Bibliotheca indosinica.
          See AA23 for complete description.
       For publications about biography, see:
       "Biographie," vol. 3: 1873-1874 (4 ref-
       erences) and "Religion--vie des missio-
       naires catholiques," vol. 3: 2043-2126
       and vol. 4: 2943-2948.
       MH

AJ2   Boudet, Paul, and Rémy Bourgeois. Biblio-
          graphie de l'Indochine française.

          See AA22 for complete description. For
          publications about biography, see, in each
          volume, the heading "Biographie," or the
          names of persons.
          MH

AJ3   *Annuaire général, administratif, commercial
          et industriel de l'Indo-Chine.

          See DG4 for complete description; con-
          tains biographical information on colonial
          officials.

AJ4   Asia who's who. Hong Kong: Pan-Asia News-
          paper Alliance, 1957-1960. 1st ed., 1957,
          712 p.;[1] 2d ed., 1958, 852 p.;[2] 3d ed.,
          1960, 939 p.[3]

          Biographical sketches of persons mostly
          in politics. Arrangement varies with each
          edition. Edition reviewed (2d ed.) listed
          62 names under RVN and 26 names under
          DRVN.
          [1]Winchell, Guide to reference books
          [2]MH [3]Nunn, Asia; a selected and annotated
          guide to reference works.

AJ5   *Barthès, L. Les 10,000 adresses; publication
          trimestrielle comprenant les adresses ex-
          actes de tous les colons et fonctionnaires
          de la colonie. Hanoi: Impr. Gallois,
          1907-1908. 4 vols.

          No. 1, May 1, 1907, 160 p.; no. 2,
          Aug. 1, 1907, 193 p., no. 3, Nov. 1, 1907,
          162 p., no. 4, Feb. 1, 1908, 302 p. (Cited
          in Boudet, Rev. indo. 1925, no. 1660)

AJ6   Brébion, Antoine. Dictionnaire de bio-
          bibliographie générale ancienne et mo-
          derne de l'Indochine française. Paris:
          Société d'Éditions Géographiques, Mari-
          times et Coloniales, 1935. 446 p. (Aca-
          démie des Sciences Coloniales. Annales,
          8)

          A major biographical and bibliographi-
          cal reference work published by Antoine

Cabaton after Brébion's death in 1917.
Contains bio-bibliographies of major persons involved in the history of Vietnam,
Laos, and Cambodia, including Vietnamese
and European rulers, authors, missionaries, explorers, and political figures.
Includes extensive listings of names of
missionaries (see entry BB17 for more
details), of Vietnamese rulers (under the
heading "Annam"), and of colonial officials (under "Annam," "Cochinchine,"
"Indochine," and "Tonkin").

          Pp. 431-466, lists of names of biog-
raphees, arranged by subject, with names
listed under as many subjects as appropriate; L. M. Cadière, for example, is
listed under "Linguistique," "Histoire,"
and several other headings. Under "Linguistique," 76 compilers of dictionaries,
grammars, or other linguistic works are
listed.

          Supersedes in part Brébion's Biblio-
graphie des voyages dans l'Indochine française du 9e au 19e siècle (1910), and
Livre d'or du Cambodge, de la Cochinchine
et de l'Annam 1625-1910 (1910), cited in
AA62 and AA63.
MH

AJ7   Bulletin des Amis du Vieux Hué.

          See AF38 for indexes. Contains num-
erous biographical articles on persons
connected with the history of Hue; a very
few examples follow: "Les Européens qui
ont vu le vieux Hué: Le Père de Rhodes"
(1915); "Brossard de Corbigny" (1916);
"Dutreuil de Rhins" (1919); "Thomas Bow-
year" (1920); "John White" (1937). "Gé-
néalogie des Nguyễn avant Gia Long"
(1920). "Les Français au service de Gia-
Long: La maison de Chaigneau" (1917);
"Le tombeau de Forçant" (1918); "Leurs
noms, titres et appellations annamites"
(1920). "Notes biographiques sur les
Français au service de Gia Long." (1917).
"Les familles illustres de l'Annam:

S. E. Nguyễn Hữu Độ" (1924). "Les grandes
figures de l'empire d'Annam: Nguyễn
Suyễn" (1926).
MH; NIC

AJ8 *Đại Nam liệt truyện [Biographies of Đại Nam].
1841-1909.

Biographies of persons from the 16th
century until 1909 and comprised of royal-
ty, concubines, loyalists, rebels, hero-
ines, hermits, and monks. Actually a series of editions: Đại-Nam liệt truyện
tiền biên (ca. 1852); Đại-Nam chính biên
liệt truyện sơ tập (1889); and Đại Nam
liệt truyện chính biên nhị tập (1909).[1]

Portions translated into quốc-ngữ by
Phan Kế Bính in Đông Dương tạp chí,
nos. 70-127, 181-203 (1916-1918).[2]

Individual biographies translated and
published, e.g., "Phan Thanh Giản et sa
famille," BSEI n.s. 16, no. 2 (1941).[3]
[1]Huỳnh Khắc Dụng, Sử-liệu Việt-Nam,
pp. 141-142. [2]Smith, "Sino-Vietnamese
sources," p. 606. [3]MH

AJ9 *Đào Văn Hội. Danh-nhân nước nhà [Vietnam
biographical dictionary]. Saigon: Lý
Công Quan, 1951. 192 p.

"A textbook of Vietnamese biography"
(Robert B. Slocum, Biographical dictionaries and related works, Detroit, 1967).

AJ10 Directory of Vietnamese studies in North
America. Ann Arbor, Mich.: Association
for Asian Studies, Southeast Asia Regional
Council, Vietnam Studies Group, 1976.
64 p.

Lists 158 persons specializing in Vietnamese studies, their disciplines, educational background, and addresses; insti-
tutional programs, resources, and libraries; and sample syllabi of courses on
Vietnam.
mgc

AJ11 Hồ Đắc Hàm, and Thái Văn Kiểm. Việt-Nam
nhân-vật-chí vựng-biên [Biographical dictionary for Vietnam]. Saigon: Nha Văn-
hóa, 1962. 2 vols. (Văn-hóa tùng thư.
13 and 14)

Arranged by personal name, with Chinese
characters added. Information is more
complete than is the compilation by Nguyễn
Huyền Anh, but the latter has more names.
MH-V; NIC

AJ12 *Indochina. Souverains et notabilités d'Indochine. Hanoi: IDEO, 1943. 112 p.

Biographical references on about 525
contemporary national figures (Jumper).

AJ13 Institut d'Étude du Viet Nam contemporain.
Guide pratique de recherche sur le Viet
Nam en France.

See DD16 for complete description. Includes brief biographical information on
37 French and Vietnamese researchers living in France.

AJ14 International biographical directory of
Southeast Asia specialists, 1969. Rob-
ert O. Tilman, project director. Inter-
university Southeast Asia Committee,
Association for Asian Studies, [n. d.]
Distributed by Southeast Asia Studies,
Center for International Studies, Ohio
University, Athens. 337 p.

Lists 950 specialists, including 156
for Vietnam (pp. 298 and 304-305 have indexes). Information for each specialist
includes nationality, formal education and
career, languages, publications and present address. Does not list any specialists from the DRVN, USSR, or Chinese people's Republic. Data given in the biographical sections are tabulated and
included in the indexes.
MH

AJ15   Nguyễn Huyền Anh. Việt-Nam danh-nhân từ
điển [Famous personalities of Vietnam].
Saigon: Hội Văn-hóa Bình Dân, 1960.
380 p. [Rev. ed. with same title], Saigon:
Khai-Trí [1967]. 559 [15] p.

   Biographical dictionary with short articles and names of books or poems. Coverage includes contemporary figures beyond
1945 (Trần Trọng Kim, Dương Quảng Hàm).
1967 edition is a revision and enlargement
of 1960 edition. Includes pseudonyms.

   Review of 1960 edition by Nicole Louis
in BEFEO, 52 (1965), 562-567, who lists
additions or corrections to about 15 biographies.

   MH-V; NIC

AJ16   Phan Huy Chú. "Nhân-vật chí" [Biography].
vol. 2, chapters 6-12 of Lịch-triều hiến-
chương loại-chí [Monographs of the institutions of the dynasties], ca. 1821.

   See AD1 for description of main work.
These volumes contain biographies of famous historical personalities.

   In addition to the translation of
vols. 6-12 as part of the translation in
Hanoi in 1960-1961 of the complete text of
Lịch-triều (AD1), two other translations
exist: 1) Translation by Nguyễn Đỗ Mục
(Hanoi? Tân Dân, 1940);[1] 2) Translation
by Nguyễn Thọ Dực (Saigon: Khối Văn-Hóa,
1973, 2 vols.)[2]
[1]Trần Văn Giáp, Lược truyện...I, 87 (BD26)
[2]Gélinas, list 033, March 15, 1975

AJ17   Southeast Asia Development Advisory Group.
SEADAG directory. New York: Asia Society, 1969- . 1968/69, 153 p.

   A list of about 250 "scholars and administrators in the United States who have
special competence or interest in Southeast Asian affairs."

   Includes biographical information for
about 50 "non-government persons associated with SEADAG;" name, position, and
address.

   MH

AJ18   Trịnh Huy Tiến. "Các loại nhân-danh Việt-
nam" [Different types of names in Viet-
nam]. VHNS, no. 61 (6/61), 540-546;
no. 62 (7/61), 694-703.

   Explains pseudonyms such as tên chính,
tên tự, hiệu, and others, with examples
from history and literature.

   MH; NIC

AJ19   Trịnh Văn Thanh. Thành-ngữ điển-tích danh-
nhân từ-điển [Dictionary of literary terms
and personnages].

   See AD3 for complete description. Includes biographical information on literary and historical figures.

   MH-V

AJ20   U.S. Central Intelligence Agency. Vietnamese personal names. [Washington, D.C.?]
1961. 36 p. [Distributed by Library of
Congress Photoduplication Service]

   Describes spelling, transcription, pronunciation, telegraphic spelling, structure, arrangement, additional names such
as pseudonyms and honorific titles, and
transliteration of Russian and Chinese.

   MH

AJ21   U.S. Dept. of State. Office of External Research. Who's who in North Vietnam.

   See CI66 for complete information.

AJ22   *Vũ Nguyên Hẫn. Đại-Nam kỳ-nhân liệt-truyện,
trad. par To Linh Thao. Hanoi: Ed.
Quang-Thịnh et Xuân-Khê, impr. Ngô Tử Hạ,
1930. 135 p.

   Celebrated personalities of Vietnam.
(Source: Boudet 3.)

AJ23   Who's who in the Republic of South Viet Nam.
See CI105 for bibliographical information. Refers to the Provisional Revolutionary Government of the Republic of
South Viet Nam.

   MH-L

AJ24 <u>Who's who in Vietnam</u>. Saigon: Vietnam Press, 1966-   . Also in Vietnamese.

Issued irregularly in looseleaf form. Volumes for 1966-1970 arranged by personal name according to the biographies completed in that year and issued in 6 volumes. Information includes birth date, pseudonyms, place of birth, education, profession, publications. Includes persons living in RVN.
MH

GENEALOGY AK

Genealogical records (<u>gia phả</u>) are primary sources for biographical research, but most of them are private and kept within the family. A few have been published in whole or in part in the <u>Bulletin des Amis du Vieux Huế</u> (<u>see</u> entry AF38 for citations of indexes), in the <u>Bulletin de la Société des Études indochinoises</u> (AF39), and in other sources cited in the bibliography of the work by Nguyễn Đức Thu (AK1). Also, according to R. B. Smith, "Sino-Vietnamese sources for the Nguyễn period: an introduction," <u>BSOAS</u>, 30 (1967), 620, the Fonds Maspero at the Société Asiatique in Paris contains a "number of copies or extracts of family registers."

AK1 [Nguyễn Đức Thu]. <u>Gia phả; khảo luận và thực hành</u> [Family registers; research, theory, and practice, by] Dã Lan Nguyễn Đức Dụ [pseud.] Saigon: Tác-gia [1971]. 372 p.

Description of traditional genealogies and suggestions for enlarging the scope of family registers. Chapters on genealogy in Europe, Asia, and Vietnam; uses of a genealogy; construction of a family book, and characteristics of some family registers. Bibliography of 55 sources, including 19 family genealogies.
ICarbS

AK2 *_____. <u>Một lối chép gia phả thật đơn giản</u> [How to construct a simple family register]. Saigon, 1973, 125 p. (Source: Thanh-long, cat. 32, févr. 1975.)

B The Humanities

PHILOSOPHY BA

Vietnamese philosophy is actually a combination of religion, geomancy, astrology, moral teachings, and history. References on philosophy may also be located in chapter BB Religion and in Connaissance du Việt-Nam, by Huard and Durand (DF3).

BIBLIOGRAPHIES

BA1 Cordier, Henri. Bibliotheca indosinica.
> See AA23 for complete description. For publications on philosophy, see vol. 3: 2127-2150 and vol. 4: 2947-2948, "Sciences morales et philosophiques."
> MH

BA2 Boudet, Paul, and Rémy Bourgeois. Bibliographie de l'Indochine française.
> See AA22 for complete description. For publications on philosophy, see "Morale" and "Philosophie" in vol. 4.
> MH

BA3 Saigon. Viện Đại Học Vạn-Hạnh. Thư-viện. Thư mục triết học, 1968-1969; philosophical bibliography; bibliographie philosophique. [Saigon? 1969?]. 91 p.
> Pp. 1-14, alphabetical listing by author of 112 publications in Vietnamese-- including original works and translations. Pp. 15-91, listing of Western publications. Information includes author, titles, imprint, pagination, size, and Dewey Decimal classification number.
> NIC

DICTIONARIES

BA4 *Phạm Xuân Thái. Danh-từ hiện đại và triết-học; vocabulaire moderne et philosophique. Phần Việt-Pháp; partie viêtnamien-français. [n. p., n. p.] 1950. (Source: SOAS.)

BA5 *Rozental, Mark Moiseevich and P. Yudin. Từ-điển triết-học, do một nhóm nghiên-cứu triết học Liên-Xô biên soạn dưới sự chỉ đạo của M. Rô-den-tan và P. I-ư-đin [Dictionary of philosophy, prepared by a group of Soviet philosophers under the leadership of M. Rozental and P. Yudin]. In lần 2. Hanoi: Sự thật, 1960. 959 p.
> English-language edition published in Moscow by Progress Publishers, 1967. Second Russian-language edition published in 1968. (Source: NIC.)

BA6 Trần Văn Hiến-Minh. Từ-điển và danh từ triết-học [Dictionary and vocabulary of philosophy]. Saigon: Tủ sách Ra Khởi, 1966. 340, 130 p.
> Section 1, Vietnamese-language dictionary, with one- or two-word definitions in French. Section 2, French-Vietnamese glossary, without definitions.
> NIC also has section 2 as separate, dated 1956.
> MH-V; NIC

RELIGION BB

Vietnamese religion is referred to as <u>tam giáo</u>, or the three religions--Buddhism (<u>Phật</u>), Taoism (<u>Lão</u>), and Confucianism (<u>Nho</u>)--in which elements of all three, as well as animism, astrology, and philosophy, are combined. The division of this chapter into sections corresponding to each religion is intended to follow the division of the available literature.

The larger number of citations for reference works on Christianity in Vietnam, compared with those for the <u>tam giáo</u>, is due to the greater availability of material on Christianity.

BIBLIOGRAPHIES

BB1   Cordier, Henri. <u>Bibliotheca indosinica</u>.

See AA23 for complete description. For citations about religion, most of which are for Christianity, see vol. 3: 1887-2128 and vol. 4: 2937-2948, "Religions;" vol. 3: 2043-2126 and vol. 4: 2943-2948, "Vie des missionaires catholiques"--an alphabetical list of 300 missionaries with biographical and bibliographical information--and vol. 3: 1959-2044, "Lettres édifiantes..."--a complete list of the contents of <u>Nouvelles lettres édifiantes</u> (Adrien Le Clerc, 1818-1823) and <u>Welt-Bott</u>, (J. Stöcklein, 1728-1761), and <u>El Correo Sino-Annamita</u> (1866-1910). See also <u>Index des matières</u> under the name of each religion or under "Indochine française--religion." See also vol. 3: 2127-2150 and vol. 4: 2947-2948, "Sciences morales et philosophiques."
MH

BB2   Boudet, Paul, and Rémy Bourgeois. <u>Bibliographie de l'Indochine française</u>.

See AA22 for complete description. For citations about religions, see, in each volume, "Bouddhisme," "Catholicisme" or "Missions Catholiques," "Caodaisme,"

"folklore," "protestantisme," "religions," "taoisme," and "morale."
MH

BB3   Vietnam (Republic). Nha Văn-khố và Thư-viện Quốc-gia. <u>Sơ-thảo mục-lục thư-tịch về Tôn-giáo ở Việt-nam; a bibliography on religion in Vietnam</u> [comp. by Vương Văn Quang]. Saigon, 1968. 78 p.

Author listing of 480 books and articles, mostly in Vietnamese and French, about religion in general, Cao-Đài; Hòa-Hao, Protestantism, Bah'ai, Islam, Subul, theosophy, yoga. Intended to complement bibliographies on other religions in Vietnam. Author index.
mgc

DESCRIPTIONS

BB4   Cadière, Léopold Michel. <u>Croyances et pratiques religieuses des Vietnamiens</u>. Hanoi: IDEO, 1944; Saigon: EFEO, 1955; Paris: EFEO, 1957. 3 vols. (Vol. 1 titled <u>Croyances et pratiques religieuses des Annamites</u>, repr. in <u>BSEI</u>, n.s. 33, 1-2 (1958).)

Collected and reprinted articles and lectures on religion and related matters among Vietnamese in Central Vietnam, originally written from 1901 to 1943. The more extensive articles are about religious or magical occurrences observed during a cholera epidemic in "Annam" (in vol. 1); religious beliefs and practices of the Vietnamese in Hue (vol. 2); popular beliefs and sayings in the valley of Nguon-son, Quang-nam province (vol. 2); and popular Vietnamese philosophy--cosmology and physical anthropology (vol. 3). Emphasis throughout is upon religion and philosophy outside of the influence of Christianity.

Vol. 3, pp. 5-40--bio-bibliography of Cadière (1869-1955). Table of contents

of all three volumes is at end of
vol. 3.

MH (BSEI); MH-P (Vols. 2-3)

BB5   [Nguyễn Văn Toán]. Nếp cũ; tín ngưỡng Việt-
       Nam [Life in Vietnam, religious beliefs,
       by] Toan Ánh. In lần thứ 2. Saigon:
       Hoa-Đăng, 1969. 2 vols. First ed., Sai-
       gon: Nam chi tùng thư, 1967, 2 v.

           Vol. 1, chapters on ancestral worship,
       anniversaries of deaths, sacrifices and
       festivals, Lao-Tze, Confucianism, Nam-
       giao ceremony, Buddhism, Hoà Hảo, Cao-Đài.
       Includes excerpts from writings of other
       authors as well as the constitution of the
       Unified Vietnamese Buddhist Congregation
       in 1964. Vol. 2, chapters on Catholicism
       and its religious orders, rites, festi-
       vals, Protestantism, Bah'ai, Islam, super-
       stitions, dreams, prophesies, stars,
       phrenology, festivals, and lunar festivals
       such as Tết Nguyên Đán, the Lunar New
       Year.

           Favorably reviewed in BEFEO, 45 (1968)
       and 46 (1969), 209.

       MH-V; NIC

BUDDHISM

BIBLIOGRAPHIES

BB6   *Lê Xuân Khoa. Thư-tịch Phật-học Việt-Nam
       [Bibliography on Buddhism in Vietnam].
       Saigon: Tủ-sách Văn-hóa Á-châu, 1963.
       56 p. (Source: Diêu; TTHTQG.)

BB7   Nguyễn Khắc Kham. Sơ-thảo mục-lục thư-tịch
       về Phật-giáo ở Việt-nam; a bibliography on
       Vietnamese Buddhism. Saigon: Nha Văn-khố
       và Thư-viện Quốc-gia, 1966. 32 p.

           Author listing of 72 Vietnamese-lan-
       guage original publications in books, 63
       French and English books and articles,
       and 76 translations from Chinese, Pali,

and Japanese into Vietnamese. Citations
omit pagination of books. Author index.

mgc; NIC

BB8   "Traductions de textes canoniques chinois,"
       and "Traductions de textes canoniques
       palis." In Présence du Bouddhisme, spe-
       cial issue of France-Asie, 16 (1959),
       1010-1013.

           List of 41 and 30 publications respec-
       tively of texts which have been trans-
       lated into Vietnamese. Information con-
       sists of original title, title in Viet-
       namese, name of translator, and publisher
       and date.

       MH

BB9   Vietnam (Republic). Nha Văn-khố và Thư-viện
       Quốc-gia. Thư-tịch về phật-giáo (thư-
       tịch Anh và Pháp văn); a bibliography on
       Buddhism (English and French [language]
       writings). Saigon, 1967. 28 p.

           Alphabetical listing of 164 books and
       articles on Buddhism. For publications
       on Buddhism in Vietnam, see items 15-18,
       27, 28, 40, 49, and 65.

       mgc

DICTIONARIES

BB10   *Danh-từ Phật-giáo (Việt-Pháp-Anh) [Diction-
       ary of Buddhism (Vietnamese-French-Eng-
       lish)]. Saigon: Việt Tấn Xã, 1963.
       (Source: KimSa.)

BB11   Đoàn Trung Còn. Phật-học từ-điển [Diction-
       ary of Buddhism]. Saigon: Phật-học tổng
       thơ, 1966-68. 3 vols. (Phật-học,
       vol. 23)

           Each entry, in Vietnamese, is followed
       by the Chinese character, romanized Pali
       or Sanskrit spelling, French translation,
       and definition in Vietnamese. Defines
       proper nouns, expressions in Buddhist

literature, and phrases with meanings applicable to religion, e.g. oan-đich (enemy).

MH-V; TTQGVN 2/3; NIC

CONFUCIANISM

BB12   Vietnam (Republic). Nha Văn-khố và Thư-viện Quốc-gia. Sơ-thảo mục-lục thư-tịch về Khổng-giáo ở Việt-Nam; a bibliography on Confucianism in Vietnam. Saigon, 1966. 41 p. In lần thứ 2. Ibid., 1967.

    Author listing of 253 books and articles in Vietnamese about Confucius and Confucianism in Asia and Vietnam, Mencius, relationships between Confucianism and Buddhism and Christianity, and influence of Confucianism in politics, education, and other areas.

mgc; NIC

CHRISTIANITY

BIBLIOGRAPHIES AND GENERAL WORKS

BB13   Anderson, Gerald H. Christianity in Southeast Asia, a bibliographical guide; an annotated bibliography of selected references in Western languages. New York: Missionary Research Library, 1966. 69 p.

    Includes a section on general bibliographies, atlases, periodicals, history and "Christianity in the area," or publications on two or more countries in Southeast Asia, as well as a separate section-- pp. 28-38--on Cambodia, Laos, and Vietnam. The latter section includes about 50 books and articles about Vietnam, some of which refer to missionary work among ethnic minorities. Annotations are brief and descriptive.

MH

BB14   Annuaire pontifical catholique. Paris, 1898-1939. 50 vols.

Includes biographical information on titular bishops, statistical and descriptive information about apostolic vicariates in Tongking and Cochinchina (until 1925), Saigon, Hue, and Quinhon (beginning in 1925). INDEX: Tables générales, 1898-1917.

MH

BB15   Bibliografia missionaria. Rome: Pontificia Universita Urbaniana de Propaganda Fide, 1933- . Editors include, variously, Giovanni [Johannes] Dindinger, G. Rommerskirchen, N. Kowalsky, and G. Metzler.

    Lists books and articles currently published in Western European languages about all aspects of missionary work. Arrangement is generally by geographic or subject: See "Indocina" for publications about Vietnam. Every three issues contain an index by personal author or geographical area: See "Annam," "Cocincina," "Indocina," "Tonchina," and "Vietnam." References include publications issued in Vietnam about Christianity in Vietnam, the state of missions there, indigenous clergy, the political situation, papal declarations, and biographical information. Anno 9 (1942) pp. 93-95 contains a bibliography of historical documents about Christianity in Vietnam.

MH

BB16   Bigaouette, Jules. "Les évêchés titulaires conférés aux missionnaires." Revue d'histoire des missions, 12 (1935)-16 (1939), 97-128. Appears in most issues. Does not seem to have been completed; last entry is Bp. of Zorolus, although the article ends with the words, "à suivre." Cf. Streit, vol. 22, p. 571, no. 3776, and Bibliografia Missionaria, vol. 6, p. 17, no. 132, which do not list articles subsequent to the article in vol. 16 listed here.

Alphabetical list of vicars apostolic--
in order of the name of the bishopric--and
short biographical notes about the missionaries appointed to those sees. (The
vicars apostolic were appointed by the
Pope beginning in 1658 and were under his
direct authority. They were appointed to
extinct sees in Asia Minor but served in
Asia and Africa; Msgr. Pallu, for example,
was Bp. of Heliopolis, and Msgr. Pigneau
de Behaine was Bp. of Adran. The program
was supported by the French court and the
French church.)

Does not include index, although one
was planned by the author. To locate a
particular bishop, one must know the name
of his see.
MH

BB17 Brébion, Antoine. Dictionnaire de bio-
bibliographie.... 1935. (See entry AJ11
for details.)

Chronological lists of missionaries who
went to Vietnam: pp. 88-93, Jesuits, from
1615-1733; pp. 122-130, Dominicans, 1693-
1910; pp. 161-164, Franciscans, 1580-1822;
pp. 354-398, Société des Missions Étrangères, 1660-1910.
MH

BB18 Metzler, Josef. "Vietnamesische Bibelüber-
setzungen." Neue Zeitschrift für Mis-
sionswissenschaft, 20 (1964), 195-202.

Bibliographical essay, with 52 references to translations of the Bible or
books and articles about religion. Includes information on dictionaries and
other works, whether manuscript or published. Scope includes the manuscript
dictionary of 1645 by Gaspar de Amaral
through translations of religious tracts
in 1964.
MH-AH

BB19 Streit, Robert, and Johannes Dindinger.
Bibliotheca missionum. Freiburg, etc.:
Herder, etc., 1916- . (In progress,
vols. 1 to 29 published as of 1973)
(Veröffentlichungen des Internationalen
Instituts für Missionswissenschaftliche
Forschung)

Annotated retrospective bibliography,
presently compiled by Johannes Rommerskirchen and Josef Metzler, of publications
by missionaries as well as publications
about missionaries. Annotations include
references to variant editions, book reviews, and short biographies of missionary
writers. Scope includes relations, letters, lists of missionaries, papal documents and letters, contents of edited
works, and references to individual documents printed in more comprehensive works.
Arrangement is chronological according to
the year under discussion.

Indexes in each volume (except vol. 1,
which lacks indexes) are by author, personal subject, topic, country, and language (for dictionaries, catechisms, etc.).

Most references to Vietnam are in
vols. 5 (Asiatische Missionsliteratur,
1600-1699); 6 (Missionsliteratur Indiens,
der Philippinen, Japans und Indochinas,
1700-1799); 11 (Indochinas Missionsliteratur, 1800-1909); and 29 (Missionsliteratur Südostasiens, 1910-1970). Additional references may be found in vols. 1
(Grundlegender und Allgemeiner Teil [gen-
eral works]); 4 (Asiatische Missionsliteratur, 1245-1599); 7 (Chinesische Missionsliteratur, 1700-1799); 8 (Missionsliteratur Indiens und Indonesiens, 1800-
1909); 12-14 (Chinesische Missionsliteratur, 1800-1950); 22 (Grundlegender und
Allgemeiner Teil, 1910-1935, und Nachtrag
zu Band 1); 23 (Grundlegender und Allgemeiner Teil, 1936-1960); and 27 (Missionsliteratur Indiens und Indonesiens, 1919-
1950).

Volumes 1, 22, and 23 are useful for their listings of collected works which include references to Vietnam, particularly the Lettres édifiantes and Nouvelles lettres édifiantes (BB21) in vol. 1 and other publications such as Catalogue des missionaires français partis du Séminaire des Missions Étrangères (cited in vol. 1, no. 1190) and general histories of missionary orders.

References in vol. 5 cover the beginnings of missionary activity in Vietnam, activities of Christoforo Borri, Alexandre de Rhodes, Lambert de la Motte, and François Pallu. In vol. 6, references include publications on missionary activity, the rise of Spanish activity after 1693, opposition of the Vietnamese governments, the Tây-Sơn era, and activities of Pigneau de Behaine. Vol. 11 covers the period of the founding of the Nguyễn dynasty, opposition by the Minh Mạng emperor and his successors to the spread of Christianity, and French intervention and colonization. Vol. 29 contains works on Christianity under French colonization and during the rise of nationalism.

Vol. 11 (originally published in 1939 and reprinted in 1966) contains 2,062 numbered entries, many of which include numerous additional references to an author's writings (the bibliography for L. M. Cadière, for example, on pp. 435-442, lists over 90 publications by him). In addition to the chronological listing of books, articles, published letters and relations, and papal documents, it includes, on pp. 565-658, an author listing of manuscripts and published grammars, catechisms, and other works on linguistics, including works in nôm, and, on pp. 659-728, anonymous works by title, including 40 periodicals on p. 725.

Vol. 29 includes 901 publications on Indochina (including Thailand), mostly

annual reports on missionary work in Compte-rendu, Société des Missions Étrangères.
MH

BB20   Vietnam (Republic). Nha Văn-khố và Thư-viện Quốc-gia. Sơ-thảo mục-lục thư-tịch về thiên-chúa-giáo ở Việt-Nam; a bibliography on Christianity in Vietnam. Saigon, 1966. 81 p.

Author listing of, mostly, Vietnamese-language books and articles. Contains 634 items, including translations into Vietnamese of works on theology, prayers, politics and Christianity, morals, missions, and Vatican II.
mgc

JESUITS

BB21   Lettres édifiantes et curieuses, écrites des missions étrangères, par quelques missionaires de la Compagnie de Jésus. Éds. Charles Le Gobien, Nicolas Maréchal, et Patrouillet. Paris, 1702-1776. 34 v. Title varies: Recueil I: Lettres de quelques missionaires de la Compagnie de Jésus, écrites de la Chine et des Indes Orientales.

Letters and reports written by Jesuit missionaries on their work in non-Christian societies during the 18th century, with observations on history, customs, religions, and government in those countries. Described by Streit as a "great publication." The letters included "practically the whole field of 18th century Jesuit missionary work, especially the French...[and] must be considered a literary event of the century." (I, 336). The letters were read with great interest not only by the faithful but also by the literati and scholars for their essays on geography and religious and secular history of foreign lands. Considered an in-

valuable source for 18th century missionary history and first-person accounts of
events in non-European societies. Subjects about Vietnam include its history
and events subsequent to the Trịnh-Nguyễn
separation, observations on Vietnamese society, and Christianity in Vietnam. The
following volumes contain material about
Vietnam: Recueil 3 (1703), pp. 1-33
(Streit no. 756); 14 (1720), pp. 485-499
(no. 820); 18 (1928), pp. 122-188
(no. 850); 24 (1739), pp. 92-187 (no. 899);
28 (1758), pp. 252-283 (no. 987); 30
(1774), pp. 37-115, 352-382 (no. 1025);
31 (1774), pp. 57-212, 373-377 (no. 1029).
Except for Recueils 30 and 31, which are
comprised of letters about Tongking and
Cochinchina, the Recueils are about Tongking only.

Four major variant editions were published. 1) Lettres édifiantes et curieuses, écrites des missions étrangères.
Nouvelle éd. Paris, 1780-1783. 26 v.
Epître signed by [Yves Mathurin de] Querboeuf. Letters from Vietnam in: Mémoires
de la Chine, v. 16 (1781), 1-149, 180-221,
245-338, with Table des lettres, pp. 435-
438; v. 18 (1781), pp. 108-115, with Table
des Lettres, p. 479-480. Contents of the
Querboeuf edition listed in Streit I:
1051, pp. 533-541. Later editions in
1810, 1819, 1829, and 1838.

2) Lettres édifiantes et curieuses concernant l'Asie, l'Afrique et l'Amérique
avec quelques relations nouvelles des
missions et des notes géographiques et
historiques...de M. L. Aimé-Martin.
Paris: Desrez, 1838. 4 v. Subsequent
editions published by Société de Panthéon
Littéraire, 1843-1847, and Daffis, 1875-
1877. Contents of the Aimé-Martin edition
listed in Cordier 3: 1959-1961.

3) Nouvelles lettres édifiantes des
Missions de la Chine et des Indes Orientales. Paris: Adrien Le Clere, 1818-

1823. 8 v. Letters from Vietnam in
Vols. 6-8, including in vol. 6, pp. I-CXIV,
a history of Tongking, chronology of kings,
and succession of French bishops and apostolic vicars of Tongking and Cochinchina.
Letters include events through the Tây-Sơn
era.

4) Allerhand So Lehr-als Geist-reiche
Brief Schrifften und Reis-Beschreibungen
Welche von denen Missionariis der Geselle-
schaft Jesu...von Joseph Stöcklein...Augs-
burg, 1725-17..? 40 v. Also known as
Neue Welt-Bott. Letters from Vietnam in
vol. 2 (letters 44 and 45); v. 6 (130,
131, 133, 137); v. 7 (204); v. 12 (298);
v. 14 (312-317); v. 25 (527); v. 36
(699-723). Summaries of letters and memoirs in Sommervogel, appendix, 2d ser.,
pp. 17-102 and III, col. 1753-1857.

In addition to cataloging these collections under the titles or the names of the
compilers, many American libraries might
also catalog them under the entry:
Jesuits. Letters. Lettres édifiantes....
[MH] Aimé-Martin ed.

BB22   Sommervogel, Carlos. Bibliothèque de la
Compagnie de Jésus. Nouv. éd. Brussels:
O. Schepens; Paris: A. Picard, 1890-1932.
12 vols. Repr., Hérvelé, Louvain: Éditions de la Bibliothèque S. J., Collège
Philosophique et Théologique, 1960.
1ʳᵉ partie: "Bibliographie," par Augustin
et Aloys de Backer. 10 vols. 2ᵉ partie:
"Histoire," par Auguste Carayon. 1 vol.
(tome 11). "Corrections et additions"...
Supplément au "De Backer--Sommervogel"
par Ernest M. Rivière. Toulouse, 1911-
1930. Also repr. 1960. 5 fasc. (tome 12).
1960 reprinted edition has cross-references to citations in other volumes of the
work. 1st ed. Liège, 1853-1871 (7 vols.);
2d ed. Liège, Louvain, Paris, and Lyon,
1869-1876 (3 vols.)

Vols. 1 to 9, alphabetical listing, by
author, of works published by or about
Jesuits, until 1900; vol. 12 consists of
5 fascicles with an index in cols. 1265-87
updating the information in vols. 1-9.
Volume 10, pp. xxvii-xxxviii contains an
alphabetical subject index, see "Asie,"
"Cochinchine," "Tonkin" which refer the
user to the subject tables in vol. 10 and
subsequently to the appropriate and complete entries in volumes 1-9.

Citations include biographical and
bibliographical information on books and
manuscripts and sources cited for works
not in hand. If one knows the author of
a particular work, one may look in
vols. 1-9 for the bio- or bibliographical
information, but must also look in the in
the index in volume 12 for information
added after the publication of vols. 1-9.
MH

BB23   Teixeira, Manuel. "Missionários Jesuítas no
Vietnão." Boletim Eclesiástico do Diocese
de Macau, 62 (1964), 815-907.

Pt. 1, "Lista dos Missionários Jesuítas
na Cochinchina;" pt. 2, "Lista dos Missionários Jesuítas no Tonquim." Chronological listing of Jesuit missionaries in
Vietnam from 1615 to 1802. Includes biographical information, dates of service in
Vietnam, and activities in Vietnam.
MH

SOCIÉTÉ DES MISSIONS ÉTRANGÈRES AND OTHERS

BB24   Launay, Adrien. Documents historiques relatifs à la Société des Missions Étrangères.
[2d. éd. Vannes, 1905.--BN.] Tome premier: Préf., 1904.

Texts of a number of documents to which
Launay referred to in his Histoire générale de la Société des Missions-Étran-
gères. Although material includes a wide
variety of references to activities of the

SME, documents about Vietnam may be located through the index, under "Annam,"
"Cochinchine," "Tonkin," "Faï-fo," "Lambert de la Motte," "Pallu, François,"
"Rhodes, P. de." and other names. Documents are reprinted in Latin with French
translation. Complements Launay's Lettres
de Monseigneur Pallu (ca. 1906).
MH

BB25   ____. Histoire de la Mission de Cochinchine
(1658-1823). Paris: Anciennes Maisons
Charles Dounion et Retaux (vols. 2 and 3
have imprint covered by label: Librairie
Oriental et Américaine Maisonneuve Frères),
1923-1925. 3 vols. At head of title:
Société des Missions Étrangères.

Biographies of missionaries, and their
correspondence. Includes reference to the
source in the archives of the SME and
footnotes. Does not translate letters
originally written in Latin. Arranged by
name of missionary in chronological order,
beginning in vol. 1 with Lambert de la
Motte (1658-1679). The section on Pigneau
de Behaine, in vol. 3, includes his accounts of the Tây-Sơn rebellion and his
intervention on behalf of Nguyễn Anh.
Appendices in vol. 3 include articles on
Christianity in Cochinchina, the persecu-
tions of 1645 and 1663, and the Franciscans in Cochinchina from 1583 to 1769.
MH

BB26   ____. Histoire de la Mission du Tonkin.
Paris: Maisonneuve, 1927. Vol. 1, 600 p.
No subsequent volumes seem to have been
published. At head of title: Société
des Missions Étrangères.

Similar format to his Histoire de la
Mission de Cochinchine. Includes biographies and correspondence of Pallu, de
Bourges, and Deydier. A basic reference
source for the SME in Vietnam. Gives

original text of documents, but does not
translate Latin texts.
MH

BB27   _____. Histoire générale de la Société des
Missions Étrangères depuis sa fondation
jusqu'à nos jours. Paris: Téqui, 1894.
3 vols.

Detailed history of the SME by one of
its major historians. A detailed table of
contents is in vol. 3, pp. 603-646. Footnotes but no bibliography.
MH

BB28   _____. Memorial de la Société des Missions
Étrangères. Paris: Seminaire des Missions Étrangères, 1912-1916. 2 vols.

Vol. 1, list of all members of the Société from 1658 to 1910. Pp. 1-513,
chronological listing of 3,067 members
with their number in the Order, name, date
and place of birth, date of ordination,
date of departure for the Orient, place of
assignment, information about change of
status (promotions or resignations), and
date and place of death. Pp. 615-677,
list by vicariate of the "établissements
communs" in Indochina. Remainder of volume 1 includes supplement for information
received from 1910 to 1912, Vietnamese
names of missionaries, and the index.
Vol. 2, Biographical and bibliographical
dictionary about missionaries. Information about Pigneau de Behaine, for example, on pp. 511 to 516, includes one
page of bio-bibliographical information.
Some biographical summaries include por-
traits.
CtY

BB29   Marcellino, da Civezza. Saggio di bibliografia geographica, storica, etnografica
sanfrancescana. Prato: R. Guasti, 1879.
698 p.

Lists books and manuscripts written by
Franciscan missionaries. Cites 819 au-

thors, arranged alphabetically; no index
by geographic area, although a partial
list of Franciscan missionaries is in
Brébion, pp. 161-164. Annotations describe the books or manuscripts, provide
biographical information, or give references to writings by other missionaries.
Manuscripts are from various archives,
including the Franciscan convent in
Manila.
MH

BB30   Meynard, André-Marie. Missions dominicaines
dans l'Extrême-Orient. Lyon and Paris:
Librairie Chrétienne de Bauchu, 1865.
2 vols.

Includes Meynard's narrative history
and long quotations from original sources.
A principal source was Historia de la Pro-
vincia del Santo-Rosario de Filipinas
(Manila, 1692-1783). Includes activities
of missionaries such as Pallu who were not
Dominicans. Concludes with 1863.

Title page lists author only as André-
Marie.
MH

OTHER SOURCES

BB31   Bibliographie bouddhique. Paris: Geuthner,
etc., 1928- .

BB32   Bulletin signalétique section 527: Sciences
religieuses. Paris: Centre national de
la recherche scientifique, 1970- . Continuation of Bulletin signalétique (1940-
1941) and other titles.

BB33   Hanayama, Shinsho. Bibliography on Buddhism,
edited by the Commemoration Committee for
Prof. Shinsho Hanayama's Sixty-first
birthday. Tokyo: Hokuseido Press, 1961.
869 p.

BB34   Missionary Research Library, New York. Dictionary catalog. Boston: G. K. Hall,
1968. 17 vols.

LINGUISTICS AND PHILOLOGY BC

This chapter includes works on grammar, ro-
manization of the Vietnamese language, and descriptive and analytical studies of Vietnamese. Although
many grammars have been published, the few listed
here should be a representative selection. See also
chapter AE Language dictionaries.

BIBLIOGRAPHIES

BC1 Cordier, Henri. Bibliotheca indosinica.
  See AA23 for complete description. For
  publications on linguistics and philology,
  see vol. 4: 2281-2326, "Langue et litté-
  rature--Origines--Lexicographie" which
  includes language dictionaries (AE).
  MH

BC2 Boudet, Paul, and Rémy Bourgeois. Bibliographie de l'Indochine française.
  See AA22 for complete description. For
  publications on linguistics and philology,
  see "Langue annamite" in vols. 1-4 and
  "Enseignement: manuels--langue annamite"
  in vol. 4. Vol. 4 has extensive citations
  for publications in Vietnamese.
  MH

BC3 Nguyễn Đình Hòa. "Reading list on Vietnamese
  language and writing." VHNS, 11 (1962),
  685-697.
  Alphabetical list, by author, of about
  200 books and articles on language dictionaries, quốc-ngữ, grammar, dialects,
  and orthography appearing as early as
  Rhodes' Dictionarium of 1651. Includes
  many articles from periodicals published
  in France. Useful for references on quốc-
  ngữ in the early 20th century.
  MH; NIC

BC4 Thompson, Laurence C., and David D. Thomas.
  "Vietnam." In Current trends in linguistics, vol. 2, Linguistics in East Asia and

South East Asia, ed. Thomas A. Sebeok,
  pp. 815-846. The Hague: Mouton, 1967.
  Bibliographic essay describing re-
  search--past and present, up to 1965--on
  all aspects of the Vietnamese language.
  Bibliography of about 185 books and periodical articles.
  MH

BC5 Vasiljev, I. V. "Les ouvrages des savants
  soviétiques sur la langue viêtnamienne."
  Archiv orientalni [Prague], 30 (1962),
  331-342.
  Bibliographical essay, including footnotes citing about 40 Russian books and
  articles.
  MH

BC6 Vietnam (Republic). Nha Văn-Khố và Thư-Viện
  Quốc-Gia. Sở-thảo mục-lục thư-tịch về
  ngôn-ngữ Việt-Nam; reading list on Vietnamese language. Saigon, 1966. 29 p.
  Author listing of 243 books and articles, including grammars, linguistics,
  textbooks, orthography, nôm, regionalisms,
  and borrowing. Excludes dictionaries.
  mgc; NIC

DICTIONARIES

BC7 Nguyễn Văn Mai. Dictionnaire des homonymes
  annamites. Saigon: [n. p.?], 1925.
  134 p.
  Offered for sale by Thanh-long (Brussels), Nov. 1971.

BC8 Nguyễn Văn Minh. Việt-ngữ tinh-nghĩa từ-
  điển. [Dictionary of synonyms]. [Sai-
  gon]: Hoa Tiên, [1973?] Preface signed
  in 1952.
  Tập hai [vol. 2], 1973, 193 p.
  Defines and explains similarities and
  differences in synonyms and different uses
  of words in compound forms. Index in
  vol. 2 refers to terms defined in volumes 1 and 2.
  MH-V

BC9 Trần Văn Điền. Dictionary of synonyms and
antonyms; tự điển đồng nghĩa và phản
nghĩa. [Saigon]: Sống Mới [1970].
581 p. Cover has title: Tự điển Anh ngữ
đồng nghĩa phản nghĩa

English-English synonyms and antonyms,
with brief Vietnamese definition.
MH-V

GRAMMARS

BC10 *Bùi Đức Tịnh. Văn phạm Việt-Nam [Vietnamese
grammar]. Saigon: Khai trí, 1968.
526 p. (Source: TTQGVN, 1; NIC [1963,
1967 eds.])

BC11 Lê Văn Lý. Le parler viêtnamien; sa structure phonologique et morphologique fonc-
tionnelle. Essai d'une grammaire viêtnamienne. 2. éd. rev. et corr. Saigon:
Bộ Quốc-gia Giáo-dục, 1960. 294 p. (Publications de l'Institut des Recherches
Historiques). 1st ed. has title, Le parler viêtnamien; essai d'une grammaire
viêtnamienne. Paris: Huong Anh [1948?]
235 p.

Analyzes phonemes, tones, and sentence
structure.
MH

BC12 *____. Sơ thảo ngữ pháp Việt-Nam [A sketch
of Vietnamese grammar]. Saigon: Trung
tâm Học liệu, Bộ Giáo Dục, 1968. 232 p.
(Source: TTQGVN, 2/3; NIC.)

BC13 Thompson, Laurence C. A Vietnamese grammar.
Seattle: University of Washington Press,
1965. 386 p.

Chapters on pronunciation, writing,
grammatical structure, compounds, deriva-
tives, substantives, predicates, particles,
sentence structure, levels of discourse,
personal names, and glossary of difficult
forms. Includes numerous examples of
usage.
MH

OTHER SOURCES

BC14 Bulletin signalétique section 524: Sciences
du langage. Paris: Centre national de la
recherche scientifique, 1969- . Continuation of Bulletin signalétique (1940-1941)
and other titles.

BC15 MLA international bibliography of books and
articles on the modern languages and literature. New York: Modern Language Association of America, 1921- .

BC16 Permanent International Committee of Lin-
guists/Comité International Permanent de
Linguistes. Linguistic bibliography of
[year]; bibliographie linguistique de
l'année ----. Utrecht: Spectrum,
1949- .

LITERATURE BD

Although Vietnamese literature was originally
written in Sino-Vietnamese characters, some of it
has been translated into quốc-ngữ or Western languages, and in the twentieth century, almost all of
it has been written originally in quốc-ngữ. The
bibliographies, selections, and histories cited in
this chapter list mostly the works which have been
translated or published in quốc-ngữ or Western
languages.

BIBLIOGRAPHIES

BD1 Cordier, Henri. Bibliotheca indosinica.
See AA23 for complete description. For
publications on literature, see vol. 4:
2327-2386 and 2969-2972, "Littérature,"
which includes editions of Kim Vân Kiều,
2353-2356 and Lục Vân Tiên, 2356-2357.
MH

LITERATURE BD

BD2　Boudet, Paul, and Rémy Bourgeois.　Biblio-
　　　　graphie de l'Indochine française.

　　　　See AA22 for complete description.　For
　　　publications on literature, see "Littéra-
　　　ture annamite" in each volume.　Volumes 3
　　　and 4 have extensive listings of works in
　　　Vietnamese, arranged according to "géné-
　　　ralités," "études et critiques," "chan-
　　　sons," "divers," "poésies," "romans,
　　　contes et nouvelles," and "théâtre."
　　　MH

IND P300　VS B9

BD3　Ross, Marion W.　Bibliography of Vietnamese
　　　　literature in the Wason collection at
　　　　Cornell University.　Ithaca:　Southeast
　　　Asia Program, Department of Asian Studies,
　　　Cornall University, 1973.　178 p.　(Its
　　　Data Paper, 90).

　　　　Alphabetical listing by author of 2,852
　　　books in Vietnamese, French, English, and
　　　Chinese on all aspects of literature--
　　　novels, short stories, poetry, drama, es-
　　　says, memoirs, humor, folk literature,
　　　etc.　Bibliographic information is com-
　　　plete and includes call number in Wason
　　　collection and designation of literary
　　　genre.　Indexes are by literary genre, by
　　　language, and by place of publication.
　　　Includes many works by writers of the
　　　1930's, 1940's, and 1950's which have been
　　　reprinted in Saigon and Hanoi in the past
　　　decade.

　　　　Differs from the Checklist of the Viet-
　　　namese holdings of the Wason collection by
　　　Giok Po Oey (AA25) in that it includes
　　　works in English and French, has indexes
　　　by place and date of publication, and is
　　　restricted to literature only.
　　　MH

TRANSLATIONS

BD4　Baruch, Jacques.　Bibliographie des traduc-
　　　　tions françaises des littératures du Viêt-
　　　　nam et du Cambodge.
　　　　See AA85 for complete description.

BD5　Jenner, Philip N.　Southeast Asian litera-
　　　　tures in translation:　a preliminary
　　　　bibliography.
　　　　See AA87 for bibliographic description.

BD6　N. G. P.　"Thư-tịch khảo về các tác-phẩm và
　　　truyện ngắn dịch từ Anh-Pháp ngữ sang
　　　Việt-ngữ (1958-1965)" [Bibliography of
　　　works and short stories translated from
　　　English and French into Vietnamese (1958-
　　　1965)].
　　　　See AA88 for annotation.

BD7　Senny, Jacqueline.　Contributions à l'appré-
　　　　ciation des valeurs culturelles de
　　　　l'Orient; traductions françaises de lit-
　　　　tératures orientales.
　　　　See AA89 for complete description.

DICTIONARIES

BD8　Diễn Hương.　Thành ngữ điển tích [Literary
　　　phrases and idioms].　In lần thứ 3.　Sai-
　　　gon:　Khai-Trí, 1961.　503 p.
　　　　1st ed., 1949.　1969 ed., 536 p., cited
　　　in Thư mục 1970.
　　　　On cover:　Tự-điển thành ngữ điển tích.
　　　　Dictionary of words, phrases, and idi-
　　　oms, with excerpts from writings.
　　　MH-V

BD9　Hải-Thanh.　"Danh-từ khảo dụng:　văn-học"
　　　[Literature terms].　Quê-hương, nos. 23-
　　　26, 28 (5/61-8/61, 10/61).
　　　　Definitions of Sino-Vietnamese terms.
　　　Each entry is arranged alphabetically in
　　　Chinese characters, quốc-ngữ, and defini-
　　　tion in Vietnamese.　Terms in each issue
　　　of QH are arranged alphabetically, but in
　　　some instances, the alphabetizing begins
　　　anew with each installment.
　　　MH

BD10　*Nguyễn Văn Minh.　Tự-điển văn-liệu [của]
　　　Long-điền Nguyễn Văn Minh.　In lần 2.
　　　[Hanoi] Á châu [1952.]　472 p.

"Dictionary of classical words and phrases from literature." (Source: Ross [BD3]). Copy at NIC.

BD11 Trịnh Văn Thành. Thành-ngữ điển-tích danh-nhân từ-điển [Dictionary of literary terms and personnages].

See AD3 for complete description. Includes definitions of literary terms.

SELECTIONS AND HISTORIES

BD12 Anthologie de la littérature vietnamienne. Intro. et notes de Nguyen Khac Vien, Nguyen Van Hoan [et] Huu Ngoc. Trad. de Nguyen Khac Vien [et al]. Hanoi: Éditions en langues étrangères, 1972- .

Vol. 1, From the beginnings to the 17th century; vol. 2, 17th, 18th, and first half of 19th centuries; vol. 3, Second half of 19th century to 1945. Other volumes are planned on literature of ethnic minorities and on folklore.

Translations into French of selected Vietnamese works. Titles of all works are also printed in Vietnamese.
MH (vol. 1); MLXBP 8/75 (vol. 3)

BD13 Cordier, Georges. Morceaux choisis d'auteurs annamites.... 1. éd., Hanoi: Lê-văn-Tân, 1932. 336 p. 2. éd., ibid., 1935.

For use in secondary schools. Text in quốc-ngữ. Includes an outline of Vietnamese history and a chart naming authors and their works. Extracts of works are prefaced by biographical notes of each author.

A revised edition of his Littérature annamite; extrait des poètes et des prosateurs. (Hanoi: IDEO, 1914. 194 p.)
MH

BD14 Dương Quảng Hàm. Việt-Nam văn-học sử-yếu. [Précis of Vietnamese literature]. Hanoi: 1943. In lần thứ 8. [Saigon]: Bộ Quốc-gia Giáo-dục, 1961. 480 p.

For secondary schools. A survey of the history of Vietnamese literature, including folk poetry and songs, Chinese influence, and classical writings. Examples are printed in nôm, romanized nôm, and quốc-ngữ. Extensive sections on literature during the 19th century. Bibliographies at end of chapters include citations of printed or translated editions of texts discussed in those chapters. Pp. 446-461, chart of literary developments and publications since the Lý dynasty (1010-1225).

Eighth edition, 1961, is a reprinting but not revision of text.
MH

BD15 Dương Đình Khuê. Les chefs d'oeuvre de la littérature vietnamienne. [Saigon: Kim Lai ấn quán, 1966-] Vol. 1, La littérature ancienne, 1966. 420 p.

Vol. 1 covers writers from Vạn-Hạnh Thiền-sư (d. 1018) to 1913. Selections of prose and poetry, with summaries of biographical and historical information. Does not mention the discoveries of the true names of Bà Huyện Thanh-Quan and Hồ Xuân Hương in the DRVN as reported in Durand and Huân (BD16). Selections are translated into French, and many poems originally written in nôm or quốc-ngữ also include the transcription in quốc-ngữ "to preserve the charm of the original text."
MH

BD16 Durand, Maurice, and Nguyễn Trần Huân. Introduction à la littérature vietnamienne. Paris: Maisonneuve et Larose, 1969. 253 p. (Collection UNESCO Introduction aux littératures orientales)

"One of the first syntheses in French of contemporary Vietnamese literature" (Huân, in preface). Durand contributed the chapters about Vietnamese literature before the arrival of the French before

his death in April 1966; Huân wrote the
section on the periods from 1862-1945,
from 1945-1963, and the bio-bibliographical dictionary on pp. 181-225. Makes note
of recent discoveries by writers in the
DRVN of what are believed to be the real
names of Bà Huyện Thanh-quan (Nguyễn Thị
Hinh) and Hồ Xuân Hương (Thị Mai). Selections are translated into French. Few
footnotes; bibliography, pp. 169-175, is
an essay rather than a list with complete
bibliographical information. Includes a
list of 13 contemporary works translated
into French as of 1963. Bio-bibliographical dictionary lists Vietnamese and French
authors; brief information for most Vietnamese authors, otherwise it serves as an
index to French authors listed in the text
and is useful as a recent guide to contemporary authors.

Extensive review by Nguyễn Đình Hòa, in
Journal of the American Oriental Society,
92 (1972), 364-368.
MH

BD17   *Hợp tuyển thơ văn Việt-Nam [Anthology of
        Vietnamese poetry and prose]. Hanoi:
        Nhà Xuất bản Văn-hóa, 1965? Vols. 2-4,
        1962-64. (Source: Kyoto, 1965, p. 314;
        NIC [vols. 3-6].)

BD18   *Lê Văn Siêu. Văn-học Việt-Nam thời Lý [Viet-
        namese literature under the Lý dynasty].
        Saigon: Hướng Dương, 1957. (Source: VN
        Buddhism.)

BD19   *Ngô Tất Tố. Việt-Nam văn-học; văn-học đời Lý
        [Vietnamese literature; literature during
        the Lý dynasty]. Saigon: Khai-trí, 1960.
        117 p. (Source: VN buddh; NIC.)

BD20   *_____. Việt-Nam văn-học; văn-học đời Trần
        [Literature during the Trần dynasty].
        Saigon: Khai-trí, 1960. (Source: VN
        Buddh.)

BD21   Nguyễn Tấn Long and Nguyễn Hữu Trọng. Việt-
        Nam thi-nhân tiền-chiến [Pre-war Vietnam-
        ese poets]. Saigon: Sống Mới, 1968- .
        Quyển thượng [vol. 1], 1968, 818 p.
        [3 vols.--NIC]

        Extensive selections, with commentary,
        of poems by 18 poets writing from about
        1932 to 1945.
        MH-V

BD22   Phạm Văn Diêu. "200 năm lịch sử văn học nhà
        Lý" [200 years of literature of the Ly
        dynasty]. VHNS, XIV, 8/9 (8/9, 1965),
        1229-1244; XIV, 12 (12/65), 1795-1830;
        XV, 1/2 (1/2, 1966), 1-38.

        Parts 1 and 2 are descriptions of the
        development of literature under the Lý;
        part 3 is short biographical sketches of
        53 writers of the period.
        MH; NIC

BD23   *Sở thảo lịch sử văn học Việt-Nam [Draft of a
        history of Vietnamese literature, by] Văn
        Tan [et al]. Hanoi: Văn Sử Địa [1957-
        1960]. 5 v.

        Vol. 1: Fables, written literature,
        and oral literature. Vol. 2: 10th to
        end of 17th century. Vols. 3 and 4:
        18th century. Vol. 5: First half of the
        19th century. (Source: NIC; CtY.)

BD24   *Trần Trung Viên, comp. Văn-đàn bảo-giám
        [Selections of Vietnamese literature].
        Pref. de Dương Bá Trạc, rev. par Trần
        Tuấn Khai. Hanoi: ed. Nam-ký, 1932.
        3 v. (Collection Văn-học tùng-thư)
        (Source: Boudet 4; NIC [1968 ed.].)

BD25   Trần Tuấn Kiệt. Thi ca Việt Nam hiện đại
        1880-1965 [Contemporary Vietnamese poetry].
        Saigon: Khai-trí, 1968. 1150 p.
        Extensive selection of poems from about
        150 writers born after 1880. Includes
        biographical sketches and real names of
        authors who write under pseudonyms.
        MH-V; NIC

BD26   Trần Văn Giáp [ed.] Lược truyện các tác giả
       Việt-Nam [Short biographies of Vietnamese
       authors]. Hanoi: Nhã Xuất bản Sử Học,
       1962- .

       Vol. 1, authors writing in Sino-Viet-
       namese characters. 1962. 576 p.[1] In
       lần 2, có sửa chữa, bổ sung, [2d. ed.,
       rev. and updated]. 1971. 521 p.[2]
       Vol. 2, authors writing in the Latin al-
       phabet (quốc ngữ and European languages);
       planned as of the time of the publication
       of vol. 1.

       Vol. 1, chronological list of 735 au-
       thors, from Khuông-Việt (d. 1011) to Đặng
       Xuân Viên (1880-1958). Includes authors
       of non-Vietnamese ethnic origin (mostly
       Chinese) as well as Vietnamese. Informa-
       tion for each author includes, if known,
       name, dates, pseudonyms, birthplace, fam-
       ily, occupation and activities, descrip-
       tion of works, and bibliography. The in-
       dexes, by family name and pseudonym and by
       title of work, are necessary to locate a
       particular author because of arrangement
       of list. (Indexes are not included in
       2d ed.) Pp. 30 ff., list of 30 sources
       used to compile the work: Việt Sử Lược,
       An-Nam Chỉ-Lược, Lịch-triều hiến-chương
       loại-chỉ, and others. Annotations of
       these sources are in some instances ex-
       tensive, with listing of individual chap-
       ters of some sources.
       [1]CtY; NIC (vol. 1); [2]MH-V

BD27   Vũ Ngọc Phan. Nhã văn hiện đại; phê bình văn
       học [Contemporary writers; a literary
       criticism]. Hanoi: Tân Dân, 1942;[1]
       Hanoi: Vĩnh Thịnh, 1951. 4 v.;[2] [In
       lần 3] Saigon: Thăng-Long, 1960. 4 v.
       in 5.[3]

       Literary criticism of 79 writers, from
       Trương Vĩnh Ký to 1942, with additional
       sections for writers living after 1942
       added by the publisher for the 3d. edi-
       tion. About 10 pages on each writer.
       [1]Cited in 3d. ed. [2]NIC [3]MH-V

NGUYỄN DU (1765-1820)

BD28   *Đào Duy Anh. Tự điển Truyện Kiều. Phụ lục:
       Văn bản truyện Kiều, do Đào Duy Anh khảo
       đỉnh [Dictionary of the Kim Vân Kiều sto-
       ry. Appendix: The tale of Kiều, edited
       by Đào Duy Anh]. Hanoi: Khoa học xã hội,
       1974. 557 p.

       Cited in Vietnam studies newsletter,
       June 1976.

BD29   Kỷ niệm hai trăm năm năm sinh Nguyễn Du
       (1765-1965) [The two hundredth anniversary
       of the birth of Nguyễn Du (1765-1965)].
       Hanoi: Nhã xuất bản Khoa học xã hội,
       1967. 500 p. At head of title: Viện Văn
       Học.

       Part 1, articles, speeches, and other
       communications of writers and government
       and Party officials observing the anni-
       versary; part 2, research articles written
       in DRVN or abroad on various aspects of
       Nguyễn Du's works. Includes bibliography
       of 95 publications written in DRVN, other
       Socialist countries, and France in observ-
       ance of the bicentenary.
       MH-V

BD30   Lê Ngọc Trụ and Bửu Cầm. Thư mục về Nguyễn
       Du [Bibliography of Nguyễn Du]. Saigon:
       Bộ Giáo-dục, 1965. 139 p. (Tủ sách Viện
       Khảo-cổ; Publications of the Institute of
       Archaeological Research; Publications de
       l'Institut de Recherches Archéologique,
       11.)

       "The first bibliography of Nguyễn Du"--
       pref., published in the year of the bi-
       centenary of his birth. Author listing of
       574 books and articles in Vietnamese, Chi-
       nese, and European languages about Nguyễn
       Du and his writings. Based on holdings of
       the Thư-viện Quốc-gia (National Library),
       the Tổng Thư-viện (General Library) in
       Saigon, and the collection of Trụ. In-
       cludes the numerous editions and transla-
       tion of Kim Vân Kiều and articles, printed

speeches, or books about Nguyễn Du's writings. References in Chinese characters include his biography in Đại-Nam chính-biên liệt-truyện (see p. 35) and numerous articles in Nam-phong. Also includes chapters in books in which Nguyễn Du is mentioned.

MH-V; NIC

BD31   Mélanges sur Nguyễn Du réunis à l'occasion du bi-centenaire de sa naissance (1765), publiés sous la direction de Maurice Durand. Paris: École française d'Extrême-Orient, 1966. 317 p. (Publications de l'École française d'Extrême-Orient, 59.)

Contains mostly articles about Nguyễn Du, Vietnamese society during his time, or his writings. Pp. 47-51, "Bibliographie: liste des ouvrages" [of or about Nguyễn Du, 38 items]; pp. 53-70, "Bibliographie: liste par auteur" [about Nguyễn Du, 205 items], both by M. Durand; and pp. 71-80, "Le Nam-phong et les études sur le Kiều," by Phạm Thị Ngoan, 80 items.

MH

FINE ARTS BE

Publications in this chapter comprise mostly works on sculpture and statuary, architecture, engraving in wood, ivory, or bronze, and pottery. See also chapter DI Archeology.

BE1   Cordier, Henri. Bibliotheca indosinica.

See AA23 for complete description. For publications on fine arts, see vol. 3: 2277-2278, and vol. 4: 2969-2970, "Beaux arts."

BE2   Boudet, Paul, and Rémy Bourgeois. Bibliographie de l'Indochine française.

See AA22 for complete description. For publications on fine arts, see "Art" and

"Archéologie" in vols. 1-4 and subheadings "Art" or "Archéologie" under "Annam," "Cochinchine," and "Tonkin" in vol. 4.

MH

BE3   Bezacier, L. L'art vietnamien. Paris: Éditions de l'Union française, [1955]. 236 p.

"The first comprehensive work on the subject" (R. Heine-Geldern, Arts Asiatiques, 1955). Chapters on religious art, funerary art, civil architecture, military architecture, and principal epochs in Vietnamese art history.

Reedition of Essais sur l'art annamite (Hanoi, 1944) (Source: Gaspardone, Journal asiatique, 1955).

MH-FA

BE4   *Vietnam (Democratic Republic). Viện Ngôn Ngữ Học. Thuật ngữ mỹ thuật, Pháp-Việt, Việt-Pháp, có chú thêm tiếng Nga [Terminology in the fine arts. French-to-Vietnamese, Vietnamese-to-French, with Russian terms added]. Hanoi: Khoa học xã hội, 1970. 62 p. (Source: Châu.)

BE5   *Vietnam (Republic). Nha Văn-Hóa. Niên-giám văn-nghệ-sĩ và hiệp-hội văn-hóa Việt-Nam [Yearbook of Vietnamese artists, writers and cultural associations]. Saigon, 1970. 815 p. [Sources: TTAPC (listed as 844 p.); Gélinas, list 033, March 15, 1975 (listed as the 1969-1970 edition, 815 p.)]

APPLIED ARTS, NUMISMATICS, AND STAMPS BF

Subjects in the applied arts include ceramics, costume and dress, metal arts, numismatics, and postage stamps. Most of the references in this chapter are for works in numismatics and stamps; for publications in the other subjects, see the bibliographies by Cordier and Boudet, the works by

Oger (BF19 and BF20), and the references in chapter BE Fine Arts.

BIBLIOGRAPHIES

BF1 Cordier, Henri. Bibliotheca indosinica.
     See AA23 for complete description. For
     publications on the applied arts, see
     vol. 3: 1883-86 and vol. 4: 2411-12,
     "Numismatiques," "Jeux," and "Monnaies,
     Poids et Mesures, Sociétés d'Argent";
     vol. 3: 2267-76 and vol. 4: 2967-68,
     "Sciences et arts--Industries diverses";
     and vol. 4: 2389-2414 and 2971-74,
     "Moeurs et coutumes."
     MH

BF2 Boudet, Paul, and Rémy Bourgeois. Biblio-
     graphie de l'Indochine française.
     See AA22 for complete description. For
     publications on the applied arts, see "Nu-
     mismatique" in vols. 1 and 4 and "Art" and
     related topics in each volume.
     MH

NUMISMATICS

MAJOR SOURCES

BF3 *Daniel, Howard A., III. The catalog and
     guide book of Southeast Asian coins and
     currency. Reston, Va.: the author,
     1975- . Pt. 1, French colonial, 1975,
     110 p.
     Catalog of French colonial coins and
     paper money issued in Indochina and by
     banks in Thailand with authorization to
     issue notes, ending in 1954.--Rev. by
     Patrick D. Hogan, T'ung Pao, Journal of
     the Society for Oriental Numismatics,
     Iowa City, Iowa, vol. 2, no. 1 (1976),
     pp. 28-29.

BF4 Daudin, Pierre. "Sigillographie sino-anna-
     mite." BSEI, 12 (1937), 1-321. Also

published separately: Saigon: Impr. de
l'Union, 1937. 321 p.
     Describes history and uses of official
seals in China and in Vietnam including
extensive descriptions and illustrations
and comparison of similarities between
China and Vietnam. Pp. 8-230, "sigillographie chinoise;" pp. 231-276, "sigillographie annamite."
MH; DLC

BF5 Gillingham, Harrold Edgar. Notes on the
     decorations and medals of the French col-
     onies and protectorates. New York:
     American Numismatic Society, 1928. 62 p.
     (Numismatic Notes and Monographs, 26)
     Describes various decorations and med-
     als and provides short accounts of the
     conditions by which they are conferred.
     For the government of Annam, describes
     and pictures nine decorations, from the
     time of the Gia-long emperor to 1928.
     Short bibliography.
     MH

BF6 Lacroix, Désiré. Numismatique annamite.
     Saigon: Ménard et Legros, 1900. 2 vols.
     (Publications de l'École française d'Ex-
     trême-Orient [1].)
     A revised and enlarged edition of Notes
     pour servir à la recherche et au classe-
     ment de monnaies et médailles de l'Annam
     et de la Cochinchine française, by
     J. Silvestre (BF10). Describes coins
     discovered subsequent to the French occu-
     pation of Tongking and as a result of re-
     search in Cochinchina. Vol. 1, text,
     discusses metals, manufacture of money,
     and describes about 500 coins and medals,
     including several coins issued by the
     French colonial government. The earliest
     coin pictured was issued by Đinh Tiên-
     Hoàng (968-980) while the latest coins
     issued by the Vietnamese are from the pe-
     riod of the Thành-Thái emperor (1889-

1907). Concludes by describing money of French Indochina, a chronological table of Vietnamese dynasties, also published separately, and an alphabetical table of coins described.

Reviewed, with corrections and additions by Éd. Chavannes in Nouvelles et Mélanges (mars-avril 1901), 361-362, and by S. W. Bushill, Journal of the Royal Asiatic Society, 33 (1901), 142-146.
MH

BF7   Novak, John A. A working aid for collectors of Annamese coins. Longview, Wash.: publ. by Ken and Creta Olmsted, printed by Daily News Press [1967]. 111 p.

Pictures of facsimiles of from 500 to 700 types of coins (Coole). Purpose of book is "to aid in attributing Annamese coins...written for numismatists seeking identification of coins in hand." Arranged according to stroke order and stroke count. Relied upon nine sources--western and Japanese--to compile list, the four Japanese sources not listed in this bibliography. Includes only coins with Chinese characters, minted up to and during the Bao Dai reign. Some annotations about historical circumstances of an issue.
DSm

BF8   Permar, Bernard J. Catalogue of Annam coins, 968-1955. Saigon [pref. signed November 1963] 73 p., plates, 71 p. text. [Distrib. by Librairie Xuân-Thu]

Chronological listing of about 625 coins, with photographs. Most coins are dated by the author. Types of coins include a commemorative coin on the occasion of what the author thinks is the victory of Trịnh Sâm over the "Chua of Hue" at Thuận Hóa in the 10th month of 1774 (no. 91); silver bars minted for commerce to compete with Mexican and U.S. silver coins (nos. 120-122); coins minted in

Europe in 1834 (nos. 81-83); coins minted by usurpers or feudatories (nos. 446-589); and charms (nos. 590-614). Reproduction of the coins is poor; the text has many errors of syntax and spelling; and not all coins are photographed on both sides. Reviewed by Philippe Langlet in "Elements bibliographiques d'histoire vietnamienne," BSEI, n.s. 45 (1970), 126, who states that this is a translation of Schroeder's Annam; études numismatiques which omits the franco-indochinese coins.

As described by Coole, pp. 345-346, "the cover gives the name Walter Lozozki as the author in two places, but the introduction" gives Permar's name. Coole also recognized this as mainly a translation without reference to Schroeder's book, and wrote to Permar, who explained that this was printed from his work sheets and is a pirate issue. Permar also stated that he had intended to publish the book and acknowledges Schroeder's basic work, which he had updated and translated into English.
NIC

BF9   Schroeder, Albert. Annam, études numismatiques; Dai Nam Hoa Te Do Luc. Paris: Leroux, 1905. 2 vols.

Extensive history of currency in Vietnam and French Indochina. Includes dynastic chronologies; inscriptions used on coins; weights and measures; manufacture of coins, including laws pertaining to their manufacture; and mining. Pp. 415-637 list descriptions of about 700 coins pictured in vol. 2 (plates). The basic work on Vietnamese numismatics.
DLC

BF10   Silvestre, J. "Notes pour servir à la recherche et au classement des monnaies et médailles de l'Annam et de la Cochinchine française." Excursions et Reconnaissances, no. 14 (1882), 305-344.

A pioneering work, later revised and expanded into two volumes by Lacroix, the purpose of which was to aid the numismatist in research and classification of money and medals by providing a means of identifying coinage of Vietnamese dynasties and by indicating principal historical events which might affect coinage. Not intended to illustrate coins.

Pp. 305-332, brief outline of Vietnamese dynastic history; pp. 332-344, chronological table of Vietnamese kings and emperors to the Tự-Đức emperor, with dates and pseudonyms of rulers.
MH-H

BF11 Toda, Ed. "Annam and its minor currency." Journal of the North China Branch of the Royal Asiatic Society, 17 (1882), 41-220. Repr. separately: Shanghai: Noronha, 1882. 261 p. German translation in Berliner Münzblatter, vols. 4, 7, 8 (1883, 1886, 1887).

Describes, with illustrations, 290 coins minted as early as the Đinh dynasty and as recent as the reign of the Tự-đức emperor. Includes coins minted by legitimate rulers, rebels, counterfeiters, and usurpers, and 45 coins known to be Vietnamese but of unknown origin. Does not identify any coins minted by the Nguyễn princes (1558-1776).

Includes chapters on Vietnamese history in brief, chronological tables of rulers, mines in Vietnam, manufacture of coins, laws and superstitions about coins, and paper money. Pp. 75-135, "history of the coinage," describes coins minted by each ruler.

Toda's descriptions and illustrations were cited in Lockhart's Currency of the Farther East (BF14).
MH

OTHER SOURCES

BF12 Bowker, Howard Franklin. A numismatic bibliography of the Far East; a check list of titles in European languages. New York: American Numismatic Society, 1943. 144 p. (Numismatic notes and monographs, 101)

BF13 Coole, Arthur Bradden. An encyclopedia of Chinese coins. Vol. 1, A bibliography on Far Eastern numismatology and a coin index. Denver, Colo.: the author, 1967. 581 p.

BF14 Lockhart, James Haldane Stewart. The currency of the Farther East from the earliest times up to the present day. Hongkong: Noronha, 1895-1898. 3 vols.

STAMPS

BF15 *Dương Hội, Louis. Mục-lục sưu tập tem Việt-Nam, Cambodge, Laos [catalog of postage stamps...]. Saigon: Maridor, 1964. 33 p. (Source: Thư mục 1965.)

BF16 *Mục lục sưu tập tem Việt-Nam, Cambodge, Laos (Catalogue de timbre-poste pour collections du Vietnam, Cambodge et Laos). [Saigon: Dung-Hà, 1971]. 50 p. TTQGVN, 13/14

BF17 Nguyễn Bảo Tung. 20 [i.e. Hai mươi] năm bưu-hoa Việt-Nam; 20 years of the Vietnamese philately; 20 ans de la philatélie Vietnamienne 1955-1971. Saigon: Phu Quốc Vụ Khanh Đặc Trách Văn-Hóa, 1971. 491 p.

Brief history of postage stamps in Indochina and in Vietnam since the establishment of the Sở Bưu Chỉnh và Viễn-Thông Việt-Nam [Postal and Telecommunications Service of Vietnam] in 1951. Summary of events in philately under French rule, 1886-1954. Catalog, with illustrations of stamps issued by RVN, 1951-1971, and

text in English, French, Chinese, and
Vietnamese. Indicates those stamps listed
in catalogs by Yvert et Tellier and by
Champion-Scott.
MH-V

BF18 *Quách Phong Vân. Sưu-tập và ỷ nghĩa tem
Việt-Nam 1960-1964, Vietnamese postage
stamps and their meaning. Saigon: [the
author] 1967. [84 p.]. (Source: NIC.)

OTHER TOPICS

BF19 Oger, Henri Joseph. Introduction générale à
l'étude de la technique du peuple annamite; essai sur la vie matérielle, les
arts et industries du peuple d'Annam.
Paris: P. Guethner, 1910. 3 vols.,
vol. 1, text; vols. 2 & 3, atlas (album
of drawings). (Archives documentaires
d'art, d'ethnographie et de sociologie de
la Chine et de l'Indo-Chine)

Limited edition of 60 copies, each
fascicle in vols. 2 & 3 composed of about
300 plates which are photocopies of wood
engravings by Vietnamese artists. According to the publication note, 40 copies
were put on sale in Europe and 20 copies
were sent to governmental archives and libraries in Indochina.

Vol. 1, text and drawings describing
the work of artisans, fishermen, butchers,
bamboo weavers, brickmakers, carpenters,
and other tradesmen on pp. 1-81; bibliography of about 250 western and Chinese
publications on pp. 82-112; analytical
tables of the contents of the atlas volumes, and subject index of the atlas volumes, pp. 154-161.

For a brief account of the writing of
this work and of the life of Oger, see
"Henri Oger (1885-1936)," BEFEO, 58
(1970), pp. 215-217, by P. Huard.
DLC, Vol. 1

BF20 *_____. Technique du peuple annamite; documents et observations rassemblés durant
le service militaire de l'auteur à Hanoi
en 1908-1909; encyclopédie de tous les
instruments, ustensiles de tous les gestes
de la vie et métiers du peuple annamite
tonkinois. Hanoi [n. p., n. d.].
(Source: Ajia.)

THEATER ARTS BG

BG1 Cordier, Henri. Bibliotheca indosinica.
See AA23 for complete description. For
publications on theater arts, see vol. 4:
2373-2380 and 2971-2972, "Théâtre."
MH

BG2 Boudet, Paul and Rémy Bourgeois. Bibliographie de l'Indochine française.
See AA22 for complete description. For
publications on theater arts, see "Théâtre"
in vols. 1-4 and "Littérature annamite--
théâtre" in Vols. 3 and 4.
MH

BG3 Huỳnh Khắc Dụng. Hát bội; théâtre tradi-
tionnel du Viet-Nam. Saigon: Kim Lai Ấn
Quán, 1970. 56 p. Text in French and
Vietnamese.

Written in order to demonstrate the
art form of hát bội, which the author
thinks is often looked down upon by West-
erners. Chapters on the origin, organization, technique, and future of hát bội,
texts of two dramas, San Hậu and Bá Ấp
Khảo. Includes colored drawings of masks
and costumes.
MH-V

BG4 *Mục lục giới thiệu ảnh các di tích văn hóa
Việt-Nam [Catalog of films showing Vietnamese culture]. Hanoi: Thư viện khoa
học xã hội.

Tập 3: (Các di tích có tên gọi từ Q-Y)
Tô ảnh Thư viện khoa học xã hội biên soạn
[Volume 3. (Films with titles from Q-Y)
Prepared by the Film Group of the Social
Sciences Library]. 1975. 772 p. (Source:
MLXBP, 10/75.)

BG5 *Vietnam (Republic). Bộ Thông-Tin. Trung-Tâm
Quốc-Gia Điện-Ảnh. Mục thư phim [Film
catalog]. Saigon, 1971. Cited in TTTV,
VQGTK, 10/72. Editions in 1960 and 1968
cited in Bibliography, documentation, and
terminology (May 1972) and in Bibliographical services throughout the world, 1965-
1969, both published by UNESCO.

MUSIC BH

BH1 Cordier, Henri. Bibliotheca indosinica.
See AA23 for complete description. For
publications on music, see vol. 3: 2279-
2280, "Musique," and vol. 4: 2406-2410,
"Chants populaires."
MH

BH2 Boudet, Paul, and Rémy Bourgeois. Bibliographie de l'Indochine française.
See AA22 for complete description. For
publications on music, see "Musique" in
vols. 1, 2, and 4, and "Littérature anna-
mite--chansons" in vol. 4.
MH

BH3 Lê Hoàng Long. Nhạc-sĩ danh-tiếng hiện-đại
[Well-known contemporary musicians]. Sai-

gon: Tự-do, 1959- . Vol. 1, 1959,
197 p.[1]
Biographies and lists of compositions
by Dương Thiệu Tước, Nguyễn Hữu Ba, Lê
Thương, Vũ Đức Thu, and Phạm Duy.
[1]MH-V; NIC

BH4 * Minh Tâm. Danh-từ âm-nhạc dẫn-giải [Expla-
nation of musical terms]. Saigon: Nhựt-
Hanh và Minh-Tâm, 1953. (Source: UNESCO:)

BH5 *Tống Ngọc Hạp. Danh-từ âm-nhạc, Pháp-Việt và
Việt-Pháp, có phụ thêm chuyên ngữ Ý, Đức,
Anh, v. v.; vocabulaire des terms de music
[in French-Vietnamese, Vietnamese-French,
with added terms in Italian, German, Eng-
lish, etc.]. Paris: Minh-Tân, 1954.
Vol. 1, Danh từ Pháp-Việt. (Source:
NIC.)

BH6 Trần Văn Khê. La musique viêtnamienne tra-
ditionnelle. Paris: Presses Universitaires de France, 1962. 348 p. (Annales
du Musée Guimet, Bibliothèque d'études,
66)
Study of the historical background of
Vietnamese music, its instruments, and its
music theory. Discussion of Vietnamese
music in the North, Center, and South--
the latter of which has not been studied
as much as have the North and Center, according to the author. Bibliography of
156 items and discography of 118 items.
Rev. by Lê Văn Hảo, BEFEO 52 (1965),
578-589.
MH

C Social Sciences

SOCIAL SCIENCES — GENERAL WORKS CA

This chapter contains reference works in more than one of the social sciences as well as in history and area studies. Although some bibliographies and indexes of periodical articles are listed here, others are in chapters AF Periodicals and DB History.

BIBLIOGRAPHIES

CA1 London bibliography of the social sciences....
London: London School of Economics, etc.,
1931- . (London School of Economics and
Political Science studies: Bibliographies,
no. 8)

Subject arrangement with author indexes of the holdings of nine London libraries. Vols. 1-3, subjects; vol. 4, author index, periodicals list, and table of subject headings, listing accessions to May 31, 1929. See entries under "Annam," "Cochin-China," "Indo-China," and "France-Colonies" as well as under subjects such as "Labour." Later volumes also have references under "Tonkin," until volume 10, when "Vietnam" appears as a heading. At end of volumes 4, 5, and 6, the section "Geography, history, and topography" includes lists of subjects and places indexed in vols. 1-3. After 1950, includes Russian-language titles. Beginning with the second supplement (1931-1936), includes, for the most part, accessions to the British Library of Political

and Economic Science and to the Edward Fry Library. Latest supplements cover 1974.
MH

CA2 Nguyễn Hùng Cường. Thư-tịch về khoa-học xã-
hội tại Việt-Nam; bibliographie des sciences sociales au Vietnam; a bibliography
of social science materials published in
Vietnam (1947-1967). Saigon: Nha Văn-
khố và Thư-viện Quốc-gia, 1970. 246 p.

Subject listing of 1,247 books, pamphlets, periodical articles, and official publications in the social sciences (corresponding to the 300 classification of the Dewey Decimal Classification). Comprises publications issued in Vietnam from 1947 to 1954 and in RVN from 1954 to 1967. Entries include complete bibliographical information, translation of Vietnamese-language titles into French and English, and indication of location in either the National Library, the General Library at the Pétrus Ký secondary school, or the Library of the Học Viện Quốc-gia Hành-chánh. Indexes articles in nine major Saigon and Hue periodicals. Cites the first issue of periodicals and official gazettes as well as of some official annual publications such as the budget and statistical yearbooks. Indexing seems to be comprehensive for all publications in scope; most numerous subjects are economics (288 entries), law (190), political science (187), public administration (123). Author index shows entries for Vietnam official headings (150), Nghiêm Đằng (32), Lê Đình Chân (31), Vũ Quốc Thúc (27), and Vũ Quốc Thông (24).

Apparently updates and supersedes earlier bibliographies by Bùi Quỳnh and Nguyễn Hùng Cường in LHKT 1959, 1960, 1962 for the 1947 to 1962 period.

MH

CA3   Rand Corporation. Index of selected publications of the Rand Corporation [Santa Monica, Calif?], 1962- . Vol. 1, 1946-1962, var. pag. (767 p.)

Abstracts of unclassified publications issued by the Rand Corporation, a major independent research organization which performs research on problems of foreign and domestic policy for various agencies of the U.S. government. During the Vietnam war, the Rand Corporation published reports on "Viet Cong" morale, interviews with captured prisoners, documents of military units (particularly the 514th Battalion of the NFL), and similar topics which influenced U.S. government policy toward Vietnam. Indexes by subject and author.

The current listing of Rand reports is: Selected Rand abstracts (quarterly, 1963-); the Rand Corporation has also published A bibliography of selected Rand publications, Southeast Asia, 1971, 55 p.

MH

CA4   Scott, James C., Howard Leichter, et al. A bibliography on land, peasants, and politics for Vietnam, Laos, and Cambodia. Madison: [Univ. of Wisconsin] Land Tenure Center, 1972. 26 p.

Listing of 241 books, periodical articles, and government reports in English on social and political aspects of social structure and peasant politics. Most references are also cited in more comprehen-

sive works such as the EARI bibliography (AA25) or the Bibliography of Asian studies (AA21). Bibliographical descriptions do not always include pagination or date of publication.

NNC

CA5   Social sciences citation index; an international interdisciplinary index to the literature of the social sciences. Philadelphia: Institute for Scientific Information, 1973- . Triennial.

Indexes about 2,240 journals, mostly in English, French, or German, published in the United States, United Kingdom, West Germany, Canada, and France and other countries. Volume titled "Citation index" is alphabetical index by name of cited author, with each entry containing references to periodical articles written by other authors who have referred to the original author. Also includes book reviews and citation of publications subsequent to original article. Volume titled "Source index" contains: 1) author index to book reviews, periodical or newspaper articles, or other publications except books, 2) corporate address index, or index by name of corporate organization to names of staff who have published articles during the year, and 3) "Permuterm subject index," or alphabetical list of significant words used in compiling the SSCI and names of authors of articles. In the Triennial index for 1973, this index listed 24 articles under "Vietnam."

Bibliographic descriptions do not include pagination of articles. Photocopies of articles cited are available for purchase from SSCI.

MH

CA6   *Tăng Thị Tị. "Mục-lục phân tích tạp chí khoa học xã-hội Việt-Nam 1958-1960, 1960-1961" [Index to Vietnamese social science peri-

odicals]. NCHC (10/61), 45-95; (3/4,
1962), 89-111; (3/63), 1-47. Also published in book form by Học-Viện Quốc-gia
Hành-chánh, 1961, 1963. (Source: KimSa;
NIC.)

CA7 Trần Thị KimSa. Bibliography on Vietnam,
1954-1964; thư-tịch về Việt-Nam, 1954-
1964. Saigon: National Institute of Administration, 1965. 255 p.

Alphabetical listing by subject of
books, periodical articles, government
publications, and institute publications
in Vietnamese, English, and French published in the RVN or other non-Communist
countries. Scope is mostly publications
in the social sciences, but includes between 10 and 50 references in culture,
literature, religion, and Vietnamese language. Titles in Vietnamese are also
translated into English. Indexes over 10
of the most important periodicals from
RVN. Author index. No annotations.
Omits pagination of books.
MH

CA8 Vietnam National Commission for UNESCO. Thư-
mục chú-giải về văn-hóa Việt-Nam; bibliographie commentée sur la culture viêtnamienne; commented bibliography on Vietnamese culture. Saigon, 1966. 226 p.

Subject arrangement of over 450 books
and articles published between about 1942
and 1964 on anthropology, biology, Vietnamese language and writing, technology,
the arts, and books and articles in French
from 1945-1954. Annotations are trilingual. Includes publications from RVN and
a few from DRVN.
mgc; NIC

DICTIONARIES

CA9 *Phan Văn Thiết. Tự-vựng của công-chức;
lexique du fonctionnaire. Phiên dịch tất

cả những danh-từ thường dùng về chính-trị,
hành-chính, kinh-tế và tư-pháp [Transla-
tion of all terms in politics, administration, economics, and justice]. Saigon:
Impr. Saigonnaise, 1952. 152 p. (Source:
NIC.)

CA10 *Quỳnh Lâm. Tự-điển chuyên-môn Việt-Anh, trên
10,000 danh-từ và từ-ngữ chính-trị hành-
chính, kinh-tế, tài-chánh, ngân-hàng và
pháp-luật. Vietnamese-English dictionary
of technical terms and phrases, covering
politics, administration, economics, finance, banking and law. [Saigon?]: Tác-
giả, 1966. 398 p. (Source: NIC.)

OTHER SOURCES

CA11 Technical Assistance Information Clearing
House. Development assistance programs
of U.S. non-profit organizations in Vietnam. New York, 1973-[1975?]. Continues
South Vietnam: Assistance programs of
U.S. voluntary organizations, Oct. 1965-
1973.

Lists names of organizations which provide assistance in Vietnam, the kinds of
programs, staffing, expenditures, and
similar features. The 13th ed., 1975,
lists for the first time organizations
which provide assistance to the DRVN and
to territories controlled by the Provisional Revolutionary Government.
MH

EDUCATION CB

BIBLIOGRAPHIES

CB1 Cordier, Henri. Bibliotheca indosinica.
See AA23 for complete description. For
publications on education, see vol. 3:
2137-2150, "Sciences et arts--enseigne-

EDUCATION CB

ment," for pre-French education, and
vol. 4: 2605-2608, "Instruction publique,"
for education during French rule.
MH

CB2 Boudet, Paul, and Rémy Bourgeois. Bibliographie de l'Indochine française.

See AA22 for complete description. For
citations about education, see "Enseignement" in each volume, "Education" and "Morale," in vol. 4, and subheading "Enseignement" under "Annam," "Cochinchine," and
"Tonkin" in vol. 4.
MH

CB3 *Vietnam (Republic). Bộ Quốc-Gia Giáo-Dục.
Trung-tâm Học-liệu. Thư mục [Catalog of
books]. Saigon, 1969. 185 p. (Source:
TTAPC.)

CB4 _____. Nha Văn-Khố và Thư-Viện Quốc-Gia.
Mục-lục thư-tịch tuyển-trạch về giáo-dục
tại Việt-Nam [Selected bibliography of
reference works on education in Vietnam].
Saigon: Bộ Quốc-gia Giáo-dục, 1964. 29 p.

Alphabetical listing by personal name
or issuing agency of 111 publications; includes publications from as early as 1872
for all of Vietnam, but only for the RVN
after 1954. Includes books and articles,
including statements by colonial officials, guidebooks to universities, curric-
ula for various levels of schools, and reports from congresses. Alphabetical author or title index.
mgc; NIC

OTHER SOURCES

CB5 Association of Southeast Asian Institutions
of Higher Learning. Handbook, Southeast
Asian Institutions of Higher learning.
Bangkok, 1965- . Annual.

Brief history, list of faculty, curriculum, and activities of universities in

Southeast Asia, including the Universities
of Hue and Saigon in the 1965, 1966, and
1967 issues, and the University of Saigon
and Vạn Hạnh University in Saigon in the
1968 issue.
MH

CB6 Chỉ nam giáo-dục cao đẳng, giới thiệu các
trường đại học, cao đẳng và chuyên nghiệp
Việt-Nam [Guide to higher education, introduction to universities, higher education, and specialty schools in Vietnam].
[Saigon]: Văn phòng Tâm lý và Hướng
nghiệp Đắc lộ, [1973]. 393 p.

For each institution, gives a short
history, the goals, organization and work,
research, and student activities. Pp. 361-
393, student enrollment at each institution by course of study. Pp. 337-351, directory of libraries, including activities
and organization.
MH-V

CB7 Institut Colonial International. L'enseignement aux indigènes; documents officiels
précédés de notices historiques. Brussels,
1910. 2 vols. (Bibliothèque coloniale
internationale, 9. sér.)

Vol. 2, pp. 219-352, texts of legislation in Indochina on indigenous education,
Quốc-học, École Pavie, École de medecine
de Hanoi, and elementary education.
Pp. 353-368, article on L'enseignement des
indigènes...1908-1909, from Journal Officiel de la République Française,
13 mars 1910, pp. 131-159.
MH-L

CB8 Reed, Charles H. Danh-từ giáo dục Anh-Việt &
Việt-Anh; English-Vietnamese & Vietnamese
English. [Saigon: Printed by M/S CORDS
Translations-Publications, 1972.] 345 p.

"An initial effort to get the basic
educational vocabulary of [Vietnamese and
English] into one book for easy reference:"

Compiled from dictionaries, official documents, and textbooks. Emphasis is upon terms in education (administration, curriculum, guidance, library, philosophy of education, psychiatry, psychology, etc.) rather than such subjects as adult education, agricultural education, elementary, secondary, and higher education, etc.
MH-V

CB9 Vietnam (Republic). Bộ Quốc-Gia Giáo-Dục. Annuaire statistique de l'enseignement: 1958/1959, 1959/1960-1970-1971[?] Saigon, 1961- .
MH; NIC

SOCIOLOGY CC

SEE ALSO ANTHROPOLOGY CD

CC1 Cordier, Henri. Bibliotheca indosinica.
See AA23 for complete description. For citations about sociology, see vol. 4: 2389-2414, 2971-2974, "Moeurs et coutumes," and vol. 3: 1769-1790, 4: 2929-2930, "Ethnographie et anthropologie."
MH

CC2 Boudet, Paul, and Rémy Bourgeois. Bibliographie de l'Indochine française.
See AA22 for complete description. For publications about sociology, see the references in this Guide under CD Anthropology and ethnology.
MH

CC3 Nguyễn Hùng Cường; Nguyễn Thị Khuê-Giung; and Nhật-Thịnh. Thư-tịch về Tết Nguyên-Đán tại Việt-Nam; a bibliography on Vietnamese customs and legends related to Tết; bibliographie des coutumes et légendes de la fête du Tết au Vietnam, 1913-1973. Saigon: Khối Văn-Hóa, 1974. 86 p.

Bibliography of 352 books, periodicals, and periodical articles on the lunar New Year festival, arranged by subject, with author and title indexes. Some subject categories are the meaning and customs of Tết, the 12-year cycle, Tết in literature and the arts, and spring flowers. No annotations.
mgc

CC4 [Nguyễn Văn Toàn]. Nếp cũ; con người Việt-Nam, phong tục cổ truyền [Life in Vietnam, traditional customs, by] Toan Ánh. In lần thứ 2. Saigon: Khai-trí [1970]. 420 p.
Chapters on the family, children, education through the centuries, military and self defense, marriage, celebrations, death and burial, royal funerals, mourning, graves. Part of a well-received series by the author.
MH-V; NIC

CC5 Phan Huy Chú. "Lễ-nghi chỉ" [Rites and ceremonies]. Vols. 20-25 in Lịch-triều hiến-chương loại-chỉ [Monographs of the institutions of the dynasties], ca. 1821.
See AD1 for description of main work. These volumes contain descriptions of rites and ceremonies in Vietnam. They have been translated into quốc-ngữ by Nguyễn Thọ Dực (Saigon: Khối Văn-Hóa, 1974, 705 p.[1]
[1]Gélinas, list 033, March 15, 1975

CC6 Vũ Văn Mẫu. Từ-điển Pháp-Việt, pháp--chính--kinh--tài--xã-hội; dictionnaire français-vietnamien des sciences juridiques, politiques, économiques, financières et sociologiques.
See CJ19 for complete description.
MH-V

ANTHROPOLOGY AND ETHNOLOGY CD

BIBLIOGRAPHIES AND DICTIONARIES

CD1   Cordier, Henri. <u>Bibliotheca indosinica</u>.

        <u>See</u> AA23 for complete description. For citations about anthropology and ethnology, see vol. 3: 1769-1790 and 4: 2929-2930, "Ethnographie et anthropologie," and vol. 4: 2389-2414 and 2971-2974 "Moeurs et coutumes."

        MH

CD2   Boudet, Paul, and Rémy Bourgeois. <u>Biblio-graphie de l'Indochine française</u>.

        <u>See</u> AA22 for complete description. For publications about anthropology and ethnology, see vols. 1 and 4, "Anthropolo-gie," "Ethnographie," "Moeurs," and volume 4, "Littérature annamite--chansons," "Littérature annamite--romans, contes et légendes," and subheadings "ethnographie" under "Annam," "Cochinchine," and "Tonkin."

        MH

CD3   Embree, John Fee, and Lillian O. Dotson. <u>Bibliography of the peoples and cultures of mainland Southeast Asia</u>. New Haven: Yale University, Southeast Asia Studies, 1950. 821 p.

        Publications in western European lan-guages, most of which were available in the Sterling Memorial Library at Yale in 1950. Emphasis is upon works in anthro-pology, ethnology, literature, and lan-guage. No index, but alphabetical ar-rangement within broad subject headings facilitates the finding of authors' names. See: "Vietnam and the Vietnamese," pp. 559-737 for most citations about Vietnamese.

        MH

CD4   Harvard University. Peabody Museum of Ar-chaeology and Ethnology. Library. <u>Author</u>

<u>and subject catalogues</u>. Boston: G. K. Hall, 1963. 53 vols. <u>Index to subject headings</u>. <u>Ibid</u>. 116 p.

        Lists books, articles, pamphlets, and serials about anthropology, archaeology, ethnology, linguistics, psychology, reli-gion, sociology, somatology, and tech-nology. The author catalogs (26 vols.) contain main entries and extensive added entries for editors, translators, spon-soring institutions, etc. The subject catalogs (27 vols.) are arranged by geo-graphical or ethnic name. In the subject catalogs, see: "Annam," vol. 2, pp. 135-150 (305 references); "Cochin-china," vol. 6, pp. 321-323 (52 items); "French Indochina," vol. 9, pp. 361-365 (91 items); "Indochina"--including the Indochinese peninsula--vol. 11, pp. 412-433 (432 citations); and "Tonkin," vol. 27, pp. 22-27 (116 items). The term "Vietnam" is not used as a subject head-ing.

_____. _____. _____. <u>First supplement</u>. <u>Author and subject catalogs</u>. Boston: G. K. Hall, 1970. 12 vols. Author cata-logs (6 vols.); subject catalogs (6 vols.).

_____. _____. _____. <u>Second supplement</u>. <u>Author and subject catalogs</u>. <u>Ibid</u>., 1972. 6 vols. Author catalogs (3 vols.); subject catalogs (3 vols.).

_____. _____. _____. <u>Third supplement</u>. <u>Author and subject catalogs</u>. <u>Ibid</u>., 1975. 7 vols. Author catalogs (3 vols.); subject catalogs (4 vols.).

        MH

CD5   Huard, Pierre, and A. Bigot. "Les caracté-ristiques anthropobiologiques des indo-chinois (rapport présenté au Congrès de l'Association de Médecine Tropicale d'Ex-trême-Orient, Hanoi 1938)." <u>Travaux de l'Institut Anatomique de l'École supé-</u>

rieure de Médecine de l'Indochine (Section anthropologique), 4 (1938). 225 p.

Presents the results of 40-odd years of anthropological and medical research in Vietnam by French doctors and other scientists. Information is intended to bring together in summary form the results of that research. Article includes statistical data from experiments and measurements, photographs, X-rays, drawings, and summaries of published articles. Footnotes and bibliography, but not a complete bibliographic record of research.
MH-P

CD6   Huard, Pierre; G. Lanchou; and Trần Anh. "Les enquêtes anthropologiques faites en Indochine et plus particulièrement au Viêtnam." Bulletin et Mémoires de la Société d'Anthropologie, tome 3, sér. 11 (1962), 372-438.

A survey of the literature; states that anthropologically speaking, Vietnam is one of the best studied and known countries in Southeast Asia. Includes genetics, somatology, physical and pathological anthropology, and miscegenation. Bibliography of about 200 books, articles, and dissertations from universities in Indochina and Vietnam.
MH-P

CD7   Nguyễn Văn Tố. "Bibliographie sommaire des travaux indochinois concernant les sciences anthropologiques et ethnologiques." Travaux de l'Institut Anatomique de l'École Supérieure de Médecine de l'Indochine (Section anthropologique), 2 (1937), 185-218.

Author listing of about 720 books and periodical articles published in Indochina or Europe. Scope includes descriptions by European travellers; works by scientists on physical anthropology, linguistics, folklore and spirits, and religion; and government reports.
MH-P

CD8   *Vietnam (Democratic Republic). Viện Ngôn Ngữ Học. Thuật ngữ sử học, dân tộc học, khảo cổ học, Nga-Việt có chú thêm tiếng Pháp [Terminology in history, ethnography, and archaeology. Russian-to-Vietnamese, with French terms added]. Hanoi: Khoa học xã hội, 1970. 133 p.
Châu

OTHER SOURCES

CD9   Bulletin signalétique section 521: Sociologie. Ethnologie. Préhistoire et archéologie. Paris: Centre national de la recherche scientifique, 1969- . Continuation of an earlier Bulletin signalétique (1940-1968) with various subtitles.

CD10   Tugby, Donald J. "Ethnological and allied work on Southeast Asia, 1950-66." Current anthropology, 9 (1968), 185-206.

CD11   Tugby, Elise. "The distribution of ethnological and allied field work in Southeast Asia, 1950-1966." Current anthropology, 9 (1968), 207-214.

(Includes 29 field trips or researchers in Vietnam, 13 of which were in DRVN.)

MAPS
SEE ALSO GEOGRAPHY CK

CD12   Akademiia nauk SSSR. Institut etnografii. Karta narodov indokitaia [map of the peoples of Indochina, ed.] S. I. Bruk. Moscow, 1959. Accompanying explanation has title: Naselenie Indokitaia, poiasnitel'naia zapiska k karte narodov. Ibid., 1959. 23 p.

Map shows location of various ethnic groups throughout mainland Southeast Asia.
MH-P

CD13   Ethnic groups of mainland Southeast Asia [by] Frank M. Lebar, Gerald C. Hickey [and] John K. Musgrave. New Haven: Human Relations Area Files Press, [1964]. 288 p.

Descriptions of ethnic groups with two maps showing geographical distribution. Section "Viet-Muong" by Gerald C. Hickey, pp. 161-171, describes briefly the Vietnamese and Mường in terms of physical characteristics, geographic settlement patterns, history, kin groups, marriage and family, sociopolitical organization, and religion. Bibliography of 45 publications, mostly from French colonial era.

Other ethnic groups living in Vietnam are described elsewhere in the book.
MH

MYTHOLOGYA CE
SEE FOLKLORE AND POPULAR CUSTOMS   CF

FOLKLORE AND POPULAR CUSTOMS   CF
SEE ALSO SOCIOLOGY CC AND ANTHROPOLOGY CD

CF1   Cordier, Henri. Bibliotheca indosinica.

See AA22 for complete description. For citations about folklore and popular customs, see vol. 3: 1769-1790 and 4: 2929-2930, "Ethnographie et anthropologie," and vol. 4: 2389-2414 and 2971-2974, "Moeurs et coutumes."
MH

CF2   Boudet, Paul, and Rémy Bourgeois. Bibliographie de l'Indochine française.

See AA21 for complete description. For citations about folkore and popular customs, see vol. 1 and 2 "Folklore," and vols. 3 and 4, "Anthropologie," "Ethnographie," "Moeurs," "Races," "Folklore," and "Littérature annamite."
MH

CF3   Nguyễn Tấn Long, and Phan Canh. Thi ca bình dân Việt-Nam; tòa lâu đài văn hóa dân tộc. [Folk songs of Việt-Nam; the cultural palace of the people]. Saigon: Sống Mới, [1969-1971]. 4 vols.

Contents: Vol. 1, Nhân sinh quan [philosophy of life]; vol. 2, Xã hội quan [view of society]; vol. 3, Vũ trụ quan [world view]; vol. 4, Sinh hoạt thi ca [songs of existence].

Extensive collection of folksongs, accompanied by text and illustrations (drawings and photographs). Attempt is to be as comprehensive as possible before folk songs are someday lost.
MH-V; NIC

CF4   Nha Trang Công Huyền Tôn Nữ. Vietnamese folklore; an introductory and annotated bibliography. Berkeley: Center for South and Southeast Asia Studies, University of California, 1970. 20, 33 p. (Its Occasional paper, 7)

Lists 198 books and articles in Vietnamese, English, and French published in the 20th century. Comprises folk narratives, folk songs, proverbs, riddles, superstitions and beliefs, customs and festivals, folk music, and games. Includes citations from 20 periodicals, among them Revue indochinoise, Bulletins et travaux of the Institut indochinois pour l'étude de l'homme, France-Asie, and BEFEO. Citations of books do not include pagination. Annotations indicate whether a particular book or article has included "contextual information," that is, information about the circumstances in which the folklore was obtained, occasions it is repeated, and the meaning ascribed to it by the people who use it.

Cites several collections of published folk tales and several anthologies of Vietnamese literature which include folklore, a few of which are listed here:

No. 35, Đỗ Vạng Lý, The stork and the shrimp, New Delhi, 1959.

No. 43 and 44, Hoàng Trọng Miên, Việt-Nam Văn-Học Toàn-Thư. Tập 1: Văn Chương Truyền Khẩu, Thần Thoại. Tập 2: Văn Chương Truyền Khẩu, Cổ Tích [An anthology of Vietnamese literature. Vol. 1, Oral

literature, mythology. Vol. 2, Oral literature, folktales]. Saigon, 1959.

No. 73, Nguyễn Đổng Chi, Kho Tàng
truyện cổ tích Việt Nam [Treasure of Vietnamese folk narratives]. Hanoi, 1958,
vol. 1.

No. 80 and 81, Nguyễn Văn Ngọc, Truyện
Cổ nước Nam. Tập 1, Người ta. Tập 2,
Muông chim. [Vietnamese folk narratives.
Vol. 1, Human tales. Vol. 2, Animal
tales]. Saigon, n. d. various editions.

No. 97, George F. Schultz, Vietnamese
legends, Rutland, Vt., 1965.

No. 102, Ruth Q. Sun, Land of seagull
and fox; folktales of Vietnam, Rutland,
Vt., 1967.

Critically reviewed by Nguyễn Thế Anh
in BSEI, n.s. 46 (1971), pp. 94-95, for
omitting several basic works on folklore
such as Cadière, Croyances et pratiques
religieuses des Vietnamiens; Connaissance
du Việt-Nam; and Phạm Quỳnh, Le paysan
tonkinois à travers le parler tonkinois
(1930).
MH

STATISTICS CG

Publications listed in this section are comprised of official statistics issued by the governments of Vietnam or Indochina or by non-Vietnamese
official sources. They are intended to include statistical periodicals and annuals, collections, census reports, and general statistical publications.
Statistics of a particular subject such as commerce
are listed with that subject.

In addition to the works cited here, one
might also find general statistics in such sources
as the Annuaire statistique de la France and Bulletin mensuel de statistiques coloniales issued by the
French government throughout the colonial era and in
the United Nations statistical yearbook, United Nations demographic yearbook, United Nations monthly
bulletin of statistics, and League of Nations sta-

tistical yearbook. The specialized agencies of the
United Nations (UNESCO, FAO, International Monetary
Fund, etc.) also issue statistics about member nations, which until April 1975 included the Republic
of Vietnam, but not the DRVN nor PRG.

POPULATION STATISTICS

Population statistics were compiled in historical times as a means of surveillance and to determine taxes and liabilities for military duty and
public works. Although the original records from
all of the dynasties have not survived, the statistics have been reconstructed in various histories
and document collections cited elsewhere in this
Guide, particularly in collections of administrative
materials. They are usually presented in terms of
numbers of households or numbers of males of an age
to perform corvée labor rather than in statistics
reflecting the entire population as presented in
modern census figures.

During French colonial rule, population surveys (évaluations) were conducted throughout Indochina in 1906, 1921, 1926, 1931, and 1936, and a
census (recensement) of the European and assimilated
population was conducted in 1937. Except for the
results of the survey of 1906, which is cited below,
the official reports (if ever published) could not
be located by the compiler of this Guide; they are
probably at the Archives centrales de l'Indochine,
in the Dépôt des Archives d'Outre-Mer in Aix-en-
Provence. Selected statistics from these surveys
are in various sources in this chapter, in the yearbooks cited in Chapter DG Yearbooks, and in publications cited in the several bibliographies in chapter AA Bibliography. A critical evaluation of the
accuracy of the 1931 survey is in: Pierre Gourou,
Les paysans du delta tonkinois (Paris, 1936; repr.,
Paris, 1965), pp. 139-198.

The Democratic Republic of Vietnam conducted
censuses in 1960 and in 1974. Unofficial reports of
the statistics are cited below because the official
government reports could not be located.

The Republic of Vietnam never conducted a
census, although it conducted surveys in 1958 and
in 1967, which are cited below. The statistics

STATISTICS CG

published in the Statistical yearbooks are taken
from birth and death registrations in the areas controlled by the RVN.

BIBLIOGRAPHIES

VIETNAM AND FRENCH INDOCHINA

CG1   Ng Shui Meng. Demographic materials on the
        Khmer Republic, Laos and Vietnam. [Singa-
        pore]: Institute of Southeast Asian Stud-
        ies, [1974]. 54 p. (Its Library bulle-
        tin, 8)
            Bibliography of 510 books, periodical
        articles, government publications, re-
        search reports, and unpublished reports.
        Emphasis is upon publications in French
        and English from the French colonial pe-
        riod because of the language limitations
        of the compiler and the nature of mate-
        rials available in the libraries used by
        the compiler; compiler does include bi-
        lingual sources such as Việt-Nam niên-
        giám thống-kê; statistical yearbook of
        Việt-Nam under the English-language ti-
        tles. Arranged alphabetically under six
        subject headings, although where necessary
        a reference is cited in more than one
        category. Includes list of bibliographies
        consulted (33) and list of periodicals
        consulted (100). Not annotated. Index by
        author.
        mgc; NNC

CG2   Population index bibliography, cumulated
        1935-1968 by authors and geographic areas.
        Boston: G. K. Hall, 1971. 8 vols.
            Photographic reproduction of catalog
        entries in the Office of Population Re-
        search, Princeton University, and pub-
        lished since 1935 as Population Index.
        Scope includes demography, population
        movements, manpower, censuses and other
        official statistics, family planning, and
        other aspects of population studies. Cov-
        erage includes books, chapters in books,

articles in composite works, festschrift-
en, government publications, and periodical articles in European languages. Many
entries include summaries of contents.
    Vols. 1-4 are author catalogs, con-
taining personal and corporate author entries. Vols. 5-8 are geographic areas
catalogs, arranged in two sequences. For
1935-54, all topics are in one part: see
"French Indo-China," in vol. 3, pp. 135-
143 (180 citations), "Southeast Asia,"
p. 251-254 (80), and "Vietnam," p. 264 (1).
For 1954-68, includes author entries except for official statistics, which are
listed in author catalogs; see "Vietnam,"
in vol. 4, p. 653 (16 entries). Entries
about Vietnam in the 1954-68 catalogs are
in vol. 5, pp. 566-67 (19 entries). Citations also include references to additional titles, but only to the numbers of
those entries; they are identifiable only
by searching through back issues of Population Index or by writing to the Office
of Population Research, as the Population
index bibliography is not arranged in numerical order.
MH

CG3   Tin tức thư-viện; nouvelles bibliographiques.
        Saigon: Viện Quốc-gia Thống-kê, 1959-
        [1975?]. Monthly.
            Accessions list of the library. In-
        cludes RVN publications as well as govern-
        ment publications and commercial publica-
        tions from Europe, the U.S., Asia, and the
        United Nations. Each issue lists about 5
        publications or less about RVN.
        MH

UNITED STATES

CG4   American statistics index; a comprehensive
        guide and index to the statistical publi-
        cations of the United States government.
        Washington, D.C.: Congressional Informa-

tion Service, 1974- . Monthly, with annual and retrospective cumulations.

A bibliography, with abstracts, of statistical publications in all subjects.
Retrospective compilation covers statistics from the early 1960's to January 1974.
Coverage of statistical publications is
more detailed than the coverage in the
Monthly catalog (AH9); in addition, the
ASI provides abstracts which help the
users determine the scope of a statistical
publication. The retrospective compilation lists 38 publications under "Vietnam," in agriculture, economic and technical assistance under AID, war casualties,
foreign trade of the DRVN, and cost of the
war. The 1974 ASI lists 16 publications
under "Vietnam."

Abstracted publications are available
on microfiche from the publishers.

SOURCES

FRENCH INDOCHINA

CG5   Brenier, Henri. Essai d'atlas statistique de
l'Indochine française. Hanoi: IDEO,
1914. 256 p. 88 graphs, 38 maps. At
head of title: Gouvernement général de
l'Indochine.

An essai, according to the author, for
various reasons. The population figures
are estimates and not from a census; the
land survey is not complete except for
Cochinchina; the budgetary figures of 1914
are used only in some instances; several
changes in administrative organization
were made in the latter part of 1913; and
Brenier did not compile this as an official atlas.

Includes figures and charts for physical characteristics of Indochina, population, administration, finances, agriculture, commerce, and industry.

MH-P

CG6   Bulletin économique de l'Indochine. Saigon
and Hanoi: IDEO, 1898-1952. Monthly.
Issued by Service de la Statistique Générale and various other agencies.

INDEX: Table de 1898 à 1922, par
L. Hautefeuille. Grenoble: J. Baratier,
1924. 260 p. INDEX: Table générale des
matières contenues dans le Bulletin économique de l'Indochine de 1923 à 1937.[1]
Monthly statistical summaries also issued
with the Bulletin: Supplément statistique
mensuel. From 1946 to 1949, 21 numbered
supplements--each with its own title--were
issued in place of the Bulletin under the
title Bulletin de renseignements économiques.

The basic source for colonial statistical and economic information on agriculture, forestry, industry, commerce, mining, prices, and demography. Contents
well-indexed, especially in Cordier and
Boudet.

MH   [1]unverified; cited in advertisement

CG7   France. Agence Générale des colonies. Statistiques de la population dans les colonies françaises pour l'année 1906. Mehun:
Impr. Administrative, 1909. 608 p. Half-
title: Statistiques coloniales pour l'année 1906.

"Indo-Chine," pp. 276-520, is divided
by colony, then by administrative division (provinces, cercles, towns, etc.).
Gives statistics for Frenchmen and other
Europeans, mixed bloods, Vietnamese, Chinese, others, including Cambodians, Indi-
ans, Minh-hương (Chinese-Vietnamese par-
entage). Does not always distinguish
indigenous ethnic groups: in Cochinchina
and Annam, refers to Moïs, Khas, but in
Tongking, gives separate figures for Mán,
Thô,[2] Nùng, etc.

MH

STATISTICS CG

CG8 _____. Ministère des Finances. Bulletin de statistique et de législation comparée. See CJ74 for complete description.
MH

CG9 _____. Ministère de la Marine et des Colonies. Statistiques coloniales. Paris: Impr. Nationale, 1837-1896. Title varies: 1839, Tableaux et relevés de population, de culture, de commerce, de navigation, etc.; 1840-81, Tableaux de population, de culture...; 1860-70 also published in or as supplements to Revue maritime. 1892-1895 published in one volume as Résumé des statistiques coloniales. Continued by the following publications issued by the Agence générale des colonies: 1) Statistiques de l'industrie minière dans les colonies françaises (1900/04-1916/17); 2) Statistiques de la navigation (1903-1916), continued as Renseignements généraux sur le commerce et la navigation des colonies françaises (1918-1924); 3) Statistiques de la population...(1906, 1911),[1] continued as Recensement de la population (1-3, 1921-1927); 4) Statistiques des chemins de fer...(1910); 5) Statistiques des finances (1895/1905-1904/1913); 6) Statistiques du commerce...(1897-1904), continued as Renseignements généraux sur le commerce... (1905-1914). Issued from 1887-1893 by the Ministère du Commerce, de l'Industrie et des Colonies.

Statistics include, in various issues, population, commerce, navigation, agriculture, education, judicial cases, budget, elections, pawnshops, and other subjects. In 1887, began including Annam and Tongking.
MH 1882-1890

[1] See citation CG7 for description of Statistiques de la population dans les colonies françaises pour l'année 1906, which reports the results of the population survey of 1906. A similar report for 1911 could not be located.

CG10 Indochina. Direction des Services Économiques. Résumé statistique relatif aux années 1913 à 1940. Hanoi: IDEO, 1941. 48 p.

"Condensed form of basic figures appearing in the first nine volumes of Annuaire statistique de l'Indochine." Appendix presents a small number of statistiques for the years of the French occupation through 1912.
MH; CtY

CG11 _____. Service de la Statistique Générale. Annuaire statistique de l'Indochine, 1913-1947/48. Hanoi: IDEO, 1927-1950 [?]. 12 vols.

The basic source for statistical information on Indochina.
MH

CG12 _____. _____. Indices économiques indochinois. Hanoi: IDEO, 1932-1948.
Sér. 1 (1932) and sér. 2 (1937), published separately. Sér. 3 (1947) and sér. 4 (1948) appear in suppléments 13 and 19 of the BEI.

Compilation of statistics appearing in BEI and presentation in retrospective format.
MH

CG13 Leurence, F. "Étude statistique sur le développement économique de l'Indochine de 1899 à 1923." BEI, n.s. vol. 28, no. 171 (1925), 127-161. Also publ. separately: Hanoi: IDEO, 1925.

Compilations of statistics showing "the economic progress of Indochina during the past 25 years," with emphasis on prices of rice, expenses for public works, government budgetary figures, commerce, and government revenues.
MH

DEMOCRATIC REPUBLIC OF VIETNAM

CG14 "Column offers major demographic statistics
       of Vietnam." JPRS, 65746; MC, July 1975:
       [10752-14]. Translated from Tổ quốc,
       no. 6 (June, 1975), pp. 42-44.

           Brief statistics on area and population
       of the administrative units in DRVN; popu-
       lation distribution by nationalities and
       sex; and economic parts in value of gross
       agricultural output. Statistics from 1974
       census.
       MH

CG15 "Official government report on the 1960 cen-
       sus in North Vietnam." JPRS, 6570,
       Jan. 13, 1961. 7 p. From Nhân Dân,
       Nov. 2, 1960. MC, 1961: 4488.

           Statistical tables giving the total
       population, distribution by age and sex,
       occupation, province, educational level,
       and race. Original government source not
       cited.
       MH

CG16 Vietnam (Democratic Republic). Bộ Giao Thông
       Vận Tải. Sơ liệu thống kê [Statistical
       data]. Hanoi: Sự thật, 1962?-- .

           Issues for 1955/60 (Hanoi, 1962) and
       for 1961 are cited by Võ Nhân Trí, in
       Croissance économique de la République
       démocratique du Viet-Nam (Hanoi: Éditions
       en langues étrangères, 1967).

           Issue for 1963 (Hanoi, 1964) is
       translated by JPRS, no. 28,726
       (February 12, 1965), MC 1965: 6414,
       120 p. Text, pp. 1-9. Tables, pp. 10-120,
       provide statistics on "Socialist reforms,"
       industry, agriculture, basic construction,
       transportation, commerce, and other sub-
       jects. Includes comparative data for 1960
       and 1962.

       MH (1963)--Readex Microprint

CG17 *____. Cục Thống-kê Trung Ương. 3 [Ba] năm
       khôi phục kinh tế phát triển văn hóa 1955-
       1957 [Three years of economic recovery
       and cultural growth, 1955-1957]. Hanoi,
       1959.

           Cited by Võ Nhân Trí as a collection of
       statistics.

CG18 *____. Cục Thống-kê Trung Ương. 5 [Năm]
       năm xây dựng kinh-tế và văn-hóa [Five
       years of building the economy and cul-
       ture]. Hanoi, 1960. 248 p.[1]

           Cited by Võ Nhân Trí as a collection of
       statistics.
       [1]Châu

STATE OF VIETNAM AND REPUBLIC OF VIETNAM

CG19 *Bắc-Việt thống-kê nguyệt-san; bulletin sta-
       tistique mensuel du Nord Viêt-Nam. Hanoi:
       Phu Thu-hiến Bắc-Việt, 1953-[1954?]
       (Source: Cường, Soc Sci.)

CG20 Vietnam (Republic). Viện Quốc-Gia Thống-Kê.
       Dân số Việt-Nam theo đơn-vị hành-chánh
       trong năm 1964 [The population of Vietnam
       according to administrative units in
       1964]. Saigon, 1965. 227 p.
       ____. ____. ____ 1965. Saigon, 1967.
       222 p.

           Population of cities, towns, districts,
       villages, and hamlets; number of adminis-
       trative units in each higher unit (number
       of ấp in each xã, for example); and male
       and female population. Where the figure
       is unavailable, usually due to lack of
       military security, only a dot (·) is given.
       Tables at end of volumes list the names of
       units for which no figures could be ob-
       tained and the changes in administrative
       boundaries during the year.
       MH-V

STATISTICS CG

CG21   * ____. ____. Điều-tra dân-số, tại Sài-gòn năm 1967 [Demographic inquiry in Saigon, 1967]. Saigon, 1969. 77 p. (Source: NIC.)

CG22   * ____. ____. Enquête démographique à Saigon en 1962. Saigon, 1963. 232 p. (Source: TTAPC.)

CG23   * ____. ____. Enquête démographique au Vietnam en 1958. Saigon, 1960. 122 p. (Source: TTAPC.)

CG24   ____. ____. Thống-kê nguyệt-san; monthly bulletin of statistics; bulletin mensuel de la statistique. Saigon, 1957- . (Latest issue at MH is 7-8-9, 1974)

    Basic statistical information about the RVN population, economy, expenses, etc.
MH

CG25   ____. ____. Tình-hình kinh tế Việt-Nam; situation économique du Việt-Nam. Saigon, 1967-1972. Annual issues for 1966-1971, published as phụ bản [supplement] to Thống-kê nguyệt-san (preceding citation). Also published separately in English: Economic situation in Vietnam.

    Continuation of Sự tiến triển của nền kinh-tế Việt-Nam; évolution de l'économie du Việt-Nam, 1957-1965 (Saigon, 1958-1966, also published separately with title in English: Economic expansion of Vietnam.)

    Statistical data with commentary on the RVN economy.
MH

CG26   ____. ____. Việt-Nam niên-giám thống-kê; annuaire statistique du Việtnam; statistical yearbook of Vietnam, 1949/50-1971. Saigon, 1951-1972[?]. Issues for 1949/50-1951/52 (1951-1953) published by Bộ Kinh-tế Quốc-Gia, Quốc-Gia Việt-Nam.

    Basic source for official statistical information.
MH; NIC

CG27   ____. Viện Thống-Kê và Khảo-Cứu Kinh-Tế. Việt-Nam kinh-tế tập-san; bulletin économique du Việt-Nam. Saigon, 1950-1956. From January, 1950-October 1955, issued by Quốc-Gia Việt-Nam [State of Vietnam].

    Includes Việt-Nam thống-kê nguyệt-san; bulletin statistique mensuel du Việt-Nam. Issued as a phụ-bản [supplement]: Tình-hình tiến-triển kinh-tế Việt-Nam; l'évolution économique du Việt-Nam, 1951-1952 (1952-1953), continued with Sự tiến-triển kinh-tế Việt-Nam; l'évolution économique du Việt-Nam, 1953-1955 (1954-1956).

    Similar to the format of Bulletin économique de l'Indochine, but much more abbreviated: Articles and statistics on the economic situation.
MH

OTHER SOURCES

CG28   U. N. Economic Commission for Asia and the Far East. Committee for the Coordination of Investigations of the Lower Mekong Basin. Annual statistical bulletin. Bangkok, 1967- . (WRD/MKG/INF/L.256, etc.) Title varies: 1967, Statistical bulletin.

    Compilation of statistical information from the four countries of the Lower Mekong Basin. Emphasis is upon agriculture and power, although other tables include population, manpower, economic resources, irrigation, commerce, health, and education. Years covered by statistics usually include 1960 and later. Sources are official statistical publications or other agencies, such as Viet-Nam Power Co.
MH

CG29   U.S. Agency for International Development. Annual statistical bulletin. Saigon, 1958- . Also Monthly statistical bulletin, as supplement to above. Issuing agency varies: 1958-1962, U.S. Operations Mission to Vietnam.

Statistics from RVN sources prepared in English for the U.S. mission.
MH

CG30 Vietnam economic data. Washington, D.C.: Office of Economic Policy, Bureau for Supporting Assistance, Vietnam Programs, Agency for International Development, 1969-Oct./Dec. 1974. Title varies: Sept. 1969-Dec. 1971, Summary of monthly economic data for Vietnam.

Statistics on prices, money and credit, national accounts, employment, and international exchange.
MH

ADDITIONAL SOURCES

The following publications of the United Nations Economic and Social Commission for Asia and the Pacific (ESCAP)--until mid-1973 the United Nations Economic Commission for Asia and the Far East (ECAFE)--are suggested as additional sources for official statistics of Vietnam. Although neither the RVN nor the DRVN were members of ESCAP, the RVN sent its statistical data to the Commission; foreign trade statistics between the DRVN and its trading partners in ESCAP (excluding China, which did not report its statistics as of this writing) were reported by the trading partners. The Socialist Republic of Vietnam joined the International Monetary Fund in September, 1976; as a condition of its membership, it must report its economic data to the IMF. It is expected that this data will be incorporated into the present IMF publications, International financial statistics and Balance of payments yearbook.

* * *

For each of the publications, only the most recent title is given, reflecting the present name of the publication; on the other hand, the beginning date of publication is that of the earliest title in the series.

CG31 U. N. Economic and Social Commission for Asia and the Pacific. Economic bulletin for Asia and the Pacific. Bangkok, 1950- . Annual.

CG32 _____ . _____ . Foreign trade statistics of Asia and the Pacific, 1962- . New York: United Nations, 1965- . Irregular.

CG33 _____ . _____ . Quarterly bulletin of statistics for Asia and the Pacific. Bangkok, Sept. 1971- .

CG34 _____ . _____ . Statistical yearbook for Asia and the Pacific, 1968- . Bangkok, 1969- . (Appendix in issues of 1970 and later includes statistics of DRVN)

ECONOMICS CH

The economic life in Vietnam covers a variety of subjects listed in this chapter as well as elsewhere in this Guide. Some of these subjects are agriculture in its economic aspects, communications and transportation, cooperatives, credit, industry, labor, land reform, landholdings, prices, state planning, and taxes. In addition to the relatively few reference works on these and other subjects cited in this chapter, the bibliographies in other chapters--especially AA Bibliography, AF Periodicals, CA Social Sciences, CG Statistics, CI Political Science and Government and EK Agriculture--include many references to publications in economics. The four bibliographies on the DRVN--Keyes (CI55), Kyriak (CI56), Phan Thiện Châu (CI48), and Transdex (AA90)--are particularly valuable for references in economics. Some statistical sources in economics are cited in this chapter, but a wider variety of sources are in chapters CG Statistics and DG General Yearbooks. As with other reference works on the DRVN, the foreign trade statistics of

ECONOMICS CH

France and the U.S.S.R. are cited in lieu of actual
publications from the DRVN, which could not be located for this Guide.

BIBLIOGRAPHIES

CH1   Cordier, Henri. Bibliotheca indosinica.

    See AA23 for complete description. For
citations about economics, see vol. 4:
2453-2478, 2975-2976, "Commerce," and
various sections under "Administration
française," e.g. vol. 4: 2575-2590, "Finances," 2613-2622, 2981-2982,"Chemins de
fer," and vol. 3: 2267-2276 and 4:
2967-2968, "Industries diverses."
MH

CH2   Boudet, Paul, and Rémy Bourgeois. Bibliographie de l'Indochine française.

    See AA22 for complete description. For
citations about economics, see "Economique," "Commerce," and "Travail," as well
as subheadings "Economique," "Banques,
institutions de crédit," "Commerce," "Communications," "Transports," and "Ports"
under "Annam," "Cochinchine," and "Tonkin," in vol. 4. In vols. 1-3, see "Economique," "Commerce," and "Travail."
MH

CH3   Kiel. Universität. Institut für Weltwirt-
schaft. Bibliothek. Kataloge; Catalogue
of the Library of the Institute for World
Economics. Boston: G. K. Hall, 1966-
1968. 207 vols.

    Catalog of the collection on all areas
of economic activity and related areas of
the social, technical, and physical sciences and the humanities. Includes a
large number of citations for periodical
articles and for government and private
sources. Includes publications in all
European languages and in Vietnamese.
Comprised of seven catalogs; each catalog

except the "Standortskartei der Periodika"
is arranged alphabetically.

    Most references to Vietnam are in the
"Regionenkatalog" (1967, 52 vols.) which
lists publications under the name of the
country, with subdivisions by subject.
About 900 publications are listed on Vietnam (Bd. 52, pp. 451-493) and about 580 on
Indochina (Bd. 22, pp. 766-794) although
some publications are listed more than
once, under different subject headings.

    The "Behördenkatalog" (1967, 10 vols.)
contains publications of governments, arranged alphabetically by country. See:
Bd. 4, pp. 570-576 for "Indochina" and
Bd. 10, pp. 507-510 for "Vietnam." Includes publications from DRVN and RVN.

    The "Standortskartei der Periodika"
(1968, 6 vols.) lists periodicals in the
order they are arranged on the shelves.
To locate information about a specific
periodical--the beginning date, changes
in title, issuing agency or editor, or
the issues in the Bibliothek--one must
first look in one of the other sets of
catalogs to obtain the shelf number of the
periodical (indicated by an arrow) and
then refer to the "Standortskartei."

    Other catalogs are the "Personenkata-
log" (1966, 30 vols.), which lists works
by or about persons; "Körperschaftenkata-
log" (1967, 13 vols.), publications by or
about corporate bodies and conferences;
"Sachkatalog" (1968, 83 vols.), subject
catalog, with subdivisions by region; and
"Titelkatalog" (1968, 13 vols.), which
lists serial and collective publications
by title.

    The Kataloge are quite comprehensive
for works on Vietnam and Indochina (particularly the latter); some works were
noted here which were not listed in any
other source cited in this bibliography.
MH

CH4   U. N. Economic Commission for Asia and the
       Far East. Committee for Coordination of
       Investigations of the Lower Mekong Basin.
       Mekong Project documentation. [Bangkok?],
       1972. 81 p. (WRD/MKG/INF/L.54 Rev.23)
       Limited [distribution].

CH5   _____. _____. _____. _____, 1957-1972 pro-
       visional list (including documents issued
       in 1973 for 1972). [Ibid?], 1973. 85 p.
       (WRD/MKG/INF/L.57/Rev.1) Limited.

           Bibliography of reports on the Lower
       Mekong Project, including committee meet-
       ings, annual and semi-annual reports, ex-
       ecutive agent reports, program reports by
       other U. N. agencies and by countries from
       outside the Mekong project area, and
       others. Most reports not available for
       general distribution and are not cited in
       United Nations documents index (CJ135 and
       CJ136).

           The 1973 edition is essentially an up-
       dated version of the 1972 edition.
       MH

DICTIONARIES

CH6   *Đào Văn Hội. Danh-từ kinh-tế và tài-chánh
       [Economic and financial terminology].
       Saigon: Võ-văn-Vân, 1954. 118 p.
       (Source: Cường, Soc Sci.)

CH7   *Lê Đình Châu. "Danh-từ kỹ-thuật" [technical
       terms]. NCHC, nos. 7/8 (7/8, 1959), 198-
       201; 9 (9/59), 162-166; 12 (12/59), 59-60;
       1 (1/60), 76-77; 6 (6/60), 57-61; 7 (7/60),
       71-73; 4 (4/61), 130-133.
           KimSa describes as "kinh-tế từ-điển"
       [dictionary of economic terms]. (Source:
       NIC.)

CH8   Nguyễn Cao Hách. "Từ-điển kinh-tế" [Diction-
       ary of economics]. LHKT, [vol. 3] (1958),
       337-342, 527-550, 781-830; [vol. 4]
       (1959), 267-308.

Definitions of English terminology in
economics in a broad sense. Definitions
and commentaries are more extensive than
in the following compilation by Hách,
some definitions being 10 pages. Arrangement varies, sometimes alphabetically by
English-language term and sometimes alphabetically by Vietnamese-language term.
MH-L; NIC

CH9   _____. "Từ điển kinh-tế Anh-Pháp-Việt."
       [English-French-Vietnamese dictionary of
       economics]. Quê-hương, no. 32 (2/62),
       305-320; 34 (4/62) to 38 (8/62) separate-
       ly paged; 40 (10/62) to 46 (4/63), sepa-
       rately paged, to p. 269. Later issues not
       available for inspection. Also published
       in LHKT, vol. 8 (1963) to vol. 9 (1965),
       separately paged, to p. 268.
           Brief definitions in French and Viet-
       namese, of English words and phrases in
       economics, budget, commerce, finance,
       business, insurance, transportation, and
       related subjects.
       MH-L; NIC

CH10   *Quỳnh Lâm. Từ điển Anh-Việt--chính-trị,
       hành-chính, kinh-tế, tài-chính, pháp-
       luật; English-Vietnamese dictionary of
       political, administrative, economic, fi-
       nancial, and legal terms and phrases.
       Saigon: Thanh-Hiền, 1968. 960 p.
       (Source: NIC.)

CH11   Vũ Văn Mẫu. Từ-điển Pháp-Việt, pháp--chính--
       kinh--tài--xã hội; dictionnaire français-
       vietnamien des sciences juridiques, poli-
       tiques, économiques, financières et so-
       ciologiques.
           See CJ19 for complete description.

CH12   Vũ Văn Mẫu; Nguyễn Văn Trác; and Đào Văn Tập.
       Từ-điển Pháp-Việt pháp-luật chính-trị
       kinh-tế; dictionnaire français-viêtnamien

ECONOMICS CH

des sciences juridiques, politiques, éco-

nomiques.

See CJ20 for complete description.

GENERAL WORKS

CH13   *Indochina. Direction des affaires économiques.
        Annuaire économique de l'Indochine. Hanoi,
        1925- .
            Compilation of financial, technical and
        commercial information on agricultural,
        industrial, and commercial undertakings
        (Boudet 1). (Source: Boudet 1, Gregory.)

CH14   *Ngân-hàng Quốc-gia Việt-Nam. Phúc trình
        thường niên về tài-khóa...[Annual financial
        report]. Saigon. 1964 ed., 1965, 119 p.
        (Source: Thư mục 1965; NIC.)

BUDGET AND REVENUE

TRADITIONAL VIETNAM

CH15   Phan Huy Chú. "Quốc-dụng chỉ" [Economic re-
        sources]. Vol. 6, chapters 29-32 In Lịch-
        triều hiến-chương loại-chỉ [Monographs of
        the institutions of the dynasties], ca.
        1821.
            See AD1 for description of main work.
            Compilation of laws and practices on
        economic resources of governments of Viet-
        nam in the Lý, Trần, and Lê dynasties.
        Two major translations exist, in addition
        to the complete translation of the main
        work in Hanoi in 1960-61 (See AD1):
        1) R. Deloustal, "Les ressources écono-
        miques et financières de l'état dans
        l'ancien Annam," Revue indochinoise 1924,
        1925; BAVH 1932[1] and 2) Vietnam (Repub-
        lic). Laws, statutes, etc. Compilations.
        Lịch-triều hiến-chương loại-chỉ. Lưỡng
        Thần Cao Nãi Quang phiên âm và dịch nghĩa.
        Saigon: Nhà in Bảo Vinh, 1957, 568, 46 p.[2]
        At head of title: Đại-học-viện Saigon.
        Trường Luật-khoa Đại-học.

Deloustal's translation includes extensive footnotes and references to Đại
Việt sử-ký toàn thư and Khâm-định Việt-sử
thông-giám cương-mục. The translation by
the University of Saigon comprises the
Chinese-language text, transcription into
romanized Vietnamese, and translation
into quốc-ngữ, pp. 365-516.
[1]MH; [2]MH-L

FRENCH INDOCHINA

CH16   Indochina. Budget général. Hanoi: IDEO,
        etc., 1899- . At head of title: Minis-
        tère des colonies.
            The annual budget statement, comprised
        of Budget général, Budget annexe de Kouang-
        tchéou-wan, Budget annexe spécial des
        grands travaux, Budget annexe de l'ex-
        ploitation des chemins de fer, Compte ad-
        ministratif du budget général, Compte ad-
        ministratif du budget de Kouang-tchéou-
        wan, Compte administratif du budget spé-
        cial des grands travaux, and Compte ad-
        ministratif du budget des chemins de fer
        (cf. JOIF 1934); earlier annexes to the
        budget varied in title and scope, e.g.
        Budget spécial des grands travaux et dé-
        penses sanitaires sur fonds d'emprunt
        (cf. Cordier). Budgets locaux were pub-
        lished for each colony, while budgets mu-
        nicipaux were published for cities.
            The text of the budgets were printed
        only in this form, although supplementary
        estimates (remaniements) and the arrêté
        enacting the budget were published in the
        JOIF. The monthly report on receipts and
        expenditures was published in the JOIF,
        although, unlike the remaniements and ar-
        rêté, it was not always indexed, since it
        was published in the "partie non-offi-
        cielle."
        Cordier 4:2575-2581; Boudet 2-4; MH-L

REPUBLIC OF VIETNAM

CH17   Vietnam (Republic). Nha Tổng Giám-Đốc Ngân-Sách và Ngoại-viện. <u>Ngân-sách quốc-gia tài-khóa...</u> [National budget for the fiscal year...]. Budgets for 1962 (Saigon, 1962, 387 p.) and for 1964 (<u>Ibid</u>., 1964, 337 p.) cited in <u>TTAPC</u>.

Less detailed budgetary figures cited in <u>CBVNCH</u> and <u>QPVT</u>, beginning with the calendar/fiscal year 1968. Prior to 1968, only gross figures for revenue and expenditure were listed, unless the budget was revised (cf. <u>CBVNCH</u> no. 27 (24/6/67), p. 3072-3075, revising the 1966 budget to show an increase of income from national resources (<u>tài nguyên quốc gia</u>) and aid from the United States (<u>viện trợ Mỹ</u>)). The budget law is usually passed as <u>Luật</u> or <u>Sắc luật</u> 001 each year.
MH-L (<u>CBVNCH</u>); NIC

See also <u>Public administration bulletin Vietnam</u> no. 33 (Nov. 1, 1966), 6-36 for discussion of the budgetary process of RVN and the changes from the 1956 constitution to the changes in 1966 providing for more detailed estimates, periodic reporting of expenditures to the <u>Quốc Hội</u>, and annual recapitulation of obligations.

A summary of the budgetary process before November 1963 is also in Nghiêm Đằng, <u>Viet-Nam: Politics and public administration</u> (Honolulu: East West Center Press, 1966), ch. 6.

CH18   *____. Tổng Nha Thuế-Vụ. <u>Tax statistics 1960-1963</u>. Saigon, 1964. 297 p. (Source: Johnson; NIC.)

BUSINESS

CH19   *<u>Annuaire des entreprises d'outre-mer</u>. Paris.
In period after World War II, was published under the Comité central de la France d'Outre-Mer. Previous title: <u>Annuaire des entreprises coloniales</u>.

Each volume contains a substantial section on Indochina and covers its commerce, industry, banks, agriculture, and other areas. (Source: DLC.)

CH20   *<u>Công-thương Việt-Nam; industrial and commercial directory; annuaire industriel et commercial</u>. Saigon: Trịnh Hưng, 1960 [?]- . (Source: NIC, Kim Sa (1960, 1962/63).)

CH21   Indochina. Direction des Services Économiques. <u>Répertoire des sociétés anonymes indochinoises</u>. Hanoi: IDEO, 1944. 235 p.
Lists of incorporated firms, published to fill the gap caused by the rupture of relations between France and Indochina because of World War II and the cessation of French metropolitan publications of this sort. Information for each company comprises date of founding, purpose, capitalization, number of shares, directors, and dividends and production from 1938 to 1941 or 1942. Alphabetical index to administrators and to companies.
CtY

CH22   *<u>Indochine adresses; annuaire complet de l'Indochine: officiel, commerce, industrie, plantations, mines, adresses particulières</u>. Saigon: Portail. 1938-39, ed. by L. Barrière and J. Dickson. (Saigon, 1938) 1215 p. (Source: DLC.)

CH23   *Saigon. Export Development Center. <u>Trade directory, 1965</u>. Saigon, 1965. 43 p.
____. Export Promotion Center. <u>Trade directory, 1968</u>. Saigon, 1968. 251 p. (Source: <u>TTAPC</u>.)

CH24   *Vietnam (Republic). Viện Quốc-Gia Thống-Kê. <u>Recensement des établissements au Viêtnam (1960)</u>. Saigon, 1962-63. Fasc. 1, méthodologie, 1962. 132 p. Fasc. 2, 1963. 289 p. (Source: <u>TTAPC</u>.)

FOREIGN COMMERCE

CH25 *Ajia Keizai Kenkyūjo, Tokyo. Asian trade statistics; statistics on foreign trade between the Asian countries and industrial nations classified by commodities, 1956-58. Tokyo: Institute of Asian Economic Affairs, 1961. 503 p. (Source: Johnson--CtY.)

CH26 _____. Asian trade statistics: export 1960. [Tokyo] 1964. 276 p.

Lists exports by country--including RVN--of about 30 commodities. Includes countries to which products are shipped. MH-HY

CH27 *Chambre de Commerce de Saigon. Situation commerciale. Statistique. Importations et exportations. Mouvement général maritime et commercial dans les différents ports de la Cochinchine pendant l'année. Saigon, 1881-1936 [?].

Boudet 4 cites: Statistiques commerciales de la Cochinchine pour l'année 1933. Mouvement monétaire. Changes. Ports. Commerce extérieur...Principales exportations. Navigations maritimes. Saigon, 1934. 327 p. (Source: Kiel: Y 2783; Boudet; Cordier 3: 1709.)

CH28 *Chambre de commerce du port de Hai-phong. Statistiques commerciales. Hai-phong, 1906-1937[?]. (Source: Kiel: X 2263; Boudet 4.)

CH29 France. Direction Générale des Douanes et Droits Indirects. Statistiques du commerce extérieur de la France. Paris, 1820- . Annual. Title varies: 1820-1928, Tableau général du commerce et de la navigation; 1928-1959, Tableau général du commerce extérieur; 1959-1967, Statistiques du commerce extérieur de la France.

Statistics on foreign trade of France and trade between France and her colonies. Since 1896, format contains, in vol. 1 of each year, one section arranged by country or colony showing each commodity imported into or exported from France and another section arranged by commodity showing the countries or colonies in which each commodity originated.

Until 1959, statistics for post-1954 Vietnam were listed only for RVN; beginning in the May 1959 issue of Statistique mensuelle du commerce extérieur, statistics for DRVN are included. Beginning in 1969, each country receives a numerical designation--688 for "Viet-Nam Nord" and 692 for "Viet-Nam Sud."

Statistics for pre-colonial years are included in various headings, e.g. for 1840, "Cochinchine" (p. 47); for 1852, "Chine, Cochinchine et Océanie" (p. 44) not differentiated. MH

CH30 _____. Office colonial. Statistiques décennales du commerce des colonies françaises, 1896-1905, publiées sous l'administration de Georges Trouillot. Documents réunis par M. P. Chemin Dupontès. Paris: Bureau de vente des publications coloniales officielles, 1910. 3 v.

Vol. 1, Statistiques générales et statistiques par colonies. Vol. 2, Importations. Vol. 3, Exportations.

Indochina, vol. 1, pp. 210-229, and vols. 2 and 3, provide statistics by product, according to each colony. Statistics are for Indochina as a whole, not divied by port. MH

CH31 Indochina (Federation). Administration des Douanes et Régies. Tableau du commerce extérieur des États Associés de l'Indochine; statistique annuelle du commerce extérieur des États associés de l'Indochine. Saigon: Lê-văn-Tân, [1950-53?]. Supersedes: Indochina, Direction des Douanes et Régies, Tableau du commerce extérieur de l'Indochine, Hanoi and Saigon, 1933-[1950?], itself a continuation of Rapport sur la navigation et le mouvement commercial de l'Indochine, issued by the Direction, 1904-1932[?] (see below).

Foreign trade statistics, also published in BEI; ca. 400 pp./year.

Statistiques mensuelles du commerce extérieur de l'Indochine issued in JOIF as annexes; ca. 1935.

MH-L (JOIF); Kiel Y 112; Boudet 4; DLC

CH32 "Rapport sur la navigation et le mouvement commercial de l'Indochine."

Appeared each year in BEI. Authors varied; were usually the director of Douanes et Régies de l'Indochine. Publication began about 1904, titled, "Le mouvement de la navigation et le mouvement commercial de l'Indochine en 1903," by M. Crayssac, BEI, 1904, 695-741. See Cordier 4:2454-59 "Commerce," for citations of other articles on commerce.

Statistics on the number of ships arriving at and leaving the ports of Indochina, types of ships, destinations, tonnage, quantities, and value of imports and exports; annual retrospective figures back to 1903; commodities imported or exported; imports and exports by country of origin or by destination; internal trade among Tongking, Annam, Cochinchina, and Cambodia; and goods transshipped to Yunnan.

MH

CH33 *Saigon. Phòng Thương-mại [Chamber of Commerce]. Danh sách hội viên các phân bộ chuyên nghiệp nhập cang và thực dụng [List of members, specializing in imports and commodities]. Saigon, 1967. 250 p.

(Source: TTQGVN.)

CH34 U.S.S.R. Planovo-Ekonomicheskoe Upravlenie. Vneshniaia torgovlia Soiuza SSR za 1955-1959 gody. Moscow: Vneshtorgizdat, 1961. 623 p.

Compilation of U.S.S.R. foreign trade statistics (export and import) arranged by country, then by commodity, corresponding to the Standard International Trade Classification. DRVN, pp. 428-439.

_____. _____. _____ 1959-1963 gody. Ibid., 1965. 483 p. DRVN, p. 342-351.

MH

CH35 _____. _____. Vneshniaia torgovlia Soiuza SSR, statisticheskii obzor. Moscow, 1958- .

Annual compilation of foreign trade statistics between the USSR and other countries. Arranged by country, then by commodity. Comprises tonnage and value of shipments.

Some years also translated by JPRS: statistics for 1957 (including 1956 and 1957 statistics) in JPRS, 526-D, Feb. 17, 1959 (MC, 1959: 4973), for 1958 (including 1957 and 1958 statistics) in JPRS, 1087-D, Dec. 30, 1959 (MC, 1960: 1914). Later years not verified.

MH

CH36 U. N. Statistical Office. World trade annual; trade of the industrialized nations with Eastern Europe and the developing nations, 1963- . N.Y.: Walker, 1964- .

Annual detailed statistics on foreign trade intended to update and cumulate quarterly statistics issued in Statistical papers series by the Statistical Office (ST/TAO/Ser.D). Arranged by commodity.

CH37 _____. Supplement to the World trade annual; trade of the industrialized nations with Eastern Europe and the developing nations, 1964- . N.Y.: Walker, 1965- .

Same as above, but arranged by country. Vol. 5, the Far East, includes statistics

ECONOMICS CH

by value in U.S. dollars and by tonnage
for the DRVN and the RVN. Does not seem
to be complete: omits statistics for
trade between the DRVN and Eastern Europe.
MH

CH38   Vietnam (Republic). Tổng Nha Quan-Thuế. Việt-
Nam Thống-kê ngoại thương [Foreign trade
statistics of Vietnam]. Saigon, [1955?-
1970?]. Also issued monthly: Thống-kê
ngoại-thương nguyệt-san.
MH; Thư-mục 1965

LABOR

CH39   *Lê Huy Lạp. Những danh-từ thông-dụng về lao-
động, Việt-Anh, Anh-Việt; common used labor terminology, Vietnamese-English, English-Vietnamese. [Saigon? n.p.], 1966.
148 p. (Source: NIC.)

CH40   *Vietnam (Republic). Sở Nghiên-Cứu Thống-Kê.
Thống-kê lao-động [Labor statistics year-
book]. Saigon.
1973 edition (27 p., 1974), cited in
TTTV, VQGTK 10-11-12/1974.

DEVELOPMENT PLANS

INDOCHINA

CH41   *France. Commission de modernisation des ter-
ritoires d'outre-mer. Sous-commission de
modernisation de l'Indochine. Premier
rapport de la sous-commission de modernisation de l'Indochine. Paris, 1948.
208 p. At head of title: Commissariat
général du plan, de modernisation et
d'équipement.
   Synthesis of reports on reconstruction
and modernization of Indochina in the
post-World War II years, as presented by
working committees. Considered as an inventory of resources in Indochina as of
that time and a "hardheaded document tak-

ing into account nearly every local as-
set--mineral, agricultural, and human."[1]
MH-L   [1]Bernard B. Fall, The two Viet-Nams,
2d rev. ed. (New York: Praeger, 1967,
pp. 170-171.)

DEMOCRATIC REPUBLIC OF VIETNAM

   From 1955 to 1967, the DRVN enacted state
plans for the years 1955-1957, 1958-1960, 1961-1965,
and 1966-1967 as well as individual years during
this period. After 1967, they enacted plans on a
yearly basis through 1975, at which time they an-
nounced the 5-year plan for 1976-1980. Although
details of the plans were seldom published, summaries
of the plans are available in articles and speeches
of party officials in Nhân Dân, Học Tập, and Vietnam
courier and other sources. The bibliographies by
Jane Godfrey Keyes and Phan Thiện Châu cited elsewhere and the index to translations from Vietnamese
sources--Transdex--contain references to the plans.
   The citations listed below are only for the
major plans in the 1955 to 1967 period. At the time
this manuscript was completed, the compiler had not
located any substantive articles about the 1976-1980
plan.

CH42   1955-1957: Economic restoration and cultural
development in the Democratic Republic of
Vietnam (1955-57). Hanoi: FLPH, 1958.
47 p.

CH43   1958-1960: Vietnam (Democratic Republic).
Quốc Hội. The three-year plan to develop
and transform economy and to develop culture (1958-1960). Hanoi: FLPH, 1959.
136 p.

CH44   1961-1965: Summary in: Nguyễn Duy Trịnh,
"North Vietnam's first five-year plan
(1961-1965), Report to the sixth session
of the Second National Assembly," JPRS,
19,952, 1963, 101 p.; MC, 1963: 14354.
(From Nhân Dân, May 3 and 4, 1963).

CH45   1966-1967: Summary in: Nguyen Con, "Eco-
       nomic construction and development for
       1966-67 and the state plan for 1966,"
       JPRS, 35,757, Translations on North Viet-
       nam's economy, no. 239, 1966, pp. 1-35;
       MC, 1966: 10700-52. (From Nhân Dân,
       April 29, 1966.)
       MH

REPUBLIC OF VIETNAM

     The RVN announced economic development plans
for 1957-1961, 1962-1966, 1966, and 1972-1975 in addition to a rural economic development plan for
1971-1975. Because of the war, the plans received
correspondingly less emphasis than did the plans of
the DRVN; nevertheless, they are cited here for the
historical record.

CH46   1957-1961: Projet de plan quinquennal (1957-
       61). Saigon: Direction Générale du Plan,
       1957. 330 p.[1]

CH47   *1962-1966: Đệ nhị kế-hoạch ngũ niên, 1962-
       66. Saigon: Nha Tổng Giám-đốc Kế-hoạch,
       1962. 254 p.[2] French-language edition
       titled Deuxième plan quinquennal 1962-
       1966. Saigon, 1962. 229 p.[3]

CH48   *1966: Kế-hoạch phát-triển quốc-gia năm 1966.
       Saigon: Nha Tổng Giám-đốc Kế-hoạch, 1966.
       171 p.[4] Outlined in Appendix 9 of: Ray-
       mond E. Kitchell, Planning and Control, a
       report prepared for the General Committee
       for Administrative Improvement, Office of
       the Prime Minister, Government of Vietnam.
       Saigon, 1966.

CH49   1971-1975: Rural economic development plan
       and Plan of action for the five-year de-
       velopment plan for rural economy. See
       EK10 for complete citation.

CH50   1972-1975: Four year national economic de-
       velopment plan 1972-1975. [Saigon] Nha
       Tổng Giám-đốc Kế-hoạch, 1972. 375 p.[5]
       [1]MH [2]Cường, Soc. Sci. [3]TTAPC; microfiche
       copy available from Inter-Documentation
       Company, Zug, Switzerland [4]Asian bibli-
       ography (Bangkok: United Nations Economic
       and Social Commission for Asia and the
       Pacific, Jan.-June 1972) [5]CtY

POLITICAL SCIENCE AND GOVERNMENT   CI

     This chapter consists of works on the admin-
istration of government, the independence and revolutionary movements, and military events. Concerning the independence and revolutionary movements, it
is difficult to maintain a clear distinction between
works on the DRVN and on the NFLSVN and PRG, so the
reader should check both sections. The major bibliography on the DRVN--Phan Thiện Châu, Vietnamese
communism, a research bibliography (CI48)--is
placed before most of the works on the DRVN primarily because its scope is wider than the DRVN.
The portion of the chapter on the DRVN also includes
the major theoretical works by leaders of the DRVN
and the revolutionary movement in Vietnam.

     Additional bibliographies and reference
sources on political science and government will be
found in chapters CJ Law and DB History.

BIBLIOGRAPHIES

CI1   Cordier, Henri. Bibliotheca indosinica.
      See AA23 for complete description. For
      citations about political science, see 3:
      1843-1848 and 4: 2933-2934, "Gouverne-
      ment," for the pre-French era, and 4:
      2557-2638 and 2979-2982, "Administration
      française," and 3: 2275-2278 and 4:
      2967-2970, "Art militaire et navigation."
      See also 4: 2505-2518, "Gouverneurs,
      etc." which includes a list of governors

and other high administrators and their
dates of service.
MH

CI2   Boudet, Paul, and Rémy Bourgeois. Bibliographie de l'Indochine française.
See AA22 for complete description. For
publications about political science, see
subheading "Administration" under "Annam,"
"Cochinchine," "Indochine," and "Tonkin,"
and subheadings "Bulletins administratifs"
or "Publications administratives" under
"Publications périodiques."
MH

CI3   Bonew, Mme. Premiers éléments bibliographiques relatifs aux problèmes actuels du
Sud-Est de l'Asie. Brussels: Centre
d'Étude du Sud-Est Asiatique, 1966.
515 p.
Book and periodical holdings on Southeast Asia in 5 research libraries in
Brussels. About 200 references on Vietnam: Indochina, pp. 307-313; North Vietnam, pp. 486-498; South Vietnam, pp. 498-
515. Bibliographic information is not
always correct or complete; pagination of
periodical articles is omitted. Scope is
centered upon current events in Southeast
Asia, published in English and French in
Western Europe and the United States.
MH

CI4   Coates, Joseph. Bibliography of Vietnam.
[Washington, D.C.] Institute for Defense
Analysis, Research and Engineering Support
Division, 1964. 52 p. (IDA/HQ 64-2253.
Internal note N-100)
Bibliography of 709 citations to books,
government publications, and periodical
articles primarily in English, compiled in
order to "provide some general orienta-
tion" to the unclassified literature on
Vietnam. A few descriptive annotations.
MH

CI5   Halstead, John P., and Serafino Porcari.
Modern European imperialism, a bibliography of books and articles, 1815-1972.
Boston: G. K. Hall, 1974. 2 v.
Vol. 2: French and other empires.
Pp. 1-31, "French empire--general."
About 720 citations to books, newspaper
and periodical articles, and government
publications on all aspects of French
imperialism. Pp. 201-225, "France in
South and Southeast Asia," and "French
Indochina." About 570 citations, mostly
under "general," "documents and papers,"
and "economic and financial," with fewer
references under "atlases," "bibliographies," and "fiction and literary comment." Languages are English and French.
No annotations or indexes.
MH

CI6   Harvard University. Law School. Library.
Current legal bibliography and Annual legal bibliography.
See CJ7 and CJ8 for complete
description.

CI7   Heaney, Judith W. Vietnam: a bibliography.
[Washington, D.C.] Bureau for Vietnam,
Agency for International Development,
1968. 25 p. MC, 1969: 4426.
Subject listing of over 300 books and
articles, mostly in English, published
within the last 20 years. Some short annotations. A few typographical errors in
names of authors and inconsistent choice
of entry, sometimes family name, other
times personal name.
MH

CI8   Hoover Institution on War, Revolution, and
Peace. The library catalogs of the Hoover
Institution on War, Revolution, and Peace;
catalog of the western-language collections. Boston: G. K. Hall, 1969.
63 vols.

C Social Sciences

A dictionary catalog of printed materials and archival files in 36 languages on political, social, and economic change in the 20th century. Although entries are found in the respective volumes under "Annam," "Cochinchina," and "Tongking," most references are in vol. 24, pp. 183-197 "Indochina;" vol. 52, pp. 757-796 "Vietnam;" vol. 59 (government documents) "Indochina;" and vol. 60 (government documents) "Vietnam." Includes several publications from the 1946-1952 period, cross-references for French-language serials published in Vietnam from "Vietnam" to "French serials drawer," and cross-references from subject headings not used, such as "Indo-China, French--Budget" to "Budget--Indo-China, French."
MH

CI9   Jumper, Roy. <u>Bibliography on the political and administrative history of Vietnam.</u>
     <u>See</u> DB9 for complete description.

CI10   Michigan State University. Vietnam Project. <u>What to read on Vietnam, a selected annotated bibliography.</u> New York: Institute of Pacific Relations, 1959. 67 p. 2d ed. <u>Ibid.</u>, 1960. 73 p.

     Second edition lists about 300 publications on contemporary Vietnam. Pp. 3-60, annotated bibliography of recent publications on Vietnam, 1955 to Fall 1958, arranged according to articles, books, and special reports--U.S. government publications, MSU, RVN, and "miscellaneous" (DRVN, ICSC, and United Nations publications). Pp. 61-66, supplement, listing publications from late 1958 to October 1959. Pp. 67-73, periodicals list, prepared by Nguyễn Xuân Đào and Richard K. Gardner, including 35 periodicals currently published and 50 which had ceased as of 1959. Đào and Gardner attempt to give birth and death dates and changes of titles;

they also translate Vietnamese titles into English or French. Scope includes periodicals of research value from colonial times to the present.
MH

CI11   O'Brien, Patricia Anne. <u>Vietnam.</u> Adelaide: South Australia State Library, 1969. (<u>Its</u> Research Service bibliographies, series 4, no. 113.) 50 p.

     Bibliography of 660 books, periodical articles, and government publications, mostly in English, published mainly between 1965 and 1970. Sources comprise citations from <u>Australian National Bibliography</u>, <u>Australian Public Affairs Information Service</u>, <u>British Humanities Index</u>, <u>Index to New Zealand Periodicals</u>, <u>Library of Congress catalog, books: subjects</u>, and <u>PAIS</u>.
MH

CI12   *Stuttgart. Bibliothek für Zeitgeschichte. Weltkriegsbücherei. <u>Kataloge der Bibliothek für Zeitgeschichte--Weltkriegsbücherei; catalogs from the Library for Contemporary History--World War Library.</u> Boston: G. K. Hall, 1968. 31 v.

     Catalog in book form of books and periodical articles on political history, foreign relations, and military affairs of the 20th century, collected since the end of World War I. Scope is not limited to German-language publications. For works on the Franco-Indochinese War and the Vietnam War, see the Systematischer (Classified) Katalog, esp. vols. 9, 18, and 19. For an alphabetical listing by author, see the Alphabetischer (Alphabetical) Katalog. (Location: MB.)

CI13   Tsuchitani, Patricia M. <u>Vietnam, a selected annotated bibliography, 1969-August 1971.</u> Washington, D.C.: Library of Congress,

Congressional Research Service, 1971.
72 p. Not in MC.

Supplements and updates Vietnam, a bibliography, by Larry A. Niksch and revised
by Walter Ochinko, dated October 1, 1970.
Divided into periodical articles, books,
and U.S. government publications. Includes periodical articles from sources
not indexed in standard indexes: Aero-
space medicine, Army, Congressional Record,
SAIS review, and U.S. Naval Institute Proceedings, among others.
MH

CI14   U.S. Dept. of the Army. Army Library Program. Vietnam, an annotated bibliography.
Washington, D.C., 1968. 57 p. Rev. ed.,
1968. 85 p.

Prepared by the Army Library Program,
Army Education and Morale Support Directo-
rate, Office of the Adjutant General,
Headquarters, Dept. of the Army.

Selective list of about 700 English-
language books, pamphlets, government reports, and periodicals. "Designed for
U.S. Army post and hospital librarians as
a buying guide..., checklist of materials,
and a reference tool...and for library
patrons as a reading guide." Includes
references to general reference books
(Jane's Fighting ships, Europa yearbook,
Air forces of the world) in which information about Vietnam may be located. Useful
for reference to JPRS, United States,
United Nations, and RAND Corporation reports. Short, one-sentence descriptive
annotations.
MH

CI15   U.S. Military Assistance Command, Vietnam.
Civil Operations for Revolutionary Development Support [CORDS]. Information Center. Accessions list. [Saigon?], 196-
Ceased publication as of 1974. Title

varies: also called CIC accessions list.
Issued monthly.

Lists, in order of accession in the
CORDS Information Center, books, articles,
and government publications about Vietnam
or of interest to the CORDS staff. Information for each entry includes author,
title, issuing agency, date, pagination,
language, security classification, and,
in some instances, abstracts. Valuable
for finding publications of JUSPAO, USAID,
MACV, CORDS, and civilian contractors reporting to the U.S. government. Includes
many manuals and handbooks on the conduct
of military or civilian assistance to the
Revolutionary Development movement of RVN
government. Not indexed.
MH

CI16   Universal Reference System. Political science, government and public policy series.
Princeton, N.J.: Princeton Research Publ.
Co., [1967-   ], 10 vols., annual supplements.

A computer-produced bibliography with
extensive indexing of the contents of
books and articles. Coverage is designed
to include a selection of classics and
20th century writings and is recommended
by the editor as a bibliography for the
"great middle group of scholars that
stands between, on the one hand, the most
general public interested in any good text
or a current informative essay, and on the
other hand, the highly specialized scholar." Recommended as the first step for
writing a senior paper, a thesis, an article, or a dissertation. The main set is
a 10-volume compilation, each with its own
title: Vol. 1--International affairs;
vol. 3--Bibliography of bibliographies in
political science, government, and public
policy; etc.

For references on Vietnam (Indochina
is not used as a "descriptor"), see

"Dictionary of descriptors" at front of each volume, which lists the number of references to Vietnam and the pages on which they are located. The citations to which these references pertain are listed in full, with an abstract of the book or article, in the section following the "Dictionary of descriptors." Most citations are for works in English, and citations on Vietnam are mostly on the Vietnamese war and the American involvement; relatively few articles or books on Vietnamese society as such seem to be listed. Annual supplements are alphabetical by subject. Number of references under "Vietnam": Vol. 1--57; vol. 2--3; vol. 3--23; vol. 4--11; vol. 5--75; vol. 6--41; vol. 7--7; vol. 8--17; vol. 9--8; vol. 10--53; 1967--133; 1968--127; 1969--123; 1970--195; 1971--250; 1972--190; 1973--190; 1974--70; 1975--130. MH

CI17   Vega Sala, Francisco. "Aportación a una bibliografía sobre el Viet-Nam." Revista de Estudios Políticas, no. 156 (1967), 409-439.

          Subject bibliography with some annotations, designed to bring English and French writings on Vietnam to the attention of Spaniards; also includes some Spanish writings. A few typographical errors: Ho Chi Manh, Nguye Ali Quoc, etc. MH

DICTIONARIES

CI18   *Bùi Quang Khánh. Tự-điển hành-chánh công-quyền Việt-Anh-Pháp. Dictionary of terms and idioms of public administration Vietnamese-English-French. Dictionnaire des termes et expressions de l'administration publique vietnamien-anglais-français. [Saigon], 1971. 361 p. (Source: NIC, April 1972.)

CI19   *L. H. Hap. Vietnamese-English military and political dictionary; tự điển Việt-Anh quân-sự và chỉnh-trị. [Saigon. Khai-trí, 1965]. 697 p. (Source: BAS 1967.)

CI20   Văn-Lâm. "Danh-từ khảo dụng: chỉnh trị" [political terminology]. Quê-hương, no. 22 (4/61) to no. 28 (10/61), various pages in each issue. Approximately 182 p.

          Definitions of Sino-Vietnamese terms. Originally planned to define terms in 28 subjects in social, natural, and physical sciences and the humanities; beginning with the installment in no. 23 (5/61) the scope was reduced to comprise only terminology used in politics.

          Each entry is given in Chinese characters, then in quốc-ngữ, followed by a definition of each word and explanation of the term. In some installments, alphabetical order begins anew; in others it continues from the previous installment. MH

CI21   Vũ Văn Mẫu. Tự-điển Pháp-Việt, pháp--chỉnh--kinh--tài--xã-hội; dictionnaire français-vietnamien des sciences juridiques, politiques, économiques, financières et sociologiques.
          See CJ19 for complete description.

CI22   Vũ Văn Mẫu; Nguyễn Văn Trác; and Đào Văn Tập. Tự-điển Pháp-Việt pháp-luật chỉnh-trị kinh-tế; dictionnaire français-vietnamien des sciences juridiques, politiques, économiques.
          See CJ20 for complete description.

TRADITIONAL VIETNAM

CI23   *Cao Xuân Dục, et al. Quốc triều khoa bảng lục [Record of successful candidates in the national examinations]. 1894, 1919.
          Names of successful candidates for the mandarinate from 1822 until 1919, rules

for entering, names of examiners, and biographical information on the candidates.
Vols. 1-3 comp. in 1894 by Cao Xuân Dục;
vol. 4, covering examinations from 1894 to
1919--the year of the last examinations
held--comp. in 1919.

Translated into quốc ngữ as Quốc triều
đăng khoa lục by Lê Mạnh Liệu (Saigon: Bộ
Quốc-gia Giáo-dục, 1962), 276 p. (Tủ sách
dịch thuật.) (Source: NIC.)

CI24   Khâm-định Đại-Nam hội-điển sự-lệ [Official
administrative repertory of texts, 1802-
1851].

See CJ44 for description and for
translations.

CI25   Ngô Cao Lãng. [Also known as Lê Cao Lãng,
and Cao Viên Trai.] Lê triều lịch khoa
tiến sĩ đề danh bi ký. [Inscriptions of
the names of successful examination candidates during the Lê dynasty].

Lists of the graduates from 1442 until
1779, arranged chronologically by date of
examinations, with village of origin and
names of officials who administered the
examinations. Compiled from names in-
scribed in the Văn Miếu [Temple of Litera-
ture] in Hanoi beginning in 1484.--Whit-
more, "Vietnamese historical sources,"
p. 381. According to T. V. Giáp, Lược
truyện, p. 95, it contains many errors and
omits names of candidates of examinations
held under the Mạc interregnum.

Translated into quốc-ngữ by Võ Oanh
(Saigon: Bộ Quốc-gia Giáo-dục, 1961-
1962), 3 vols.[1]

Also cited, but not examined: Ngô Cao
Lãng, Lịch triều tạp ký, tập 2. Người bổ
sung [Completed by]: Xiển Trai. Hoa Bằng
dịch và chú giải [Translated and annotated
by Hoa Bằng]. Hanoi: Khoa học xã hội,
1975. 326 p.[2] An edition of 340 p., re-

vised and edited [hiệu đính] by Văn Tân
is also cited but not examined.[3]

[1]MH-V (vols. 2, 3); NIC [2]MLXBP, 9/75
[3]MLXBP, 11/75

CI26   *Nguyễn Hoản. Đại Việt lịch triều đăng khoa
lục [Record of the successful candidates
in the examinations of Đại Việt]. 1779-
1862. Also termed Đăng khoa lục (Whitmore, "Vietnamese historical sources,"
p. 381).

Names of successful candidates and
biographical information arranged chronologically by the date each candidate
passed the examinations, beginning in
1075. Although the prefatory chapter was
signed in 1779, supplements to the work
itself carry the record up to 1862, as
enumerated in T. V. Giáp, Lược truyện,
p. 97.

Translated into quốc ngữ by Tạ Thúc
Khai (Saigon, 1962), covering 1075 to
1691 (Whitmore, p. 381).
Cited in Whitmore; T. V. Giáp; and Gaspardone, "Bibliographie annamite."

CI27   Phan Huy Chú. "Quan-chức chỉ" [Government].
Vol. 3, chapters 13-19. In Lịch-triều
hiến-chương loại-chỉ [Monographs of the
institutions of the dynasties], ca. 1821.

See AD1 for description of main work.
Government regulations and practices
under the Lý, Trần, and Lê dynasties. In
addition to the complete translation in
Hanoi, 1960-61 (See AD1), it has also
been translated in Saigon: Vietnam (Republic). Laws, statutes, etc. Compilations.
Lịch-triều hiến-chương loại-chỉ. Lương
Thần Cao Nãi Quang phiên âm và dịch nghĩa
[translator]. Saigon: Nhà in Bảo Vinh,
1957, 568, 48 p. At head of title: Đại-
học-viện Saigon. Trường Luật-khoa đại
học. Pp. 3-363 comprise photographs of

the original Chinese-language text, the
romanized transcription, and the translation into quốc-ngữ.
MH-L

FRENCH INDOCHINA

CI28   Almanach national; annuaire officiel de la
       République française. Paris: 1872-1919.
       Began as Almanach royal in 1709 and issued
       under various titles (Almanach royal et
       national, Almanach national, and Almanach
       impérial) until 1872.
          Microtext edition available from Indi-
       anhead Editions (formerly NCR Microcard
       Editions), Englewood, Colorado.
          Lists the organizational structure of
       colonial governments and names of colonial
       officials under the names of the colonies.
       Lists the structure and names of officials
       of the Ministère des Colonies and its
       predecessors under the heading "Colonies."
       MH

CI29   *Annam. Rapport d'ensemble sur la situation
       du Protectorat de l'Annam. Hue. (Source:
       Boudet 3, 4 (lists 1929-1934/35 reports);
       NN.)

CI30   *____. Chambre des representants du peuple
       de l'Annam. Procès-verbaux des séances.
       Hue.
          Name of issuing body in Vietnamese:
       Trung-kỳ nhân-dân đại-biểu viện. [Title
       in Vietnamese: Tập kỷ-yếu các công việc
       hội-đồng thường-niên.] (Source: Boudet,
       2, 3, 4 [lists 1927-1935 reports].)

CI31   *____. Conseil des intérêts français éco-
       nomiques et financiers. Compte-rendu des
       séances. Hue.
          Proceedings of the Conseil, an official
       advisory body to the French Résident.
       Some years issued as Procès-verbal.
       (Source: Boudet 2, 3, 4 [lists 1929-1935
       reports].)

CI32   *Cochinchina. Rapport au Conseil colonial,
       avec carte et statistique sur l'état de
       la Cochinchine. Saigon.
          Reports for 1928/29 and 1929/30 are
       listed in Boudet 2 and 3; each report
       ca. 740 p.

CI33   *____. Conseil Colonial. Procès-verbaux du
       Conseil colonial. Saigon, 1880- .
          Proceedings of the Conseil, an advisory
       body to the Governor of the colony.
       (Source: Gregory; NUC; Cordier 4: 2567;
       Boudet 4.)

CI34   *Dictionnaire administratif et judiciaire de
       l'Indo-Chine publié sous la surveillance
       du Procureur Général, Chef du Service Ju-
       diciaire avec la collaboration des Magis-
       trats et Fonctionnaires de la Colonie.
       Hanoi: Impr. Express, 1907- .
          Tome I, Les officiers ministeriels en
       Indochine, par M. Monlezun, 1907, 58 p.
       (Cordier 4: 2600 [only volume located].)

CI35   *Indochina. Rapports au Conseil de Gouverne-
       ment. Hanoi, 1913- .
          Issued annually in two parts: 1, Si-
       tuation générale de l'Indochine; 2, Fonc-
       tionnement des divers services indochi-
       nois.--Gregory, Boudet 1 ("Conseils"),
       2 ("Administration").
          Also cited in Boudet 4: Indochina.
       Conseil de Gouvernement. Rapport au Grand
       Conseil des intérêts économiques et fi-
       nanciers de l'Indochine et au Conseil de
       gouvernement. Not verified for similarity
       with Rapports au Conseil de Gouvernement.

CI36   *____. Conseil de Gouvernement. Discours
       prononcé par M. le Gouverneur général à
       l'ouverture de la session. Hanoi.
          Annual policy message by the Gouverneur
       général, usually published separately, al-
       though at least one discours (for 1909)
       was published in JOIF, 13 décembre 1909,
       1974-2025. Discours by P. Pasquier

(1931-1933) and R. Robin (1934, 1935) are listed by author in Boudet 4 under the heading "Conseil de gouvernement."

CI37 *_____. Conseil supérieur. Rapport. Hanoi, 1903-1910.

Reports by the Conseil, superseded in 1911 by the Conseil de Gouvernement. (Source: Gregory, Cordier 4: 2565-2567.)

CI38 _____. Gouverneur général. Situation de l'Indochine.

Reports for 1897/1901, by Paul Doumer (Hanoi, 1902), 554 p.; 1902/1907, by Paul Beau (Saigon, 1908), 2 v.

Reports to the Conseil supérieur de l'Indochine on economic and political conditions in Indochina. Annexes include reports on specific topics such as public works and communications and on the work of various government agencies such as the Administration des Douanes et Régies. MH (Doumer)

CI39 Landron, André. "Divisions administratives de la Cochinchine." BSEI, n.s. 20 (1945), 15-32.

Lists the changes in administrative organization from 1832, changes in names of administrative divisions, and changes in territory. Includes the source of the official text in JOIC, BOIC, etc. MH

CI40 *Tonkin. Rapport sur la situation administrative, économique et financière du Tonkin. Hanoi. (Source: Boudet 3, 4 [lists 1929/30-1934/35 reports].)

CI41 *_____. Chambre des representants du peuple du Tonkin. Compte-rendu des travaux de la session. Hanoi.

Name of issuing body in Vietnamese: Bắc-kỳ nhân dân đại-biểu viện. Title in Vietnamese: Tập ký-yếu các công việc hội-

đồng thường-niên. (Source: Boudet 2, 3, 4 [lists 1929-1935 reports].)

CI42 *_____. Conseil des intérêts français économiques et financiers du Tonkin. Procès-verbal des séances. Hanoi:

An advisory body to the Résident. (Source: Boudet 2, 3, 4 [lists 1929-1935 reports].)

INDEPENDENCE AND REVOLUTIONARY MOVEMENTS

CI43 Boudarel, Georges. "Bibliographie des oeuvres relatives à Phan Bội Châu éditées en Quốc Ngữ à Hanoi depuis 1954." BEFEO, 56 (1969), 151-176.

Lists 95 books and articles about Phan Bội Châu, new editions of works originally written by him in nho or nôm, or anthologies.

A similar article is planned for works in RVN; the principal examples of the latter are cited in an appendix. MH

CI44 Breaking our chains; documents on the Vietnamese revolution of August 1945. Hanoi: FLPH, 1960. [106 p.] French edition titled Brisons nos fers.... (Ibid., 1959)

Edition published in Australia: Documents of the August 1945 revolution in Vietnam, trans. by C. Kiriloff, ed. by Rima Rathausky (Canberra: Australian National University, Research School of Pacific Studies, Department of International Relations, 1963), 70 p., translated from Razobem Okovy-Dokumenty Avgustovskoi Revoliutsii 1945 goda vo Vietname (Moscow: Foreign Literature Publishing House, 1960).

Contains documents issued by the Communist Party of Indo-China, the Viet Minh, the Revolutionary Military Conference of North Vietnam and other groups, from March 1, 1945 to September 2, 1945. In-

cludes the Declaration of Independence of
DRVN, September 2.

MH

CI45 Đảng Lao-Động Việt-Nam. _Thirty years of_
struggle of the Party. Hanoi: FLPH,
1960. Vol. 1, 102 p.

The official history of the Indo-Chi-
nese Communist Party.--R. Rathausky, in
Documents of the August 1945 revolution in
Vietnam.

Updated by _An outline history of the_
Viet-Nam Workers' Party (Hanoi: FLPH,
1970, 183 p.), a translation of _Bốn mươi_
năm hoạt động của Đảng (Hanoi: Sự Thật,
1970), which itself has been translated in
part and published as "Forty years of Party activity," _Viet-Nam documents and re-_
search notes, no. 76 (March 1970),
pp. 1-105.

MH

CI46 Indochina. Direction des Affaires Politiques
et de la Sûreté Générale. _Continuité de_
la politique française du protectorat en
Annam-Tonkin avant et après l'avènement de
Sa Majesté Bao Daï. [Hanoi: IDEO, n.d.].
152 p. (_Its_ Documents politiques, 1)

Publication of legislation, reports,
and correspondence for 1921-1933.

MH

CI47 _____. _____. _Contribution à l'histoire des_
mouvements politiques de l'Indochine fran-
çaise. Hanoi: IDEO, 1933-34. 6 v.

Vol. 1: Le "Tân Việt Cách Mệnh Đảng"
ou "Parti Revolutionnaire du Jeune Annam"
(1925-1930). 63 p. Prepared by Hoàng
Đức Thi, one of the founders of the Party.

Vol. 2: Le "Việt-Nam Quốc-Dân Đảng" ou
"Parti National Annamite du Tonkin" (1927-
1932). 52 p.

Vol. 3: Le "Việt-Nam Quốc-Dân Đảng" ou
"Parti National Annamite" des emigrés en
Chine (1930-1933). 62 p.

Vol. 4: Le "Đông Dương Cộng Sản Đảng"
ou "Parti Communiste Indochinois" (1925-
1933). 138 p.

Vol. 5: La Terreur Rouge en Annam
(1930-1931). 307 p.

Vol. 6 not published.

Vol. 7: Le Caodaïsme (1926-1934).
112 p.

Official colonial government sources on
political movements, undertaken as a result of nationalist agitation and uprisings. Source materials include interviews and interrogations and documents
seized by the Sûreté.

Microfilm available from Service International de Microfilm, Ministère des Affaires Étrangères, Paris.

MH; NIC

CI48 Phan Thiện Châu. _Vietnamese communism, a_
research bibliography. Westport, Conn.:
Greenwood Press, 1975. 359 p.

Classified listing of 3,467 books, periodical and newspaper articles, government publications, and political party
publications in Vietnamese, English and
French on all aspects of Vietnamese communism, based upon cataloged and uncata-
loged materials at Cornell and Yale Universities and The Library of Congress.
Scope includes works on predecessors of
the Indochinese Communist Party, the Vietnam Workers' Party, the DRVN, the NFLSVN,
and the PRG and affiliated groups. Subjects include reference works (including
works on communism in general as well as
those specifically relating to Vietnam);
Hồ Chí Minh (over 100 citations); social
conditions, government and politics, land
policy and agriculture, and the non-agri-
cultural economy in the DRVN; military
affairs; and The South. Particularly
valuable for extensive listings of Vietnamese-language publications, some of
which are translated by JPRS.

Author and subject indexes. No annotations. Titles of works in Vietnamese are not translated into English.

Pp. 3-19, "Vietnamese communism, an introductory bibliographic guide," an annotated bibliography of about 100 major primary and secondary sources and major North Vietnamese serials. Annotations of Vietnamese-language works include citations to English or French translations that have been published by FLPH or its French-language counterpart, Éditions en langues étrangères. Compiler includes about 10 references to materials translated by the U.S. Embassy in Saigon in the Viet-Nam documents and research notes series which supplement original material from the DRVN, NFLSVN, and similar sources.
MH-HY

CI49   Trần Huy Liệu, et al. Tài liệu tham khảo lịch sử cách mạng cận đại Việt Nam [Reference documents on the history of the contemporary revolutions in Vietnam]. Hanoi: Văn Sử Địa, 1956-58. 12 vols.

Narrative history and reproductions of Communist Party, Việt Minh, and other nationalist documents. Each volume has separate title. Volumes include such topics as: the Văn-thân movement, Yên-thế and mountain minority groups uprisings, revolutionary movements from the beginning of the 20th century to the end of World War I, democratic and other movements from 1918-1930, the Tân Việt Cách Mạng Đảng and Việt Nam Quốc Dân Đảng, struggles of 1930-31 and 1931-35, the Popular Front, Vietnamese society under Franco-Japanese occupation (1939-1945), French surrender to Japan, economic and social situation after World War II, antifascist movements of Bắc Sơn, Nam Kỳ, and Đô Lương, the growing uprisings, and the general August uprising.
NIC

CI50   U.S. Congressional Research Service. World communism, 1964-1969, a selected bibliography, volume II. Washington, D.C.: GPO, 1971. 420, 32 p. Committee print, 92d Congress, 1st session, Committee on the Judiciary, United States Senate.

Continuation of an earlier bibliography. "South and Southeast Asia" and "Vietnam," pp. 285-315, about 530 references in books, pamphlets, newspaper and periodical articles, and U.S. government publications. Full bibliographic citation and Library of Congress call numbers. No annotations. Author index.

Earlier bibliography has very few citations on Vietnam.
MH

CI51   U.S. Dept. of State. "Working paper on the North Vietnamese role in the war in South Viet-Nam." Viet-Nam documents and research notes, no. 37 (June 1968), 1-23. Appendices issued separately, in 250 copies only.

The "working paper" describes, from documents captured from DRVN forces operating in RVN or from NLF units, the background of the war from 1954, political changes among the DRVN government as they affected the NLF, and relationships between the DRVN governments and the NLF.

Appendices entitled "Captured documents and interrogation reports" contain information gathered from documents captured from NLF and DRVN troops, and interrogation of NLF and DRVN defectors. The earliest document, "The expansion of the party," dates from 1948, although most of the documents date from the post-1954 period. Documents of a reference nature include such subjects as the historical development of the Lao Động party, descriptions of the organization of the NLF, and regulations of the NLF. Arrangement is not in any particular order. Com-

prised of documents numbering up to
no. 303, but contains less than 303
documents.

MH

CI52   _____. Division of Research for the Far
East. Office of Intelligence Research.
Political alignments of Vietnamese nation-
alists. Washington, D.C., 1949. 168 p.
(O.I.R. report no. 3708.) Written by
I. Milton Sacks.

A history of the nationalist movements
since 1884, with emphasis on Communist
movements, the Việt Minh, and the Bảo Đại
restoration movement. Charts include the
development of Communist organizations in
Indochina and the ICP international con-
nections in 1930. Index of names,
pp. 162-168.

MH

CI53   _____. Office of Intelligence and Research.
Programs of Japan in Indochina, with index
to biographical data. Assemblage no. 56
(2d. ed. of Assemblage no. 26 & 40). Honolulu, 1945. 369 p. (Its R & A no. 3369)

Contains transcriptions of broadcasts
from Radio Tokyo and affiliated stations
as intercepted by the U.S. Federal Communications Commission from December 1941
to May 24, 1945. Useful for information
on political and economic situation in
Indochina. Excludes information of a
purely military nature. Pp. 367-369, index to biographical data, is list of names
of persons mentioned in broadcasts.

MH

CI54   *Vietnam (Republic). Viện Khảo Cổ. Việt Nam
tranh đấu độc-lập trong thời kỳ Pháp xâm-
chiếm đất đai [The independence movement
in Vietnam during the French occupation].
Saigon, 1960. 14 p.

Contains 204 works in Vietnamese, Chinese, and European languages and indicates

the principal periodicals which deal with
the independence movement (Jumper).

DEMOCRATIC REPUBLIC OF VIETNAM

BIBLIOGRAPHIES

CI55   Keyes, Jane Godfrey. A bibliography of
[North] Vietnamese publications in the
Cornell University Library. Ithaca:
Southeast Asia Program, Cornell University, 1962. 116 p. (Its Data Paper, 47)
_____. A bibliography of Western-language
publications concerning North Vietnam in
the Cornell University Library. Ibid.,
1966. 280 p. (Its Data paper, 63)

Books, periodical articles, government
publications, and dissertations in European languages. The 1962 bibliography is
useful for publications about the nationalist and Communist movements of the period during and after the 1930's and the
beginnings of the DRVN. The 1966 bibliography updates the 1962 bibliography and
has an extensive section of translations
by JPRS. No indexes. Annotated.

mgc

CI56   Kyriak, Theodore E. North Vietnam, 1957-
1961: a bibliography and guide to contents of a collection of United States
Joint Publications Research Service translations on microfilm. Annapolis, Md.:
Research and Microfilm Publications
[1962?] 62 p.

Annotated bibliography of North Vietnamese, Russian, and East European newspaper and periodical articles on North
Vietnam. Arrangement is by subject--eco-
nomics, sociology, and politics. Although
this is a guide to contents of the microfilm collection, it may also be used, in
conjunction with Index to Readex Microprint Edition of J.P.R.S. Reports (AA86),
to locate the respective publications is-

sued as Readex Microprint edition of U.S. government publications (non-depository). Continued by Kyriak's Asian developments, a bibliography (1962-1966), Catalog cards in book form for United States Joint Publications Research Service translations (1966-June 1970), and Transdex; bibliography and index to United States Joint Publications Research Service translations (AA90).

MH

GOVERNMENT

CI57   Đảng Lao Động Việt-Nam. National Congress, 3d, 1960. Documents of the Third National Congress of the Việt-Nam Workers' Party. Hanoi: FLPH, 1960. 4 v.[1]

Includes addresses by Pres. Hồ Chỉ Minh and members of the Party's Central Committee; reports on the first Five Year Plan; addresses by top Party members on various aspects of political, social and military events--including liberation of the South--and addresses by visiting delegates from the Communist bloc.

Original title: Đại hội Đại biểu Toàn quốc lần thứ ba Đảng Lao Động Việt Nam: Văn Kiện Đại Hội. (Hanoi: Ban Chấp Hành Trung Ương Đảng Lao Động Việt Nam, 1960); available on microfilm at Cornell: Wason Film 2584, No. 66A, B, C.[2]

A selection of documents has been published as "Documentary record of the 3d National Congress of the Vietnam Lao Dong Party, North Vietnam," JPRS 7137 (Jan. 23, 1961); MC 1961: 10803. 430 p.[1]

[1]MH [2]Châu, "Bibliographic guide"

CI58   [Đặng Xuân Khu.] The resistance will win. Hanoi: FLPH, 1960. 150 p. Facsimile edition published as: Primer for revolt: The Communist takeover in Viet-Nam. A facsimile edition of The August revolution and The resistance will win, by Truong

Chinh. New York: Praeger [1963] 213 p. (Praeger publications in Russian history and world communism, 133)[1] Original title: Kháng chiến nhất định thắng lợi (Hanoi, 1947)[2]

Basic works on the Communist revolution in Vietnam, analyzing the reasons for success of the takeover of Hanoi by the Viet Minh in 1946 and establishing the "three-stage" theory of resistance: contention, equilibrium, and general counter-offensive.

[1]MH [2]Châu, "Bibliographic guide"

CI59   The Democratic Republic of Vietnam. Hanoi: FLPH, 1960. 159 p.

An official compendium published to cover the post-Geneva period until 1960 (Keyes).

MH

CI60   Democratic Republic of Vietnam: party and government structure. Washington, D.C.: Central Intelligence Agency. (Its Reference Aid A(CR) series) Latest is August 1975, A (CR) 75-31.

Fold-out chart with pictures of politburo members and names of ministers and the government ministries and commissions.

Available to non-government users from Documents Expediting Project, Library of Congress.

MH

CI61   Fall, Bernard B. The Viet-Minh regime; government and administration in the Democratic Republic of Vietnam. Ithaca, N.Y.: Cornell Univ., Dept. of Far Eastern Studies, and New York: Institute of Pacific Relations, 1954. 134 p. (Cornell University, Dept. of Far Eastern Studies, Data Paper, no. 14)

_____. _____. Rev. and enl. ed. Ithaca: Southeast Asia Program, and New York: Institute of Pacific Relations, 1956. 196 p.

MH

CI62   . Le Viêt-Minh; la République Démocratique du Viêt-Nam, 1945-1960. Paris:
Colin, 1960. 376 p. (Cahiers de la Fondation Nationale des Sciences Politiques,
106).

Revised, enlarged, and translated edition of his The Viet-Minh regime (CI6).
History, organization, and administration
of the DRVN. Annexe reprints the Constitution of January 1, 1960.
MH

CI63 Hồ Chỉ Minh. Selected works. Hanoi: FLPH,
1960-1962. 4 v.[1]

Writings and speeches from 1920 to
1960. Includes speech at Congress of
Tours of the Third International in 1920;
the English translation of French colonization on trial, originally written as Le
procès de la colonisation française; and
other basic documents. Arrangement is
mostly chronological; speech at Tours is
in vol. 2, although vol. 1 covers the
1922-1926 period.

Original Vietnamese-language edition:
Hồ Chỉ Minh tuyển tập (Hanoi: Sự Thật,
1960, 815 p.).[2]

Reprinted, with some poems and nine
speeches or articles from 1960-1966 as Ho
Chi Minh on revolution, selected writings,
ed. Bernard B. Fall (New York: Praeger,
1967, 368 p., Praeger publications in Russian history and world communism, no. 190;[1]
and New American Library Signet Books,
1968, 368 p., paperback).

Condensed and updated as Selected writings (1920-1969), (Hanoi: FLPH, 1973,
368 p.,[1] originally published as Vì độc
lập tự do, vì chủ nghĩa xã hội [For independence and freedom, for socialism].
(Hanoi: Sự Thật, 1970, 344 p.).[2]
[1]MH [2]Phan Thiện Châu, "Bibliographic
guide."

CI64 *Hoàng Văn Chỉ. From colonialism to communism: A case history of North Vietnam.
New York: Praeger, [1964]. 252 p.

Description of government and society
in the DRVN and during the Franco-Indochinese War by a non-Communist who es-
caped to the South after 1954. Criticized
by some nationalists as having been subsi-
dized by the U.S. Central Intelligence
Agency, it also propounded the theory of
the "bloodbath" thought to have been per-
petrated when the Communists established
the DRVN after 1954.

The "only comprehensive published study
of North Viet Nam by a non-Communist Vietnamese" (Châu, "Bibliographic guide").
MH

CI65 Lê Duẩn. The Vietnamese revolution: funda-
mental problems, essential tasks. Hanoi:
FLPH, 1970. 195 p.[1]

(A "re-edited" version published with the
same title, New York: International Publishers, 1971, 151 p.)[2] Also available
as: "Under the glorious party banner, for
independence, freedom, and socialism, let
us advance and achieve victories," Viet-
Nam documents and research notes, no. 77
(April 1970), 120 p.[1] Original title:
Dưới lá cờ vẻ vang của Đảng, vì độc lập,
tự do, vì chủ nghĩa xã hội, tiến lên
giành những thắng lợi mới (Hanoi: Sự
Thật, 1970, and Nhân Dân, Feb. 14, 1970).[3]

A major policy statement on the progress
of the war in the South, economic problems
and policies in the DRVN, and the role of
the Party in the Vietnamese revolution.
Received much editorial comment in DRVN.
[1]MH [2]DLC [3]Châu, "Bibliographic guide"

CI66 U.S. Dept. of State. Office of External Research. Who's who in North Vietnam.
[Washington, D.C.?], 1972. 342 p.

POLITICAL SCIENCE AND GOVERNMENT CI

Summary biographic data on 207 North Vietnamese party, government, and military leaders, collected prior to July 1972 and prepared from files in the Central Intelligence Agency. Information includes birth place and date, current and previous positions, and dates of appointment, travel, and major speeches and publications. Supplementary background sketches on fifty of the top leaders, dated 1969, are also included. Pp. xi-xxiv, officials of the Lao Động party, DRVN government, People's Army of Vietnam, and various mass organizations. MH; original at ICRL

CI67 "VWP-DRV leadership 1960-1973." Viet-Nam documents and research notes, no. 114 (July 1973), 2 parts, 138 p.

Pt. 1, biographical sketches of members of the Central Committee of the Viet-Nam Workers' Party (Đảng Lao Động Việt-Nam), government officials, and military leaders in the DRVN. Some sketches are 2-3 pages long. Pt. 2, names of party, government, and military officials from 1960 to 1973.

Information compiled from various sources available to the U.S. mission in Saigon.
MH

CI68 *Vietnam (Democratic Republic). Thư-Viện Quốc-Gia. Thư mục Chu tịch Hồ Chí Minh (các nước ngoài viết về Hồ Chu tịch) [Bibliography of Chairman Ho Chi Minh (works written in foreign countries about Chairman Hồ)]. Hanoi, 1975. 42 p. (Source: MLXBP, 8/75.)

CI69 Võ Nguyên Giáp. Banner of people's war, the party's military line. New York: Praeger [1970] 118 p.[1] Also available as "The party's military line is the ever-victorious banner of people's war in our country," Viet-Nam documents and research notes, no. 70 (Jan. 1970), 82 p.,[1] and in

Daily report, U.S. Foreign Broadcast Information Service, no. 31 (Feb. 13, 1970), suppl. 5, 68 p.[1] Originally serialized in Vietnamese in Nhân dân and Quân đội nhân dân, Dec. 14-17, 1969.

Articles commemorating the 25th anniversary of the Vietnam People's Army. Emphasizes flexibility, creativity, and determination in fighting a people's war in which the enemy has vastly superior weapons and manpower, reflecting the military situation in Vietnam as of 1969-1970.
[1]MH

CI70 _____. Big victory, great task: North Vietnam's Minister of Defense assesses the course of the war. New York: Praeger [1968] 120 p.[1] Issued in French as: Victoire totale, tâche grandiose (Paris: Didier, 1969, 112 p., (Collection Forum))[2]

Considered a major exposition of the Lao Động Party's military line,[3] this was written to stimulate North Vietnamese resistance to heavy bombing by the U.S. by pointing out the dissension in American society over the continued war, the failure of the U.S. and RVN to wage a limited war, and the eventual victory of the DRVN and NFL.
[1]MH [2]BAS 1969 [3]Viet-Nam documents and research notes, no. 70 (January, 1972), p. i.

CI71 _____. People's war, people's army. Hanoi: FLPH, 1961. 217 p. Facsimile edition published as: People's war, people's army; the Viet Công insurrection manual for underdeveloped countries. New York: Praeger [1962]. 217 p. (Praeger publications in Russian history and world communism, no. 119).[1] Translation of Chiến tranh nhân dân và quân đội nhân dân (Hanoi: Sự Thật, 1959).[2] Published in French as: Guerre du peuple, armée du

peuple (Paris: Maspéro, 1966, 232 p.
(Cahiers libres, 82)).[1]

Collection of four articles on the
Franco-Indochinese war, developing the
"three-stage" theory of guerilla war probably first expounded by Trường Chinh.
[1]MH [2]Châu, "Bibliographic guide"

NATIONAL ASSEMBLY (QUỐC-HỘI)

Printed proceedings of the National Assembly
of the DRVN have not been located by the compiler
except for the two selections of documents printed
by the FLPH. The translations series by the JPRS
and in Viet-Nam documents and research notes (Saigon: Joint United States Public Affairs Office) includes translations of portions of the proceedings.

CI72 Vietnam (Democratic Republic). Quốc-Hội.
Some documents of the National Assembly of
the Democratic Republic of Vietnam; 3d
Legislature, 1st session, June–July 1964.
Hanoi: FLPH, 1964. 121 p.

Reports on economic and political
events in the DRVN; war in RVN; speech by
President Hồ Chí Minh.
MH

CI73 _____. Against U.S. aggression; main documents of the National Assembly of the Democratic Republic of Vietnam, 3d Legislature, 2d session, April 1965. 2d ed. Hanoi: FLPH, 1966. 102 p.

Pp. 9–74, report by Prime Minister Phạm
Văn Đồng on the extension of the war into
the DRVN by United States forces.
MH

STATE OF VIETNAM

CI74 Vietnam (State). Laws, statutes, etc.
Hành-chính pháp điển [Administrative
code]. Saigon: Nhà in các Công-báo,
1953. 657 p. Second section has title
and text in French: Code administratif.

Part 1, Organic texts of the State of
Vietnam; pt. 2, General administration;
pt. 3, Public institutions and representative bodies.

Basic public documents from
March 26, 1948 to Sept. 30, 1953 on
the legal status of the State of Vietnam
within the French Union, the organization of the central government, and the
establishment of governments in the separate regions and municipalities.
MH-L

REPUBLIC OF VIETNAM

GOVERNMENT

CI75 Các văn-kiện tổ-chức cơ-cấu quốc-gia tại
Việt-Nam Cộng-hòa sau cách-mạng 1-11-63
(từ ngày 1-11-1963 đến ngày 19-6-1965)
[Documents on the organization of the
structure of the Republic of Vietnam after
the revolution of 1 November 1963 (from
1 November 1963 to 19 June 1965]. [Sai-
gon]: Học-Viện Quốc-gia Hành-Chánh,
1965. 227 p. Also issued in Nghiên-cứu
hành-chánh, số đặc-biệt [special issue]
3&4, 1965.

_____, 19-6-1965 đến ngày 1-4-1967. Issued
in Nghiên-cứu hành-chánh, số đặc-biệt
11 no. 1 (1st quarter 1968), 185 p.

Contains: 1) daily chronology from
1:30 p.m., November 1, 1963 until
June 19, 1965 (and from June 19, 1965
until April 1, 1967), 2) a list of decrees
by the various governments after November 1, 1963, and 3) texts of decrees.
Other sections include names of cabinet
officers. The 1965 to 1967 compilation
includes lists of members of the Quốc-Hội
Lập-Hiến [Constituent Assembly] and the
rules of the Quốc-Hội Lập-Hiến and the
text of the 1967 Constitution.
MH-V

CI76 *Đào Văn Hội. Lịch trình hành chánh Nam Phần
[Administrative chronology in South Viet-
Nam]. Saigon, 1961. (Source: Kim Sa;
NIC.)

CI77 *"Những văn kiện hành chánh quan trọng công bố
trong đệ---lục cá nguyệt". [Important administrative documents promulgated during
the---semester]. NCHC 9/57 to 12/58,
various pagings in most issues.
KimSa, Tạp-chỉ, pp. 196-197; might be continued in NCHC (1/59 and later issues) as
"Những văn kiện quan trọng..."; see KimSa,
p. 197.

CI78 Public administration bulletin Vietnam,
nos. 1-52. Saigon: U.S. Agency for International Development, Public Administration Division, Dec. 1962-Dec. 1971.
Contains summary results of elections;
reports of new government publications (of
RVN); information on population; lists of
administrative units, cabinet members and
provincial and district officials; translations of RVN proclamations and other
laws; and other information such as budgetary figures.
INDEX: "Index of all GVN legislation
published in Public Administration Bulletin Vietnam, nos. 1-48," PABV no. 49
(June 1, 1969), 68-95.
INDEX: "Index of all GVN legislation...
nos. 49-53," Ibid., no. 54 (Sept. 1, 1970),
84-93.
MH

CI79 Rose, Dale L., and Vũ Văn Học. The Vietnamese civil service system. Saigon: MSU,
Vietnam Advisory Group, 1961. 467 p.
Vietnamese-language edition: Hệ-thống
Công-vụ Việt-Nam. 470 p.
Describes the organization of the civil
service after 1949 and includes extracts
of documents listing organization of various agencies.
mgc

CI80 Saigon. Học-viện Quốc-gia Hành-chánh. Niên-
giám hành-chánh [Yearbook of administra-
tion]. Saigon, 1957- . Published in
1957, 1959, 1963, 1967, and 1971.
Contains text of constitutions, organization of government, names of government
bureaus, and enabling legislation. 1963
ed. (477 p.) lists proclamations issued
between November 1 and November 22 (date
of publication); organization of the government is given as of 7.7.1963. 1967 ed.
(505 p.) contains constitution of
April 1, 1967, provisional constitution
of June 19, 1965, organization tables of
the government, and enabling legislation.
1971 ed. (443 p.) contains organizational changes in the RVN government since the
promulgation of the Constitution of 1967.
MH-V; NIC

CI81 *Tài liệu quan trọng về cuộc Cách Mạng ngày 1
tháng 11-1963. Saigon: Việt-Nam Thông-
Tấn-Xã, 1964-69. 6 vols. ca. 190 p.
English-language edition published as:
Major documents on the Revolution of
November 1, 1963. Saigon: Việt-Nam
Press, 1964. 7 vols. (Source: NIC;
Cường, Soc. sci.)

CI82 Vietnam (Republic). Bộ Ngoại-Giao. Liste
diplomatique et consulaire. Saigon,
1959- .
Names of RVN diplomats and the countries to which they are accredited and
names of foreign diplomats stationed in
RVN. Also published in Le Vietnam et ses
relations internationales; Vietnam in
world affairs (Saigon, 1956-).
KimSa; MH-L

CI83 *____. Bộ Thông-Tin. Tổng kết thành-tích
đệ nhị chu niên của chính-phủ Việt-Nam
Cộng-Hòa [Summary of accomplishments of
the Vietnam Republic on its second anni-
versary]. Saigon, 1966. 330 p. (Source:
TTAPC.)

CI84 *____. ____. Nha Tổng Giám-đốc Thông-tin. Thành-tích --- năm hoạt-động của chính-phủ Việt-Nam. Saigon, 1955-1963.

Also published in French and in English: --- years of the Ngo Dinh Diem administration; and Bilan des réalisations gouvernementales.

The official yearbook of the government. Issues for most years are listed in TTAPC; pagination of the 1959, 1961 and 1962 issues were over 1000 pages.

Succeeded by Thành-tích hoạt-động của nội-các chiến-tranh [Activities of the War Cabinet] Saigon, 1965-1967. (Source: TTAPC; NIC.)

CI85 *____. Nha Tổng Giám-đốc Công-Vụ. Sưu tập các văn kiện nguyên-tắc về quản-trị nhân-viên chính ngạch [Collection of documents relating to the organization and classification of civil service personnel]. Saigon: Xã Hội Ấn Quán, 1960. 2 vols.

Basic regulations since 1950 (Jumper).

CI86 *____. Tổng-Thống. Message of President Nguyễn Văn Thiệu to the joint session of the National Assembly November 2, 1968. Saigon, 1968. 14 p.

Probably issued also in Vietnamese and French and in years subsequent to 1968; above edition is only edition listed in TTAPC.

CI87 *____. ____. Message of the President of the Republic to the National Assembly. Saigon: Nha Tổng Giám-đốc Thông-Tin, 1957[?] to 1962. Vietnamese-language edition: Thông điệp của Tổng-Thống Việt Nam Cộng Hòa đọc tại Quốc-hội; French-language edition: Message de Son Excellence Monsieur le Président Ngô Đình Diệm à l'Assemblée Nationale de la République du Việt-Nam.

The annual message, usually given in the first week of October. (Source: TTAPC.)

CI88 Viet Nam government organization manual, 1957-1958. Saigon: National Institute of Administration, 1958. 275 p.

Text of the 1956 constitution, outline of legislative and executive branches, with names of National Assembly deputies and committees, names of high-ranking executive-branch officers, and responsibilities of executive agencies.

____. Supplement to Government organization manual, 1957-1958. Saigon, 1960. 174 p. MH-L; DLC; TTAPC

ELECTIONS

CI89 Penniman, Howard R. Elections in South Vietnam. Washington, D.C.: American Enterprise Institute for Public Policy Research, and Stanford: Hoover Institution on War, Revolution and Peace, 1972. 246 p. (AEI-Hoover Policy study, 4; Hoover Institution Studies, 38) Available in hardcover and paperback.

"Presidential election returns, 1967 and 1971," pp. 231-237. Summary statistics for each candidate by province or region in Saigon.
MH

Statistics of the elections of 1967 and 1970 are in the following sources:

CI90 "The village elections," Public administration bulletin Vietnam, special issue, no. 38 (June 1, 1967), 74 p.;

CI91 "The hamlet elections," Ibid., special issue, no. 40 (August 15, 1967), 35 p.;

CI92 [Presidential, Vice-Presidential, Senatorial, and Lower House]. Ibid., no. 41 (November 30, 1967), 129 p.;

CI93 [Saigon prefecture, province, and city council elections and Senate elections].

POLITICAL SCIENCE AND GOVERNMENT CI

Ibid., no. 54 (September 1, 1970),
72-83.
MH

CI94 *Vietnam (Republic). Bộ Thông-Tin. Bầu-cử
Tổng-Thống và Phó Tổng-Thống nhiệm kỳ
1961-1966 [Results of the Presidential and
Vice-Presidential election for the 1961-
1966 term]. Saigon: Nha Tổng Giám-Đốc
Thông-Tin, 1961. 417 p. (Source: TTAPC.)

CI95 *_____. Nha Kế-Hoạch Tâm-Lý-Chiến. Tài-liệu
về cuộc bầu cử Tổng-Thống, Phó Tổng-
Thống, Nghị Sĩ Thượng Nghị Viện ngày
3-9-1967 [Documents about the election for
President, Vice President, and Representative on September 3, 1967]. Saigon, 1967.
48 p. (Source: Thư-mục 1967.)

NATIONAL ASSEMBLY (QUỐC HỘI)

CI96 Nguyễn Văn Nam, and Phương Nam. Niên-giám
Quốc-Hội Việt-Nam; Quốc-Hội Lập-Pháp,
pháp-nhiệm khóa hai, 1959, tập II [Year-
book of the National Assembly; Legislative
Assembly, second session, 1959, vol. II].
[Saigon?: Phương Nam Văn Nghệ, 1959?].
202 p.
    Biographical information about
legislators.
MH-V

CI97 Phương Nam. Niên-giám Quốc-Hội Việt-Nam,
1956. [Yearbook of the National Assembly, 1956]. Saigon: Phương-Nam Văn Nghệ,
[1956?]. 180 p.
    Brief history of political events in
Vietnam from 1945 until the election of
Ngô Đình Diệm as president in 1955 and
the formation of the National Assembly in
1956; organization of the National Assembly in 1956; and pp. 52-180, biographical
sketches of the representatives.
MH-V

CI98 Vietnam (Republic). Quốc Hội. Công-báo Việt-
Nam Cộng-Hòa (Ấn-bản Quốc-Hội) [Official
gazette of the Republic of Vietnam (National Assembly edition)]. Saigon: Nhà
in các Công báo, 1955- . Available on
microfilm from 3M/IMPress, New York City.
    Verbatim record of the proceedings of
the Quốc-Hội, and during the period before
the establishment of the Second Republic,
in April 1967, of the Constituent Assembly and its immediate predecessors.
MH; NIC

CI99 *_____. Niên-giám Quốc-Hội Lập-hiến
11-9-1966 [Yearbook of the Constituent Assembly September 11, 1966]. Saigon, 1967.
123 p. (Source: Thư mục 1966.)

CI100 _____. _____. Hạ-Nghị-Viện. Niên-giám Hạ-
Nghị-Viện, pháp nhiệm I, 1967-1971 [Year-
book of the Lower House for the first legislative period, 1967-1971]. [Saigon?,
1971?] 190 p.
    Results of the elections of
October 22, 1967, texts of speeches
by the Speaker of the House and by
President Nguyễn Văn Thiệu, and biographical summaries of members of the
Lower House.
MH-V

CI101 _____. _____. Thượng-Nghị-Viện. Niên-giám
Thượng-Nghị-Viện nhiệm kỳ I, II, và III
1967-1968, 1968-1969, và 1969-1970 [Year-
book of the Upper House for the first
three years]. [Saigon: Văn-phòng Thượng-
Nghị-Viện], 1970. 148 p.
    Names of members of the Upper House,
their committee assignments and party af-
filiations, and biographies. About 1 or
2 pages of biographical information about
each member.
MH-V

NATIONAL FRONT FOR THE LIBERATION OF SOUTH
VIETNAM AND PROVISIONAL REVOLUTIONARY
GOVERNMENT OF THE REPUBLIC OF SOUTH VIETNAM

CI102 "The leadership of the PRG, the NFLSV and
their affiliated organizations, 1973."
Viet-Nam documents and research notes,
no. 111 (April 1973), 102 p.

Biographical sketches of 16 members of
the PRG, NFLSV, etc. and lists of offi-
cials in various affiliated organizations
down to the provincial level. Replaces
"Leaders of the PRG-NLF and affiliated or-
ganizations, May 1972," ibid., no. 105
(May, 1972), and a supplement to "The
'Provisional Revolutionary Government of
South Vietnam,' pt. 2, The founding con-
ference of the PRG," ibid., no. 101
(January, 1972), pp. 12-15.
MH

CI103 Pike, Douglas. Viet Cong; the organization
and techniques of the National Liberation
Front. Cambridge: MIT Press, 1966.
490 p. (Center for International Studies,
Massachusetts Institute of Technology.
Studies in international communism, 7)
Published in paperback edition, 1967.

A study emphasizing the organizational
structure of the NLF, based upon documents
captured from the NLF and now available in
microfilm from the Center for Research Libraries, Chicago. Pp. 421-436, "Biographical notes." Generally favorably reviewed,
but critically reviewed by Huỳnh Kim Khánh
in Pacific affairs 42 (1969), 58-67.
MH

CI104 "South Viet Nam: from the N.F.L. to the Provisional Revolutionary Government." Vietnamese studies, 23 (1970) whole issue,
428 p.

Includes documents on the organization
and programs of the NFLSVN, the Vietnamese
Alliance of Nationalist, Democratic, and

Peace Forces, and the Provisional Revolu-
tionary Government of the Republic of
South Viet Nam.
MH

CI105 Who's who in the Republic of South Viet Nam
[n. p., Giai Phong editions, 1969]. 54 p.

Biographical sketches and pictures of
the 37 members of the Provisional Revolutionary Government of the Republic of
South Viet Nam and of the Advisory Council.
MH-L

FRANCE

The Parliamentary debates and documents of
France are necessary for studying the colonial policies of France. The Débats contain the text of
speeches and record of daily business in the Parlia-
ment. The Documents parlementaires contain the
texts of proposed legislation (projets de loi and
propositions) and reports of the legislative committees after studying the proposals.

To find the debates and documents on a particular subject, it is necessary to use the indexes
which are published annually as Tables du Journal
officiel de la République française, Débats parlementaires, Assemblée nationale (or Sénat). During
the Third Republic (1871-1942) cumulated indexes
were published from time to time and are listed below as Tables analytiques des Annales.

The texts of laws passed by the Parlement are
published in the Journal officiel de la République
française, Édition Lois et décrets.

The National Union Catalog, pre-1956 imprints,
lists the various publications of the French Parlement in vol. 180, under the headings "France. Assemblée nationale" or "France. Parlement (1946-)."

The major published sources for debates until
1881 are:

CI106 Archives parlementaires de 1787 à 1860 (Paris, 1867-1913, 2 series: Première série,
1787-1799; Deuxième série, 1814-1860.

Repr., Paris: Centre National de la Recherche Scientifique (in progress), and
microfilmed by ACRPP (in progress));

CI107 France. Chambre des Députés. Procès verbaux. (Paris, 1818-1848);

CI108 ____. Chambre des Pairs. Procès verbaux.
(Ibid.);

CI109 ____. Corps législatif. Annales du Sénat
et du Corps législatif. (Paris, 1861-
1870);

CI110 From 1869 until 1880 the Journal officiel de
la République française contained laws and
decrees and the reports of debates in the
Assemblée nationale. This has been microfilmed by ACRPP.

Before 1880, the debates were also published
as:

CI111 France. Assemblée nationale. Annales de
l'Assemblée nationale (Paris, 1871-1876).

Beginning in 1881, the débats were published
as separate éditions of the Journal officiel de la
République française. Current issues are available
from the Imprimerie des Journaux officiels, Paris,
while back issues are available on microfilm from
ACRPP.

CI112 France. Assemblée nationale (1871-1942).
Chambre des députés. Annales de la Chambre
des députés. Débats parlementaires.
(Paris, 1881-1940);

CI113 ____. ____. Sénat. Annales du Sénat.
Débats parlementaires. (Paris, 1881-
1940).

A non-official summary of the debates was
also published:

CI114 Journal des débats politiques et littéraires
(title varies: Journal des débats et décrets, 1789-1805; Journal de l'Empire,
1805-1815), (Paris, 1789-1944), microfilm
available from ACRPP.

From 1946 to the present, the debates of the
Parlement are published as:

CI115 France. Parlement (1946-). Assemblée nationale. Débats parlementaires, Assemblée nationale. (Paris, 1946-);

CI116 ____. ____. Conseil de la République.
Débats parlementaires, Conseil de la République. (Paris, 1946-1958), superseded
in the Fifth Republic by:

CI117 ____. ____. Sénat. Compte-rendu des débats du Sénat. (Paris, 1958- .)

The major published sources for Documents
parlementaires, also known as Impressions, are:

CI118 France. Assemblée nationale (1871-1942).
Annales du Sénat et de la Chambre des Députés. Documents parlementaires, annexes
aux procès-verbaux des séances (Paris,
1876-1880);

CI119 ____. ____. Chambre des Députés. Annales,
documents parlementaires. (Paris, 1881-
1940);

CI120 ____. ____. Sénat. Annales, documents
parlementaires. (Paris, 1881-1940);

CI121 French Union. Assemblée. Documents de l'Assemblée; annexes aux procès-verbaux des
séances. (Paris, 1947-1958);

CI122 France. Parlement (1946-). Assemblée nationale. Documents parlementaires, annexes aux procès-verbaux des séances.
(Paris, 1946-23 mars 1971), continued by:

CI123 ____. ____. ____. Impressions. (Paris,
       1971-);

CI124 ____. ____. Conseil de la République.
       Documents parlementaires. (Paris, 1946-
       sept. 1957), continued as Its Impressions
       (Oct. 1957-juin 1958), superseded in the
       Fifth Republic by:

CI125 ____. ____. Sénat. Impressions. (Paris,
       1958-).

CI126 INDEXES: [Table alphabétique et analytique
       du Journal officiel de la République fran-
       çaise, 1871-1965.] Microfilmed by ACRPP
       from annual volumes of Tables;

CI127 France. Assemblée nationale (1871-1942).
       Chambre des députés. Tables analytiques
       des Annales, 3.-16. législature, 1881/85-
       1936/40. (Paris, n. d.) Index to Débats
       and Documents.[1]

CI128 ____. ____. Table alphabétique (nomina-
       tive et méthodique) des Impressions du
       Sénat et de la Chambre des Députés,
       12 fév. 1871/31 déc. 1875-1 juin 1936/
       31 mai 1942. (Paris, n. d.)[1,2]

CI129 ____. Parlement (1946-). Assemblée na-
       tionale. Table du Journal officiel de la
       République française. Débats parlemen-
       taires. Assemblée nationale. Paris:
       Impr. des Journaux officiels. Annual.
       Includes index to Documents parlementaires
       of the Assemblée nationale.

CI130 ____. ____. Sénat. Table du Journal of-
       ficiel de la République française. Débats
       parlementaires. Sénat. Paris: Impr. des
       Journaux officiels. Annual. Includes in-
       dex to Documents parlementaires of the
       Sénat.
       [1]NUC (cites copy at DLC) [2]Available on
       microfilm from ACRPP

CI131 U.S. Central Intelligence Agency. Chiefs of
       state and cabinet members of foreign gov-
       ernments. Washington, D.C., [1969?]- .
       Monthly. (Its Reference aid A (CR)
       series)
           Names of government officials at the
       ministerial level. Includes DRVN and
       RVN. No other biographical data included.
           Available on microfilm from the Library
       of Congress, Photoduplication Service,
       Dept. C-220, and in published form from
       the Documents Expediting Project of The
       Library of Congress.
       MH

CI132 U.S. Congress. Congressional record. Wash-
       ington, D.C.: GPO, 1873- . Title varies
       before 1873.
           The daily transcript, with revisions,
       omissions, and additions, of speeches
       made in Congress or presented in writing
       to Congress. Also contains texts of Pres-
       idential messages and records of votes, as
       well as newspaper or periodical articles,
       letters from constituents, and other ma-
       terial requested by Congressmen, e.g. Na-
       tional Security Study memorandum no. 1
       (May 10, 1972, pp. E 4975-5005, and
       May 11, 1972, pp. E 5009-5066: the "Kis-
       singer memo" on Vietnam, not available
       elsewhere. Does not index Congressional
       hearings, committee prints, or documents,
       but reports concerning legislation are
       listed. (See Monthly catalog... (AH9) and
       CIS/Index (AH5)). Index is bi-weekly and
       cumulated annually, by name and subject
       and by number of bill or resolution. In-
       dexing is not always consistent: Index
       for 1971 listed speeches, articles, and
       resolutions about the Pentagon Papers
       under several headings.
       MH

POLITICAL SCIENCE AND GOVERNMENT CI

CI133 *U.S. Operations Mission to Vietnam. Organization and functions manual. Saigon,
1961. (Source: KimSa.)

CI134 _____. Report for the fiscal year. Saigon,
[1957?-].

General report on activities by the
U.S. government agency responsible for ad-
ministering the foreign assistance program. Name of agency changed to Agency
for International Development in 1962.

Each annual report also has separate
title. Useful for statistical report on
RVN economy.

MH-SPA

MILITARY

BIBLIOGRAPHIES

CI135 Air University Library index to military periodicals. Maxwell Air Force Base, Ala-
bama: Air University Library, 1949- .
Title varies: 1949-1962, Air University
periodical index.

Subject index to articles, news items,
and editorials in English-language military and aeronautical periodicals not indexed in most commercial indexing serv-
ices--Pref. As of 1976, 69 periodicals
(U.S. and foreign) were indexed, although
none published in Vietnam, thereby omitting several magazines isued by U.S. military organizations. Includes numerous
references under "Vietnam" and "Vietnamese" and "Indochina." It is not restricted to articles on military science only,
but includes subjects on prisoners of war,
psychology, public opinion, troop withdrawal, etc.

MH

CI136 L'Armée française en Indochine. Rédigé par
le colonel breveté Charbonneau. Paris:
Impr. Nationale, 1932. 2 vols. At head
of title: Exposition coloniale interna-

tionale de Paris de 1931. Les armées
françaises d'outre-mer.

Revision of Histoire militaire de
l'Indochine française (CI141). Revised in
order to be similar in format to other volumes in the collection Les armées françaises d'outre-mer, which are on other aspects of the French military organization
in Indochina and the other colonies and
contain information on the cavalry, engi-
neers, artillery, and supply.

Information does not supersede the material in the previous work; both should
be consulted if available.

MH

CI137 Caruso, Bruno; Daniela Viglione; and Silvia
DeBenedetto. Vietnam; bibliografia e
documenti sull' aggressione imperialista
contro il popolo vietnamita. Rome: Al-
fani Editore, [1972]. 90 p. (Interventi,
3)

Alphabetical listing by author of about
2,000 books, documents, and committee or
conference reports, in European languages,
mostly from the past three decades. Special kinds of publications include anti-
war pamphlets, books translated into
Italian, DRVN publications from Editions
en langues étrangères and the Ministry of
Foreign Affairs, and South Vietnamese
publications from Giai Phóng [Liberation]
Editions. No indexes or annotations.
Does not include periodical articles.

NjP

CI138 *Direr, Françoise, and Edith Bouché. Vietnam
1954-1971: essai d'une bibliographie pratique. Paris: Association d'Amitié
franco-vietnamienne, 1972. 35 p.

About 800 citations (Besterman).

CI139 Favitski de Probobysz, A. de. Répertoire bibliographique de la littérature militaire
et coloniale française depuis cent ans.
Paris: G. Thone, 1935. 363 p.

Author listing of 8,021 publications, of which several hundred are about Indochina. Includes works on the colonizations by the French as well as military operations published in books, periodicals, and government publications. Part 2 is a subject-geographical index.
MH

CI140   France. Ministère d'État Chargé de la Défense Nationale. État-Major de l'Armée de Terre. Service Historique. La campagne d'Indochine (1945-1954), bibliographie. [Comp. by] Michel Désiré. Chateau de Vincennes, 1971- . To be in 3 vols.

Vol. 1, 1971, 131 p.--chronology, events before 1940, basic documentation, and events from 1940-1945. A total of 465 citations to books, articles, and official publications.
mgc

CI141   Histoire militaire de l'Indochine française, des débuts à nos jours (juillet 1930), établie par les officiers de l'État-major du général de division Aubert...2. éd., revue et complétée. Hanoi: IDEO, 1930 [1931] 2 vols. On cover: Exposition coloniale internationale de Paris de 1931. First edition, 1921-22, by Officers of the État-Major du Général Puypéroux.

Description of military events from the time of Pigneau de Behaine (during the campaigns of Nguyễn Ánh). Includes tactics and strategy of battles with numerous illustrations including French officers and administrators, battle areas, walled cities, aerial photographs, and 19th century Chinese and Vietnamese drawings. Revised and issued as L'Armée française en Indochine (CI136).
MH

CI142   Hornung, Jacques. "Der Krieg in Indochina 1945-1954 in der Literatur." In Jahresbibliographie der Bibliothek für Zeitgeschichte, 33 (1961), 599-625.

Bibliographic essay, listing 194 books, periodical articles, and government publications, mostly in French or English.
MH

CI143   "Krieg in Indochina und Vietnam 1945- ." Appears in each issue of Jahresbibliographie der Bibliothek für Zeitgeschichte (Stuttgart) under the rubric "K Geschichte: F 606-609." See also "Indochina" and Vietnam" in each issue under "L Länderteil: L 227 Indochina" and "L 277 Vietnam."

Lists books, periodical articles, and newspaper articles on the war which have appeared in European languages during the year. Useful for locating articles in military periodicals. Volume for 1966 (Jahrgang 38) lists about 120 publications under F 609 (pp. 196-203) and 18 publications under L 277 (pp. 366-367).

Format varies in years previous to the mid-1960's.
MH

CI144   Legler, Anton, and Frieda Bauer. Der Krieg in Vietnam, Bericht und Bibliographie (Oktober 1968-September 1969). Frankfurt am Main: Bernard & Graefe, 1971. 146 p. (Schriften der Bibliothek für Zeitgeschichte, heft 11)

Similar to format to works by Legler and Hubinek: Pp. 3-91, narrative account of military operations in the war; pp. 93-140, bibliography of 650 titles, with emphasis on articles published in military periodicals and in German newspapers and periodicals.
MH

CI145 Legler, Anton, and K. Hubinek. Der Krieg in Vietnam; Bericht und Bibliographie bis 30.9.1968. Frankfurt am Main: Bernard & Graefe, 1969. 384 p. (Schriften der Bibliothek für Zeitgeschichte, Heft 8)

Pp. 3-226, description of the military situation--command structure, weapons, battles, size of military forces, Tết offensive of 1968--from about 1966 to 1968. Pp. 231-373, bibliography of about 2,000 books, periodical articles, and newspaper articles in European languages about the war, mostly published from 1966 to 1968. Includes many references to articles in military periodicals. Numbers at end of each entry are location numbers in the Weltkriegsbücherei in Stuttgart.

Includes 21 maps and illustrations of troop deployment, the Tết offensive, command structure, terrain affected by monsoons, area controlled by the different armies, etc.

A revised version of Bibliographie. Der Krieg in Vietnam. Stand: 1 Okt. 1966. (Vienna: Heeresgeschichteliches Museum, 1966) 94 p., hektographed.
MH

CI146 _____. "Der Krieg in Vietnam; Literaturbericht und Bibliographie bis 13.12.1966." In Jahresbibliographie der Bibliothek für Zeitgeschichte, 38 (1966), 401-480. Frankfurt am Main: Bernard & Graefe [1968].

Pp. 401-433, description of the military situation in RVN in 1965 and 1966. Pp. 343-480, bibliography of 662 books, periodical articles, and newspaper articles, mostly published in 1965 and 1966, in European languages. Titles of some books and articles in English are translated into German. Entries include location numbers of publications in the Weltkriegsbücherei (World War Library) of the Bibliothek für Zeitgeschichte (Library for Contemporary History) in Stuttgart. For

the published catalog of the Weltkriegsbücherei, see entry CI12 in this Guide.
MH

CI147 Leitenberg, Milton, and Richard Dean Burns. The Vietnam conflict; its geographical dimensions, political traumas, & military developments. Santa Barbara, Calif.: ABC Clio Press [1973]. 164 p. (Its War/Peace bibliography series [3])

Subject listing of 2,367 books, periodical and newspaper articles, government publications, and pamphlets, mostly in English or French. Intended as a working bibliography to introduce readers to the varied aspects of the war rather than as a comprehensive bibliography. Includes large number of U.S. Congressional publications, RAND corporation reports, and books and articles from the FLPH in Hanoi. Bibliographic descriptions are complete except for pagination of books.
mgc

CI148 Melin, Karin. Vietnamkonflikten i svensk opinion, 1954-1968. Bibliografi. Stolkholm: Rabén & Sjögren, 1969. 59 p. (Dokumentation och data, 1)

List of 17 periodicals, 55 books and pamphlets, 233 periodical articles, and 243 newspaper articles published in Sweden about the war in Vietnam. Includes works translated into Swedish, most of which are books originally written in the United States. Author index.
MH

CI149 *Schwanitz, Edith. Literatur über den Kampf der Völker gegen die Amerikanische Aggression in Vietnam; Auswahlbibliographie über Literatur, die 1961-1968 in der DDR und Westdeutschland erschienen ist. Leipzig: Fachschule für Bibliothekare an Wissenschaftlichen Bibliotheken, 1968. 83 p. Cited in Bibliographische Berichte, 1969, no. 2166.

CI150 U.S. Library of Congress. Congressional Research Service. Foreign Affairs Division. Impact of the Vietnam war. Prepared for the use of the Committee on Foreign Relations, United States Senate. Washington, D.C.: GPO, 1971. 36 p. 92d Congress, 1st session, committee print.

Summary statistics on expenditures, casualties, refugees, property damage, inflation, agriculture, forestry. Includes footnote references to other U.S. government publications.
MH

CI151 Varma, J., and K. Gopal. "India and the conflict in Vietnam; a select bibliography." International studies, 12 (1973), 621-655.

Lists about 900 books, periodical and newspaper articles, pamphlets, and government publications on Indian foreign policies and on expression of Indian opinion on the war from 1954-1973. Includes reports of ICSC issued by the Ministry of External Affairs, Parliamentary debates on Vietnam, and political party literature. All publications are in English. Includes publications about India's policies whether issued in India or in other countries.
MH

CI152 "Vietnam bibliography." New York University law review, 45 (1970), 749-759.

Lists 178 books and articles in English, mostly about events in Vietnam since 1954; emphasis is on writings on the Vietnam war from the standpoint of international law.
MH-L

DICTIONARIES

CI153 *Đỗ Thiếu Liệt. Tự-điển quân-sự pháp-anh-việt; French-English-Vietnamese military dictionary. Saigon: Ziên-Hồng, [1957]. 529 p. (Source: DLC SAAL, Mar. 59.)

CI154 *Nguyễn Hữu Trong. Danh-từ quân sự, chuyên môn Việt-Anh, Anh-Việt. Vietnamese-English, English-Vietnamese military subjects, technical terms. Saigon, Đời mới, 1969-71. 2 vols. (Source: Thư-mục 1969; Thanh-long, cat. no. 27, Mai 1973; NIC.)

CI155 *Nhóm Hoài-Bão. Đặc ngữ quân-sự Mỹ-Việt [American-Vietnamese military terms]. Saigon: Minh Tâm, 1967. 186 p. (Source: TTQGVN, 1.)

CI156 U.S. Military Assistance Command, Vietnam. VC/NVA terminology glossary. 3d. ed. Saigon, 1971. 2 vols.

Vietnamese--French--English glossary, with definitions based upon interpretations derived from usage in captured documents. Additional information, vol. 2, pp. 335-610: historic dates, military ranks and positions, political and military abbreviations, weapons abbreviations, and map symbols.
MH-V

CI157 *Vũ Anh Tuấn. Danh từ quân sự Anh-Việt; English-Vietnamese military terminology. Saigon: Văn-Nghệ, 1968. 380 p. (Source: Thư mục 1968.)

CI158 Vũ Văn Lê. The military interpreter; danh từ quân sự Anh-Việt; English-Vietnamese military handbook. Saigon: Khai-trí, 1967. 244 p.

Divided into 22 sections: command and staff, activities in the office, training centers, exercise, air force, navy, artillergy, etc. Brief phrases with corresponding term in Vietnamese.
MH-V; NIC

WEAPONS

CI159 U.S. Dept. of the Army. Guide to selected Viet Cong equipment and explosive de-

vices. Washington, D.C.: [GPO], 1966.
100 p. (DA Pam 381-11)

Illustrated catalog of 45 grenades,
mines, demolitions, and traps used by the
armies of the National Front for the Liberation of South Vietnam.
MH

CI160 ____. Handbook on the North Vietnamese
armed forces. [Washington, D.C.? 1961]
70 p. (Its DA Pam 30-53) Unclassified
from Confidential.

General information on the armed forces.
About 60 photographs of training, weapons
and materiel, and uniforms and insignia.
DAL

CI161 ____. Recognition guide of ammunition avail-
able to, or in use by, the Viet Cong.
Washington, D.C.: [GPO], 1966. 148 p.
(DA Pamphlet 381-12)

Illustrated catalog of 65 types of am-
munition and mines, mostly of Russian or
Chinese Communist manufacture.
MH

CI162 ____. Weapons and equipment recognition
guide, Southeast Asia: Communist China,
North Vietnam, South Vietnam, Cambodia,
Laos, Thailand, Burma, Malaya. Washington, D.C.: GPO, 1966. 318 p. (DA Pam
381-10)

Illustrated catalog of weapons--omit-
ting hand weapons--and vehicles, mostly of
European or United States origin. Includes only 2 weapons manufactured in
DRVN, none from RVN.

Substantially the same text has been
published as Guide to combat weapons of
Southeast Asia, ed. Donald B. MacLean
(Forest Grove, Ore.: Normount Technical
Publications, 1971), 348 p.
MH

CI163 Vietnam (Republic). Bộ Quốc-Phòng. Bộ Tổng
Tham Mưu. Quân Lực Việt-Nam Cộng Hòa.
Phòng 2. Chiến-cụ do Cộng-sản Bắc Việt
xử-dụng tại miền Nam hoặc có thể đang
được xử dụng tại miền Bắc Việt-Nam; War
materiel used by the Vietcong in South
Vietnam or presumably available to North
Vietnam. [Saigon? 1968?]. 406 p. Updated edition of a publication originally
issued in 1966. Text in Vietnamese and
English.

Pictures and descriptions of weapons
(hand guns, field guns, missiles, and
mines), vehicles, and other materiel
(compasses, boats, protective masks, flame
throwers, and radios). Text includes
statement of known use by "Viet-Cong" and
name of country where manufactured.
MH

LAW CJ

In this Guide, a distinction is made between
works on government and on law that does not neces-
sarily exist in Vietnamese society. This chapter
includes sources for texts of laws (bibliographies,
treatises, indexes, compilations, and official gazettes) and treaties. The major category of legal
publication that is excluded--for reasons of space--
is legal codes. Instead of listing several dozen
legal codes from the Gouvernement général de l'Indochine to the present day, this Guide lists the indexes to legislation, compilations of laws, and
bibliographies which refer to the codes. On the
other hand, judicial codes during the French colonial era have been included because of their importance
in restructuring Vietnamese law and society.

As with political science, the best sources
for law in the DRVN are the bibliographies by Jane
Godfrey Keyes and by Phan Thiện Châu and the index
to translations by JPRS--Transdex--which are cited
elsewhere in this Guide.

C SOCIAL SCIENCES

BIBLIOGRAPHIES

MAJOR SOURCES

CJ1   Cordier Henri. _Bibliotheca indosinica._

      See AA23 for complete description. For
publications on law, see 3: 1847-1860 and
4: 2933-2934, "Jurisprudence," for pre-
French law, and 4: 2591-2602, 2979-2980,
"Justice," for law under the French.
    MH

CJ2   Boudet, Paul, and Rémy Bourgeois. _Biblio-
graphie de l'Indochine française._

      See AA22 for complete description. For
publications on law, see "Droit" and "Législation" in each volume.
    MH

CJ3   Blaustein, A. P. "Current legal bibliography: Vietnam." _Law library journal_, 61
(1968), 20-22.

      Lists 9 serials published in the Repub-
lic of Vietnam and 29 basic texts on RVN
law.
    MH-L

CJ4   Bongert, Yvonne. "Indochine." In _Introduc-
tion bibliographique à l'histoire du droit
et à l'ethnologie juridique; bibliographical introduction to legal history and eth-
nology_, ed. John Gilissen, vol. 3, section E.11. Brussels: Université Libre de
Bruxelles, Éditions de l'Institut de Sociologie, 1967.

      Lists about 660 publications on Indo-
china and Vietnam. Includes compilations
of laws and other legal publications.
Comprises mostly French-language entries.
Entries are not always verified and some
are listed twice with different titles or
descriptions. Useful for citations on
law, legal history, administration, family
law, and social classes.
    MH-L

CJ5   Ginsburgs, George. "Soviet sources on the
law of North Vietnam." _Asian Survey_, 13
(1973), 659-676, 980-988.

      Bibliographic essay of about 70 books
and periodical articles on law in the
DRVN, 1945-1972. Writer observes that of
74 titles published during that time, 55
were published between 1955 and 1964 and
42 were about constitutional law. Commentary includes enumeration of legal
texts translated into Russian.
    MH

CJ6   Grandin, A. _Bibliographie générale des sciences juridiques, politiques, économiques
et sociales de 1800 à 1925/26._ Paris:
Sirey, 1926. 3 vols. _Suppléments 1-19,
1926/27-1950. Ibid._, 1928-1950.

      Subject listing of French-language
books, theses, government publications,
periodicals, and periodical articles if
separately published. Entries are complete, except for pagination. Considered
to be one of the most important bibliographies for French legal and political
publications. In main volumes, vols. 1
and 2 are the classified bibliography,
vol. 3 is the index volume, arranged by
author, title, and subject.

      Most citations about Indochina are in
vol. 2, pp. 267-327, under "Colonies françaises," under various subheadings, including "Indochine," pp. 318-325. Other
citations may be located in vol. 2, "Table
alphabétique par ordre de matières," under
subject headings such as "Questions politiques (Chine)," "Extrême-Orient," "Monnaies coloniales," "Protectorats," "Immi-
gration," or "Statistiques coloniales."
Extensive cross-references from subjects
such as "Chemin de fer," "Budget," "Tribunaux," "Question indigène," "Impôt en
Annam," and "Femme annamite" to "Indochine."

LAW CJ

Citations for an author's works may be located in vol. 3, pp. 237-691, in the "Table alphabétique par noms d'auteurs, des anonymes et des publications périodiques," although works about that person will be found in the "Table alphabétique par ordre de matières."
MH

CJ7   Harvard University. Law School. Library. Current legal bibliography. Cambridge, Mass. 1960- . Nine times yearly.

CJ8   ____. ____. ____. Annual legal bibliography. Ibid., 1961- . annual.

Classified subject listing of books and periodical articles received in the Library. Annual issue includes geographical (country) index. Coverage of legal subjects is broad in scope and includes constitutional law, social law, politics and government, commerce and industry, public administration, international relations, and the Vietnam war. Includes articles and books in all European languages. Citations are not always bibliographically complete, especially for U.S. Congressional publications.

CJ9   Jumper, Roy. Bibliography on the political and administrative history of Vietnam.
See DB9 for complete description.
MH

CJ10   Nguyen Nhu Dung. "Vietnamese law." Quarterly journal of the Library of Congress, 23 (1966): 337-339.

Bibliographic essay, listing 22 legal publications in the Library of Congress for studying French Indochina and the Republic of Vietnam.
MH

CJ11   [Szladits, Karoly, 1911- .] A bibliography on foreign and comparative law books and

articles in English [by] Charles Szladits. Dobbs Ferry, N.Y.: Oceana Publications, for the Parker School of Foreign and Comparative Law, Columbia University, 1955- . At head of title: Parker School Studies in Foreign and Comparative Law.

Contents: Vol. 1 (1955) is retrospective listing until 1952; vol. 2, 1953-59 (1962); vol. 3, 1960-65 (1968); vol. 4, 1966-71 (1975); supplement for 1973 published separately (1976); other annual supplements to be in American journal of comparative law, in section titled, "Foreign law in English."

Classified subject listing, with geographic index in each volume. Vol. 1 has no references under "Vietnam" but vols. 2 to 4 have about 50 references each. Useful for finding references to texts of legal decisions, constitutions, tax and patent decisions in international law reviews, such as the International Labour Office legislative series.
MH-L

OTHER SOURCES

CJ12   Index to foreign legal periodicals and collections of essays. London: Institute of Advanced Legal Studies, University of London, 1960- .

CJ13   Index to legal periodicals. New York: Wilson, 1909- .

DICTIONARIES

CJ14   Huỳnh Khắc Dụng. Mục-lục hình-sự [Contents of jurisprudence]. Saigon: Khai-Trí, [1970]. 2 vols.

Glossary of terms in jurisprudence, with references to the law in force or to earlier statements of the law under the French. In many instances, the text of the law is reprinted, e.g. "Báo-chỉ" [The press], vol. 1, pp. 95-111, includes references to laws passed between 1881 and 1941 and the text of the Press laws of 1956 and 19 February 1964. Coverage is broad, including topics such as public security, breach of contract, rental of cyclos, black markets, associations [hụi nợ], fish sauce, and Supreme Court.

Is not an index to judicial decisions, although some decisions are given. Sources include Vietnamese and French official publications and non-official publications such as Penant and Dalloz.
MH-L

CJ15   Trần Thúc Linh. "Danh từ pháp luật lược giải" [Explanation of legal terminology]. Quê hương, nos. 25 (7/61) - 44 (2/63 [?].

Alphabetical list of French legal terms, translated into Vietnamese, with lengthy explanations and examples in Vietnamese or foreign law. Appears in each issue listed above; no issues after no. 44 available for verification.
MH; KimSa, Mục-lục...; NIC has book edition: Saigon: Khai-Trí, 1965. 1274 p.

CJ16   Trương Tiến Đạt. "Tự-ngữ La Việt [Latin-Vietnamese dictionary]. PLTS, 18, no. 2 (1965), 1-50, separately paged; 18 no. 3 (1965), 51-62 sep. pag., 18 no. 4 (1965), 63-80 sep. paged.

Translations of Latin words and phrases into Vietnamese. According to the preface, the work was to have been in three parts: a Latin-to-Vietnamese dictionary, a subject index in Vietnamese, and an index in French to the Vietnamese terms in part 2. No more had been published in PLTS through the issues for vol. 23 (1970). Ends with definition for custodia honesta.
MH-L

CJ17   *Viện Luật Học, Hanoi. Từ điển thuật ngữ luật học Nga-Trung-Pháp-Việt [Russian-Chinese-

French-Vietnamese legal dictionary]. Hanoi: Khoa-học Xã-hội, 1971. 336 p. (Source: NIC Aug. 1972.)

CJ18   *Vietnam (Republic). Bộ Tư-Pháp. Tự vựng danh-từ pháp luật thông dụng [Dictionary of juridical terms]. Saigon: Phương Nam văn nghệ, 1956. 66 p. (Source: Cường, Soc Sci.)

CJ19   Vũ Văn Mẫu. Từ-điển Pháp-Việt, pháp--chính--kinh--tài--xã-hội; dictionnaire français-vietnamien des sciences juridiques, politiques, économiques, financières et sociologiques. Saigon: Viện Đại-học Vạn Hạnh, 1970. 895 p.

Translation of French terms into Vietnamese, with numerous examples of usage. Revision of 1955 work (CJ20).
MH-V

CJ20   Vũ Văn Mẫu; Nguyễn Văn Trác; and Đào Văn Tập. Từ-điển Pháp-Việt pháp-luật chính-trị kinh-tế; dictionnaire français-vietnamien des sciences juridiques, politiques, économiques. [Saigon?] Université nationale du Viêtnam, 1955. 3 vols.

Terms given in French, with translations into Vietnamese. No explanation of usages. Revised in 1970 (CJ19).
MH-L

GENERAL WORKS

TRADITIONAL VIETNAM

CJ21   Phan Huy Chú. "Hình-luật chí" [Penal code]. Chapters 33-38 of Lịch-triều hiến-chương loại-chí [Monographs of the institutions of the dynasties].

See AD1 for description of main work. Penal codes of the Lý, Trần, and Lê dynasties. Translated in three versions: the complete work published in quốc-ngữ in Hanoi in 1960-61 (See AD1); chapters

33-38 by R. Deloustal in 1903; and chapter 33 by Cao Nãi Quang in 1957.

Deloustal's translation is titled: Recueil des principales ordonnances royales edictées depuis la promulgation du Code annamite et en vigueur au Tonkin, annotée et complétée d'une table alphabétique et analytique de ce recueil et du Code annamite (traduction Philastre) par Gabriel Michel. Hanoi: Schneider, 1903. 221, 32 p.[1]

Cao Nãi Quang's translation is titled: Lịch-triều hiến-chương loại-chỉ. Lương Thần Cao Nãi Quang phiên âm và dịch nghĩa. Saigon: Nhã in Bao Vinh, 1957. 568, 48 p. At head of title: Đại Học Viện Saigon, Trường Luật-khoa Đại Học. Chapter 33 is translated on pp. 517-563, along with photographs of the original Sino-Vietnamese text and romanized transcription of that text.[2]

[1]Cited in Huỳnh Khắc Dụng, Sử-liệu Việt-Nam, p. 70 [2]MH-L (Entry under: Vietnam (Republic). Laws, statutes, etc. Compilations.)

FRENCH INDOCHINA

CJ22   Dareste, Pierre. Traité de droit colonial. Paris: Recueil Dareste, 1931. 3 vols.

History and description of French colonial law. Footnotes refer to Dareste's Recueil Dareste de législation, de doctrine et de jurisprudence coloniale. Contains chapters on the government of the colonies, local- and colony-level administration, indigenous institutions, metropolitan legislation as it affects the colonies, public colonial law, judicial organization, administrative law, civil service, taxes, property, labor legislation, mining, public health, and other topics. Index, pp. 845-877.
MH-L

CJ23   Girault, Arthur. Principes de colonisation et de législation coloniale. 5. éd. Paris: Sirey, 1927-30. 5 vols.[1]; 1. éd. Paris, 1894; 6. éd. Paris, 1943. 202 p.

The fifth edition, the most extensive edition, contains material on French Indochina in vols. 1-3. Includes a history of colonization by the French and a description of the legal and administrative system.
[1]MH

CJ24   Institut Colonial International. Les lois organiques des colonies; documents officiels précédés de notices historiques. Brussels, 1906-22. 6 vols. (Bibliothèque coloniale internationale, 8. sér.)

Vol. 2, pp. 485-580, contains texts of the organic law of Cochinchina, Indochina as a whole, Tongking, and Saigon, in that order. Subjects include the composition of the Conseil superieur de l'Indochine and Conseil privé de la Cochinchine and the organization of the colonial administration, 1887-1900. The reader is referred to the Ordonnances of 1825 and 1827 on the administrative organization of the Antilles and Réunion which were the basis of administration in the French colonies (pp. 59-136). Texts on pp. 21 to 54 give legislation passed by the Ministère des Colonies and Conseil supérieur des Colonies. Legislation passed referring to other colonies but which might also have had an effect upon Indochina are in vols. 2 and 3 and should be consulted. Additional references are in vol. 3, pp. 121-133: "Conseil colonial en Cochinchine."
MH-L

CJ25   _____. Le régime des protectorats. Brussels, 1899. 2 vols. (Bibliothèque Coloniale Internationale, 4. sér.)

Vol. 1, pp. 147-502, texts of treaties--
beginning with the treaty between Louis XVI
and "Gia Long," 28 November 1787--decrees,
circulars, arrêtés, and other legal notices
issued in the protectorates in Indochina
and in some instances in Cochinchina. Includes a 10-page historical introduction
by J. Chailley-Bert. Contains documents
on the government of the protectorates,
functioning of administration, control of
résidents, European or indigenous consultative bodies, and administration of
justice.
MH-L

DEMOCRATIC REPUBLIC OF VIETNAM

CJ26 *Nhã nước và pháp luật [The government and the
law]. [Hanoi?]: Nhã Xuất bản Lao Động,
[1971-]. v. 1-4. "Tập nghiên cứu pháp
lý của Hội Luật Gia Việt-Nam."

Vol. 1, Discussion of the constitution
of 1959; vol. 2, Lenin and law in Vietnam;
vol. 3, Hồ Chí Minh's role in building socialism in Vietnam; vol. 4, 25 years of
building a legal system in V.N. (Source:
NIC Sept. 1972.)

CONSTITUTIONS

Where possible, an original and a secondary
source in Vietnamese and French and/or English is
cited.

DEMOCRATIC REPUBLIC OF VIETNAM

CJ27 Vietnam (Democratic Republic). Constitution,
1946.
[Vietnamese-language official text not
located.]
_____. _____. _____. Constitution of the
Vietnam Democratic Republic, adopted by
the National Assembly at its meeting on
November 8th, 1946, at Hanoi, capital of
the Democratic Republic of Vietnam and
proclaimed on November 9th, 1946. New

York: Vietnam news service, [1947?].
7 p. At head of title: Vietnam Americain
[sic] Friendship Association.

See index for other sources which reprint the DRVN constitution of 1946.
MH

CJ28 _____, 1959.
[Vietnamese-language official text not
available.]
_____. _____. _____. Constitution of the
Democratic Republic of Vietnam. Hanoi:
FLPH, 1960. 69 p. Also in French.
_____. _____. _____. "Constitution de la
République Démocratique du Vietnam
(31 décembre 1959)." Notes et études
documentaires, no. 2989 (10 mai 1963).
16 p.
MH

STATE OF VIETNAM

CJ29 Vietnam (State). Constitution, 1949. "Dụ số
1 ngày mồng 1 tháng bảy năm 1949 tổ-chức
và điều-hành các cơ quan công quyền Việt-
Nam" [Ordinance number 1, July 1, 1949,
for the organization and operation of public institutions of Vietnam], and "Dụ số
2 ngày mồng 1 tháng bảy năm 1949 tổ chức
qui chế các công-sở" [Ordinance number 2,
July 1, 1949, relating to the organization
of the public administration]. In Vietnam (State), Laws, statutes, etc., Hành-
chính pháp điển [Administrative code],
(Saigon, 1953), pp. 65-76.[1]

French-language text in ibid.,
pp. 385-398.[1]

English-language translation in Peaslee, Amos J., Constitutions of nations,
2d ed., (The Hague, 1956), pp. 727-749.[2]

Supersedes the sắc-lệnh [Decree-law] of
23-5-1948, establishing the Central provisional government of Vietnam [Chính-phủ
trung-ương lâm-thời Việt-Nam], the Vietnamese and French texts of which are re-

printed in H<u>ành-chính pháp-điển</u>, pp. 25-43
and 345-363.
[1]MH-L [2]MH

REPUBLIC OF VIETNAM

CJ30 *Trương Tiến Đạt. <u>Hiến pháp chú thích</u> [The
Constitution annotated]. Saigon: [the
author], 1967. 472 p. (Source: <u>Thư mục
1967.</u>)

CJ31 *Vietnam (Republic). Constitution, 1955.
"Hiến-ước tạm thời số 1" [Provisional
charter no. 1]. <u>CBVNCH</u>, Oct. 26, 1955,
p. 2.

Cited by Trần Ngọc Chi in <u>Pháp-quy
chính-yếu mục-lục</u> (CJ88).

CJ32 ____, 1956. "Hiến-pháp Việt-Nam Cộng-Hòa"
[Constitution of the Republic of Vietnam].
<u>CBVNCH</u>, 26-10-1956, p. 2661.

____. ____. <u>Hiến-pháp Việt-Nam Cộng-Hòa</u>.
Saigon: Bộ Thông Tin, 1956. 35 p.[2]

____. ____. <u>Constitution</u>. [Saigon: Kim
Lai Ấn Quán], 1956. 63 p. Also includes
rules of the National Assembly, pp. 27-64.[3]

____. ____. <u>Constitution, tr. by the
Bureau of the Constituent Assembly</u>. [Sai-
gon] 1956. 35 p.[3]

____. ____. <u>The constitution of the Re-
public of Vietnam</u>. Saigon: Secretariat
of State for Information, [1956?]. 40 p.[3]

____. ____. <u>The constitution of the Re-
public of Vietnam, October 26, 1956</u>.
Washington, D.C.: Embassy of the Republic
of Viet-Nam [1956] 3, 14 p. Also in <u>News
from Vietnam</u>, published by the Embassy,
vol. 3, no. 4 (November 17, 1956).[3]

____. ____. "Constitution de la République
du Viet-Nam, 26 octobre 1956." <u>Notes et
études documentaires</u>, no. 2278
(2 avril 1957).[4]
[1]Trần Ngọc Chi [2]Cường, Soc sci [3]MH-L
[4]MH

CJ33 ____, Nov. 4, 1963. "Hiến-ước tạm-thời số 1,
4-11-1963" [Provisional charter no. 1,
4-11-1963]. <u>CBVNCH</u>, 4-11-1963, p. 4;
<u>QPVT</u>, 6 (1963), 120-121. English-language
text ("Provisional charter no. 1"), in
<u>Constitutions of Asian countries</u>.
MH-L; NIC

CJ34 ____, July 2, 1964. "Hiến-ước tạm-thời
số 2, tu chỉnh Hiến-ước tạm-thời số 1 ngày
4-11-1963" [Provisional charter no. 2,
replacing provisional charter no. 1 of
4-11-63]. <u>CBVNCH</u>, 2-7-1964, p. 478; <u>QPVT</u>,
7 (1964), 22-23. English-language text in
<u>Constitutions of Asian countries</u>.
MH-L; NIC

CJ35 ____, Aug. 16, 1964. "Hiến-chương Việt-Nam
Cộng-Hòa ngày 16 tháng 8 năm 1964" [Pro-
visional charter of the Republic of Viet-
nam, 16-8-1964]. <u>CBVNCH</u>, 16-8-1964,
p. 3044-51; <u>QPVT</u>, 7 (1964), 202-216.
English-language text ("Charter of
August 16, 1964") in <u>Constitutions of
Asian countries</u>.
MH-L; NIC

CJ36 ____, Oct. 20, 1964. "Hiến-chương lâm thời
ngày 20-10-1964" [Provisional charter of
Oct. 20, 1964]. <u>CBVNCH</u>, 20-10-1964,
p. 3878-82; <u>QPVT</u>, 7 (1964), 225-243.
English-language text ("Provisional
charter of October 20, 1964") in <u>Consti-
tutions of Asian countries</u>.
MH-L; NIC

CJ37 ____, 1965. "Ước pháp tạm thời, 19-6-1965"
[Provisional constitution of 19-6-1965].
<u>CBVNCH</u>, 19-6-1965, p. 2663; <u>QPVT</u>, 8
(1965), 87-95. English-language text
("Provisional constitution") in <u>Constitu-
tions of Asian countries</u>.
MH-L; NIC

CJ38 _____, 1967. "Hiến pháp Quốc Hội Lập-hiến"
[Constitution of the Provisional Assembly].
CBVNCH, 18-3-1967, p. 1586; QPVT, 10
(1967), 37-71.

_____. _____. _____. "Hiến-pháp Việt-Nam
Cộng-Hòa ban hành ngày 1 tháng 4 năm 1967."
In Niên-giám hành-chánh 1967 [Yearbook of
Administration 1967]. Saigon: Học Viện
Quốc-gia Hành Chánh, 1967.

_____. _____. _____. Constitution of the
Republic of Vietnam, promulgated
April 1, 1967. [Saigon: Ministry of In-
formation and Chiêu Hồi, 1967]. 24 p.
Also a Vietnamese-language version pub-
lished by this Ministry. 46 p.

_____. _____. _____. Constitution of the
Republic of Vietnam. Prepared by the Of-
fice of the Staff Judge Advocate, USMACV,
[n. p., 1967] 26 p. "Unofficial American
Embassy translation, 1 April 1967."
MH-L; NIC

GENERAL WORKS

CJ39 Blaustein, Albert P., and Gisbert H. Flanz.
Constitutions of the countries of the
world. Dobbs Ferry, N.Y.: Oceana,
1971- .

English-language texts of constitutions
currently in force, with a constitutional
chronology and annotated bibliography for
each country. DRVN constitution of 1959
is edited by Benjamin R. Beede, with a
bibliography of 19 English- and French-
language publications on the constitutions
of 1946 and 1959 and the government of the
DRVN. RVN constitution of 1967 is edited
by Nguyễn Văn Huyền; the bibliography of
21 English- and French-language publications includes references to previous
constitutions back to 1956.
MH-L

CJ40 Peaslee, Amos J. Constitutions of nations.
2d. ed. [The Hague: Nijhoff, 1956].
3 v.

English-language texts of constitutions;
Vietnam (Associated State) constitution of
1949 on pp. 727-749. DRVN not listed.
First edition of Peaslee, 1950, does not
include constitutions of Vietnam.

_____. _____. Rev. 3d. ed. [Ibid., 1966]
3 v.

Constitution of DRVN (1959), vol. 2,
pp. 1194-1215; Constitutional Charter of
RVN, June 19, 1965, pp. 1216-1223.
MH

OTHER SOURCES

CJ41 Constitutions of Asian countries, prepared by
the Secretariat of the Asian-African Legal
Consultative Committee, New Delhi. Bombay: Tripathi, 1968. 1171 p. (English-
language texts of constitutions and provisional charters of RVN, 1963-1965, and
of 1959 Constitution of DRVN.)

CJ42 Puget, Henry, ed. Les constitutions d'Asie
et d'Australie. Paris: Éditions de
l'Épargne, 1975. 925 p. (Travaux et recherches de l'Institut de Droit Comparé
de l'Université de Paris, XXVI). (French-
language texts of 1956 Constitution of RVN
and amendments of 1960 and of 1959 Constitution of DRVN.)

LEGISLATION

INDEXES TO LAWS

It is necessary to use indexes to locate specific laws because of the large number of laws which
have been promulgated during the centuries and because laws are published chronologically in the official gazettes as enacted. In addition to publication in official gazettes, laws may be found in
compilations, either published annually or spanning
several years, and in the bibliographies at the beginning of this chapter.

The arrangement in this section is according
to historical periods: First, the compilations of
historical times until the beginning of French rule

in Cochinchina, followed by indexes, compilations, and official gazettes and administrative bulletins during the colonial government, governments from 1945 to 1954 under colonial rule, the DRVN, and the RVN and predecessors.

Official gazettes and administrative bulletins are cited at length because of their importance to legal research. They contain laws and decrees as they are issued; regulations and decisions of the ministries which are applicable to the laws; changes in government organization; proclamations; announcements concerning the government budget; notices of awards to individuals; and other legal notices.

Only one citation is listed for an official source for laws of the DRVN, although the bibliographies by Keyes, Phan Thiện Châu, and JPRS do refer to separately published laws.

TRADITIONAL VIETNAM

CJ43   Đại-Nam Hoàng-Việt Luật-lệ [Laws and regulations of the Emperor of Đại Nam].

Generally referred to as the "Gia-long code," promulgated in 1812. Two translations, both in French, are all that seem to exist at present: 1) Annam. Laws, statutes, etc. Codes. Hoàng-Việt Luật-lệ; code annamite, lois et règlements du royaume d'Annam, trad. du texte chinois original par G. Aubaret.... Paris: Impr. Nationale, 1865. 2 vols., and 2) Annam. Laws, statutes, etc. Codes. Le Code annamite. Nouv. trad. complète...par P. L. Philastre. Paris: Leroux, 1876. 2 v. (Études sur le droit annamite et chinois). Second edition, ibid., 1909. Repr. of second edition, Taipei: Ch'eng-wen Publ. Co., 1967. Vol. 2 of the Philastre translation contains: G. Michel, "Table alphabétique et analytique des matières contenues dans le code annamite (trad. Philastre) et dans le Recueil des ordonnances des rois d'Annam en vigueur au Tonkin au 1er janvier 1902." Hanoi: Schneider, 1902. 32 p.

The index by Michel is also included in Deloustal, Raymond. Recueil des principales ordonnances.... (CJ21). MH-L; DLC

CJ44   Khâm-định Đại-Nam hội-điển sự-lệ [Official administrative repertory of organic texts of the Six Ministers and the special services of the capital promulgated from 1802-1851]. Also known as Đại-Nam hội-điển sự-lệ, or Hội-điển sự-lệ.

"The major primary source for the study of traditional Vietnamese government."-- Alexander B. Woodside, Vietnam and the Chinese model (Cambridge, 1971), p. 324. Contains all the important statutes and administrative occurrences of Vietnamese history from 1802 to 1851. Divided into bureaucratic commissions, finance, education and foreign affairs, military problems, judicial matters, and public works-- ibid.

Books 132-136, on the protocols for reception of foreigners at Hue, nomination of ambassadors, and diplomatic ceremonies and banquets, reprinted and translated as: "Nhu viễn" trong Khâm-định Đại-Nam hội-điển sự-lệ, Bửu Cầm & Tạ Quang Phát dịch. (Saigon: Viện Khảo Cổ, 1965-1966), 2 vols. (Tủ sách Viện Khảo Cổ, 10, 13) Text in quốc-ngữ and in Sino-Vietnamese characters.[1]

Books 128-131 on relations with China in the 19th century, translated and reprinted as: "Bang giao" trong Khâm định Đại-Nam hội-điển sự-lệ, dịch giả Nguyễn Đình Diệm. (Saigon: Phu Quốc-Vụ-Khanh Đặc trách Văn-hoá, 1968). 381 p. (Tủ sách Viện Khảo Cổ, 16) Text in quốc-ngữ and in Sino-Vietnamese characters.[2]

Revised summary of Khâm-định Đại-Nam hội-điển sự-lệ written in 1909 in Sino-Vietnamese as Đại-Nam điển-lệ toát-yếu [A summary of the statutes of Đại-Nam]. Nguyễn Sĩ Giác phiên âm và dịch nghĩa

(Saigon: Viện Đại Học Saigon, Trường Đại-
Học Luật-khoa, 1962). 571 p.[3]
[1]MH-V [2]MH-V [3]NIC

CJ45 *Minh Mệnh. Minh Mệnh chính yếu [Edicts of
the Minh Mệnh Emperor]. Comp. in 1898 by
the Quốc-sử-quán, the Bureau of National
History, comprised of 12 volumes, 25 chapters.[1]

Modern translation into quốc-ngữ, with
the original Chinese characters reprinted,
in Saigon, Khối Văn-Hóa, 1972-1974.[2]

Vol. 1, Laws and edicts about rites,
first part, trans. by Hoàng Du Đồng and Hà
Ngọc Xuyển (1972, 535 p.); Vol. 2, Rites,
second part, trans. by Vũ Quang Khanh and
Võ Khắc Văn (1972, 410 p.); Vol. 3, Agriculture, rites, music, and education,
trans. by Võ Khắc Văn and Lê Phục Thiện
(1974, 731 p.); Vol. 4, Army organization,
justice, finance, trans. by Đào Vũ Luyện
and Hồ Tánh (1974, 509 p.); Vol. 5, Administration, culture, wars, trans. by Hà
Ngọc Xuyển and Đào Vũ Luyện (1974, 559 p.);
Vol. 6, National defense and foreign affairs, trans. by Hoàng Văn Hoè and Nguyễn
Quang Tô (1974, 729 p.).
[1]Huỳnh Khắc Dụng, Sử-liệu Việt-Nam,
p. 138 (DB8) [2]Gélinas, List 033,
March 15, 1975

CJ46 Tự Đức. Tự Đức thánh chế văn tam tập [Edicts
of the Tự Đức Emperor].

Modern translation into quốc-ngữ by Bùi
Tấn Niên, with the original Chinese char-
acters reprinted, in Saigon, Phủ Quốc-Vụ-
Khanh Đặc Trách Văn-Hóa, 1971- .

Vol. 1 (chapters 1-8), edicts of the
Emperor from about 1876 to 1882 (1971,
275 + CCCLXX p.);[1] Vol. 2 (chapters 9-14),
administrative documents--including funer-
al orations, proclamations, petitions--
and names of princes (1972, 572 p.);[2]
Vol. 3 in preparation.[2]
[1]MH-V [2]Gélinas, list no. 033

CJ47 Vietnam. Laws, statutes, etc. Quốc-triều
hình luật. (Original publication date in
dispute.)

Collection of laws of the later Lê dynasty (1428-1788).

Two major translations exist: 1) Quốc-
triều hình-luật (Hình-luật triều Lê),
Lưỡng-Thần Cao Nãi Quang phiên âm và dịch
nghĩa [translator]...[Saigon]: Trường
Luật-khoa Đại-Học, [1956]. 524 p.; at
head of title: Việt-Nam Đại-Học-Viện.

Comprised of romanized Sino-Vietnamese,
quốc-ngữ, and of photographs of original
text of ms. A. 341 in collection of EFEO.
Extensive introduction by Vũ Văn Mẫu discusses the historical background and various dates ascribed to its publication,
usually thought to have been 1776 to 1787;
concludes (p. xiii) that work was probably
first completed under Lê Thánh Tông and
merely reprinted in later years.

2) Deloustal, Raymond. "La justice
dans l'ancien Annam: traduction et commentaire du code des Lê." BEFEO, 8
(1908)-22 (1922); see Jumper no. 651 for
list of page references or BEFEO 22 (1922),
1-40 for index to material in text. Publication began as translation of book 33
of "Hình-luật chí" [penal code] of Lịch-
triều hiến-chương loại-chí by Phan Huy
Chú (AD1). Beginning with BEFEO 9 (1909),
91, Deloustal translated the text of Quốc-
triều điều-luật, a variant edition of
Quốc-triều hình-luật, discovered in 1908.
Deloustal's footnotes and comments on
other historical works are extensive.
MH

FRENCH INDOCHINA

Indexes

CJ48 *Indochina. Laws, statutes, etc. Répertoire
chronologique et alphabétique des lois,
décrets, ordonnances, etc., promulgués ou

appliqués en Indochine depuis l'occupation
de la Cochinchine (1861) jusqu'au 31 décembre 1917, par H. Petitjean. Saigon:
A. Portail, 1918. 913 p.

Continued by Répertoire by Nicolas for
1919-1925 (CJ49*). (Source: DLC, NN.)

CJ49 *____. ____. Répertoire chronologique et
alphabétique des lois, décrets, ordonnances, etc., promulgués en Indochine du
1er janvier 1919 au 31 décembre 1925.
Hanoi: IDEO, 1926. 326 p. [Comp. Raoul
Nicolas.]

Succeeds Répertoire by Petitjean
(CJ48*)--"Notice" in Recueil général,
1927-28 (CJ62).

CJ50 *____. ____. Répertoire chronologique et
alphabétique des lois, décrets et arrêtés
ministériels promulgués en Indochine du
1er janvier 1926 au 1er janvier 1935, par
Raoul Nicolas. Hanoi: IDEO, 1935.
565 p.

Continuation of Répertoire by Nicolas
(CJ49*); continued by a Répertoire by Ni-
colas for 1935-1944 (CJ51*). (Source:
DLC; NIC.)

CJ51 *____. ____. Répertoire chronologique et
alphabétique des lois, décrets et arrêtés
ministériels promulgués en Indochine du
1er janvier 1935 au 1er janvier 1944, par
Raoul Nicolas. Hanoi: IDEO, 1943- .

1re ptie., Partie chronologique, 1943.
513 p. Continuation of other Répertoires
by Nicolas (CJ50*). (Source: Bongert,
DLC.)

CJ52 *Marty, F. Répertoire analytique de législation et de réglementation de la Cochinchine et du Cambodge. Saigon: Impr. Coloniale, 1896-97. 2 vols. 1er fasc., du
1er janvier 1889 au 31 décembre 1895;
2e fasc., Répertoire [etc.] de la Cochinchine, Cambodge et du Bas-Laos, du
1er janvier au 31 décembre 1896.

Does not include texts of legislation.
"Notice" in Recueil général...1928.
(Source: BN.)

CJ53 *Michel, Gabriel. Répertoire des lois, décrets et ordonnances rendus applicables à
la colonie et publié au Bulletin officiel depuis l'occupation de la Cochinchine jusqu'au 1er janvier 1892. Saigon:
Rey, Curiol et Cie, 1892. 103 p.;
3 supp., 1892-98.

1st part, dates of promulgation; 2nd
part, chronological table; 3rd part, alphabetical table (Cordier). (Source:
BN.)

CJ54 *____. Répertoire des lois, décrets et ordonnances rendus applicables aux possessions françaises de l'Indochine depuis
l'occupation de la Cochinchine jusqu'au
1er janvier 1902. [n.p., n.d.] 1. supp.,
1902-07, [n.p., n.d.] 2. suppl., 1908-13
[n.p., n.d.] (Source: Bongert.)

CJ55 *____. Répertoire des lois depuis l'occupation jusqu'au 1er janvier 1914. Saigon,
[n.p.]. 1914.
Cited in Nguyễn Thế Anh (DB13); not verified elsewhere. Possibly the same as
2. supplément to Michel's Répertoire des
lois, décrets et ordonnances.... (See
above).

Compilations

CJ56 *Cochinchina. Laws, statutes, etc. Recueil
de la législation et réglementation de la
Cochinchine au 1er janvier 1880 [par Bataille, Secrétaire général de la Direction de l'Intérieur]. Saigon: Impr. Nationale, 1880-81. 2 vols.

Revised and updated by Laffont and
Fonssagrives (CJ65).
Cordier

CJ57 *Ganter, D. Recueil de législation en vigueur en Annam et au Tonkin, depuis l'Origine du protectorat jusqu'au 1er mai 1895. 2. éd. Hanoi: Schneider, 1895. 695 p.

_____. Supplément; décisions intervenues en cours d'impressions. [Hanoi: Schneider, 1895]. 8 p.

_____. Supplément à la 2. éd. Paris, 1899. 401 p. (Source: BN; NN (1895).)

CJ58 *_____. Recueil des lois, décrets, arrêtés, décisions et circulaires en vigueur en Annam et au Tonkin depuis le 7 juin 1883 jusqu'en 1899. Hanoi: Schneider; Paris: Leroux, 1895-99. 5 vols. Also cited as Recueil [etc.] depuis le 7 juin 1883 jusqu'au 1er juillet 1890 collationés sur les documents officiels et classés dans l'ordre alphabétique et chronologique. Hanoi: Schneider, 1891. 375 p.; and Recueil [etc.], fasc. 3-6, avril 1891- mars 1892. Hanoi: Schneider [n.d.]. (Source: Boudet; BN.)

CJ59 *Indochina. Laws, statutes, etc. Recueil général des actes relatifs à l'organisation et à la réglementation de l'Indochine parus avant le 29 janvier 1919. Comp. [Antoine Baptiste] Arrighi de Casanova. Hanoi: IDEO, 1919-24. 3 vols. First edition, 1904; second edition, 1909.

The sections of the most important texts are reproduced fully, while those of secondary importance have only the title and a reference to the Journal officiel or Bulletin officiel in which they appeared. ("Notice" in Recueil general, 1927-28.) Continued by: Indochina. Laws, statutes, etc. Recueil général périodique des actes.... 1923 (CJ61).

Contains legislation beginning in June 1776. (Source: DLC.)

CJ60 *_____. _____. Recueil général permanent des actes relatifs à l'organisation et à la réglementation de l'Indochine. Hanoi-Haiphong: IDEO, 1909. 1449, 247 p.

_____. _____. 1.--supplément. Hanoi: Schneider, 1905-- .

Continued by Recueil général périodique... (CJ61). (Source: DLC.)

CJ61 *_____. _____. Recueil général périodique des actes législatifs et réglementaires applicables en Indo-Chine et des circulaires, instructions, avis s'y rapportant.... Hanoi: IDEO, 1923-1929. At head of title: Service de Législation et d'Administration.

Vols. 1, 2, 8, citing legislation of 1919/1921 and of April/June 1923 listed in Grandin 2: 324.

Intended to complete at regular intervals the Recueil général permanent--verso of cover, jan.-juin 1919. (Source: DLC.)

CJ62 _____. _____. Recueil général de la législation et de la réglementation de l'Indochine à jour au 31 décembre 1925. [Hanoi] Service de Législation d'Administration du Gouvernement Général, 1927-28. 4 pts. in 7 vols.

_____. _____. _____. Supplément de 1926-27. 1930-31. 2 v.

_____. _____. _____. Supplément de 1928. 1931. 1 v.

_____. _____. _____. Supplément de 1929. 1932. 1 v.

_____. _____. _____. Supplément de 1930. 1932. 1 v.

An index to laws, decrees, arrêtés, ministerial circulars, local administrative circulars, and royal ordinances, beginning in June 1778. Contains texts of legislative acts or regulations in force as of the end of the year. Omits codes, which have been published separately. Continued by next publication.
NN; MH-L

LAW CJ

CJ63 *____. ____. Recueil général de la législation et de la réglementation de l'Indochine. Répertoire chronologique et alphabétique des lois, décrets, ordonnances
royales, arrêtés, décisions et circulaires
publiés de 1931 à 1937, précédé d'un répertoire chronologique et alphabétique des
textes antérieurs à 1931, promulgués, modifiés ou abrogés entre le 1er janvier 1931
et le 31 décembre 1936.... Hanoi: IDEO,
1938-39. 4 vols. At head of title: Direction des Archives et des bibliothèques.

    Contents: Vol. 1, pt. 1, Répertoire
chronologique des textes antérieurs à 1931
promulgués, modifiés ou abrogés entre le
1er janvier 1916 et le 31 décembre 1936;
pt. 2, Répertoire alphabétique [etc.];
vol. 2, Répertoire chronologique des textes
législatifs et réglementaires 1931-1937;
vols. 3 and 4, Répertoire alphabétique
[etc.] (Source: DLC; NN; CtY-L.)

CJ64 *Jean, Marie Louis. Abrégé de législation coloniale générale et régime législatif administratif et judiciaire de l'Indochine.
Vinh: Impr. du Nord Annam, 1943. 500 p.[1]
    Also cited as: Legislation.... Ibid.,
1939. 524 p.[2]
    "Designed to prepare candidates for
competitive entrance examinations for
various services."--Jumper
[1]Jumper [2]Bongert

CJ65 *Laffont, E., and J.-B. Fonssagrives. Répertoire alphabétique de législation et de
réglementation de la Cochinchine, arrêté
au 1er janvier 1889, par E. Laffont (de
l'origine à 1886 inclus) et J.-B. Fonssagrives (pour les années 1887 & 1888).
Paris: Rousseau, 1890. 7 vols. Revised
and updated version of compilation by
Bataille. (Source: Lorenz.)

CJ66 *Outrey, Ernest. Recueil de législation can-
tonale et communale annamite de Basse-

Cochinchine. Saigon: A. Bock, 1888.
81 p.
    ____. Nouveau recueil de législation can-
tonale et communale annamite de Cochinchine. Saigon: Ménard et Rey, 1905.
254 p. Also in Vietnamese: Tân thơ tổng[2]
lý qui điều...diễn quốc ngữ Thơ Ký Trần-
văn-Sơm.... Ibid., 1905. 220 p.
    ____. ____, éd. nouv. mise au courant de
la législation en vigueur au 1er janvier 1928, par Julien de Villeneuve....
Saigon: J. Viet, 1928. 474 p. Also in
Vietnamese: Tân thơ tổng lý qui điều...[2]
mới in lại có Ông Julien de Villeneuve...
dọn theo lệ luật đang thông dụng ngày
1er janvier 1928.... Ibid., 1928. 362 p.
(Source: BN.)

Official Gazettes and Administrative Bulletins

CJ67 *Annam. Bulletin officiel du Protectorat de
l'Annam et du Tonkin, 1883-1886. (Cordier,
1667-1668, lists a publisher only for the
1885 volume: Hanoi: Impr. du Gouvernement.) Continued by Indochina. Bulletin
officiel de l'Indochine française, deuxième partie, Annam et Tonkin. Hanoi:
Schneider, 1889-1901, itself continued as:
Indochina. Bulletin officiel de l'Indochine française. Hanoi: Schneider, and
IDEO, 1902-1940? (Source: ACRPP.)

CJ68 *Bulletin administratif de l'Annam. Hue,
1902-40 [?]
    See annotation for Bulletin administra-
tif du Tonkin. (Source: Gregory--NN;
ACRPP.)

CJ69 *Bulletin administratif de la Cochinchine.
Saigon, 1902-40 [?]
    See annotation for Bulletin administra-
tif du Tonkin. (Source: Gregory--DLC;
ACRPP.)

CJ70   Bulletin administratif du Tonkin. Hanoi,
        1902-40.

        "Partie officielle" contains arrêtés
        and decisions circulaires from the Gouver-
        nement Général, Résidence Supérieure and
        other authorities; notices of deportations;
        and various civil service changes in per-
        sonnel. "Partie non-officielle" contains
        miscellaneous notices not related to the
        government.
        MH-L; DLC

CJ71   *Cochinchina. Bulletin officiel de la Cochin-
        chine française. Saigon, 1861-88. Title
        varies: 1861-64, Bulletin officiel de
        l'Expédition de Cochinchine. Chinese-
        language edition was also planned, titled,
        Bulletin des communes.[1] A second edition
        of the Bulletin officiel, 1862-71, was
        published in Paris by Challamel, 1871-73.[1]

        Indexes: Table générale analytique,
        alphabétique et chronologique...1861 à
        1867. 2. éd. Paris: Challamel, 1872.
        clxii, 249 p.; Table...1868 à 1871. 2. éd.
        Ibid., 1873. clxxxvii, 108 p.[1]

        Continued by: Indochina. Bulletin of-
        ficiel de l'Indochine française, première
        partie, Cochinchine et Cambodge. Saigon,
        1889-1901. Continued by Indochina. Bul-
        letin officiel de l'Indochine française.
        Hanoi, 1902-[1950?] (CJ75).
        ACRPP [1]Cordier

CJ72   *____. Journal officiel de la Cochinchine
        française. Saigon, 1879-89. Preceded by
        Courrier de Saigon, 1864-79.--Cordier
        1750.

        A translation into quốc-ngữ was also
        published: Gia-định báo (available on
        microfilm from ACRPP). (Source: Cordier;
        Gregory.)

CJ73   *France. Ministère des Colonies. Bulletin
        officiel de l'Administration des Colonies.
        Paris, 1887-1893. Continued by: France.
        Ministère des Colonies. Bulletin officiel

du Ministère des Colonies. Paris, 1894-
1953. Continued by: France. Ministère
de la France d'Outre-Mer. Bulletin officiel. Paris, 1954- .

CJ74   ____. Ministère des Finances. Bulletin de
        statistique et de législation comparée.
        Paris: Impr. Nationale, 1877-1940.
        128 vols. Indexes: Vols. 1-10, 1-20,
        21-30, 1-40, 41-60, 61-128.

        Contains budget, foreign trade, finan-
        cial, and other statistics and texts of
        legislation or references to legislation
        published during the month. Indexes are
        published with the June and December is-
        sues; the section "Indochine française"
        lists legislation and references to the
        Journal officiel (France). Most refer-
        ences are about metropolitan France and
        legislation in other countries. Each is-
        sue also contains a chronological table of
        financial and economic legislation issued
        during the month, some of which is re-
        printed in the Bulletin. Includes texts
        of laws on organization of the colonial
        government, budgets, tariffs, and the
        Conseil Colonial.
        MH

CJ75   *Indochina. Bulletin officiel de l'Indochine
        française. Saigon, 1889-1901; Hanoi,
        1901-13. Continuation of: Cochinchina,
        Bulletin officiel de la Cochinchine fran-
        çaise; and of: Annam, Bulletin officiel du
        Protectorat de l'Annam et du Tonkin. From
        1889-1901, published in two parts: pt. 1,
        Cochinchine et Cambodge; pt. 2, Annam et
        Tonkin. (Source: Gregory; ACRPP.)

CJ76   ____. Journal officiel de l'Indo-Chine
        française. Saigon, 1889-1901; n.s., Ha-
        noi, 1902-1946[?]. Continuation of, vari-
        ously, Journal officiel de la Cochinchine
        française (CJ72), Bulletin officiel du
        Protectorat de l'Annam et du Tonkin (CJ67)
        and Courrier de Saigon.

LAW CJ

Comprised of "Partie officielle" which
listed laws and decrees and "Partie non-
officielle" which listed a variety of information over the years; e.g., "Compte
rendu sommaire des séances, Conseil supérieur de l'Indochine," <u>JOIF</u>, 8 mars 1909,
346-367; "Discours prononcé par M. le
Gouverneur général à l'ouverture de la
session du Conseil de Gouvernement," <u>JOIF</u>,
13 décembre 1909, 1974-2025; and monthly
reports on official revenues and
expenditures.
MH-L; ACRPP

CJ77　*Tongking.　<u>Bulletin officiel en langue indigène; công báo</u>. Saigon, 1936 [?]-1940 [?].
ACRPP entry: France. Protectorat du Tonkin.
Might also be cited as <u>Băc-kỳ bao-hộ
quôc-ngữ công-báo</u> [official journal of the
protectorate of the North, in <u>quôc-ngữ</u>],
1931-[40?] (Source: ACRPP.)

GOVERNMENTS FROM 1945 TO 1954

CJ78　*Cochinchina (Republic). <u>Journal officiel de
la République de Cochinchine</u>. Saigon,
1946-49.
Continued by <u>Công-văn Tập-san Nam Việt</u>
(CJ94). (Source: Cường <u>Soc Sci</u>.)

CJ79　*France. Commissariat Général en Indochine.
<u>Bulletin officiel</u>. Saigon: Impr. des
Journaux officiels, 1951-1954. Weekly.
Issued 5 juillet 1951 to 14 mai 1953 by
the Haut Commissariat de France en Indochine. (Source: DLC <u>SAAL</u>, Apr. 1957.)

CJ80　*_____. Commissariat de la République française dans le Nord Việt Nam. <u>Bulletin of-
ficiel</u>. Hanoi, 1948-1951. Bimonthly.
Issued 1948-49 by the Commissariat de
la République française au Tonkin. Available on microfilm from ACRPP. (Source:
DLC <u>SAAL</u>, Jan. 1957.)

CJ81　*_____. Commissariat dans le Centre Việt Nam.
<u>Bulletin officiel du Commissariat de la
République française dans le Centre Việt
Nam</u>. Hue, 1947-51.
Title as in ACRPP: <u>Bulletin officiel
du Commissariat de la République française
en Annam</u>. Available on microfilm from
ACRPP. (Source: Cường & Quỳnh.)

CJ82　Indochina (Federation). <u>Journal officiel de
la Fédération indochinoise</u>. Saigon, 1945-
[1951?]
Copy at MH-L dated 15 novembre 1945,
but Cường no. 931 gives beginning date as
2 janv. 1947.
MH-L

DEMOCRATIC REPUBLIC OF VIETNAM

CJ83　*Việt-Nam Dân-Quốc Công-báo [Official gazette
of the Democratic Republic of Vietnam].
(Source: Bongert.)

REPUBLIC OF VIETNAM AND PREDECESSORS

<u>Indexes</u>

CJ84　<u>Các văn-kiện tô-chức cơ-cấu quốc-gia tại
Việt-Nam Cộng-hòa sau cách-mạng 1-11-63
(từ ngày 1-11-1963 đến ngày 19-6-1965)</u>.
[Documents on the organization of the
structure of the Republic of Vietnam after
the revolution of 1 November 1963 (from
1 November 1963 to 19 June 1965)].
See CI75 for complete description.
MH-V

CJ85　*Cung Đình Thanh. "Mục lục phân tích văn kiện
lập pháp và lập qui" [Index to legislative
and executive documents]. NCHC, nos. 6-7
(6-7/64), 163-197. (Source: KimSa, <u>Mục-
lục</u>....; NIC.)

CJ86 "Những văn-kiện quan-trọng công-bố trong
[quarter]" [Important official documents
promulgated during the quarter]. Appears
in each issue of: Luật-học kinh-tế,
1956-58, 1960; Nghiên-cứu hành-chánh,
1959; Pháp-lý tập-san, 1961- .

Alphabetical arrangement by subject or
governmental department, summarizing documents appearing in Công-báo Việt-Nam Cộng-
hòa and Công-báo Việt-Nam Cộng-hòa (Ấn-ban
Quốc-Hội). Listing of individual articles
appears in KimSa, Mục lục phân-tích tạp-
chí Việt-ngữ (AF18).
MH-L; NIC

CJ87 Public administration bulletin Vietnam.
See CI78 for complete description, including index of all RVN legislation
translated and published in PABV, nos. 1-
53.
MH

CJ88 Vietnam (Republic). Laws, statutes, etc.
(Indexes).
Pháp-quy chỉnh-yếu mục-lục; các bản-văn
quan-trọng về lập-pháp, lập-quy ấn-hành
trong Công báo Việt-Nam từ 1948 đến hết
năm 1971. In lần thứ hai. Cập-nhật-hóa
đến Công-báo số cuối tháng 6 năm 1972
[Table of contents of essential legislation, important legislative and administrative texts published in the Official
Gazette of Vietnam from 1948 until the end
of 1971. Second edition. Updated through
the end of June 1972]. [Saigon] Trung-tâm
nghiên-cứu luật-pháp, Bộ Tư-pháp, 1972.
565, 34, 35 p.

Compiled by Trần Ngọc Chi. Alphabetical index by subject to legislation published in the Công-báo Việt-Nam Cộng-Hòa
(CJ86).
MH-L

Compilations

CJ89 Pháp-lý tập-san. "Số đặc-biệt, gồm các
thông-tư và công-văn đã đăng trong 5 năm
qua (từ 1-1-1955 đến 31-12-1959)" [Special
issue, comprising official circulars and
official documents published from 1955-
1959]. [Saigon?], 1960. 453 p.

A complementary publication to a compilation of documents in PLTS in 1954 on
the organization of justice in RVN.
MH-L; NIC

CJ90 Vietnam (Republic). Laws, statutes, etc.
Index, alphabetical-subject and chronological of GVN decrees & related Vietnamese legal documents. Prepared and distributed by the Office of the Staff Judge
Advocate, USAMACV. [Saigon? 1968] 145 p.

A listing of Vietnamese and Indochinese legal documents which have been
translated into English and are on file
in the office of the Staff Judge Advocate
of the U.S. mission in Saigon. Entries
list date of law, short description, subject, and citation of original document.
Most documents are those published after
1955, although a few are as early as 1895
and the early twentieth century.
MH-L

CJ91 ____. ____. Quy pháp vựng tập; recueil
des lois et règlements. Saigon: Sở Công
báo ấn-hành, 1960- .
Volume 1, 1955/58 (1960); subsequent
compilations are annually.

Includes texts of laws [luật], decrees
[sắc-lệnh, nghị-định], and resolutions
[quyết-định, quyết-nghị] as originally
published in CBVNCH.

Arranged according to legislative ac-
tions--Văn-kiện lập-pháp--and regulatory

actions--Văn-kiện lập-quy. Indexes are
essential to use, since arrangement in
each section is chronological; indexes are
chronological and by subject.
MH-L

CJ92 _____. Quốc-Hội. Hạ-Nghị-Viện. Công-tác
lập-pháp, niên khóa 1967-1968, 1968-1969
[Legislative record, 1967-1968, 1968-1969].
[Saigon? 1969?]. 172 p.

Texts of laws passed by the National
Assembly, arranged in chronological order.
Unlike the contents of Quy-pháp vựng-tập
(CJ91), this excludes texts of decrees and
other laws not passed by the National As-
sembly.

Issues for subsequent years not located.
MH-V

Official Gazettes

CJ93 *Vietnam (Central Provisional Government).
Công-báo Việt-Nam [Official Gazette of
Vietnam]. Saigon: Ministère de la Jus-
tice du Gouvernement Central provisoire du
Việt-Nam, Impr. des Journaux officiels,
1948-49. Available on microfilm from
ACRPP.

CJ94 *Vietnam (State). Công-văn Tập-san Nam-Việt;
bulletin officiel du Sud Việt Nam. Saigon: Impr. des Journaux officiels,
1949-50. Title varies: Bulletin officiel du Sud Việt Nam--Cochinchine; Công-
văn tập-san Nam-phần Việt-Nam.

Continuation of Journal officiel de la
République de Cochinchine (CJ78) (cf.
Cường Soc. Sci., 932).

CJ95 Vietnam (Republic). Công-báo Việt-Nam Cộng-
Hòa [Official gazette of the Republic of
Vietnam]. Saigon: Nhà in các Công-báo,
1955- . Weekly, with quarterly index.
Edition containing the proceedings of the
National Assembly is: Công-báo Việt-Nam

Cộng-Hòa (Ấn-bản Quốc-Hội) (CI98). Available on microfilm from 3M/IMPRESS.
MH-L

OTHER SOURCES

CJ96 Penant; recueil général de jurisprudence, de
doctrine et de législation coloniales et
maritimes. Paris: Penant, 1901- . Continuation of La tribune des colonies et
des protectorats, 1891-1898.

CJ97 Recueil Dareste de législation, doctrine et
de jurisprudence coloniales. Paris: Dareste, 1898-1939.

CJ98 Sol, Bernard, and Daniel Haranger. Recueil
général et méthodique de la législation
et de la réglementation des colonies françaises; textes émanant du Pouvoir central
(lois, décrets, arrêtés, circulaires et
instructions ministérielles), recueillis,
classés et mis à jour. Paris: Société
d'Éditions Géographique, Maritime et Coloniale, 1930-1938. Vols. 1-5, pt. 1.

CJ99 Table annuelle de [year] pour les journaux
officiels d'outre-mer, comp. Nguyen Huu
Khang. In Revue juridique et politique
de l'Union française, 1947-1951.

JURISPRUDENCE

FRENCH INDOCHINA

CJ100 *Gentile, N. de. Petit recueil de jurisprudence indochinoise en matière civile française, civile indigène et commerciale,
1915-24. Hanoi: IDEO, 1925. 187 p.
(Source: Grandin.)

CJ101 *Indochina. Conseil d'État. Jurisprudence
du Conseil d'État en matière indochinoise
de 1922 à 1936. Hanoi, 1938. 700 p.
Comp. by C. Leonardi. Contains texts
of decisions of the Conseil d'État (BMC).

CJ102 _____. Laws, statutes, etc. Code judiciaire de l'Indochine; lois, décrets et arrêtés concernant le Service judiciaire et applicables par les cours et les tribunaux de l'Indochine, par Gabriel Michel. Hanoi: Schneider, [Later IDEO] 1904-13. 4 vols. Covers 1776-1913.

Chronological arrangement of laws of metropolitan France, as applicable to Indochina with date of promulgation in Indochina, and of laws specifically passed in Indochina.
MH-L; NIC; MiU-L

CJ103 _____. _____. Recueil des circulaires, instructions et avis concernant le Service judiciaire de l'Indo-Chine émanant du Ministère de la Justice, du Ministère des Colonies, du Gouverneur et du Parquet Général de l'Indo-Chine, avec une table alphabétique et analytique par Gabriel Michel...de l'année 1819 au 1er janvier 1895. Saigon: Impr. Commerciale Rey, Curiol et Cie, 1895. 2 vols.

_____. Recueil des circulaires, instructions et avis concernant le Service judiciaire de l'Indo-Chine émanant du Ministère de la Justice, du Ministère des Colonies, du Procureur général près la Cour de cassation, du Lieutenant-Gouverneur de la Cochinchine et des Résidents Supérieurs de l'Annam, du Tonkin, du Cambodge et du Laos, par Gabriel Michel.... Saigon; Hanoi, 1896-1908. 9 supplements.

Supplements comprise legislation from 1895 to 1907 (Source: Cordier 2595).
MH-L

CJ104 Journal judiciaire de l'Indochine française. Saigon, 1890-1939, 1947-1953. Monthly.

Issued by Directeur de l'Administration judiciaire en Indochine (to 1939) and by Commissariat général de la France en Indochine (in 1953).

Published all decisions of the Cour de Cassation, Conseil d'État, and other courts in Indochina which ruled on colonial jurisprudence.
MH-L

CJ105 Lasserre, F. Recueil de jurisprudence en matière indigène, années 1880-1885; lois, décrets et arrêtés sur la justice en vigueur dans la colonie. Répertoire méthodique et alphabétique de législation, de doctrine et de jurisprudence indigène. Saigon, Guilland & Martinon, 1884. 371 p. At head of title: Cochinchine française. 1re partie. (Source: Grandin.)

CJ106 *Michel, Gabriel. Code judiciaire de la Cochinchine; lois, décrets et arrêtés concernant le Service judiciaire et applicables par les cours et tribunaux de la Cochinchine. Saigon: Impr. Coloniale, 1896. 798 p.

Chronological collection of legal texts covering 1862 to 1896 (Jumper).

_____. Code judiciaire de la Cochinchine; lois...de la Cochinchine et du Cambodge. 2. suppl. Hanoi: Schneider, 1901. 307 p. For 1898-1901; 1st supplement not listed in BN, Jumper, Cordier.

_____. Code judiciaire de la Cochinchine et du Cambodge; lois [etc.] Hanoi: Schneider, 1902-03. 3. and 4. suppl, covering 1901-02. (Source: Cordier; BN [described as 5 vols., 1896-1902].)

CJ107 * _____. Code judiciaire de l'Annam, du Tonkin et du Laos; lois, décrets et arrêtés concernant le Service judiciaire et applicables par les cours et tribunaux du Tonkin, de l'Annam et du Laos. Hanoi: Schneider, 1902. 1. and 2. suppl, covering 1901 and 1902. (Source: Cordier; Boudet 1.)

LAW CJ

CJ108 *_____. Jurisprudence générale de la Cour de Cassation, du Conseil d'État et des cours, tribunaux et Conseils du contentieux de l'Indochine en matières civile, commerciale, criminelle, administrative et indigène, concernant les possessions françaises en Extrême-Orient. Hanoi: Schneider, 1901. 555 p. (Source: Cordier.)

CJ109 *_____. Recueil analytique des circulaires, instructions et avis concernant l'administration de la justice en Indo-Chine émanant du Ministère de la justice, du Ministère des colonies, du gouvernement et du Parquet-général de l'Indo-Chine. Hanoi-Haiphong: Impr. L. Gallois, 1907. 1671, lxxvi p., date on cover, 1908. (Source: DLC.)

CJ110 "Tóm tắt án lệ" [Summary of procedure]. Pháp lý tập-san, 1 (1961), 133-55; 2 (1961), 135-57; 3 (1961), 155-63. No more published.

Summaries of selected court decisions in about 100 subjects from 1890 to 1953. References include the name of the court handing down the decision, the date, and the source in which the complete text may be found. References are in French, under headings "Droit administratif," "Droit civil," "Droit criminel." Compiled in order to bring older decisions to the attention of the legal profession.
MH-L; NIC

CJ111 *Tongking. Recueil des avis du Comité consultatif de jurisprudence annamite sur les coutumes des annamites du Tonkin en matière de droit de famille, de succession et de biens cultuels. Hanoi: Trung-Bắc tân-văn, 1930. 182 p. (Source: Boudet 3.)

STATE OF VIETNAM AND REPUBLIC OF VIETNAM

CJ112 "Án-lệ hành-chánh" [Administrative jurisprudence]. Appeared in each issue of Luật-học kinh-tế, 1956-1959.

Summaries of cases decided by the Tham-chính-viện [State Council].
MH-L; NIC

CJ113 "Án-lệ tư-pháp" [Judicial jurisprudence]. Appeared in each issue of Luật-học kinh-tế, 1956-1959.

Abstracts of decisions of courts at various levels.
MH-L; NIC

CJ114 [Ngũ niên mục-lục về án lệ tư pháp và án lệ hành-chánh (1948-1952)] [Five-year index to legal and administrative decisions]. PLTS, 6 (1953), whole number, 111 p.

Summaries of decisions, list of articles on decisions, and list of laws published in PLTS.
MH-L; NIC

CJ115 Nguyễn Khắc Nhân. "Mục lục ôn tập; những án lệ và bài khảo-luận phổ-thông về tư-pháp Việt-Nam in trong các tạp-chí từ 1946 đến hết 1957" [Index to jurisprudence and general essays on justice in Vietnam, appearing in periodicals published from 1946 through 1957]. Luật-học kinh-tế, no. 2, 3/4 (1958, pp. 1-66, 67-142, separately paged.

Alphabetical index by subject; includes court decisions and articles published in journals. Index, pp. 137-42.
MH-L; NIC

CJ116 Pháp-lý tập-san. Saigon: Bộ Tư-Pháp, 1947- .

Similar in scope to Journal judiciaire de l'Indochine (CJ104). Divided into four main sections: "Án-lệ tư-pháp" [judicial jurisprudence], records of decisions of

Tòa Phá Án [Supreme Court of Appeals], Tòa
Thượng Thẩm [Court of Appeals], Tòa Sơ
Thẩm [Courts of First Instance], and Tòa
Hòa-Giải Rộng-Quyền [Justices of the
Peace]; "Khảo-cứu" [Research], articles on
jurisprudence; "Luật-pháp" [Law], texts of
laws relating to the Bộ Tư-Pháp and the
government of RVN; and "Thông-tư và Công-
văn," Presidential messages to the Quốc-
Hội, circulars and official letters from
the Bộ Tư-Pháp and other official communiqués. Beginning with vol. 14 (1961), includes "Những văn kiện quan trọng công
bố...(CJ86).
MH-L; NIC

CJ117 Trần Đại Khâm. Án lệ vựng tập; recueil de
jurisprudence 1948-1967. Saigon: Khai-
trí [1969]. 694, 69 p.

Summaries and classification of ver-
dicts in civilian, military, and administrative law, with references to official
sources. Pp. 1-66 at end of book is an
alphabetical index by subject.
MH-V

CJ118 Vietnam (Republic). Bộ Tư-Pháp. Tổ-chức tư-
pháp Việt-nam Cộng-hòa [Organization of
the judicial system of the RVN]. [Saigon],
1962. 596 p.

Description of the judicial system.
Pp. 7-121, text in Vietnamese with summary in French; pp. 122-580, texts of laws
and decisions establishing courts and civil procedures, including--pp. 476-548--the
decree of 16 February 1921 reforming the
magistrate system in Indochina.
MH-L; NIC

CJ119 _____. Tổng Bộ Tư-Pháp. Chế-độ tư-pháp [The
system of justice]. Saigon, 1967. 192
[198] p.

Organization of the judicial system of
RVN. Supplements include organizational
charts and map of the locations of courts

throughout the country. Description of
legal education system.
MH-L; NIC

TREATIES

The following section contains mostly sources
for collections of treaties. Individual treaties
are often published separately by the participating
governments, in the official gazettes, and in an
annual cumulation of laws or of treaties. Texts of
the Geneva agreements of 1954 are cited in Chapter
DE Documents, which includes documentation on the
conference. Texts of the Paris agreements of January and March 1973 are also cited in Chapter DE.

FRANCE AND VIETNAM (HISTORICAL)

CJ120 *Abor, Raoul. Conventions et traités de droit
international intéressant l'Indochine.
Hanoi: IDEO, 1929. 170 p.

Agreements concluded between France and
Asian states during the 19th and 20th centuries (Jumper).

CJ121 De Clercq, Alexandre Jean Henri, and Jules de
Clercq. Recueil des traités de la France,
publié sous les auspices du Ministère des
affaires étrangères. Paris: Durand et
Pedon-Lauriel, 1864-1919. 23 vols.

Contains treaties, decrees, and minis-
terial-level reports to the President of
France on subjects as organization of colonial administration. Index: in tome 16,
Tables générales 1713-1885--see p. 144,
"Annam et Tonkin" for treaties in tomes 11,
14, 15; p. 184, "Cochinchine," tomes 8, 9,
15. In tomes 17-23, see headings "Annam-
Tonkin," "Indo-chine," "Colonies françaises," and "Colonies et possessions
françaises," in the Table alphabétique par
ordre des puissances at end of each volume.
Beginning with tome 17, some references in
the Tables have asterisks, which refer to
documents which are cited but for which no

LAW CJ

text is given. References usually include
the citation to the Journal officiel.
MH

CJ122 France. Treaties, etc. Recueil des traités
conclus par la France en Extrême-Orient,
1684-1907. Paris: Leroux, 1902-07.
2 vols. At head of title: L[ucien] de
Reinach.

Chronological arrangement of treaties,
with index by country at end of each volume. Includes various treaties, including
postal and telegraphic Conventions and
some background information such as correspondence. For treaties relevant to Vietnam, see "Table des matières--Annam, Cambodge, Chine" (especially pp. 198-202,
300-302, 328-330, 346-348), and "Cochinchine" in vol. 1 and "Indo-Chine" in
vol. 2.
MH

DEMOCRATIC REPUBLIC OF VIETNAM

Official DRVN sources for treaties could not
be located by the compiler, but the official texts
should be in the official gazette, Việt-Nam Dân-
Quốc Công-Báo. The official Party newspaper, Nhân
Dân [The People], publishes the texts of treaties,
which might be translated by JPRS and indexed in
Transdex. The World treaty index and the United Nations treaty series lists treaties, but only the
UNTS publishes the text of treaties. The sources
listed below may be used to locate treaties between
the DRVN and some of the countries with which it has
signed treaties, but they do not publish the full
text of treaties. The texts of the Paris agreements
on Vietnam, January and March, 1973, are published
in United States treaties (CJ134).

CJ123 Institut für Asienkunde, Hamburg. Verträge
der Volksrepublik China mit anderen
Staaten. Frankfurt am Main: Alfred Metz-
ner Verlag, 1962-1971. 5 vols. (Schrift-
en des Instituts für Asienkunde im Ham-

burg, Bd. XII) (See Teil 5: Verträge mit
kommunistischen Staaten, 1971, pp. 556-622
and 643-659.) Updated by:

CJ124 Bartke, Wolfgang. Agreements of the People's
Republic of China with other countries,
1969-1972. Hamburg: Instituts für Asienkunde, 1973. 50 p. (Mitteilungen des
Instituts für Asienkunde, Hamburg, 52)

CJ125 Johnston, Douglas M., and Hungdah Chiu.
Agreements of the People's Republic of
China, 1949-1967, a calendar. Cambridge:
Harvard University Press, 1968. 286 p.
(Harvard studies in East Asian Law, 3)

CJ126 Slusser, Robert M., and Jan F. Triska. A
calendar of Soviet treaties, 1917-1957.
Stanford: Stanford University Press,
1959. 530 p. (Hoover Institution on War,
Revolution, and Peace. Documentary series, 4)

CJ127 U.S. Dept. of State. Bureau of Intelligence
and Research. Major political treaties
and agreements between Communist countries. Washington, D.C., 1960. (Its Intelligence Report, no. 8264, May 20, 1960)

REPUBLIC OF VIETNAM

The official text of treaties is published in
CBVNCH and in QPVT and indexed under thỏa-ước, qui-
ước, hiệp-ước, or the subject of the treaty, and
sometimes includes the text in both languages, e.g.
"Hiệp ước thân-hữu và liên-lạc kinh-tế giữa Việt-Nam
Cộng-hòa và Hiệp-chung-quốc Hoa-kỳ; Việt-Nam--United
States treaty of amity and economic relations,
2 November 1961," QPVT 4 (1962), 603-638.

Selected treaties are published in the series Văn-kiện ngoại-giao (CJ129).

Nguyễn Hùng Cường (CA2), pp. 56-58, cites 9
treaties signed in 1959 and 1960 including Japanese
reparations, economic and financial cooperation between RVN and France, and the question of landed

property owned by French citizens living in RVN, and
includes the references to the text in CBVNCH.

CJ128 *Vietnam (Republic). Treaties, etc. Accords
et conventions de 1954. Saigon: IDEO,
1955. 198 p. (Source: Jumper.)

CJ129 _____. _____. Văn-kiện ngoại-giao [Documents
on foreign relations]. Saigon: Bộ Ngoại-
Giao, Sở Thư-viện và Văn-Khố. Irregular.
French- or English-language texts of
treaties to which the RVN was a party.
Date of deposit in the library of the Ministry of Foreign Affairs is included on
last page of treaty. Among these are:
Accord Franco-Vietnamien du 8 mars 1949
(6-VKNG, Loại A: XII, [deposited]
15-2-1970); Convention franco-vietnamienne
du 16 août 1955 sur la nationalité (97-
VKNG, Loại A: LXLVII, 15-4-1970); Convention sur les relations entre le trésor
français et le trésor vietnamien,
17-8-1955 (98-VKNG, Loại A: XCVIII,
25-4-1970); and Traité d'indépendance du
Việt-Nam et traité d'Association entre le
Việt-Nam et la France, 4 juin 1954 (68-
VKNG, Loại A: XI, 20-11-1969).
MH-L

FRANCE

Treaties of France are published in the Journal officiel de la République française, as projets
de loi of the Documents parlementaires of the Assemblée nationale at the time they are submitted for
ratification, or as separate publications by the
Ministère des Affaires étrangères if considered
important.
In 1962, the Ministère des Affaires étrangères began to publish:

CJ130 Recueil des traités et accords de la France,
starting with treaties ratified in 1958.

OTHER SOURCES

CJ131 Rohn, Peter H. World treaty index. Santa
Barbara, Calif.: ABC-Clio Press [1974].
5 v.
Bibliographic listing and indexes of
several thousand treaties mostly signed
between 1920 and July 1970, of which 328
are listed under "Vietnam," "Vietnam,
North," and "Vietnam, South." Volumes 1-
3 are main entry listings of treaties,
vol. 4 includes index by name of country,
and vol. 5 is an index by topic. Information in main entry section comprises type
of treaty (bilateral or multilateral, and
treaty, protocol, convention, etc.); published source; dates of signing and entering into force; number of articles; languages; headnotes; concepts; signatory
countries; and procedure (amendment, ter-
mination, or other action). Information
in vol. 4 comprises names of countries;
date of signing; topic; citations to published source; and reference number in
main entry section.
Use of the Index requires careful reading of the Introduction in order to follow
abbreviations and to determine in which
volume of the main entry section a particular treaty is located: Reference numbers 300001-304834 (citations to the League
of Nations Treaty series) are in vol. 1;
100001-106485 (United Nations Treaty series) are in vol. 2; and 106486-200657
(UNTS) and 403001-496103 (national treaty
series) are in vol. 3.
For treaties signed by the various
modern governments in Vietnam, the listing
in volume 4 does not always specify which
government was the signatory: The first
34 treaties listed under "Vietnam" are
multilateral treaties signed by the RVN
or the State of Vietnam, but which neither
that listing nor the complete reference in
the main entry section specifies. Con-

versely, some treaties signed by the State of Vietnam from 1949 until October 26, 1955 are listed under "Vietnam, South."

Coverage of DRVN treaties with the People's Republic of China is narrower in scope than is the coverage by Douglas Johnston and Hungdah Chiu (CJ125) which includes agreements of all kinds: This Index lists 49 treaties with PRC, all of which have as their source the references in Johnston and Chiu. It lists 26 treaties with the USSR (most of which were taken from Slusser and Triska, listed above). No DRVN publications are listed as sources.

Coverage of RVN treaties as listed under "Vietnam, South" includes 38 treaties with France between 1950 and May 22, 1963, among them some signed by the State of Vietnam and later accepted by the Republic of Vietnam; 53 with the U.S. signed between September 7, 1951 and May 15, 1970: and 16 with Japan. The Văn-kiện ngoại-giao (see above) is listed as the RVN source.

The Index was compiled from information eventually stored in the computer data bank at the Treaty Research Center at the University of Washington and is being updated and is able to provide information about the treaties of a country on a more detailed basis than listed in the Index. MH

CJ132   United Nations treaty series; treaties and international agreements registered or filed and recorded with the Secretariat of the United Nations. Vol. 1- , 1946/47- . New York, 1947- . Issued irregularly. Abbrev. as UNTS.

Original-language texts of treaties and other international agreements entered into by a member of the United Nations; as such, it includes treaties of the DRVN

and the RVN which are concluded with member states.

INDEX: Cumulative index. Indexes for UNTS, no. 1-700 publ. as of 1976. MH

CJ133   Statement of treaties and international agreements registered or filed and recorded with the Secretariat. N.Y., 1947- . Monthly. (ST/LEG/Ser.A)

Includes titles, but not texts, of treaties which will later be published in UNTS and ratifications, accessions, prorogations concerning treaties and international agreements registered with the United Nations Secretariat or with the League of Nations Secretariat. Does not cumulate, but partly fills the gap between the signing of a treaty and its publication in UNTS.

The May, 1974 issue of Statement of treaties (ST/LEG/Ser.A/327) lists the Geneva accords on Indochina of 1954 (assigned the number 13295ab, under which it will appear in the UNTS); the Paris agreements and protocols of January 27, 1973 (no. 13295a, 13295b, and 13296 to 13299); the Act of the International Conference on Vietnam, March 2, 1973 (no. 13300); and the Joint Communique Implementing the Agreement and Protocols of 27 January 1973 on Ending the War and Restoring Peace in Vietnam, June 13, 1973 (nos. 13301 and 13302). MH

CJ134   U.S. Treaties, etc. United States treaties and other international agreements, 1950- . Washington, D.C.: GPO, 1952- . Annual. Issued by Dept. of State. Cited as UST.

The official record of publication of treaties, agreements, exchanges of notes, etc. of the United States. Individual

copies of treaties are also issued in
Treaties and other international acts series, 1946- (TIAS). For a list of
treaties concluded with each country, see
Treaties in force published annually by
the Dept. of State, arranged by country
for bilateral treaties and by subject for
multilateral treaties.

Treaties in TIAS are indexed under name
of country in the Monthly catalog (AH9).

Treaties concluded with France concerning Indochina are not indexed; the researcher must read each treaty with France
to determine from the text whether it applies to Indochina. A retrospective compilation of Franco-U.S. treaties is:
Treaties and other international agreements of the United States of America,
1776-1949, comp. Charles I. Bevans. Washington, D.C.: GPO, 1971. (Vol. 7, Denmark to France) (Dept. of State Publication 8566).

A 20-year cumulative index to UST has
been published by Igor I. Kavass and Adolf
Sprudzs: UST cumulative index 1950-1970;
cumulative index to United States Treaties
and Other International Agreements 1950-
1970, 1 UST-21 UST, TIAS nos. 2010-7034.
Buffalo, N.Y.: Hein & Co., 1973. 4 vols.
Vol. 3, index by country.

It lists 84 bilateral treaties under
"Vietnam."
MH

INTERNATIONAL LAW

CJ135 United Nations documents index. New York;
Dag Hammarskjold Library, United Nations,
1950-1973. Monthly, with annual index,
1950-1962; with annual cumulation, 1963-
1973. Superseded in 1974 by UNDEX (see
following entry). Abbreviated as UNDI.
CUMULATED INDEX: United Nations documents
index, U.N. and specialized agencies docu-

ments and publications. Cumulated index,
volumes 1-13, 1950-1962. New York:
Kraus-Thomson, 1974. 4 v.

The United Nations documents index was
a listing of documents issued by the United Nations, arranged by issuing agency,
with an index by subject and country in
each issue. From 1950-1962 it contained
documents by the United Nations and the
specialized agencies (FAO, UNESCO, etc.);
from 1963-1973 it contained only documents
by the United Nations itself. Each of the
specialized agencies subsequently became
responsible for issuing lists of its own
publications.

Although neither the DRVN nor the RVN
were members of the United Nations, and
the United Nations was not directly involved in the Vietnam war, UNDI does list
many documents about political, economic,
and social developments in RVN and, under
"Viet-Nam situation," about political and
diplomatic events in the war. The RVN had
observer status in the General Assembly
and was a member of the Economic Commission for Asia and the Far East, the Trade
and Development Board, and the Industrial
Development Board of the United Nations,
and of most of the specialized agencies.

Publications issued by the United Nations before 1950 are listed in the Checklist of United Nations documents (1949- ,
in progress). Publications of the United
Nations are available in depository libraries throughout the world, in countries
which are members of the United Nations.
There are about 43 depository libraries in
the United States. There are none in
Vietnam.

Some publications of the United Nations
("Sales publications") are available for
sale through the United Nations or its
sales agents. The Readex Microprint Corp.,
New York City, sells microform copies of

LAW CJ

most United Nations publications except
those of the Secretariat (with ST/ symbols). The United Nations Archives sells
microfilms of all United Nations publications through 1970. The United Nations
Sales section sells microfiches of certain
categories of United Nations publications.
MH

CJ136 UNDEX; United Nations documents index. New
York: Dag Hammarskjold Library, 1970- .
Irregular until 1974, then issued monthly.

Computer-produced listing of United Nations publications, available in three series as of 1974: Subject index (ST/LIB/
Ser.I/A.1 etc.); Country index (ST/LIB/
Ser. I/B.1 etc.); and List of documents
issued (ST/LIB/Ser. I/C.1 etc.). Complete
bibliographic information is only in List
of documents issued.
MH

GEOGRAPHY CK

BIBLIOGRAPHIES

MAJOR SOURCES

CK1 Cordier, Henri. Bibliotheca indosinica.
See AA23 for complete description. For
citations about geography, see 3: 1551-
1770 and 4: 2919-2930, "Géographie," and
4: 2415-2454, 2973-2976, "Voyages." Maps
and charts are cited in 3: 1573-1620.
The sections "Voyages" include books on
description and travel, from missionary
accounts to diaries and official reports
such as the Pavie Mission and the Mission
Lyonnaise to China.
MH

CK2 Boudet, Paul, and Rémy Bourgeois. Bibliographie de l'Indochine française.

See AA22 for complete description. For
citations about geography, see, in
vols. 1-3, "Géographie" and "Cartogra-
phie," and in vol. 4 "Géographie" and
its subheadings, "Service géographique,"
and subheadings "géographie" under "Annam,"
"Cochinchine," and "Tonkin."
MH

CK3 American Geographical Society. Library. Research catalogue. Boston: G. K. Hall,
1962. 15 vols.

Reproductions of catalog cards of one
of the major collections of geographical
publications; lists books, pamphlets, articles, government publications, and maps.
Vol. 13, "Asia," lists "Vietnam" and
"Southeast Asia" on pp. 9519-9555, sections 43e-43x (906 items).
MH

CK4 ____. Map Department. Index to maps in
books and periodicals. Boston: G. K.
Hall, 1968. 10 vols.

Arranged in one alphabet by geographical and political divisions in chronological order, by subject, and by author of
books or periodical article. Vol. 1,
"Annam" (p. 309, 7 references); vol. 2,
"Cochin China" (p. 621, 12 references);
vol. 5, "Indochina" (pp. 245-251, about
110 references); vol. 9, "Tongking"
(pp. 536-537, 29 references); vol. 10,
"Vietnam," (pp. 278-280, 40 references).
A few references are under the names of
cities: Hanoi, Hue, Saigon, Tourane.
Many citations to maps in various issues
of BEI and BSGI. Information includes
scale of map, type of map, and bibliographical information about book or article.
MH-Map

CK5 Bibliographie cartographique internationale,
1936- . Paris: Colin, 1938- . Annual.
Title varies, 1936-1945, Bibliographie
cartographique française.

Lists sheet maps, whether published individually or as part of larger series,
such as World cartographic series. Information includes scale, projection, type of
map, and size. To 1959, index listed maps
on Vietnam under "Indo-Chine," in the
"Asie" section; since then, index lists
"Vietnam." Indexing lists the publications of the Service Géographique de l'Indochine until the early 1950's; since then
it lists Army Map Service and commercial
maps such as National Geographic and C. S.
Hammond.

MH-Map

CK6　Bibliographie géographique internationale,
1891- . Paris: Colin, 1894- . Annual.
Vols. 1-24 (1891-1913/14) issued as
part of Annales de géographie. About a
two- or three-year lag in publication.
Geographical subject listing of books,
periodical articles, government publications, festschriften, and conference proceedings. Lists many contents of series
and composite works. Particularly useful
for locating French publications on Vietnam and book reviews. Includes references
to citations in previous years' bibliographies.

MH

CK7　Carlson, Alvar W. A bibliography of the geographical literature on Southeast Asia,
1920-1972. Monticello, Illinois: Council
of Planning Librarians, 1974. 127 p.
(Its Exchange bibliography, 598, 599, and
600)
Subject arrangement of over 1,300 books,
articles, reports, and unpublished masters' and doctoral theses in English, of
which about 90 are on Indochina. Scope
includes human geography, agriculture,
medical geography, and physical geography.
Contents are limited to English-language publications, therefore omits basic

bibliographies for Vietnamese studies such
as those by Cordier, Boudet and Bourgeois,
and the Bibliographie géographique internationale as well as important French and
Vietnamese works. Also omits Area handbooks on North and South Vietnam. Section
on bibliographies and source materials
omits the extensive work by Harvey Vogel
(CK14).

MH

CK8　"Französische Besitzungen." Geographisches
Jahrbuch, 42 (1927), 28-38.
Bibliographical essay, listing about
150 books, articles, journals, and book
reviews about Indochina. Citations are
in abbreviated form and might not be
readily identifiable. Journals cited include many which are not usually considered as having geographical articles.
Most references are to publications in
French.

MH

CK9　*Indochina. Service géographique de l'Indochine. Catalogue des plans et cartes.
Hanoi: IDEO, [1903?--]. Issued irregularly; cited in Cordier 3: 1603 and
Boudet 1-4.

CK10　*＿＿＿. ＿＿＿. Compte-rendu annuel des travaux exécutés. Hanoi, 1905- .
Progress report on mapping completed
or under way during the year. Geographical, geological, ethnographical, and
practical information on the regions sur-
veyed; table of principal series of published maps (Boudet 4).

CK11　Sternstein, Larry, and Carl Springer. An
annotated bibliography of material concerning Southeast Asia from Petermanns
Geographische Mitteilungen, 1855-1966.
[Bangkok ?]: Siam Society, 1967. 389 p.

Divided into 7 parts, according to type
of publication, such as articles and supplementary papers; notes; maps; etc. See:
pp. 84, 99-101, 371-376. Index to book
reviews, pp. 371-376, is particularly valuable for extensive listing of books published during French colonial rule.
MH

CK12   U.S. Library of Congress. Map Division. A
       list of geographical atlases in the Library
       of Congress. Washington, D.C.: GPO,
       1909- . 8 vols. published to 1976.
          Vols. 1-4 comp. by Philip Lee Phillips,
       vols. 5 and 6 by Clara Egli LeGear. Ex-
       tensive listings of atlases and maps, with
       complete bibliographical information.
       Vols. 1-4 have majority of listings about
       Indochina, indexed under that name.
       Vols. 7 and 8 contain references for the
       Western Hemisphere only.
       MH-Map

CK13   *U.S. Military Assistance Command, Vietnam.
       MACV map catalog, Vietnam catalog of maps,
       charts, and related products. [n. p.]
       USARV Engineer section, M&I Division,
       1968. 87 p. (Source: BAS 1969.)

CK14   Vogel, Harvey. An inventory of geographical
       research of the humid tropic environment.
       Dallas: Texas Instruments, Inc., proc-
       essed for Defense Documentation Center,
       Defense Supply Agency, 1965-66. [Distrib.
       by the U.S. National Technical Information
       Service, Dept. of Commerce]. 2 vols.
       (AD 625 426)
          Volume 1, KWIC Index: Humid tropic en-
       vironmental literature. Volume 2, Com-
       pendium and appendices. A multidisci-
       plinary bibliography and survey of the
       state of the art, compiled over a 35-
       month period, with 130 man-months of ef-
       fort involved. The purposes of the proj-
       ect were to provide information to the

U.S. Army about the humid tropics and to
make this information available to the
scientific community (Pref., vol. 2).
   Volume 1 lists about 260 references for
Vietnam (pp. E-169 to E-173) and about 330
for Indochina and Southeast Asia (E-209 to
E-216). Includes books, articles, government publications, maps, and reports from
research contractors in English, French,
Russian, and a few other European languages. Especially useful for finding
publications of the U.S. Army, Navy, and
Central Intelligence Agency and translations by JPRS. Most of the publications
are about geology, ground water supplies,
soils, irrigation and canals, weather, and
climate. In addition to references on the
pages above, other references may be found
by looking in section C, under author, or
in section D, under subject. Of the 17
entries on page C-10 for Pierre Gourou,
for example, 9 are for publications about
subjects other than Vietnam, but might
nevertheless contain information about
Vietnam that is not ascertainable from
the title. Complete bibliographic citations include personal author, full title,
full publishing information, pagination,
and series notes. Bibliographic citations
are not always complete, and Vietnamese
names are not entered consistently. The
symbol "xx" is not explained, but seems to
be used to indicate a corporate author--
which is then listed as the publisher--or
unavailable publishing information.
   Volume 2 includes an evaluation of the
bibliographic state of information about
humid tropics, "an identification of authorities and depositories, an inventory
of maps and aerial photographs,...and the
identification of research gaps and recommendations for future research." Pp. 233-
302 lists the names of 1,115 "authorities
of the humid tropic environment" and their
addresses and areas of research; 23 names

are listed for Vietnam on the chart on
pp. 252-53. It does not list any authorities from the DRVN, Peoples' Republic of
China, USSR, or any other Socialist-bloc
countries. Pp. 303-368 lists 333 "principal depositories"--libraries, museums, and
collections--by country in which they are
located. Each entry includes name of depository, address, size of collection, and
description of holdings. It does not list
any depositories in Vietnam. Pp. 369-488,
index of aerial photography and mapping
coverage of the humid tropics, with Vietnam listed on pp. 471-73.

MH

OTHER SOURCES

CK15   New York (City) Public Library. Map Divi-
        sion. Dictionary catalog. Boston: G. K.
        Hall, 1969. 10 vols.

ATLASES AND MAPS

See also Anthropology CD for maps of ethnic
or linguistic distribution, Geology EE for geological maps, and Meteorology EE for climatological maps.

TRADITIONAL VIETNAM

CK16   Hồng-đức ban-đồ [Atlas of Hồng-đức]. Com-
        piled in 1490.

        Maps of the administrative units, lists
of the administrative units in each province, and the numbers and different types
of villages in each unit of the thirteen
provinces and the capital region of the
empire of the Hồng-đức emperor (Lê-Thánh-
Tông).

        Published in Saigon by the Bộ Quốc-gia
Giáo-dục, 1962, in the series Tu-sách Viện
Khảo Cổ, Publications of the Institute of
Historical Research, 3: 31, 276 p. Pho-
toreproduction of the microfilm in the
Toyo Bunko. Briefly described by John K.

Whitmore in "Vietnamese historical sources
for the reign of Le Thanh-Tong (1460-
1497)," JAS, 29 (1970), 375, 379.
        Pp. viii-xix and xxii-xxx of the intro-
duction by Trương Bửu Lâm are in Vietnamese and French respectively and explain
the circumstances of the compilation of
the Atlas. Pp. 203-237, appendix listing
administrative units of the provincial
governments from 1428 until the present
day RVN.

MH-HY

FRENCH INDOCHINA

CK17   *Chabert-Ostland, [?] de, and L. L. J. Gallois.
        Atlas général de l'Indochine française;
        atlas de C.-L. G. contenant 169 cartes ou
        plans, documents puisés au Service géo-
        graphique à la Direction générale de
        l'Agriculture, des Forêts et du Commerce,
        renseignements de l'Annuaire général de
        l'Indochine, entièrement remis à jour.
        Avec une préface de M. Cl.-E. Maitre. Ha-
        noi: IDEO, 1909. 169 maps. (Source:
        NN; NIC; Ajia.)

CK18   France. Service Géographique de l'Armée.
        Carte de l'empire colonial français.
        Paris: G. Lang, imprimeur, 1931. 210 p.
        ([État-major de l'armée] Les armées fran-
        çaises d'outre-mer. [II. 8]) At head of
        title: Exposition coloniale internatio-
        nale de Paris, 1931.
        Pp. 95-121, La carte de l'Indochine.
        Discussion of cartographic work by the
        French after 1862, with summaries of pub-
        lication as a result of surveys or explo-
        rations. Organization of Service Géo-
        graphique de l'Indochine and names of
        European personnel.

MH

GEOGRAPHY CK

CK19   Grandidier, G. Atlas des colonies françaises. Paris: Société d'Éditions Géographiques, Maritimes et Coloniales [1934]
various pag.

"Indochine," by E. Chassigneux,
pp. 1-19: maps no. 30-34, depict Indochina as a whole, Cochinchina, the Tongking delta, geologic and rainfall maps,
and smaller maps of Hue, Hanoi, Saigon and
Saigon-Cholon.
MH-Map

CK20   *Indochina. Service Géographique de l'Indochine. Atlas de l'Indochine. Hanoi,
1928. 54 sheets, various scales.
(Source: Boudet 4.)

CK21   *_____. _____. Carte de l'Indochine. Hanoi,
Various topographical series were published, among them:

Carte de l'Indochine au 1:500,000.
Hanoi, 1899-1935, 21 sheets.
_____ au 1:100,000. Hanoi, 1907-1935.
244 sheets.*
Carte des deltas de l'Annam au
1:25,000. Hanoi, 1904-1935. 108 sheets*,
nos. 0-107.
Carte de Cochinchine au 1:25,000. Hanoi, 1922-1935. 239 sheets.*
Carte du delta du Tonkin au 1:25,000.
Hanoi, 1901-1935. 78 sheets.*
*Number of sheets refers to numbering as-
signed by Service géographique (i.e. some
maps are issued as 167, 167 bis, 167 ter,
168) and does not refer to the total number of sheets produced in each series.
(Source: Boudet 4.)

A list of 52 maps and charts produced
by the colonial government, the French and
British Admiralties, and other sources is
in: Gt. Brit., Naval Intelligence Division, Indo-China, pp. 450-455.

CK22   *Manen, L. Atlas de la Basse-Cochinchine ou
Nam-ki et du royaume de Cambodge ou de

Khmer. Paris: A. Bry, 1863. 19 maps.
At head of title: Ministère de la Marine
et des Colonies. (Source: DLC/Phillips.)

CK23   Pollacchi, Paul. Atlas colonial français.
Paris: L'Illustration, 1929. 318 p.
Pp. 205-236, "Indochine." Has 7 maps
on various scales, from 1:5,000,000 of
Indochina as a whole to 1:75,00 and
1:65,000 of Hai-phong, Tourane, Hue, and
Saigon-Cholon. Maps contain physical,
economic, and political information.
MH

CONTEMPORARY VIETNAM

CK24   Atlas of physical, economic, and social resources of the lower Mekong basin. Prepared under the direction of the United
States Agency for International Development, Bureau for East Asia, by the Engineer Agency for Resources Inventories and
Tennessee Valley Authority for the Committee for Coordination of Investigation
of the Lower Mekong Basin..., United Nations Economic Commission for Asia and
the Far East. Washington, D.C.: GPO,
1968. 257 p. 42 maps. At head of title:
United Nations. Title page and text also
in French. Distributed to depository libraries of the U.S. government.

Collection of 42 maps of the area as a
whole, each on a scale of 1:2,000,000,
covering 38 topics, with separate narrative texts referring to each topic. Topics include physiography, climatology,
geology, land resources, water resources
development, human resources (population,
ethnography, education, and health), social and economic infrastructure (urban
development, industries, fisheries, tour-
ism, and energy), transportation and communications, development activities, and
mapping and photography. P. 253, list of
city plans, with references to map series,

scale, date, authority, and distributor.
Lists 25 maps for RVN. Narrative text includes statistics on topics covered in the
atlas. Draft bibliography for this project included about 7,000 entries. Does
not include DRVN, which does not partici-
pate in the Mekong Basin project.
MH-Map

CK25   Atlas of South-East Asia. Introduction by
D. G. E. Hall. New York: St. Martin's
Press, 1964. 84 p.

Includes 22 maps showing Vietnam: 11
with Southeast Asia as a whole (scale
1:30,000,000) and 11 with Thailand or
Cambodia and Laos (scales 1:8,000,000 or
1:16,000,000). Maps show physical features, land use and economic aspects, and
population. Ethnology maps refer to "Annamese" and to "Khas" and "Moïs."
MH

CK26   Nguyễn Ngọc Bích. An annotated atlas of the
Republic of Viet-Nam. Washington, D.C.:
Embassy of Viet-Nam, 1972. 62 p.

Instead of an atlas, is rather a collection of summary information on various
aspects of the RVN. No bibliography.
Quality of reproduction of maps is poor,
many of them printed by Xerography from
Xerographed copies.
MH

CK27   South Viet Nam provincial maps. Santa Monica,
Calif.: Rand Corp., 1964. 43 maps. Microfiche copy available from NTIS: AD
457991. Compiled by J. A. Wilson and
M. Penzo--Vogel. Alternate catalog entry:
U.S. Central Intelligence Agency, dated
1967.

Administrative maps, showing cities,
towns, villages, capitals, village boundaries, roads, railroads, airfields, waterways at a scale of 1:200,000 for most

areas. No detailed maps for cities, no
index, no text, no topographical
information.
MH-Map

CK28   U.S. Defense Mapping Agency. Topographic
Center. Indochina and Thailand, series
L 509. Washington, D.C., 1958- . 37
sheet maps.

Scale 1:250,000. Publication began
under Army Map Service, as predecessor of
Defense Mapping Agency. Series revised
from time to time since 1958.

For accompanying gazetteer, see U.S.
Army Map Service, Gazetteer to AMS
1:250,000 maps of Indochina (CK40).

Not sold; for U.S. map depository
libraries.
MH-Map

CK29   U.S. Engineer Agency for Resources Inventories. Vietnam subject index maps; research files of the Engineer Agency for
Resources Inventories and Vietnam Research
and Evaluation Information Center, Bureau
for Vietnam. [Eds. Robert E. Gensler and
Larry B. Staley. Washington, D.C.?],
1970. 182 p.

Compilation of photoreproduction of
182 maps, most of which are reproduced
from U.S. government and AID contractors'
reports. Subjects include resources and
development possibilities of the Plain of
Reeds and of An Giang Province, population, rainfall, highways, inland water
routes, airports, tides, crop production,
soils, climate, water resources, land utilization, population, ethnic and linguistic
groups, education, industries and economic
activity, refugees, rural development,
landholdings, forests, and cities. Maps
83-89 show areas which have been mapped,
beginning with the Cadastral Survey of
Cochinchina in 1872 and continuing until
1967 surveys. Includes nine maps of the

GEOGRAPHY CK

Plain of Reeds, 14 maps of An Giang Province. Reproduction of several maps--such as those of Saigon on pp. 145-147--is poor. Includes mostly maps of RVN, almost none of DRVN.
MH-Map

CK30 "Viet Cong political geography of South Viet Nam, January 1971." Viet-Nam documents and research notes, no. 93, March 1971. 28 p.

Maps and text showing changes in administrative boundaries of NFLSVN and of Việt Minh in comparison with boundaries of RVN as of January 1971. Similar in scope to "Viet Cong political geography" by Albert E. Parmerlee, ibid., no. 23 (March 1968), 10 p., for the 1960-1967 period.
MH

CK31 Vietnam (Republic). Nha Địa Dư Quốc-Gia. [Name of province]. Saigon, 1971. Series of 44 maps--one of each province--scale is either 1:100,000, 1:150,000, or 1:200,000.

Area and population figures for each village in each province, based upon 1970 Hamlet Evaluation Survey. Maps include physical and geographical features (roads, waterways, airports) and political boundaries. Contours shown for Kontum and Darlac.
MH-Map; NIC

GAZETTEERS OF PLACE NAMES

CK32 Bửu Cầm. Quốc hiệu nước ta từ An Nam đến Đại Nam [The names of our country from the time of An Nam until Đại Nam]. [Saigon]: Phu Quốc Vụ Khanh đặc trách Văn Hoá, 1969. 143 p. (Tu sách sử-học)

Describes the changes in names and political boundaries from about A.D. 220 until 1838. Extensive footnotes and references to Cương-mục and Đại Việt sử-ký tiền biên.
MH-V

CK33 *India. Survey of India Department. Gazetteer of Indo-China, published under the authority of the Director of Survey (India) Nov. 1945. [New Delhi?, 1946?]. 498 p.[1]
Contains nearly 100,000 place names.[2]
Publisher and series note also given as: Gt. Brit., War Office. General Staff, Geographical Section. (Its Hind misc., 7419).[3]
[1]DLC SAAL, Oct. 1953; [2]Gazetteer no. 79 (CK46); [3]DLC SAAL, Jul. 1954.

CK34 Murzayev, E. M. "The geographical names of Vietnam." Soviet geography: review and translation, 9 (1970), 809-821. Translated from Toponimika vostoka, issledovaniya i materialy (Moscow: Nauka, 1969), pp. 3-18.

Analysis of the structure of Vietnamese place names and the derivation of their names and discussion of similarities with place names in Chinese and languages from other Southeast Asian areas.
MH

CK35 *Ngô Vĩ Liễn. Nomenclature des communes du Tonkin, classés par cantons, phu, huyện ou châu et par provinces, suivie d'une table alphabétique detaillée contenant la transcription des noms en caractères chinois et divers renseignements géographiques. Hanoi: Lê Văn Tân, 1928. 426 p.
Rev. by E. Gaspardone, BEFEO, 28 (1928), 283-284. Lists of the administrative units, with names and geographical characteristics of each.

CK36 *Nguyễn Khắc Ngữ, and Phạm Đình Tiếu. Từ-điển địa-lý [Geographical dictionary]. Saigon: Nhóm Nghiên-cứu Sử Địa Việt-Nam, [1970]. 323 p. (Source: Thư mục 1970.)

CK37 Permanent Committee on Geographical Names for Official Use. Vietnamese. London, 1963. [13 p.] (Its glossaries, 10)

Refers only to maps printed wholly in the Vietnamese language. Defines 300 terms found on maps.

MH-Map

CK38   Schroeder, T. P. Vietnamese glossary, pre-liminary listing. [Washington, D.C.?: Army Map Service, 1968?] 1 vol., various pag. (33 p.).

Handwritten list of about 200 Vietnam-ese terms and translations into English.

MH-Map

CK39   Trung-Tâm Tỉnh-báo Hỗn-hợp Việt-Nam; Combined Intelligence Center, Vietnam-U.S. VC/NVA--RVN gazetteer. Saigon, 1967. 2 vols. On cover: Bộ Tổng-tham-mưu, Quân-lực Việt-nam Cộng-hòa, Phòng Nhì [and] Headquarters, U.S. Military Assistance Command Vietnam, Office of Assistant Chief of Staff-12.

Alphabetical listings of 21,594 place names in RVN with NLF/DRVN map coordinates, RVN names, UTM coordinates, and L 7014 map sheet numbers. Vol. 1 is alphabetical listing by NLF/DRVN names, vol. 2 is by RVN names, with sections listing corre-sponding NLF/DRVN and RVN names and the NLF/DRVN names which do not have corre-sponding RVN names. No diacritical markings.

MH-Map

CK40   U.S. Army Map Service. Gazetteer to AMS 1:250,000 maps of Indochina (Series L 509) 1958. Washington, D.C., [1959]. 305 p.

Alphabetical listing of names of physi-cal features and populated areas as they appear on maps, with grid references, lat-itude and longitude, and sheet number. No diacritics.

MH-Map

CK41   *____. Glossary of Indochinese terms. Washington, D.C.: GPO, 1945. 34 p. Cited in Johnson.

____. Glossary of Indochinese terms. Ibid., 1951. 84 p. (Its AMS technical manual no. 51) Cited in MC (1951).

CK42   U.S. Board on Geographic Names. South Viet-nam; official standard names approved by the United States Board on Geographic Names. Prepared in the Geographic Names Division, U.S. Army Topographic Command. Washington, D.C.: [GPO], 1971. 337 p.

Gazetteer of place names. Includes diacritics in place names.

MH-Map

CK42   ____. Southern Vietnam [and China Sea], official standard names approved by United States Board on Geographic Names. Pre-pared in the Geographic Names Division, U.S. Army Topographic Command. Washing-ton, D.C.: GPO, 1961. 248 p. (Gazet-teer no. 58)

Cited by Van Peenen (EC123) as National intelligence survey gazetteer of South Vietnam (Washington, D.C.: Dept. of the Interior, 1962, 248 p.) but not made available for public distribution in that edition.

Listing of place names with geographic locations in latitude and longitude. Omits diacritics in place names.

MH

CK44   U.S. Hydrographic Office. Gazetteer (no. 12); French Indochina and South China Sea. Washington, D.C.: GPO, 1943-45. (Its Publication no. 892)

About 26,000 names. No diacritics. Pp. 243-246, list of 232 sources consulted including U.S. Hydrographic Office and Army Map Service charts, British Admiralty charts, French charts as early as 1864, and Japanese, German, and Spanish charts.

MH-Map

GEOGRAPHY CK

CK45 *U.S. National Security Agency. Indochina
place name list. Washington, D.C., 1957.
2 parts in 6 vols.
Derived from Army Map Service 1:100,000-
scale maps.--Gazetteer 79 (CK46).

CK46 U.S. Office of Geography. Northern Vietnam,
official standard names approved by the
United States Board on Geographic Names.
Washington, D.C.: Dept. of the Interior,
1964. 311 p. (Its Gazetteer no. 79)
About 22,250 entries for places and
physical features in DRVN. No diacritics.
Coverage corresponds approximately to that
on maps at the scale of 1:250,000 or
larger.
MH

CK47 *U.S. Operations Mission to Vietnam. Provinces of Viet Nam; alphabetical listing
with names of subordinate districts and
cantons and numbers of villages in each.
[Saigon? 1958?] 16 p. At head of title:
USOM/Pub. Adm. Div. Unofficial as of
Dec. 15, 1958. (Source: DLC.)

CK48 *Vietnam (State). Sở Địa Chỉnh và Địa Hình
Bắc Việt. Danh sách các làng Bắc Việt Nam
[Name list of all places in North Vietnam].
Hanoi, 1953.
Lists about 8,000 place names.--Gazet-
teer no. 79 (CK46).

TELEPHONE DIRECTORIES

CK49 *Danh bạ điện thoại tự động Hà-nội 1975 [Tele-
phone subscribers in Hanoi, 1975]. Hanoi:
Bưu điện thành phố, 1975. 392 p.
(Source: MLXBP, 11/75.)

CK50 Điện-thoại niên-giám, Nam phần và Cao nguyên
Trung phần. Saigon: Bưu điện Việt-Nam.
Title varies: earlier editions, at NIC,
titled: Điện-thoại niên-giám Nam Việt và
Hoàng-Triều Cương-thổ; annuaire du télé-
phone du Sud Viêt-nam et des P.M.S.
Includes names and addresses of tele-
phone subscribers, particularly of govern-
ment agencies.
MH-V (1970); NIC

D History and Related Subjects

HISTORY — GENERAL WORKS   DA

This chapter contains the major classical works on Vietnamese history as well as a selection of contemporary histories.

CLASSICAL HISTORIES

DA1   Đại-Nam thực-lục [Veritable relations of Đại-Nam]. 1841-1910 [?]. Also called Đại-Nam thật-lục. Abbreviated DNTL.

The history of the Nguyễn family from 1558 and of dynastic events after 1802, compiled to serve as source material for later histories. Comprise of Đại-Nam thực lục tiền-biên, from 1558-1778, and Đại-Nam thực-lục chính-biên, from 1778-1886/1888. The Đại-Nam thực-lục chính-biên is "the single most important source for early nineteenth century Vietnamese history."-- Woodside, Vietnam and the Chinese model, p. 323. It is comprised of records of the Tây Sơn revolution and, for the period of the Nguyễn dynasty, of the day-to-day business of the court, daily conversations of the emperors, imperial appointments lists, detailed anatomies of diplomatic crises or of provincial problems received in Hue but written by bureaucrats serving on the scene.--Woodside, p. 324.

Two modern translations of the Chính biên exist: 1) Đại Nam thực lục. Tô Phiên dịch Viện Sử Học phiên dịch [Translated by the staff of the Historical Research Institute]. Hanoi: Nhã Xuất-bản Khoa-học, 1962- .[1] Vol. 32, covering 1870-1873, was published during 1975.[2] 2) Đại Nam thực lục. Saigon: Bộ Văn-Hóa Giáo-Dục và Thanh-Niên, Viện Khảo Cổ, 1971. 248 p. (Tủ sách Viện Khảo Cổ, 21)[3]

[1]MH-V (incomplete set; includes vol. 22); NIC [2]MLXBP, 6/75 [3]Gélinas, list 033, March 15, 1975.

DA2   Đại Việt sử-ký toàn thư [The complete book of the historical records of Đại Việt]. 1479, 1663, 1698, ca. 1800.

The official history of the Lê dynasty, written to cover Vietnamese history from the Hồng Bàng dynasty (3d century B.C.) until 1675. Comprised of ngoại-ký, for events until A.D. 967 (the end of the period of the 12 feudal lordships (Thập nhị Sứ-quân)), and ban-ký, for events from 968 to 1428. Based upon the Đại Việt sử-ký by Lê Văn Hưu in 1272, then revised as Sử-ký toàn thư by Ngô Sĩ Liên in 1479, it was revised and updated by Phạm Công Trứ (or Phạm Văn Trứ) in 1663 as Việt-sử toàn thư and extended from 1428 to 1662. The last two chapters (from 1428 to 1662) are also known as Việt-sử toàn thư ban-ký tục-biên, Ban-ký tục-biên, or Tục-biên, for they are continuations (tục-biên) of the ban ký portion of the Sử-ký toàn thư for A.D. 968-1428.

(The Việt-sử toàn thư was supplemented for 1663-1675 by Lê Hi and Nguyễn Quý Đức as Sử-ký tục-biên or Tục-biên in 1698.

This was continued for the 1697-1786 period as Đại-Việt sử-ký tục-biên under the Tây Sơn emperor Nguyễn Quang Toản, ca. 1800, at which time the text for the period 1428-1697 was also revised.)[1]

Three major translations exist: 1) Ngô Sĩ Liên. Đại Việt sử ký toàn thư, do Cao Huy Giu phiên dịch và Đào Duy Anh hiệu đính, chú giai va khao chứng [Đại Việt sử ký toàn thư, translated by Cao Huy Giu and revised, edited, and verified by Đào Duy Anh.] Hanoi: Nhã Xuất ban Khoa học Xã hội, 1967. 4 v. Translated into quốc-ngữ. Vols. 1 and 2 contain the Sử-ký toàn-thư by Ngô Sĩ Lien; vols. 3 and 4 are the Ban-ky tục-biên by Lê Hi and Nguyễn Quý Đức. This edition has extensive footnotes and an index of names at the end of vols. 2 and 4.[2] 2) Ngô Sĩ Liên. Đại Việt sử-ký toàn thư (Ngoại ky): từ đời Hồng Bàng đến Ngô sứ quân, cua Ngô Sĩ Liên và các sử-thần đời Lê. Ban dịch cua Mạc Bao Thần [và] Nhượng Tống. Bo khuyết theo Khâm-đinh Việt-sử và các sách ngoài. [Đại-Việt sử-ký toàn thư (Ngoại ky): from the Hồng Bàng era until the feudal time of the Ngô, by Ngô Sĩ Liên and official historians of the Lê dynasty. Translated by Mạc Bao Thần and Nhượng Tony, prepared from the Khâm-đinh Việt-su and other works.] Saigon: Tân Việt, 1965. 320 p. (Tu sách sử học Tân Việt)[3] 3) Le Văn Hứu and Ngo Sĩ Lien. Đại Việt sử ký toàn thứ, [vol.] 1, Đại Việt sử ký ngoại kỹ toàn thứ. [Trans.] Tạ Quang Phát. Saigon: Phu Quốc-Vụ-Khanh Đặc-Trách Văn-Hóa, 1974. 598 p. Vol. 2 in preparation.[4] Text in Chinese characters and in quốc-ngữ. [1] Huỳnh Khắc Dụng, Sử-liệu Việt-Nam, pp. 27-31, 37-39, 45-47. [2] MH-V [3] NIC [4] Gélinas, list no. 033, March 15, 1975

DA3 Khâm-đinh Việt-sử thông-giám cương mục [Text and commentary of the complete mirror of Vietnamese history as ordered by the Emperor]. 1856-1884. 53 books. Also called Cương mục.

Written by a group of scholars under Phan Thanh Gian, then revised by the Quốc Sử Quán from 1871 until 1884, when they published the edition called Khâm-đinh Việt-sử thông-giám cương-mục thinh tự. A history of the Vietnamese from the time of the legendary Hồng Bàng dynasty until 1789, compiled at the order of the Tự Đức emperor. Provides a commentary on people and events mentioned in the Toàn thư (see above). Contents of each chapter listed in Huỳnh Khắc Dụng, Sử-liệu Việt-Nam, pp. 143-148.

Comprised of a quyển thu [prefatory chapter]--the royal instructions for writing the history and reports of the historians, methodology, and table of contents and names of the editors--the tiền biên [preliminary part], and the chỉnh biên [principal part].

The tiền biên covers the history of Vietnam from the Hồng Bàng dynasty until the War of the Twelve Lords (945-967), in 5 vols. The chỉnh biên continues with the reign of Đinh Tiền Hoàng until 1789, in 47 vols.

Several translations exist: 1) Complete original text, reprinted by photographic reproduction in Chinese, in Taipei, the National Central Library, 1969.[1] 2) Complete text, translated into quốc-ngữ, by the Viện Sử Học (Hanoi: Nhã Xuất ban Văn Sử Địa, 1957-1960), 20 vols.[2] 3) Complete original text in Chinese, with a translation into quốc-ngữ and transliteration of the Chinese words in quốc-ngữ by the Viện Khao Cổ (Saigon: Bộ Quốc-Gia Giáo-Dục, 1965-1974, in progress): a) Khâm-đinh Việt-sử thông-giám cương-mục, quyển thu. Phiên dịch và chú-thích cua Bửu-Cầm [et al.]. (Saigon, 1960.) 234 p. (Tu sách Viện Khao Cổ, 2a [written IIa])[3] b) Khâm-đinh Việt-sử thông-giám cương-mục tiền biên, quyển nhất [preliminary part, vol. 1]. Phiên dịch và chú thích cua Trương Bửu Lâm [et al.]. (Ibid., 1965.)

148 p. (Tủ sách Viện Khảo Cổ, 9)[3]

c) [Same as above], quyển nhì [vol. 2].
Phiên dịch và chú thích Tạ Quang Phát,
hiệu đính Bửu Cầm. (Ibid., 1967.) 267 p.
(Tủ sách Viện Khảo Cổ, 14)[3] d) [Same as
above], quyển ba [vol. 3]. [No translators' names listed] (Ibid., 1970) 295 p.
(Tủ sách Viện Khảo Cổ, 20)[3] Also cited as
vols. 3 and 4 (Saigon, 1974), 129 p. (Tủ
sách Viện Khảo Cổ, 20)[4] e) [Same as
above], quyển năm [vol. 5]. Tôn-Nữ Thương-
Lãng phiên dịch, Tạ Quang Phát hiệu đính
và chú thích. (Saigon: Bộ Văn-Hóa Giáo-
Dục và Thanh-Niên, Viện Khảo Cổ, 1974),
129 p. (Tủ sách Viện Khảo Cổ, 22)[3,4]
f) Khâm-định Việt-sử thông-giám cương-mục
chính-biên, quyển một [principal part,
vol. 1]. Tôn-Nữ Thương-Lãng phiên dịch,
Tạ Quang Phát hiệu đính và chú thích.
(Ibid., 1974) 177 p. (Tủ sách Viện Khảo
Cổ, 23)[3,4]

Partial translations: (1) Abel Des
Michels, Les annales impériales de l'Annam,
traduit en entier pour la première fois du
texte Chinois. (Paris: Leroux, 1889-
1894). 3 vols. Comprised of "tiền biên"
only and does not include "quyển thu."
Extensive footnotes. Text only in French.[5]
(2) Maurice Durand, Texte et commentaire
du miroir complet de l'histoire du Việt;
Khâm định Việt sử thông giám cương mục.
(Hanoi: Impr. Munsang, 1950). 82 p.
(French text), pp. f 1--f 34 (Sino-Vietnamese text). (École française d'Extrême-
Orient. Bibliothèque de diffusion, 1).
Comprised of "quyển thu" and "tiền biên,
quyển 1." Includes photographs of original Sino-Vietnamese text.[6] (3) Maurice
Durand, "Cương mục, quyển II," BEFEO 47
(1953), 369-434, plates 28-43 Sino-Vietnamese text. Includes extensive footnotes
to Đại Việt sử-ký, Đại Việt sử-ký toàn-
thư, Đại Nam nhất-thống chí and Chinese
sources.[7] (4) Philippe Langlet, "La tra-
dition vietnamienne; un Etat national au

sein de la civilisation chinoise d'après
la traduction des 33 et 34e chapitres du
Khâm định Việt sử thông giám cương mục
(Texte et commentaire du miroir complet de
l'histoire viet, établi par ordre impé-
rial)," BSEI n.s. 45, no. 2 & 3 (2e et
3e trimestres 1970), 395 p. and "volume
supplémentaire comprenant le texte original en caractères chinois," 62 p.
Pp. 1-85 of French translation, background
and commentary on Vietnamese history and
society in the latter half of the 17th century, the period covered by Langlet's
translation; pp. 88-268, translation of
Cương-mục, with extensive footnotes;
pp. 269-292, bibliography of 140 publications; pp. 295-395, annexes, including
comparison of Vietnamese and Chinese
calendars, 5 maps of Vietnam from the
17th century to 1962, index of translated
terms, and general organization chart of
Đại Việt government in the late 17th century.[8] Presented as thèse de 3e cycle,
le 2 juillet 1969, Faculté des Lettres et
Sciences Humaines de Rennes.
[1,2]Cited by Langlet [3]MH-V; NIC [4]Gélinas,
list 033, March 15, 1975 [5,6,7,8]MH

DA4 Lê Quý Đôn. Đại Việt thông sử [History of
Đại Việt]. 1749. Also cited as Lê triều
thông sử; Hoàng Việt thông sử; and Tiền
triều thông sử.

Considered one of the most important
works on Vietnamese history. Comprised of
history of the Lê dynasty from 1428 to
1527; biographies of the Mạc dynasty rulers; and bibliography of historical works,
"Nghệ-văn chí" (AA13). At least three
different manuscripts exist and are cited
by Huỳnh Khắc Dụng, p. 56.

Modern translation by Lê Mạnh Liêu
(Saigon: Bộ Văn Hóa Giáo Dục và Thanh
Niên, 1973; 308 + CD pp.). On title page:
Nguyên tác là bản chép tay lưu trữ tại
Viện Khảo Cổ dưới số VS-15 [Original manu-

script preserved in the Viện Khảo Cổ, no. VS-15]. Text contains Chinese characters and translation into quốc-ngữ. Omits "Nghệ-văn chỉ." No translator's preface, therefore does not explain reason for omitting "Nghệ-văn chỉ" or source of manuscript. MH-V

DA5   Lê Tắc. An-nam chỉ lược [Sketches of An-Nam]. ca. 1333.

The oldest known example of dã sử, or histories by private individuals (as distinct from official histories). (Others are Lê Quý Đôn, Đại Việt thông-sử; Phan Huy Chú, Lịch-triều hiến-chướng loại-chỉ; and Trịnh Hoài Đức, Gia-định thông-chỉ.-- Lê Thành Khôi, Le Việt-Nam, p. 67.)

Written in China by a Vietnamese official from Nghệ-An who had returned with the Mongol invaders in 1285 to China, where he eventually died.

Translated into French by Camille Sainson, Mémoires sur l'Annam, Ngann nan tche luo (Peking: Impr. du Pe-tang, 1896), 581 p.[1]

Translated into quốc-ngữ and published in Hue: (Viện Đại Học, 1961), 307, 183 p.[2] Text in quốc-ngữ and Sino-Vietnamese.
[1]MH [2]MH-V; NIC

MODERN HISTORIES

DA6   Buttinger, Joseph. The smaller dragon; a political history of Vietnam. New York: Praeger, [1958]. 535 p.

A frequently-quoted synthesis of Vietnamese history, written from French-language works. Major part of work covers history up to 1900; a summary and chronology for the 1900-1957 period is included. Long and frequent footnotes and extensive bibliography of Western-language works, a characteristic of this and other books by the author.
MH

DA7   Lê Thành Khôi. Le Việt-Nam, histoire et civilisation. Paris: Editions de Minuit [1955-   ]. Vol. 1, Le milieu et l'histoire. 1955, 587 p. German-language ed.: 3000 [i.e. Dreitausend] Jahre Vietnam. Schicksal u. Kultur e. Landes. Aus. d. Franz. übertrg. v. Wolfgang Helbich. Bearb. u. urg. v. Otto Karow. Munich: Kindler, 1969. 579 p.

The first attempt to synthesize the history of Vietnam--avant-propos. Relying upon original Vietnamese source materials as well as research by Europeans, author has written a history of Vietnam from the Vietnamese rather than the usual European viewpoint. Well documented, index includes personal names, with chronological table and 16 maps. A second volume, on Vietnamese civilization, is planned.--author.

Rev. by Roy Jumper, JAS 16 (1957), 450-452: "a pioneer attempt at a broad, integrated history of Vietnam." Critical of author for not consistently showing the inequalities of pre-French society and for allowing his Marxist background to influence the text.
MH

DA8   *Lịch-sử Việt-Nam [History of Vietnam]. Hanoi: Nhã Xuất Bản Khoa Học Xã Hội, 1971-   . Vol. 1, 1971, 438 p.

Issued by Ủy Ban Khoa Học Xã Hội Việt-Nam [Social Science Council of Vietnam].

Uses the results of archaeological research performed in the past two decades by Vietnamese scholars; folklore and legends; maps and photographs of art and architecture, especially of folk art; and a Marxist framework to produce a new work of scholarship on Vietnamese history, important for its perspective from the viewpoint of the peasantry. The archaeological evidence as presented here makes outdated most of the work conducted by Europeans during the French colonial pe-

riod.--rev., Keith Taylor, JAS, 33 (1974),
338-340.

DA9 Nguyễn Văn Thái, and Nguyễn Văn Mừng. A short
history of Viet-Nam. Saigon: The Times
Publ. Co. for the Vietnamese-American Association, [1958]. 350 p.

Primarily a history of political and
military events. Based on Vietnamese
sources, although bibliography is mostly
works in English or French.
MH

DA10 Phạm Văn Sơn. Việt sử tân biên [New history
of Vietnam]. Saigon: Trần Hữu Thoán,
1956. 6 [?] v. A later edition, unavailable for inspection, published in Saigon:
Khai-Trí, 1968- .

A standard history of Vietnam.
NIC (1956 ed.); Thư-mục (1968 ed.)

DA11 Trần Trọng Kim. Việt Nam sử lược [Outline of
Vietnamese history]. Hanoi: Impr. Vĩnh
Thành (?) 1928. 2 v. In lần thứ 4. Hanoi: Tân Việt, 1951. 585 p. (Published
in Saigon). In lần 7. Saigon: Tân Việt,
1964. 582 p.

A standard political history covering
from antiquity until the early twentieth
century.
NIC (1928, 1951, 1964 editions)

HISTORY — BIBLIOGRAPHIES DB

The bibliographies cited in this chapter are
those which are primarily about Vietnamese history
only. In addition to these bibliographies, the researcher should also consult chapters AA Bibliography
and AF Periodicals and CA Social sciences for reference to articles in periodicals. Because history is
so wide in scope, some researchers might find it
necessary to check other chapters, such as CI Political science and government and CJ Law, particularly
for works on the history of French Indochina.

DB1 Cordier, Henri. Bibliotheca indosinica.

See AA23 for complete description. For
publications on the history of Vietnam,
see 3: 1859-1886 and 4: 2933-2938, "Histoire," as well as rest of volumes 3 and 4
for works in various subjects considered
from an historical standpoint.
MH

DB2 Boudet, Paul, and Rémy Bourgeois. Bibliographie de l'Indochine française.

See AA22 for complete description. For
publications on the history of Vietnam,
see "Annam," "Cochinchine," and "Tonkin"
in each volume and "Histoire d'Annam" in
vol. 4.
MH

DB3 Annual bibliography of Oriental studies.
Kyoto: Kyoto University, Research Insti-
tute of Humanistic Studies, 1935- .
See AA19 for annotation.

DB4 Association for Asian studies. Cumulative
bibliography of Asian studies, 1941-1965.
_____. _____, 1966-1970.
See AA20 for complete description.
MH

DB5 Aurousseau, Léonard [Bibliographic essay on
sources for Vietnamese history from the
16th to the 19th century]. In BEFEO, 20
(1920), 73-120.

Published with a review of Charles B.
Maybon, Histoire moderne du pays d'Annam
(1592-1820), Paris, 1920. For Maybon's
rejoinder and Aurousseau's reply, see
BEFEO, 22 (1922), 391-400.
MH

DB6 Cady, John F. "Beginnings of French imperialism in the Pacific Orient." Journal
of Modern History, 14 (1942), 71-87.

Bibliographic essay, including discussion of the writings of Henri Cordier and

Abbé Launay and other writers of the turn
of the century and their views on French
imperialism until 1861. About one-half of
the article is concerned with French activities in Indochina, the rest is on
China.
MH

DB7   Hay, Stephen N., and Margaret H. Case, eds.
       Southeast Asian history; a bibliographic
       guide. New York: Praeger, [1962]. 138 p.
          Lists 632 books, articles, and disser-
       tations on Southeast Asia, of which 72 are
       about Vietnam. Annotations usually in-
       clude a citation to a book review or an
       annotation supplied by the editors. Em-
       phasis is upon English-language publica-
       tions; vernacular publications are ex-
       cluded, as this guide is intended for the
       beginning college student or teacher.
       MH

DB8   Huỳnh Khắc Dụng. Sử-liệu Việt-Nam [Materials
       on the history of Vietnam]. [Saigon]:
       Nha Văn Hóa, 1959. 187 p. (Văn-hóa tùng-
       thư, 1)
          Bibliographical, biographical, and his-
       torical essay, with summaries of over 30
       historical and literary writings; selec-
       tions include An-Nam Chí-lược, Đại Việt
       Sử ký Toàn Thư, Đại Việt Thông Sử, Lịch
       Triều Hiến Chương Loại Chí, and Chinh-Phụ
       Ngâm. Other portions of the book include
       a chronological list and chart of dynas-
       ties and biographical notes on emperors.
       mgc; Jumper

DB9   Jumper, Roy. Bibliography on the political
       and administrative history of Vietnam,
       1802-1962. Saigon: Michigan State Uni-
       versity Vietnam Advisory Group, 1962.
       179 p.
          Lists 964 books and articles in Western
       and Vietnamese languages. Annotations are
       descriptive. Titles in Vietnamese include

a translation into English. Includes many
Vietnamese-language publications which
have appeared since Boudet 4, especially
those published in Saigon. A major source
in compiling this Guide.
MH

DB10   Lê Đình Tường. "Thư mục về cuộc bành trướng
       quốc thổ Việt-Nam; bibliography on Viet-
       namese geopolitical expansion." Canh Tân
       Đất Việt, số 4, Đông/Xuân 1972 [No. 4,
       Winter/Spring 1971-72]. 52 p.
          Pp. 3-22, overview of Vietnamese geo-
       political expansion; text in Vietnamese.
       Pp. 25-47, bibliography of about 450 books
       and articles on expansion, citing articles
       from a variety of periodicals from the co-
       lonial era as well as contemporary peri-
       odicals from Hanoi and Saigon. Biblio-
       graphic citations are not always complete.
       Author index.
       MH-V

DB11   Morrison, Gayle, and Stephen Hay. A guide to
       books on Southeast Asian history (1961-
       1966). Santa Barbara, Calif.: American
       Bibliographical Center--Clio Press, 1969.
       105 p. (Bibliography and reference se-
       ries, 8)
          A supplement and sequel to bibliography
       by Hay and Case (DB7), except that arti-
       cles and dissertations are omitted.
       Sources are the "Bibliography" issues of
       the JAS. Lists 61 French- and English-
       language books on Vietnam, with excerpts
       from reviews, or annotations by Morrison.
       MH

DB12   Nguyễn Khắc Kham [et al.]. "Bibliography on
       the acceptance of Western cultures in
       Vietnam from the sixteenth to the twenti-
       eth centuries." East Asian Cultural
       Studies, 6 (1967), 228-249.
          List of about 280 books and articles in
       Vietnamese and European languages. Cita-

tions include archival sources; bibliographies, dictionaries, grammars, novels, and scholarly works translated into Vietnamese; and writings in Vietnamese on the acceptance of western cultures. Includes several writings by Phan Bội Châu and Phạm Quỳnh.

Substantially the same as his Thư-mục về sự hấp-thụ văn-hóa Tây-phương tại Việt-Nam; a bibliography on the acceptance of western cultures in Vietnam (Saigon: Nha Văn-khố và Thư-viện Quốc-gia, 1966, 35 p.).
MH-HY

DB13 Nguyễn Thế Anh. Bibliographie critique sur les relations entre le Viêt-Nam et l'Occident (ouvrages et articles en langues occidentales). Paris: Maisonneuve & Larose, 1967. 310 p. Thèse de Doctorat de 3e cycle.

Extensive listing of 1,627 items. Descriptive and some critical annotations, particularly useful for listing of certain pages or chapters about Vietnam from larger works. Pp. 43-60 contain, for example, a list of the documents about Vietnam in the Dutch Kolonial Archief. Should be consulted for listings of archival materials in Europe. Author indexes and cross-references.
MH

DB14 _____. "Les publications de documents historiques dans la République du Viêtnam depuis 1955." BSEI, n.s. 43, 1 (1968), 53-60.

Lists reprinted editions of historical texts from Saigon and Hue in the early 1960's, comprised of Mục lục châu bản triều Nguyễn*, Hai-ngoại ky sự, An-Nam chỉ-lược*, Khâm-định Việt-sử thông-giám cương-mục*, Ban-triều bạn-nghịch liệt-truyện, Quốc-triều hình-luật*, Hồng-Đức thiện-chính thư, Lễ triều chiếu lịnh thiện-chính, portions of Lịch-triều hiến-

chương loại-chỉ*, Đại-Nam điển-lệ, Hồng-Đức bản-đồ*, Quốc-triều đăng-khoa-lục*, Ô-Châu cận lục, Phương-Đình dư địa chỉ, Đại-Nam nhất-thống chỉ*, and "Nhu Viễn" of Khâm-định Đại-Nam Hội-điển sự-lệ*.

This Guide lists those texts which are starred (*).
MH

DB15 Phan Gia Bền. La recherche historique en République Démocratique du Vietnam, 1953-1963. Hanoi: Éditions Scientifiques, 1965. 99 p.

Bibliographical essay of publications issued since 1963, with emphasis upon articles in Nghiên-cứu lịch-sử and Văn Sử Địa.
MH

DB16 Smith, Ralph B. "Sino-Vietnamese sources for the Nguyen period: an introduction." Bulletin of the School of Oriental and African Studies, 30 (1967), 600-621.

Survey of historical developments affecting the source materials, history of the production of those materials, and lists of materials reprinted since the end of the Nguyễn period. Includes governmental and private sources, with a description of the records produced by the Nguyễn administrations.
MH

DB17 Tavernier, Émile. De la nécessité d'écrire l'histoire de l'ancien empire d'Annam. Saigon: Portail, 1933. 24 p.

Text of a lecture, with a list of 149 principal sources for the study of Vietnamese history, most of which have been taken from the citations in Cadière and Pelliot and from Aurousseau. List only gives title and translation in French, with annotations in a few instances. Tavernier proposed a history of Vietnam based on these sources and comprising

about 10 volumes, each about 800 pages
long.
MH

DB18   Trần Anh Tuấn. "Thư tịch về cuộc Nam Tiến
       của dân tộc Việt Nam" [Bibliography on the
       Southward Advance of the Vietnamese peo-
       ple]. Sử địa, Bộ 5, số 19-20 (7-12,
       1960), 288-301.

       Bibliography of about 60 publications
on a topic which, in the author's opinion,
has not been the subject of many books or
articles, considering its importance in
Vietnamese history. References include
source materials (two royal decrees and a
genealogy), historical geography, history,
specific phases of the Nam tiến, and cultural influences from Chams and Khmers.
Appendix following page 300 contains maps
of Vietnam through the years.
       mgc; CtY

DB19   Tregonning, Kennedy G. Southeast Asia, a
       critical bibliography. Tucson: The Uni-
       versity of Arizona Press, [1969]. 103 p.

       Arranged by country, then by era or by
subject, with a section on Southeast Asia
in general. Mostly English-language
books, with some periodical articles. See
items 809-1018, "Vietnam" and "North Vietnam." Short descriptive annotations,
omits pagination of books. Inconsistent
in entries: omits BSEI; includes Le Thanh
Khoi's Le Việt-Nam: Histoire et civilisation with the Cambodia section; misspells
Lê Bá Khanh, Lê Bá Kông, Nguyễn Đức Hiệp,
Lyautey; omits the initial of the first
name of I. Milton Sacks; and lists the
name of Chen Ching-ho and the name he uses
when writing in Vietnamese, Trần Kinh Hòa,
without indicating that these names refer
to the same author.
       MH

DB20   *Vietnam (Democratic Republic). Viện Ngôn Ngữ
       Học. Thuật ngữ sử học, dân tộc học, khao
       cổ học, Nga-Việt có chú thêm tiếng Pháp
       [Terminology in history, ethnography, and
       archaeology: Russian-to-Vietnamese, with
       French terms added]. Hanoi: Khoa học xã
       hội, 1970. 133 p. (Source: Châu.)

DB21   Whitmore, John K. "Vietnamese historical
       sources for the reign of Le Thanh-tong
       (1460-1497)." JAS, 29 (1970), 373-394.
       _____. "A note on the location of source ma-
       terials for early Vietnamese history."
       Ibid., 657-662.

       Also available in the Reprint series,
no. 41, Yale University, Southeast Asia
studies, 1970.

       Bibliographical essays about Sino-Viet-
namese-language sources in history, geography, government, administration, belles-
lettres, and encyclopedias. Mentions any
works that have been discussed by other
scholars and reprinted in recent times,
whether in Vietnam, China, or Japan. Observes that, because of the large number
of source materials sent from Hanoi, Huế,
and Saigon to France during the colonial
era, "Paris is the best place outside of
Hanoi for research into Vietnamese history before 1800."

       The latter article cites 67 Sino-Viet-
namese historical texts and locations of
of the manuscripts, printed editions, or
microfilms in eight major libraries.
       MH

CHRONOLOGY DC

HISTORICAL CHRONOLOGY

DC1   Bùi Quang Tung. "Biểu nhất lãm áp-dụng cho
       lịch-sử Việt-Nam." VHNS, no. 53 (8/60),
       859-900. Issued in French as "Tables

synoptiques de chronologie viêtnamien,"
BEFEO, 51 (1963), 1-78.

Table I, alphabetical list of Vietnamese rulers, by niên-hiệu [dynastic title].
Includes dates of reign, dynastic name,
and other titles. Table II, chronological
list, from 111 B.C. to A.D. 939 of Chinese
rulers. Includes dates and niên-hiệu of
rulers. Tables III and IV, chronological
list of Trịnh and Nguyễn princes, including
dynastic titles, posthumous titles, and
length of rule. Table V, table of conver-
sion of lunar calendar into European dates.
Table VI, chronological list of Vietnamese
rulers, including niên-hiệu, length of
reign and of niên-hiệu, and contemporary
Chinese rulers. Indexes by proper names
(of Vietnamese) and by stroke (of Sino-
Vietnamese names).

Succeeds Georges Maspero, "Lược biên
Nam Việt sử ký...", Cadière, "Tableau...",
Deloustal, Calendrier..., Nguyễn Bá Trác,
Hoàng Việt giáp tý niên-biểu, and G. Cor-
dier, Concordance..., all of which are
listed in this section.
MH; NIC

DC2 Cadière, Léopold Michel. "Tableau chronologique des dynasties annamites." BEFEO, 5
(1905), 77-145.

Gives the title of the name of the family or dynasty in romanized Vietnamese or
in Sino-Vietnamese characters, dates of
reign, events during reign, and references
to Vietnamese texts from which information
has been compiled.
MH

DC3 *Cordier, Georges, and Lê Đức Hoạt. Concordance des calendriers lunaires et solaires
(table de concordance des dates du calendrier annamite et du calendrier grégorien
de 1802 à 2010 avec une liste chronologique des Rois d'Annam). Hanoi: Chân-
phương, 1935. 251 p. (Source: Boudet 4.)

DC4 *Deloustal, Raymond. Calendrier annamite-
français de 1802 à 1916. Hanoi: IDEO,
1908. 153 p. (Source: Jumper.)

DC5 Maspero, Georges. "Lược biên Nam-việt sử-ký
lịch tsiêu [sic] niên-kỷ; tableau chronologique des souverains de l'Annam."
T'oung Pao, 5 (1892), 43-62.

Lists, for each ruler beginning with Lê
Đại Hành (981-1006), date of accession to
throne, private name (huỷ), name of reign,
(ky-nguyên), and dynastic title (tôn-
hiệu). Includes name in Chinese characters as well as transcription in quốc-ngữ.
Last emperor listed is Thành Thái, but
Maspero could not obtain the private names
of the emperors after Tự Đức; beginning
with the Tự Đức emperor, dynastic titles
were not used. Includes same information
for Mạc, Trịnh, Nguyễn princes and Tây-sơn
rulers. Appendix-list of 13 works in
French and Vietnamese on the history of
Vietnam.
MH

DC6 Nguyễn Bá Trác. Hoàng Việt giáp tý niên biểu
[Chronology of Imperial Việt-Nam]. Phiên
dịch và chú thích Bửu Cầm [et al.]. Saigon: Viện Khảo Cổ, 1963. 31, 454 p.
(Tủ sách Viện Khảo Cổ, 4)

Chronology of Vietnamese history and of
world history from the Hồng Bàng dynasty
until 1925--the date of the original com-
pilation--and updated to 1960. Text in
Chinese characters and in quốc-ngữ. Includes dynastic tables of the Nguyễn
emperors.
NIC; MH-V

DC7 *Nguyễn Như Lân. 200 [i.e. Hai trăm] năm
dương lịch và âm lịch đối chiếu (Calendrier solaire-lunaire pour 200 ans, 1780-
1970). Saigon: Impr. Man Sanh, 1961.
240 p. (Source: Jumper.)

DC8   Schroeder, Albert. Chronologie des souve-
       rains de l'Annam. Paris: Impr. natio-
       nale, E. Leroux, 1904. 28 p.
           "Extrait de l'Ouvrage intitulé: 'Annam,
       études numismatiques' en cours d'impres-
       sions."
           Lists chronological tables of sover-
       eigns, usurpers, princes, and an alpha-
       betical list of sovereigns and usurpers.
       Includes transcription in Sino-Vietnamese
       characters, dates of reigns, and posthu-
       mous title.
       MH

DC9   *Vietnam (Democratic Republic). Vụ Bảo tồn
       bảo tàng. Niên biểu Việt-Nam; đối chiếu
       với năm dương lịch và niên biểu Trung quốc
       [Chronology of Vietnam, comparison of the
       solar calendar with Chinese chronology].
       In lần 2. Hanoi: Nhà xuất bản Khoa học
       xã hội, 1970. 130 p. (Source: NIC.)

MODERN HISTORY

DC10   "A brief chronology of momentous facts and
       events in the history of the Democratic
       Republic of Vietnam, 1945 to 1970." Viet-
       Nam documents and research notes, no. 84,
       Sept. 1970. 132 p.
           Chronology, pp. 4-50; appendices of
       related facts and events for DRVN and Lao
       Động party, 1930-1970, pp. 51-132. Trans-
       lated from DRVN sources by U.S. mission in
       RVN.
       MH

DC11   A chronicle of principal events relating to
       the Indo-China question, 1940-1954. Pe-
       king, Shihchieh Chihshih, 1954. 73 p.
           Translation from special issue of no. 8
       (Apr. 20, 1954) of Shihchieh Chihshih
       [World Culture].
           Not annotated, lists only brief sum-
       maries of events.
       MH

DC12   U.S. Congress. Senate. Committee on Foreign
       Relations. Background information relat-
       ing to Southeast Asia and Vietnam.
           See DE30 for annotation; includes
       chronology from June 1948 to August 1973
       on pp. 1-180.

DC13   Vietnam (Democratic Republic). Commission
       for Investigation of the U.S. Imperial-
       ists' War Crimes in Vietnam. Chronology
       of the Vietnam war. [Hanoi, 1968--]
       Distr. by Association d'Amitié Franco-
       Viêtnamienne, Paris. Book 1, 1941-1966.
       126 p.[1] Book 2, 1967.[2]
           Contents: Pp. 7-82, chronology of
       important political, diplomatic, and mil-
       itary events; pp. 83-121, "documents,"
       including Declaration of Independence of
       DRVN, extracts from letters and speeches
       by heads of states or other public offi-
       cials, and extracts of decrees by Vietnam
       governments.
       [1]MH [2]NIC

DC14   Vietnam, Laos, and Cambodia: chronology of
       events 1945-68. London: prepared for
       British Information Services by the Cen-
       tral Office of Information, 1968. Un-
       paged. R.5755/68.
           Updated for 1968-1970, ibid., 1970,
       [20 p.]
           Chronology in tabular form indicating
       political events in each country.
       MH

CURRENT EVENTS

       See also Chapter Newspapers AG for indexes to
       newspapers which may be used for information about
       current events.

DC15   Asia research bulletin. Singapore: Asia Re-
       search (Pte) Ltd., 1971- . Monthly.
           Abstracts and summaries of news arti-
       cles, broadcasts, periodical articles, and

government publications. Subjects include
politics, economics, production, communications, and related fields.
MH

DC16 Asian recorder; a weekly digest of outstand-
ing Asian events with index. New Delhi,
1955- .
   Summaries of news dispatches and abstracts of government releases. Annual
index by country. Sources include the
Times (London), New York Times, Tass, Consulate General of DRVN in New Delhi, International Herald Tribune (Paris), and
Far Eastern Economic Review. Emphasis is
on news about India, but does include articles about Vietnam.
MH

DC17 British Broadcasting Corporation. BBC Monitoring Service. Summary of world broadcasts. London, 1939- ; available on
microfilm from University Microfilms, Ann
Arbor, Mich.
   Title varies: The daily digest of
world broadcasts; Digest of world broadcasts; Digest of world broadcasting.
Pt. 5 of Summary of world broadcasts is
the Far East (Source: Robert Collison,
"The news as broadcast," RQ, 11 (1972),
293-296).

DC18 Documentation on Asia. Eds. Girja Kumar and
V. Machwe. New Delhi: Allied Publishers
and Indian Council of World Affairs and
Indian School of International Studies,
1965- . Annual.
   Vol. 1, 1960; vol. 2, 1961; vol. 3,
1962; vol. 4, 1963.
   Lists articles and official documents
published in periodicals and newspapers in
English. Arranged by geographic area,
then by country. Useful for citations
from Socialist-bloc countries and for information from radio broadcasts from those

countries as monitored by Western countries. Is not comprehensive in coverage,
although vol. 3 contains over 100 citations in the "Vietnam" section and numerous other citations in such sections as
"China," "Laos," and "Thailand." Supersedes Documents on Asian Affairs, 1957 and
1958 (1960-61) and complements Select articles on current affairs.
MH

DC19 Keesing's contemporary archives; weekly diary
of important world events...reports, statistics and data selected, condensed,
translated, summarized, and indexed from
newspapers, periodicals, and official publications of the United Kingdom, the Commonwealth, and foreign countries, as well
as from information supplied by International Organizations and recognized foreign news agencies. Bristol, Eng.:
Keesing's Publications, 1931- .
   Summaries of information about current
events not readily available elsewhere.
See "Indochina" or "Vietnam" in indexes
beginning with vol. 3, 1937-40. Particularly useful for information about 1944-49
period in Indochina.
MH

DC20 South Vietnam: U.S.-Communist confrontation
in Southeast Asia. New York: Facts on
File, Inc., 1966-1972/73. Annual. 7 vols.
   Compilation of reports from weekly issues of Facts on file, itself based on
events reported in the news media or in
public documents. Emphasis is upon political and military events in Vietnam.
MH

DC21 Television news index and abstracts; a guide
to the videotape collection of the network
evening news programs in the Vanderbilt
Television News Archive. Nashville, Tenn.:
Joint University Libraries, 1972- .

Index and abstracts of evening news broadcasts of the ABC, CBS, and NBC networks and of other programs about major news events. The News Archive includes videotapes of broadcasts beginning with August 5, 1968, although the published Index and abstracts begins with broadcasts of January 1972. Videotapes of broadcasts may be rented, although just the Index and abstracts is a daily guide to major events in Vietnam as reported in the television news.
MH

DC22   U.S. Foreign Broadcast Information Service. Daily report, foreign radio broadcasts-- Far Eastern section. Washington, D.C., 1941- .

_____. _____. Radio report on the Far East, no. 1-81, Aug. 24, 1942-Oct. 14, 1945. Cited as FBIS reports or FRB.

Typescript summaries of radio broadcasts of news, editorials, newspaper articles, and government announcements, with some speeches reprinted in full if considered important (such as the speech on formation of a new government by the Bao Đại emperor on Aug. 17, 1945). Arrangement varies over the years, but basic arrangement is by continent, with broadcasts from Vietnam under "Southeast Asia" or "Far East." Coverage from Indochina and Vietnam is sparse until about 1947; does not include, for example, any reference to the declaration of independence of the DRVN or any direct reference to the abdication of the Bao Đại emperor on August 30, 1945. Although broadcasts since 1955 are mostly from DRVN and other socialist countries, the monitoring reports originally included allied as well as enemy broadcasts. (During 1954, the reports included broadcasts of the Cao Đại--the "Free Voice of Authentic Vietnamese Nationalists.")

Broadcasts about Vietnam originating from other countries are included with the broadcasts from that country, e.g. much of the information about the events of the Fontainebleau meetings of September 1946 is available only in the section of broadcasts from France; extensive comment and the text of the final declaration of the Geneva conference of 1954 are in the China section.

Beginning in 1947, the complete Daily report is issued in a classified edition and in an abbreviated edition which is available on microfilm. As of 1975, issues for 1947-1951 had been declassified and sold on microfilm. Articles from the classified edition--identified by its yellow covers--are cited in the Southeast Asia subject catalog of the Library of Congress. Examples are statistics on the foreign trade of DRVN, FBIS no. 39 (Feb. 28, 1961), pp. EEE 23-31 and statistics on the development of the DRVN, ibid., no. 44 (Mar. 7, 1961), pp. EEE 5-15.

Researchers may apply to the FBIS, P.O. Box 2604, Washington, D.C., 20013, for permission to read the full edition.

Until 1975, the microfilms were sold by the Library of Congress, Photoduplication Service. Beginning in 1975, the microfiche and paper copy of the complete edition is sold by the National Technical Information Service, U.S. Dept. of Commerce.

The Vietnam courier, published in Hanoi and available on subscription from China Books and Periodicals, San Francisco, publishes the text of speeches which have been monitored by the FBIS as well as other information of a similar nature about the DRVN.

ARCHIVES DD

Archival sources are basic for research. In order to use them, the documents must be organized and cataloged and be open to researchers. Because of the volume of documents, however, organizing and cataloging is difficult and time-consuming; and for political considerations, most archives remain closed for 30 years or longer.

The publications listed in this chapter are mostly guides to government archives, although they do include references to missionary and business archives. Documents themselves are listed in chapter DF Documents.

OFFICIAL ARCHIVES IN THE REPUBLIC OF VIETNAM

The situation prior to the fall of the Republic of Vietnam in April 1975 is described below. Since that time, it has been reported that high government officials shipped abroad for sale "treasures from the Vietnamese National Archives" (Source: Nguyễn Thế Anh, "National archives of the Republic of Vietnam: A case of the scattering of historical documents," American archivist, 38 (1975), 581-582).

The Imperial Archives of the Nguyễn dynasty are in Dalat, having been transferred from Huế in 1961-62. The archives of the reigns of the Gia Long and Minh Mạng emperors have been microfilmed, and microfilms are available in the United States at the Harvard-Yenching Library, Cambridge, Mass. The catalogs have been published as: Mục-lục châu-bản triều Nguyễn (DD5). The archives occupy about 33 meters of shelves and are bound in 602 volumes, 9 other volumes as described by Smith (DB16), p. 615, having been lost. There are also about 25 unbound volumes of the Bảo Đại archives and 6 of the Tự Đức archives.

A branch of the Directorate of National Archives and Libraries is located in Dalat. It contains collections of "common Chinese-language books;" "30,000 woodplates of old Chinese-language books printed in Vietnam;" cadastral records since the reign of the Gia-Long emperor; and administrative records of the Bảo Đại emperor mostly for the 1950-1954 period.

The Saigon repository of the National Archives and Libraries contains records of the colonial government of Cochinchina. No guide has been printed.

The Saigon repository also contains the Archives Centrales de l'Indochine and the Archives du Tonkin--Kinh-lược, Ministères du Gouvernement Bảo-Đại, and Dossiers des Mandarins.

DD1 *Boudet, Paul. "Les archives des empereurs d'Annam et l'histoire annamite." BAVH, 1943, no. 3. Also in Cahiers de la Société de Géographie de Hanoi, 39 (1942), 31 p., 19 photographic plates.

Describes the official records, among them the records and seals in the Cẫn-Thành palace, or the private residence of the emperors; the châu-bản, or records of daily reports annotated by the emperors; and the địa-bộ, or records of land and taxation (Smith, pp. 614-617). (Source: NIC.)

DD2 Bùi Quang Tung. "Pour une meilleure conservation des archives viêtnamiennes." France-Asie, 11, issue no. 109-110 (1955), 742-746.

An essay of basic source materials and summary of attempts to conserve Vietnamese historical documents.
MH

DD3 Chen, Ching-ho [Trần Kinh Hòa]. "Introduction to the archives of the Nguyen dynasty." In Mục-lục châu-bản Triều Nguyễn [Catalog of the Nguyễn dynasty records], vol. 1. Hue: Đại-học, Ủy-ban Phiên-dịch sử-liệu Việt-Nam, 1961. Reprinted in JSEAH, 3 (1962), 111-128.

Describes the various archives of the Nguyễn dynasty and the court procedures for recording documents and transmitting the commentaries of the emperor.
MH

DD4   Kuntikov, I. N.   "Das Archivwesen in der
        Demokratischen Republik Vietnam." Archiv-
        mitteilungen, 5 (Juli 15, 1965), 183-185.
        From Anlass des 20. Jahrestages der Demo-
        kratischen Republik Vietnam, from Voprosy
        archivovedenija (Fragen der Archivwissen-
        schaft), 2/1964, pp. 88-90.
            Summary of the history and description
        of the archives of DRVN, emphasizing devel-
        opments since 1954. Includes a list of
        classification headings and of various of-
        ficial archives in the country.
        MH

DD5   Mục lục châu-bản triều Nguyễn [Catalog of of-
        ficial papers bearing the imperial remarks
        of the Nguyễn emperors]. Hue: Viện Đại
        Học Huế, Ủy-ban Phiên-dịch sử-liệu Việt-
        Nam, 1961- . Vol. 1, Triều Gia Long,
        1961, 198 p.; vol. 2, Triều Minh Mạng,
        1962, 256 p., only volumes published.
            Guide to the Nguyễn triều châu bản
        [Vermilion books of the Nguyễn dynasty]
        giving brief title, date, and location in
        the archives at Đà-lạt. The châu bản were
        the documents signed or annotated by the
        emperors in vermilion [châu] ink. Micro-
        films of some of the châu bản are at the
        Harvard-Yenching Library, Harvard Univer-
        sity.
        MH-V

DD6   Nguyễn Hùng Cường. Lưu-trữ hồ-sơ [Conserva-
        tion of archives]. [Saigon]: Học-Viện
        Quốc-gia Hành-chánh, 1965. 199 p.
            Practical information on organizing an
        archival collection, history of legisla-
        tion on archives in Indochina and RVN, and
        explanation of system begun by Boudet--
        under whom Cường studied--for organizing a
        collection. By way of illustration, au-
        thor uses examples from archives in RVN,
        thereby providing some information about
        archives there. (See DD9, Manuel de l'ar-
        chiviste, for the Boudet manual.)
        MH-V

FRENCH INDOCHINA

DD7   Cohen, Eldon Scott. "French archives in
        Indo-China." The American archivist, 17
        (1954), 313-316.
            General history of archival legislation
        and of attempts to establish archives in
        Indochina.
        MH

DD8   Ferry, Ferréol de. "Les archives de l'Indo-
        chine." Gazette des Archives, n.s. 8
        (1950), 34-42.
            Description of public and private ar-
        chival collections in Indochina, usually
        giving address, areas of collection, and
        any publications about the collection
        described.
        MH

DD9   Indochina. Direction des Archives et des
        Bibliothèques. Manuel de l'archiviste;
        instructions pour l'organisation et le
        classement des Archives de l'Indochine.
        Hanoi: IDEO, 1934. 159 p. 2. éd. Ha-
        noi: Impr. Levantan, 1945. 133 p.
            Pp. vii-xiv, historical resumé by Paul
        Boudet; pp. 2-36, instructions for setting
        up the archives--equipment, classifica-
        tion, inventories, and storage--pp. 37-91,
        outline of classification, including a
        listing of official publications and out-
        lines of administrative structures or
        other official and semi-official organs;
        pp. 93-133, alphabetical index to the
        classification scheme.
        mgc; DLC--2. ed.

DD10 Nguyễn Hùng Cường. "État des documents d'ar-
        chives en langue française dans la Répu-
        blique du Viêt-Nam." BSEI, 44 (1969),
        107-121.
            Brief descriptions of over 20 archives
        in RVN, the most extensive descriptions
        being the former Archives Centrales de
        l'Indochine and Archives de l'Ancienne

Résidence Supérieure au Tonkin (formerly in Hanoi, now in Saigon); the former Archives de la Cochinchine, in Saigon; the Trung-Tâm Văn-Khố, Bộ Tổng Tham-Mưu Quân-Lực Việt-Nam Cộng-Hòa [Archives of the Armed Forces of RVN]; and the archives of the EFEO, in Hanoi. For other archives, only a brief description of their contents is given.

MH

DD11 *Trần Văn Kỷ. Les archives du Gouvernement de la Cochinchine. Hanoi: Impr. Tonkinoise, 1915. 52 p.

Describes the organization of the Services des Archives and the classification drawn up by the author (Boudet 1).

DD12 [Vietnam (Republic). Nha Văn-Khố. Preliminary listing of Fonds Kinh-lược. Saigon? n.d. 1971?, 16 p.]

Brief listing of 316 documents from the archives, sample entry: "Bắc-giang, Rapports des autorités provinciales: Personnel, Rites, Guerre, 1897." Arranged alphabetically by province or by central government, with a few listings for Hanoi and Hải-phòng. Does not list entries in Vietnamese language, although most of the Fonds Kinh-lược not reproduced here are in Vietnamese. Listings are year by year. Period generally covers 1885 to 1897. Subjects include reports and correspondence between provincial authorities and Kinh-lược, Cơ-mật, etc. in Hanoi. Materials are presently in Saigon at the Nha Văn-Khố.

MH-V

FRANCE

Most official documents relating to Vietnam and Indochina are in five archives: The Archives nationales de France, Section Outre-Mer; Archives nationales de France; Archives de la Marine; Service Historique de L'Armée de Terre, Section Outre-Mer; and Archives du Ministère des Affaires étrangères. Each archive has its own regulations for access to documents and application must be submitted separately to each archive. The Archives nationales de France, Section Outre-Mer is the "single most important collection of manuscript documents for Cochinchina and Vietnam during the colonial period."-- Milton Osborne, The French presence in Cochinchina and Cambodia (Ithaca, 1969), p. 355.

The Dépôt d'Archives d'Outre-Mer, in Aix-en-Provence, retains the "archives de souveraineté" repatriated from Indochina.

The Archives de la Marine, Ministère de la Marine, Section Historique, contains several series and sub-series with material about Indochina and Vietnam: B^1, B^3, B^4, B^7, BB^1, BB^2, BB^3, BB^4, DD^2, 3JJ, 4JJ, 5JJ, 6JJ, GG2. Only the inventories of series DD^2, 4JJ, and 5JJ have been published, concerning ports and city planning, ships' logs, and hydrographic missions. A few volumes of série B^7, concerning foreign countries, commerce, and consulates, have been published, but do not yet contain material on Vietnam.

The main series on Vietnam in the archives of the Ministère des Colonies are series C^1, sections $C^1$1-6 (Cochinchine) and $C^1$22-27 (Siam), the inventories to which have been published (DD13).

The Service Historique de l'Armée de Terre, Section Outre-Mer, contains archival holdings on the Franco-Indochina war, 1946-1954. They will probably remain closed for several years.

The Archives of the Ministère des affaires étrangères contains documents on Vietnam until about 1860, when the Ministère de la Marine et des Colonies became responsible for French policy in Indochina. Archival materials for Vietnam to 1864 are cited in its Inventaire sommaire... (DD19). Correspondence about Vietnam is available in the following series: "Chine," vols. 1-28 (1841-1860); "Espagne," vols. 1350-1368 (1857-1864); and "Mémoires et documents, Asie," vols. 27-29 (1857-1859) (John F. Cady, Roots of French imperialism in Eastern Asia [Ithaca, 1954], p. 248).

ARCHIVES DD

DD13   Ferry, Ferréol de. La série d'Extrême-Orient du fonds des Archives coloniales conservé aux Archives Nationales (Registres $C^1$1 à $C^1$27). Paris: Impr. Nationale, 1958. 208 p.

At head of title: Ministère de l'Education Nationale. Direction des Archives de France.

This series is the basic source for the records of the archives before 1800. Pp. 9-14 describe other series in the archives and certain publications about the archives. Most of the documents about Indochina are in Registre $C^1$1 to $C^1$6, "Cochinchine," although others may be located through the index. Several documents listed here have been published by Henri Cordier, especially those in $C^1$1 and $C^1$2 in 1748-1750. Includes documents by Pierre Poivre (d. 1786).
MH

DD14   France. Ministère des Affaires Étrangères. Inventaire sommaire des archives du Département des Affaires Etrangères. Mémoires et documents. Paris: Impr. nationale, 1892. 3 vols.

Listing is alphabetically by area; for materials on Vietnam, see index in vol. titled "Fonds divers" under "Cochinchine," "Indochine," "Tonkin," "Indes orientales," and "Hué." Most references about Vietnam are on pp. 87-93, "Asie." See also vols. titled "Fonds France" and "Fonds divers-supplément." Covers 1664 to 1808.
MH

DD15   _____. _____. Archives. État numérique des fonds de la correspondance consulaire et commerciale de 1793 à 1901. Paris: Impr. Nat., 1961. 137 p.

Includes references to "Cochinchine (Hué-Tourane)" 2 vols., 1816-1831 (vol. 1) and 1821 (vol. 2). Does not list contents.
MH

DD16   Institut d'Etude du Viet Nam contemporain. Guide pratique de recherche sur le Viet Nam en France. Paris: Centre d'Etude des Relations Internationales, 1972- .

Founded in 1970 by about 40 researchers living in France, the Institut hopes to promote and develop knowledge about Vietnam and to publish guides to the location of materials in France and other research aids.

Vol. 1 (1972, 73 p.) describes about 26 libraries, archives, and museums in Paris and the nearby region which have research materials on Vietnam; lists about 225 periodicals and other serial publications and their locations in various libraries in Paris and the National Library and the Central Library in Saigon; and names 37 French and Vietnamese who are performing research on Vietnam and lists their home addresses and scholarly affiliation.

Vol. 2 (1976?, 41 p.) updates the information about the Archives d'Outre-Mer and map and photograph collections: It includes a brief outline of materials of the Gouvernement Général de l'Indochine and of the provincial government materials (with the exception of the Cochinchina archives, which remained in Saigon).

The Guide is more complete for listing materials about Vietnam in France, but is less readily available in the United States than is Libraries and archives in France, a handbook, by Erwin K. Welsch (Pittsburgh: Council for European Studies, 1971), which was compiled primarily for graduate students studying French history and culture. The Handbook may nevertheless be used as a beginning source.
mgc

DD17   Gut, Christian, and Ferréol de Ferry. Etat des microfilms conservés aux Archives Nationales (Service Photographique, Section Outre-Mer et Dépôt des Archives d'Outre-

Mer). Paris: S. E. V. P. E. N., 1968.
279 p. At head of title: Ministère des
Affaires Culturelles. Direction des Archives de France.

List of archival materials which have
been microfilmed and are located in the
Archives Nationales, the Dépôt des Archives
d'Outre-Mer in Aix-en-Provence, and the
Service Historique de la Marine. Entry
includes title of document, location number, and length of film, available for
purchase. Text is arranged by name of archives, making it necessary to use the Index for items about Vietnam: about 17
entries are listed under "Annamite" (journal de bord), "Cochinchine," "Extrême-
Orient," "Hué," "Indochine," "Saigon."
P. 236 lists the Fonds cochinchinois, documents relatifs à la Cochinchine française
(1872-1874), in Aix-en-Provence (Aix Mi 13),
13.50 metres. Most of the other collections
seem to be relatively minor in comparison.
MH

DD18 Taillemite, Etienne. "Les Archives de la
France d'Outre-Mer." La gazette des archives, n.s., no. 22 (1957), 6-22.

A survey of materials in the Archives,
by the Archiviste. Includes a history of
the archives and the problems of inventory
and preservation. Describes briefly the
system organized by Boudet (p. 18) and its
successful application in France.
MH

DD19 Tantet, Victor. Inventaire sommaire de la
correspondance générale de la Cochinchine
(1686-1863). Paris: Challamel, 1905.
30 p. At head of title: Archives coloniales.

Chronological list of papers, letters,
and diplomatic correspondence in the Archives about French attempts to establish
trade relations with Vietnam, assistance
to Nguyễn Ánh, trading and diplomatic mis-

sions to Southeast Asia, correspondence
about M. Chaigneau--one of the "French
mandarins" under the Gia-long and Minh-
mạng emperors--and events leading up to
the French intrusion.

Henri Cordier has published correspondence listed in Section I: Cochinchine
(1686-1748), and some other documents have
been published by others such as Taboulet
(see chapter DE Archives). Documents of
bibliographic interest are "Inventaire de
papiers relatifs à l'expedition" [du Ma-
chault, in 1750], p. 12, "Liste des cartes
et plans adressés au ministre par M. de
Kergariou" in 1818, p. 25, and "Liste de
documents sur la Cochinchine communiqués
en 1862 au cabinet du ministre" p. 29.

No annotations, each entry lists only
the title of the document and the page in
the correspondence file.
DLC

EUROPE

DD20 Cabaton, Antoine. "Liste de documents relatifs à l'Indochine conservés aux Archives
de l'État à La Haye." Revue d'Histoire
des Colonies, 2 (1914), 198-215.

Summary, giving titles only and listing
by date and folio number, of documents in
the State Archives in the Hague. Period
covers only 1637 to 1681. Published as
appendix to "Les Hollandais au Cambodge au
XVIIe siècle."
MH

DD21 _____. "Notes sur les sources européennes de
l'histoire de l'Indochine." Bulletin de
la Commission Archéologique de l'Indochine, 1911, 58-84.

Essay and list of the archival and
other sources in Spain, Portugal, and
Italy considered by Cabaton to be the most
important repositories for the study of
the history of Indochina. A survey of

sources in England and Holland was planned,
but does not seem to have been completed.
Useful for locating documents from early
travelers, explorers, and missionaries.
MH

DD22 Nguyễn Khắc Xuyên. "Sưu tầm tài liệu cổ tại
Âu Châu" [Investigation of old documents
in Europe]. Việt-Nam Khảo Cổ Tập San, 1
(1960), 138-149.

Brief listing of the kinds of books,
manuscripts, or other documents in six
repositories--Vittorio-Emmanuel Archives,
Vatican Archives, Jesuit Archives, and Archives of the Society for the Propagation
of the Faith in Rome, and the Bibliothèque
Nationale and Archives of the Société des
Missions Étrangères de Paris. Observes
that the Bibliothèque Nationale has many
works in nôm as well as many books or manuscripts by Girolano Maiorica, Alexandre de
Rhodes, and Philippe Binh.
MH-V

DD23 Nguyễn Thế Anh. Bibliographie critique sur
les relations entre le Việt-Nam et l'Occident (ouvrages et articles en langues
orientales). See DB13 for complete description.

Annotations about archival materials
are included as follows: France,
pp. 34-43; Netherlands, pp. 43-62; England, pp. 63-69; Portugal, pp. 69-73;
Spain, pp. 73-75; and Italy, pp. 75-77.
A variety of French archival sources are
included: Archives nationales, Archives
de la France d'Outre-Mer, Archives du
Ministère des Affaires Étrangères, Archives du Ministère des Armées, Archives
des Missions Étrangères, Bibliothèque nationale, Bibliothèque Mazarine, Bibliothèque de l'Arsenal, Bibliothèques de la
Marine, and Bibliothèque de la Ville de
Lyon.
MH

BRITISH ARCHIVES

Official British involvement in Vietnam has
not been constant nor extensive, but as a result of
Britain's trading interests in the 17th century, her
political and commercial influence in China and
Thailand in the 19th century, and her political role
in Vietnam in 1944-47, the researcher should inves-
tigate the archives of the India Office, the Foreign
Office, and the Cabinet Office (most files over 30
years old are open to researchers as well as available for purchase on microfilm).

The India Office archives contain most of the
archival material on Vietnam before about 1850; a
partial inventory has been published by Maybon (DE8),
and guides to other materials have been listed in
Nguyễn Thế Anh (DD23), pp. 63-68. The major series
in the India Office are Home miscellaneous series;
Marine records; Original correspondence; Calendar of
state papers, colonial series; and Factory records,
especially vol. 17 (1672-1697) and vol. 18 (1753-
1778).

Beginning about 1850, the Foreign Office became responsible for most diplomatic relations with
Indochina, primarily through British contacts with
France and China. After the establishment of a
consulate in Saigon, the Foreign Office reports on
Indochina through 1905 are included with General
correspondence--France (F. O. 27); beginning in 1906,
they are in the General correspondence, political
(F. O. 371) and are described more fully in The
records of the Foreign Office, 1782-1939, below.
These are deposited in the Public Record Office.

Records of Cabinet meetings are also deposited
in the Public Record Office and are important for
policy decisions. For the period of World War II,
these comprise the War Cabinet Minutes (Cab. 65) and
Memoranda, or papers presented for discussion
(Cab. 66, 67, 68). The Minutes have been indexed
and published as:

DD24 Cabinet Office subject index of War Cabinet
Minutes, 1939 Sept.-1945 July (London:
List and Index Society, 1972, vols. 73
and 74).[1]

[1] MH (index and microfilm of Minutes and
Memoranda

DD25 Gt. Brit. Public Record Office. The records of the Foreign Office, 1782-1939. London: HMSO, 1969. 180 p. (Public Record Office Handbooks, 13)

Describes the various series of the Foreign Office and organization of the records. As the organization and indexes of the records have changed over the years, it is necessary to understand the indexes to the series titled "General correspondence" (until 1906) and "General correspondence, political" (beginning in 1906).

From 1850 to 1906, the major series for Indochina and Vietnam are "General correspondence--China" (F. O. 17), "General correspondence--France" (F. O. 27), and "General correspondence--Siam" (F. O. 69), which are indexed in Registers (Library series) and Indexes of general correspondence, 1808-1890 (F. O. 802, microfilm edition--F. O. 605), Indexes to general correspondence, 1891-1905 (F. O. 804), and Registers of general correspondence, 1817-1920 (F. O. 566).

From 1906-1919, the only index to correspondence is a card index in the PRO, although the series F. O. 566 may be used as a general guide to the material.

From 1920 to date, the series "General correspondence, political" (F. O. 371) is the main file and is indexed in: Gt. Brit., Public Record Office, Index to general correspondence of the Foreign Office and Index to "Green" or secret papers of the Foreign Office (Nedeln, Liechtenstein: Kraus-Thompson, 1967- , 107 vols. published through the indexes for 1945). Arrangement is by name of subject or country (see "Indo-China"); each entry includes name of document and file number of document. File numbers may be converted into the number of the volume in the PRO by consulting the appropriate file number and year in: Gt. Brit., Public Record Office, Lists and indexes, supplementary series no. XIII, List of Foreign Office records, vols. 10 and 11 (New York: Kraus Reprint Co., 1966). Contents include reports on commercial conditions, nationalism, finances of the colony, relations with China and Japan, and plans for post-World War II government.
MH

DD26 Lo, Hui-Min. Foreign Office confidential papers relating to China and her neighboring countries, 1840-1914, with an additional list, 1915-1937. The Hague: Mouton, 1969. 280 p. (Maison des Sciences de l'Homme. Matériaux pour l'étude de l'Extrême-Orient moderne et contemporaine. Travaux, 4)

Chronological listing of papers, about 40 of which refer to Indochina. Most printed papers on Indochina are in the Confidential Print--Siam (F. O. 422) series, although a few are in the Confidential Print--China (F. O. 405) and Confidential Print--Europe, Western (F. O. 425) series. The papers on Indochina cover 1883 to 1908 and include topics such as the French incursion into the North, building of the Yunnan railway, and Vietnamese nationalism. Indexed.
MH

UNITED STATES

Most government archival materials are declassified after 30 years and transferred to the National Archives. Certain exceptions are made for purposes of national security, although under the Freedom of Information Act amendments (5 U.S.C. 552) and Executive Order 11652 fewer materials than previous may be withheld from the public. Selections from the Dept. of State records are published as Foreign relations of the United States (DE17), and a catalog of documents declassified under the above legislation is published commercially as Declassified documents quarterly catalog (DE18). Because no comprehensive guide exists to government archives, the researcher should determine which agencies have the relevant records for research and then apply to the National Archives or the agencies instead of relying only upon the published guides.

DD27   U.S. National Archives and Records Service. Guide to the National Archives of the United States. Washington, D.C.: General Services Administration, 1974. 884 p.

Descriptions of records transferred to the National Archives as of June 30, 1970, consisting of records no longer needed by the various agencies in the conduct of their current business. General cut-off date for transferring records is 1950. A few agencies that contain records on Vietnam are Dept. of State, Agency for International Development and predecessors, Office of Foreign Assets Control, Assistant Secretary of Defense (International Security Affairs--for Military Assistance Advisory Groups), Central Intelligence Agency, and Foreign Broadcast Information Branch.
MH

DD28   U.S. National Archives. Federal records of World War II. Washington, D.C.: GPO, 1950 [i.e. 1951]. 2 v.

Vol. 1, Civilian agencies; vol. 2, Military agencies.

Describes organization and work of government agencies with general information about their official records. For Indochina, see vol. 1, pp. 80-89, "White House Office," for description of papers of President Franklin D. Roosevelt and his Secretary of State, Harry L. Hopkins, both of which are now in the Roosevelt Presidential Library, Hyde Park, New York; vol. 1, pp. 707-708, "Dept. of State, Office of Far Eastern Affairs;" vol. 2, pp. 14-29, "Office of Strategic Services;" vol. 2, pp. 56-57, "Strategic Bombing Sur-

vey;" and vol. 2, pp. 796-814, "China-Burma-India Theater."

Except for the papers of Pres. Roosevelt and Secy. Hopkins, the records described here are in the National Archives.
MH

DOCUMENTS   DE

TO 1862

DE1   Cadière, Léopold Michel. "Documents relatifs à l'époque de Gia Long." BEFEO, 12, 7 (1912), 1-82.

Letters and diplomatic correspondence from the Archives de la Société des Missions Etrangères. Correspondence is among French diplomats or between the French mandarins in the service of the Gia Long emperor. Period covers 1774-1825.
MH

DE2   Cordier, Henri. Le consulat de France à Hué sous la restauration; documents inédits tirés des archives des départements des Affaires Etrangères, de la Marine et des Colonies. Paris: Leroux, 1884. 134 p. Repr., Mélanges d'Histoire et géographie orientales 3 (1922), 211-368. Also publ. in Revue de l'Extrême-Orient, 2 (1883), 139-262).

Publishes 74 documents, from treaty of 1787 between the King of France and Nguyễn Ánh until 1832.
MH

DE3   _____. La correspondance générale de la Cochinchine (1785-1791). Leiden: Brill, 1906-1907. 236 p. (Extr. from T'oung pao, 2. sér., vol. 7, no. 5 and vol. 8, no. 4)

Documents from the Archives of the Ministère de la Marine et des Colonies:

"Extrême-Orient.--Cochinchine, 1785-1791, IV." Correspondence is mainly concerned with French assistance to Nguyễn Ánh.
MH

DE4 _____. "Mémoires divers sur la Cochinchine (1686-1748)." Revue de l'Extrême-Orient, 2 (1883), 304-398.

Documents from the archives of the Ministère de la Marine et des Colonies: "Colonies. Extrême-Orient.--Cochinchine, 1686-1748, I." Includes mémoires by Pierre Poivre in his attempts to establish trading relations with Vietnam.
MH

DE5 _____. La politique coloniale de la France au début du Second Empire (Indo-Chine, 1852-1858). Leiden: Brill, 1911. 264 p. (Extr. from T'oung pao, vols. 10-12).

Documents and comments by Cordier on French activities in Vietnam and Siam.
MH

DE6 Devéria, Gabriel. La frontière Sino-annamite, description géographique et ethnographique d'après des documents officiels chinois. Traduits pour la première fois. Paris: Leroux, 1886. 182 p. (Publications de l'Ecole des langues orientales vivantes, 3. sér., vol. 1)

Translations of Chinese texts and reproductions of Chinese and Jesuit maps describing the China-Vietnam border area. Mostly of use for Chinese-centered history, as it does not list Vietnamese sources.
MH

DE7 _____. Histoire des relations de la Chine avec l'Annam-Vietnam du XVIᵉ siècle, d'après des documents chinois. Paris: Leroux, 1880. 102 p. (Publications de l'Ecole des langues orientales vivantes [1. sér.] vol. 13). Repr., Farnborough, Eng.: Gregg, 1969.

Translation into French of 61 official documents from China. Subjects include the founding of the Lê dynasty in 1428, the Mạc-Trịnh-Nguyễn civil war of the sixteenth century, relations with Vietnam during the Ming dynasty, the Tây-sơn period (about one-half of the documents), establishment of the Nguyễn dynasty, routes to Vietnam, and products of Vietnam. Almost no references to sources of original texts are listed.
MH

DE8 Maybon, Charles B. "Une factorerie anglaise au Tonkin au XVIIᵉ siècle (1672-1697). I.--Inventaire des documents manuscrits de l'India Office." BEFEO, 10 (1910), 1959-204.

A list of documents in the Marine Records, Factory Records, and General Records, with extensive footnotes. Most references are from dispatches about Java, China, and Japan.
MH

DE9 Taboulet, Georges. La geste française en Indochine; histoire par les textes de la France en Indochine des origines à 1914. Paris: Adrien Maisonneuve, 1955-56. 2 vols.

Reprints texts of 231 official documents or extracts from books or articles by persons involved in the historical events of French involvement in Vietnam. Includes texts of treaties, royal edicts, accounts by missionaries, traders, the "French mandarins," soldiers, and diplomats. Includes source material about contemporary life in Vietnam as well as about French policy. Source of each document is indicated, although not all references are from the original source. Epilogue: "L'indépendance du Cambodge, du Laos et du Viêtnam," texts of the exchange of let-

ters, March 8, 1949 between France and the
Bao Đại emperor.
MH

1862-1940

DE10   France. Commission de Publication des Documents Relatifs aux Origines de la Guerre
1939-1945. Documents diplomatiques français, 1932-1939. Paris: Impr. Nationale,
1963- . (in progress). At head of title:
Ministère des Affaires Etrangères. Published in 2 series: 1re série, 1932-1935;
2e série, 1936-1939.

Source documents on the French involvement in the beginnings of World War II
from the Ministère des Affaires Etrangères and Ministère de la Guerre, de l'Air,
et de la Marine. Each volume has a section
on the Far East, although tomes 7-9,
2e série, contain documents on events and
problems involving Indochina from 1937 to
1939 such as arms shipments through Indochina to China, occupation of the Spratley
and Paracel Islands, French preparations
for defense of their colonies, French involvement in the Sino-Japanese War, and
Franco-Japanese relations.
MH

DE11   _____. Ministère des Affaires Etrangères.
Documents diplomatiques. Affaires du Tonkin. Paris: Impr. Nationale, 1883.
2 vols.
    1re partie, 1874-déc. 1882. 2e ptie.,
déc. 1882-1883.
    _____. _____. _____. Exposé de la situa-
tion: Octobre 1883. Ibid. 31 p.
    _____. _____. _____. Convention de Tien-
tsin du 11 mai 1884. Ibid., 1884. 76 p.
    _____. _____. _____. Affaires de Chine et
du Tonkin, 1884-1885. Ibid., 1885.
330 p.
    N°s. 1-324, 23 juillet 1885-
12 décembre 1885.

_____. _____. _____. Chine [1885-1894,
1898-oct. 1901] Ibid., 1885-1901. 6 vols.
Basic published diplomatic documents from
the period of French intervention in the
North. Cordier, col. 2545 lists all collections published, including those which
refer to Siam, Laos, and Great Britain.
Also known as "Livres jaunes."
MH

1940-1954

DE12   Cameron, Allan W. Viet-Nam crisis, a documentary history. Ithaca: Cornell University Press, [1971-]. Vol. 1, 1940-1956.
1971. 452 p.

Reproduction of the texts of 190 official documents concerning "the international diplomacy of the Viet-Nam crisis
since World War II, and especially the development of American policy." Begun as a
revision of Allan B. Cole's Conflict in
Indochina (DE13), but eventually revised
completely into the present form; Cameron's work omits some documents found in
Cole's collection and includes many others
pertaining only to Vietnam. It emphasizes
the international relations of Vietnam
rather than its internal affairs. A relatively small percentage of documents are
from the DRVN and RVN; most documents cited are from the United States, French, or
British governments. All documents are
translated into English; none seem to have
been originally published in Vietnamese.

Vol. 1 is organized around five questions: the policy of the Western allies
from 1940-1945; the independence of Vietnam from France; the formation of the
DRVN and its relations with the Socialist
bloc; the Geneva Conference of 1954; and
the emergence of the RVN under Ngô Đình
Diệm. Documents included are some of the
"complete texts of a number of documents

which mark the development of the Vietnamese Communist movement."

Portion of text on the Geneva Conference observes that the New Times (Moscow)
published complete English translations of
the speeches by Communist delegates in the
plenary sessions throughout the conference
and that there are differences in text between the British and French minutes of the
proceedings of the eighth plenary session,
July 21, 1954, the final conference session.

Critically reviewed by Malcolm Caldwell
in Journal of Southeast Asian studies, 3
(1972), 330–332 for the selection of documents and compiler's perception of the nationalist revolution in Vietnam; the roles
of the U.S. and British in supporting the
French return in 1945; the significance of
the Việt-Minh revolution in Southeast
Asia; and the American refusal to sign and
respect the Geneva agreements; and the effects of these upon Cameron's commentary
and choice of documents.
MH

DE13   Cole, Allan Burnett, ed. Conflict in Indochina and international repercussions; a
documentary history, 1945–1955. Ithaca:
Cornell University Press, 1956. 265 p.
(The Fletcher School Studies in International Affairs)

Contains about 100 documents, including
news items judged to be significant, British Parliamentary Debates, translations
from Pravda, official French and U.S.
Dept. of State publications, and press
releases from governments in Vietnam.
Translations by Cole or co-editors.
MH

DE14   Lévy, Roger. L'Indochine et ses traités,
1946. Paris: Centre d'Etudes de Politique Etrangère, Paul Hartmann, Editeur,
1947. 105 p. (Its Section d'Information.
Publication n°· 19)

Pp. 41–102 reprints texts of Franco-
Indochinese accords of 1946, of accords
signed between France and states bordering
Indochina, and of the French constitution
of 1946. Title VIII of the latter per-
tains to the Union française.
MH-HY

DE15   Mercier, André François. Faut-il abandonner
l'Indochine? Paris: Ed. France Empire,
1954. 446 p.

Part 1, impressions of the author, a
conservative member of the French Assemblée Nationale. Part 2, pp. 261–441,
"Documents" include texts of press conferences, official statements, and treaties
and accords, beginning with "Situation de
l'Indochine avant et après le 9 mars 1945,"
by Trần Văn Tỷ (1947) and ending with
"Déclaration de Ho Chi Minh de décembre
1953," "Déclaration de M. Letourneau à
Paris le 15 janvier 1954," and "Discours du
Président du Conseil français du 27 octobre 1953."
MH

DE16   U.S. Dept. of State. American foreign policy,
1950–1955; basic documents. Washington,
D.C.: GPO, 1957. 2 v.

Documents of public statements by United
States officials, including the texts of
some other public documents, such as the
text of the Geneva agreements. Documents
on Indochina and Vietnam are in vol. 1,
pp. 750–788 and vol. 2, pp. 2363–2405 and
include such topics as U.S. foreign aid to
Indochina and Vietnam, Franco-Indochina
war, Geneva Conference, recognition of the
RVN in 1955, and SEATO.
MH

DE17   _____. Foreign relations of the United
States. Washington, D.C.: GPO, 1861– .
Issued by Bureau of Public Affairs, Histo-
rical Office. Title varies: Papers re-

lating to the foreign relations of the
United States, etc.

INDEX: General index to the published
volumes of the Diplomatic correspondence
and foreign relations of the United States
1861-1899. Washington, D.C.: GPO, 1902.

INDEX: Papers relating to the foreign
relations of the United States, general
index, 1900-1918. Washington, D.C.: GPO,
1941.

The annual official record of the foreign policy of the United States. Based
on diplomatic documents--telegrams and
other correspondence from U.S. diplomatic
mission overseas to the State Dept., instructions from the State Dept. to U.S.
and foreign diplomats, and confidential
memoranda of officials--held classified
for 25 years.

Documents on Vietnam are published in
volumes for the Far East, although the indexes for 1861/1899 and 1900/1918 list a
few documents on Vietnam under "France."
Beginning with volumes 3 and 4 of 1937,
documents on Vietnam are concerned with
ammunition shipments to China in the following volumes: 1937, as stated; vol. 3
of 1938; vol. 3 of 1939; vol. 4 of 1940.
Volumes 4 and 5 of 1940 and of 1941 concern the Japanese advance into Southeast
Asia and Indochina. Few documents about
Indochina are in the volumes for 1942 and
1943. Vols. 3, 5, and 6 of 1944 concern
the progress of the war in Indochina and
the Vietnamese nationalist movements.
Vols. 6 and 7 of 1945, vol. 8 of 1946,
vol. 6 of 1947, and vol. 6 of 1948--the
latest as of 1975--publish documents on
the efforts at a post-war settlement between the French and Vietnamese nationalist groups.
MH

1954 TO DATE

DE18 Declassified documents quarterly catalog.
Washington, D.C.: Carrollton Press,
1975- . First issue, Jan.-Mar. 1975.

"Descriptions of documents contained in
the microfiche collection of the Declassified Documents Reference System and cited
in volume 1, number 1 of its Cumulative
subject index" [to the Declassified documents quarterly catalog].--title page.

Catalog of United States official documents declassified as a result of Executive Order 11652 and of the Freedom of
Information Act amendments, 5 U.S.C. 552.
Documents consist of telegrams, diplomatic
correspondence, field reports, background
studies, minutes of cabinet and National
Security Council meetings, and other materials originally classified as secret,
top secret, confidential, restricted, or
other categories. Excludes documents
automatically declassified in bulk after
30 years, documents published in other
sources such as in parts of the Pentagon
Papers and in Foreign Relations of the
United States, and documents considered
by Carrollton Press to be of marginal interest to anyone other than the person who
has requested the declassification.

A retrospective collection, covering
several thousand documents declassified
since 1972, is also planned. All declassified documents listed in the Declassified documents quarterly catalog are
available in microfiche from Carrollton
Press.

In the issue under review (Jan./Mar.
1975), 37 references were listed under
"Indochina" or "Vietnam," including the
subjects "Viet Cong infrastructure, 1968,"
"PAVN, 1961," "U.S. support for Ngo Dinh
Diem, 1961," and "strategic hamlets,
1961." Entries consist of the title or a
summary of the document, pagination, orig-

inal security classification, originating office (usually either Central Intelligence Agency, Dept. of State, Dept. of Defense, or National Security Council), and date of declassification.
MH

DE19   France. Ministère des Affaires Etrangères. Direction des Services d'Information et de Presse. La France et le Vietnam: recueil des principales déclarations françaises depuis août 1963. [Paris, 1971?]. 81 p.

Texts of public statements--primarily by Pres. de Gaulle, Foreign Minister Couve de Murville, and Foreign Minister Michel Debré--through October 7, 1968. Comprised mostly of excerpts of longer statements such as press conferences at which topics other than Vietnam were also mentioned.
MH

DE20   Geneva. Conference, 1954. [Conference documents, IC series, IC/1-IC/55, distributed by the Conference secretariat on July 24, 1954.] 308 p. Copy in Records Services Division, U.S. Dept. of State.

English-language texts of documents presented to the conference, some of which are reprinted in the annexes of the French collection on the conference and a few of which are reprinted in the British collections, both of which are listed below. Documents IC/2, IC/15 (concerned with Korea only), and IC/50 are not reprinted in either the British or French collections.
MH film

DE21   _____. _____. Conférence de Genève sur l'Indochine, 8 mai-21 juillet 1954; procès-verbaux des séances, propositions, documents finaux. Paris: Impr. Nationale, 1955. 470 p. At head of title: Ministère des Affaires étrangères.

"Includes not only all the speeches at plenary sessions and the final documents

of the Conference but also summary transcripts of proceedings of the restricted sessions."--Cameron. A second volume on the Conference, dealing with meetings between the Foreign Ministers outside the formal Conference framework [and mentioned in the Introduction as being planned for publication] remains classified by the French government (Cameron, p. 249, n. 3).

Contents are more complete than the documents published by the British government (Documents relating to the discussions... and Further documents relating to the discussions...) (See below.)
MH; DLC

DE22   Gt. Brit. Parliamentary Papers, vol. 31 (Accounts and papers, vol. 12, 1953-54). Documents relating to the discussion of Korea and Indochina at the Geneva Conference, April 27-June 15, 1954. London: HMSO, 1954. 168 p. (Cmd. 9186. Miscellaneous no. 16, 1954)

_____. _____. Further documents relating to the discussions of Indochina at the Geneva Conference, June 16-July 21, 1954. London: HMSO, 1954. 42 p. (Cmd. 9239. Miscellaneous, no. 20, 1954)

Selections of speeches and documents of the Geneva Conference. Text is much more limited than is the collection of documents published by the French (see above), although it does include the Final Declaration and other agreements and communiques of the final session which are so often quoted.

Collection includes only extracts from the verbatim records of most of the plenary sessions and does not include any record of the restricted sessions, whereas the French collection includes verbatim records of the plenary sessions and extensive summaries of the restricted sessions. British text of the 8th plenary session, corresponding to the 31st meet-

ing, omits the opening speech by Trần Văn
Đỗ of the State of Vietnam and the reply by
Mendes-France about partition of Vietnam,
disarmament, occupation of territory held
by the Việt Minh, and the setting of dates
for elections, all of which is included in
the French text.

MH

DE23 _____. Parliamentary Papers, vol. 7 (Accounts
and papers, vol. 14, 1965-66). Documents
relating to British involvement in the
Indo-China conflict 1945-1965. London:
HMSO, 1965. 268 p. (Cmnd. 2834. Miscellaneous no. 25, 1965)

A 41-page narrative, followed by 174
documents illustrating "how Britain came
to be concerned with Indo-China and [de-
scribing] the policies pursued by succes-
sive British governments since 1945."
Documents include extracts from ICSC reports and Parliamentary debates, diplomatic correspondence, and messages of the
Co-Chairmen of the Geneva Conference on
Indochina. Sources of most documents, except for ICSC reports and debates, are not
cited.

MH

DE24 _____. Parliamentary Papers, vol. 33 (Accounts and papers, vol. 10, 1964-65).
Recent exchanges concerning attempts to
promote a negotiated settlement of the
conflict in Viet-Nam. London: HMSO,
1965. 129 p. (Cmnd. 2756. Vietnam no. 3,
1965)

Reprint of the texts of 63 documents,
not all of which are British in origin,
concerned with "efforts at negotiation
made by Her Majesty's Government and others
in recent months." An interim step in what
is planned to be the publication of a more
comprehensive collection of documents.
Documents include diplomatic correspondence, radio broadcasts from Radio Hanoi,

and official statements of policy by heads
of state or foreign ministers.

MH

DE25 International Commission for Supervision and
Control in Viet Nam. [Interim reports,
1955-1961, Special reports, 1962.] Lon-
don: HMSO, 1955-1962. Issued in Gt.
Brit., Parliamentary papers, Accounts and
papers, Papers by command: Cmd. 9461,
Cmd. 9499, Cmd. 9654, Cmd. 9706, Cmnd. 31,
Cmnd. 335, Cmnd. 509, Cmnd. 726,
Cmnd. 1040, Cmnd. 1551, Cmnd. 1755,
Cmnd. 2609, Cmnd. 2634.

Reports by the Commission--usually referred to as the ICC--to the British government, as co-chairman (with Russia) of
the Geneva Conference of 1954 on Vietnam.
Reports discuss the organization of the
ICSC, problems encountered in enforcing
and observing the cease fire, withdrawal
of troops, prisoners of war, investigations of alleged violations of the Geneva
accords by the various governments involved (DRVN, RVN, USA).

MH

DE26 [Paris Peace Talks, 1968-1973]. [Texts of
statements at the plenary sessions of the
Paris meetings on Viet-Nam, 1969-
January 18, 1973.]

Copies of transcripts, including unofficial translation of statements by Vietnamese officials, made by the Department
of State, Bureau of East Asian and Pacific
Affairs.

MH

DE27 _____. [Texts of statements at the official
conversations between the United States
and North Vietnam, 1968.]

Copies of transcripts, including unofficial translation of statements by DRVN
officials, made by the Department of State,
Bureau of East Asian and Pacific Affairs.

MH

DE28   The Pentagon papers: the Defense Department
        history of United States decision making
        on Vietnam. The Senator Gravel ed. Bos-
        ton: Beacon Press, [1971]. 5 vols.

        "Consists of public documents drawn from
        the official record of the Senate Subcom-
        mittee on Public Buildings and Grounds"
        presented at a hearing of that Subcommittee
        on June 29, 1971, at which time portions
        of the documents were read into the record
        and the remainder of the set was later in-
        corporated into the record and released to
        the press. The documents were not printed
        by the Government Printing Office, for the
        full Committee on Public Works of the
        Senate did not consent to pay the printing
        costs.

        Arrangement and physical appearance are
        superior to that of the official edition:
        Documents are arranged chronologically and
        the pages have been typeset. Chapters ti-
        tled "Justification of the war--public
        statements" are placed in the latter half
        of each volume containing the related docu-
        ments; in the official edition, those
        chapters are collected into Books 7-12,
        out of chronological sequence. (See
        entry DE31 for the edition by the Govern-
        ment Printing Office.)

        Volume 5, Critical essays edited by
        Noam Chomsky and Howard Zinn and an index
        to volumes one-four, also contains brief
        comparisons of the three editions of the
        Pentagon Papers, a table showing the com-
        parative arrangement of chapters in the
        official edition and the Gravel edition,
        and a note on omissions from the official
        edition as compared with the Gravel edi-
        tion. The complete Pentagon Papers is
        more complete than is the Gravel edition,
        which contains about 4,100 pages compared
        with 7,800 pages.

DE29   Sheehan, Neil, et al. The Pentagon papers as
        published by the New York Times: based on

investigative reporting. New York: Ban-
tam, 1971. 677 p.

        Comprised of the texts of the newspaper
articles about the contents of the Pentagon papers, excerpts of the Papers as published in the Times, editorials from the
Times concerning the Papers, court records about the government injunction
against publication, and an index to "key
documents."
MH

DE30   U.S. Congress. Senate. Committee on Foreign
        Relations. Background information relat-
        ing to Southeast Asia and Vietnam. 7th
        rev. ed., Dec. 1974. Washington, D.C.:
        GPO, 1975. 660 p. At head of title:
        93d Congress, 2d session, committee print.

        Previous editions: January 14, 1965;
        rev. ed., June 16, 1965; 2d rev. ed.,
        March 1966; 3d rev. ed., July 1967; 4th
        rev. ed., March 1968; 5th rev. ed.,
        March 1969; 6th rev. ed., June 1970.

        Chronology, pp. 1-180, begins with
        June 1948 (the signing of the Hạ-Long Bay
        agreements) and ends with August 1973
        (the end of U.S. bombing in Cambodia).
        Official documents, pp. 181-660, covers
        February 1950 (U.S. recognition of Viet-
        nam, Cambodia, and Laos) to March 1974 (a
        statement on the Indochina situation by
        U.S. Secretary of State Henry Kissinger).
        Pp. 579-660 contain statements by Viet-
        namese and Cambodian officials of the
        various sides on such issues as peace
        negotiations and cease-fire proposals,
        particularly those from the NFLSVN, as
        well as texts of the Paris agreements on
        Vietnam of January 27, 1973, the U.S.-
        North Vietnamese communique of
        February 14, 1973, and the Declaration
        of the International Conference on Viet-
        nam, March 2, 1973.
MH

DE31   U.S. Dept. of Defense. United States-Vietnam
relations, 1945-1967. Washington, D.C.:
GPO, 1971. 12 vols. Published as U.S.
Congress, House Committee on Armed Services, Committee Print, 92d Congress,
1st session. Known as the "Pentagon Papers."

Photoprinted copies of original typescript of the study prepared by the Vietnam Task Force, Office of the Secretary of
Defense from 1967 to 1969. Texts consists
of unsigned narrative chapters written by
members of the Task Force, classified U.S.
and foreign government documents, unclassified public documents--reports, proclamations, treaties, etc.--and excerpts from
books and periodicals. The 12-volume edition contains the first 43 volumes of the
original 47-volume study, the difference
being one of format--several volumes of
the original study have been combined to
form one of each of the 12 volumes of the
published edition. The four remaining
volumes--the "diplomatic volumes"--were
not released at the same time as the others
because they dealt with peace negotiations
which were still in progress at that time.
They were, however, entered in evidence at
the trial of U.S. vs. Ellsberg and Russo
in Los Angeles in 1972 on a confidential
basis. They were also declassified in
1975 and released in slightly "sanitized"
form; this version is available on microfilm as part of the "Declassified Documents Reference System" (see DE18 for description). See last paragraph of this
annotation for citations of Congressional
Staff Committee Prints of the Pentagon
Papers.

Quality of reproduction of the GPO edition is only fair: Typescript is not always as legible as if it were typeset,
maps in color in the original edition are
only black or gray and white, and photocopies of original documents are almost

illegible. Arrangement is approximately
chronological in Books [volumes] 1-7 and
again in Books 7-12; by contrast, the arrangement of the Gravel edition (DE28) is
chronological from the beginning. No indexes are available either to each volume
or to the complete study; no footnotes
are printed in this edition, for they are
still classified. Pagination is not consecutive even within a volume; a suggested
form of citation is to book, section,
chapter, and page, e.g. "Toward a negotiated settlement," Book 1, II.A.1,
pp. B-1--B-13.

The staff of the Senate Committee on
Foreign Relations issued a series of committee prints based on the Pentagon Papers, beginning in March 1972: Staff
study no. 1, Vietnam commitments, 1961;
no. 2, The United States and Vietnam,
1944-1947; no. 3, U.S. involvement in the
overthrow of Diem, 1963; no. 5, Bombing as
a policy tool in Vietnam: effectiveness.
Staff Study no. 4, Negotiations 1964-1965,
was not released as of 1973; it is based
on the then-classified "diplomatic volumes." The preface and table of contents
and chronology and exchanges of letters
between the Committee and the Department
of State on the release of the study are
printed as an appendix to Staff Study
no. 5. The Washington Post, June 26, 1972,
published "large portions" of the classified portions of the diplomatic volumes
(Sen. J. W. Fulbright, appendix, p. 23).

Newspaper articles about the Pentagon
Papers and excerpts from the Papers published in newspapers in the United States
were reprinted in the Congressional record, June 14-July 8, 1971 on various
pages between 19565 and 20076. The annual
index of the Congressional record does not
list all references to the Pentagon Papers
under one heading but under various subheadings of "Department of Defense" such

as "Remarks in House," "Remarks in Senate,"
"Studies--United States--Vietnam relationships, 1945-1967," and "Articles and edi-
torials--Pentagon Papers."
MH

DE32 U.S. Dept. of State. Historical Division.
      Bureau of Public Affairs. American for-
      eign policy: current documents. Washing-
      ton, D.C.: GPO, 1956- . Annual.

      A "collection of official papers which
      indicate the scope, goals, and implementa-
      tion of the foreign policy of the United
      States." Sources are usually public
      statements and documents: United Nations
      documents; Department of State bulletin;
      U.S. Congressional hearings; New York
      Times; Peking review. Sources for state-
      ments of officials of DRVN are usually
      "Department of State files." Footnotes
      give extensive references to earlier vol-
      umes of American foreign policy. Volume
      for 1967 (latest published as of 1975)
      contains documents on Vietnam on pp. 818-
      1057.
      MH

DE33 Vietnam (Democratic Republic). Ministry of
      Foreign Affairs. Press and Information
      Department. Documents related to the
      implementation of the Geneva agreements
      concerning Viet-Nam. Hanoi, 1956. 202 p.

      Text of the Geneva Agreements, declara-
      tions made by representatives at the last
      session, and subsequent statements made by
      DRVN, RVN, and U.S. relating to the "re-
      fusal [by the U.S. and the RVN] to abide
      by the Geneva agreements."--pref.
      MH

DE34 Vietnam (Republic). Bộ Thông-Tin. The prob-
      lem of reunification of Vietnam. Saigon,
      1958. 105 p.

      "A collection of official statements,
      communiques, and messages" (Jumper).

DE35 "Viet-Nam." In Select documents on interna-
      tional affairs. Canberra: Dept. of For-
      eign Affairs, 1964- .

      Contents: "Viet-Nam since the Geneva
      agreements," Select documents on interna-
      tional affairs, no. 1 of 1964; "Viet-Nam,
      first half of 1965," Ibid., no. 2 of 1965;
      later issues in Ibid., n.s. no. 7, 9, 11,
      13, 18 (the latest dated July 1972, cover-
      ing January 1968-December 1969).

      Texts of selected documents--press
      releases, interviews, broadcasts, official
      speeches, and diplomatic correspondence--
      showing the "record of Communist subver-
      sion" and "Communist rejection" of U.S.
      and RVN efforts to end the war (no. 1 of
      1964) and "efforts toward a political set-
      tlement" (no. 18).

      Continued as "Indo-China, January 1970-
      June 1971," in ibid., no. 20, 1973,
      182 p. Later issues not located.
      MH

HANDBOOKS AND GUIDEBOOKS DF

HANDBOOKS

DF1 American University, Washington, D.C. For-
     eign Area Studies Division. Area handbook
     for Vietnam. Washington, D.C.: GPO,
     1962, repr., 1964. 513 p. (Dept. of the
     Army pamphlet, DA Pam 550-40) Rev. ed. of
     1957 ed.
     _____. _____. Area handbook for South Viet-
     nam. Ibid., 1967. 510 p. (DA Pam
     550-55)
     _____. _____. Area handbook for North Viet-
     nam. Ibid., 1967. 494 p. (DA Pam
     550-57)

     Intended as introductions; English-
     language bibliographies at end of each of
     sections, no footnotes. Latter two hand-
     books are revisions of 1962 handbook.

Bibliography in Area handbook for North Vietnam lists numerous translations by JPRS.

MH

DF2   Gt. Brit. Naval Intelligence Division. Indo-China. [London?], 1943. 535 p. (B. R. 510, Geographical handbook series)

Synthesis of information on most aspects of Indochina (physical features, flora and fauna, population, health, government, economics, agriculture, etc.) intended for more than military purposes. Based on French sources such as Gourou, Robequain, and colonial government publications, particularly Bulletin économique de l'Indochine. Many maps of coastal features and settlement patterns and illustrations and photographs of village scenes, cities, waterways, and factories.

MH

DF3   Huard, Pierre, and Maurice Durand. Connaissance du Việt-Nam. Paris: Impr. Nationale; Hanoi: Ecole française d'Extrême-Orient, 1954. 356 p.

A handbook on Vietnamese civilization as it existed at the beginning of the 20th century, "before it was submerged by Western civilization." Brief chapters on virtually all aspects of material and spiritual life in Vietnam, with bibliographies at end of each chapter. Contains 132 drawings, mostly from Dumoutier (1907), Tissot (1908), and Nordemann (1914). Extensive use of Vietnamese terms and phrases to supplement the French text. Indexes by illustrations, subjects, Vietnamese words, Sino-Vietnamese characters, personal names, and place names.

MH

DF4   Lévi, Sylvain, ed. Indochine; ouvrage publié sous la direction de Sylvain Lévi. Paris: Société d'éditions géographique, maritime et coloniale, 1931. 2 vols. At head of title: Exposition coloniale internationale, Paris, 1931. Commissariat général.

Vol. 1, articles by Robequain, Przyluski, Finot, André Masson, A. Mus, Dufresne, G. Coedès, P. Mus, and V. Goloubew on the inhabitants, history, religions, literatures, and art and archaeology of Indochina. Bibliographies at the end of each chapter. Vol. 2, official documents on the government of Indochina.

Rev. by J. Tramond in Revue d'histoire des colonies françaises, Mémento colonial, 1932, 137-141.

MH

DF5   Maspero, Georges, ed. Un empire colonial français, l'Indochine. Paris: Van Oest, 1929-1930. 2 vols.

Articles by G. and Henri Maspero, H. Mansuy, Przyluski, Coedès, Cadière, G. Lamarre, and others. Vol. 1, "Le pays et ses habitants, l'histoire, la vie sociale." Vol. 2, "L'Indochine française, L'Indochine économique, L'Indochine pittoresque."

MH

DF6   [Nguyễn Bảo Trị, and Nguyễn Văn Toán]. Người Việt, đất Việt [Vietnam: The land and people, by] Cửu Long Giang và Toan Ánh [pseuds.] [Saigon]: Nam Chi Tùng Thư, [1967]. 528 p.

A collection of articles on various aspects of life in Vietnam, by writers living in RVN. Subjects include history, culture, geography, tourist attractions, literature and fine arts, religion, and other topics. A feature is the articles by numerous writers on their home areas (quê hương). Similar in coverage to Connaissance du Việt-Nam (DF3), although includes more information from history and from individual writers.

MH-V

DF7   Teston, Eugène, and Maurice Percheron.
      L'Indochine moderne; encyclopédie adminis-
      trative, touristique, artistique et écono-
      mique. Paris: Libr. de France, [1932?].
      1,028 p.
         Articles on history, government, social
      life, military events, geography, tourism,
      economic life, and other aspects of Indo-
      china.
      MH

GUIDEBOOKS

DF8   *About, Pierre-Edmond. Indochine: Cochin-
      chine, Annam, Cambodge, Laos. Paris:
      Société d'éditions, géographiques, mari-
      times et coloniales, 1931. 337 p.
      (Guides des colonies françaises) (Source:
      DLC.)

DF9   *Guide G. B. indochinois. Hanoi: IDEO.
         Editions of 1927 (232 p.) and 1928-
      1929 (236 p.) cited in Boudet 3. Also
      cited: Indicateur G. B. indochinois,
      1929 (Hanoi: Publications G. B., 1929,
      155 p.)

DF10 Madrolle, Claudius. Indochine du Nord:
      Tonkin, Annam, Laos. 2. éd. rev. et
      augmentée. Paris: Hachette, 1925.
      369 p.
      _____. Indochine du Sud: Cochinchine, Cam-
      bodge, Bas-Laos, Sud-Annam, Siam. Paris:
      Hachette, 1926. 344 p.
      _____. Indochina: Cochinchina, Cambodia,
      Annam, Tonkin, Yunnan, Laos, Siam....
      Paris, London: Hachette, 1930. 280 p.
      (Madrolle guides, English series)
      _____. Tonkin du Sud, Hanoi. Paris: Comité
      de l'Asie française, 1907.
      MH; DLC

DF11 *Norès, Georges. Itinéraires automobiles en
      Indochine. Guide du touriste. Hanoi:
      IDEO, 1930. 3 vols.

Vol. 1, Tonkin, 110 p. Vol. 2, Cochinchine, Cambodge, 142 p. Vol. 3, Annam,
Laos, 146 p. (Source: Boudet 3.)

YEARBOOKS DG

DG1   *Annuaire annamite de la Cochinchine; lịch
      Annam thông dụng trong Nam-Kỳ. Saigon,
      1885- . At head of title: République
      française. (Source: Cordier 3: 1761-
      1763 (1885-1907).)

DG2   *Annuaire de la Cochinchine. Saigon: Imp.
      impériale, etc., 1865-1888[?]. Title
      varies: 1865-1871, Annuaire de la Cochin-
      chine française. Beginning in 1889, issued
      as Annuaire de l'Indo-Chine française
      (1re ptie.) (DG4).
         Volume for 1880 contains agricultural
      almanac, chronological list of French
      commanders-general, outline of government
      administration, and list of European and
      Asian merchants. (Source: Cordier 3:
      1745; Gregory; MH (1880).)

DG3   Annuaire des Etats-Associés: Cambodge, Laos,
      Viêtnam. Paris: Diloutremer et Havas,
      1953. 578 p.
         Short descriptions of the history of
      each country, an outline of the government
      and foreign representation, lists of busi-
      ness establishments and professional
      groups, and economic statistics.
      MH

DG4   *Annuaire général, administratif, commercial
      et industriel de l'Indo-Chine. Hanoi:
      Schneider, 1889-1907; IDEO 1907-[1950?].
      Title varies: Annuaire de l'Indo-Chine
      (1re ptie., Cochinchine et Cambodge;
      2ème ptie., Annam et Tonkin); Annuaire de
      l'Indo-Chine française (1re ptie., Cochin-
      chine; 2ème ptie., Cambodge; 3ème ptie.,

Annam et Tonkin); Annuaire commercial et
administratif de l'Indo-Chine française;
Annuaire général de l'Indo-Chine française;
Annuaire général, commercial et administratif de l'Indo-Chine française; Annuaire
général, commercial, administratif et industriel de l'Indo-Chine; Annuaire général
de l'Indo-Chine; Annuaire général, administratif, commercial et industriel de l'Indo-
Chine.

Compendium of administrative and non-
official information. Volume for 1938/39
lists French government agencies which
deal with Indochina affairs, including
names of chief administrators, and persons
in government service in each agency.--DLC.
Pagination of most issues is over 500
pages, with volumes for 1905-1912, listed
in Cordier, about 1,500 pages. Issues for
1905-1915 also include detailed monographs
on the provinces (Boudet). (Source: Cordier 3: 1661-1663, 1745; Gregory; DLC.)

DG5 *Annuaire général du Vietnam; tổng niên giám
Việt-Nam; general directory of Vietnam.
Saigon: A. V. T., Bureau d'études tech-
niques et économiques, 1952/53- .
(Source: DLC.)

DG6 The Far East and Australasia. London:
Europa Publications, 1969- . Annual.
Directory of businesses, state enter-
prises, learned institutions, newspaper or
broadcasting stations, banks, and other
institutions; outlines of history and government; and summary statistics of various
countries. Includes DRVN, pp. 639-656;
RVN, pp. 657-680 (1969 edition).
MH

REGIONAL AND LOCAL HISTORY DH

SEE ALSO GEOGRAPHY--GAZETTEERS CK

DH1 Cordier, Henri. Bibliotheca indosinica.
See AA23 for complete description. For
publications on regional and local history,
see 3: 1619-1678 and 4: 2923-2928, "Géo-
graphie--Tonkin" (including Hanoi and Hải-
phòng), 3: 1679-1690 and 4: 2927-2928,
"Géographie--Annam" (including Hue), and
3: 1689-1768 and 4: 2927-2928, "Géogra-
phie--Cochinchine" (including Saigon).
MH

DH2 Boudet, Paul, and Rémy Bourgeois. Bibliographie de l'Indochine française.
See AA22 for complete description. For
publications on regional and local history,
see "Annam," "Cochinchine," "Tonkin," and
the names of cities or provinces. In
vol. 4, maps issued by the Service Géographique de l'Indochine are included in
the listing for each city or province.
MH

DH3 *L'Annam. Hanoi: IDEO, 1931. 227 p. At
head of title: Exposition coloniale internationale, Paris, 1931. Indochine
française.
Also published in BAVH, 18 (1931) and a
new edition by the Société de Géographie
de Hanoi, as fasc. 5 of Inventaire général
de l'Indochine (IDEO, 1931).
Chapters on the land, people, products,
and the work of the French by B. Bourotte,
A. Sallet, L. M. Cadière and others.
Notice in BEFEO, 31 (1931), 504-506.

DH4 Baudrit, André. "Contribution à l'histoire
de Saigon, extraits des registres des dé-
libérations de la ville de Saigon (Indochine française) 1867-1916." BSEI, n.s.
10, 1-3 (1935), 3-376; suite, ibid.,
3-347. Also publ. separately, Saigon:
Testelin, 1935. 2 vols.

Reprinting of the discussions of the Conseil Municipal de Saigon about all aspects of municipal affairs. Summaries, in italics, are given where a document is not reproduced.
MH

DH5 * ___ . Guide historique des rues de Saigon. Saigon: [n. p.], 1943. 532 p.

Biographical and bibliographical information about the personnages for whom the streets, places, and buildings in Saigon were named (Jumper). Of historical interest, as French names of streets and places were changed after independence.

DH6 Bouchot, Jean. Documents pour servir à l'histoire de Saigon, 1859-1865. Saigon: Portail, 1927. 527 p. Rev. by L. Finot, BEFEO, 28 (1928), 279-280.

___ . Recueil de documents pour servir à l'histoire de Saigon (1858-1868). Saigon: Portail, 1928. 400 p.

Includes texts already published elsewhere but gathered here; unpublished documents from archives; and administrative documents, "now forgotten and deemed valuable to reprint." Sections on the description of Saigon, Saigon as a port, Saigon as a commercial center, Cochinchina as seen from France, the Botanic Gardens, and the palace of the governor.

DH7 ___ . "La naissance et les premières années de Saigon, ville française." BSEI, n.s. 2 (1927), 63-138. Also issued separately, Saigon: Portail, 1927, 80 p.

Reprinted texts of official documents on the history of Saigon. A related publication is "Documents sur le Vieux-Saigon, rapports officiels," BSEI, n.s. 2 (1927), 27-33.
MH

DH8 Cochinchine 1931. Publiée sous le patronage de la Société des Etudes indochinoises. Saigon: Impr. S. I. L. I., éd. P. Gastaldy, 1931. 168 p. Issued in place of BSEI, n.s. 7, no. 2 (1932). At head of title: Exposition coloniale internationale, Paris, 1931. Indochine française. General survey and description.
MH

DH9 Đại-Nam nhất-thống-chí [Geography of Đại-Nam]. 1865-1882. [Another ed.], 1909.

The national gazetteer of Vietnam in the 19th century, with chapters on the geography, climate, customs, cities and villages, schools, fields, history, taxes, markets, temples, historic personnages, and natural resources of each province. The 1865-1882 edition comprised monographs on all of Đại Nam, including the Lục-tỉnh, or the six provinces ceded to France from 1862-1867. The 1909 edition, compiled under Cao Xuân Dục, included revised texts for only the provinces then under the protectorate of Annam, or Trung-Bộ.

Two major translations into quốc-ngữ exist: 1) Đại-Nam nhất-thống-chí, Phạm Trọng Điềm phiên dịch. Hanoi: Nhà Xuất-bản Khoa học Xã hội, 1969- . Text only in quốc-ngữ.[1] (Set at MH-V incomplete) 2) Đại-Nam nhất thống chí. (Saigon: Nha Văn-hóa, Bộ Quốc-Gia Giáo-Dục, 1959-1973.) 29 vols. in 34 pts. (Văn-hóa Tùng-thư, 2-6, 9-12, 20-29, 31-33, 36-37, 38[a], 38[b], 39-42, 52-54)[1,2]

Translators include Trần Tuấn Khải, Đặng Chu Kính, Nguyễn Tạo, and Lê Xuân Giáo. Text in Chinese characters, romanized transliteration, and quốc-ngữ text. [1]MH-V; [2]Gélinas, list 033, March 15, 1975 (description of vols. in Văn-hóa Tùng-thư, 41, 42, 52-54--Quang-Yên, Thái-Nguyên, and the Lục-tỉnh: Biên Hòa, Gia Định, Định Tường, Vĩnh Long, An Giang, and Hà Tiên)

DH10   Goodman, Allan, and Vũ Mạnh Phát. "Vietnam," in Urban Southeast Asia; a selected bibliography of accessible research, reports and related materials on urbanism and urbanization..., ed. Gerald Breese. [New York: Southeast Asia Development Advisory Group, 1973], pp. 136-159.

    Bibliography of about 450 publications in Vietnamese, English, and French on urbanism and urbanization as part of modernization as well as (in the RVN) the result of war. Kinds of publications include books, periodical articles, government contract reports for AID or other agencies, translations by JPRS and the Joint U.S. Public Affairs Office (Saigon) in Viet-Nam documents and research notes, government publications, and manuscripts. Topics include economic growth, political and military events, education, land reform, statistics, population growth, harbor facilities, refugees, water supply, electricity, transportation, and maps.

    Citations to urbanization in Asia and Southeast Asia and to bibliographies on urbanization are on pp. 1-11 and 161-165.
MH

DH11   *Lược sử tên phố Hà-nội [History of the names of streets in Hanoi]. [by] Lê Thước, Vũ Tuấn Sán [et al]. Hanoi: [n.p.], 1964. 332 p.

    Rev. in NCLS, no. 95 (2/67), 54-60, by Hoa Bằng.

DH12   [Malleret, Louis, and Georges Taboulet]. "La Cochinchine dans le passé." BSEI, n.s. 17 (1942), 9-135.

    Catalog of an exhibition on Cochinchina from 1833 to the 20th century. List of 901 items on display, including protohistory and prehistory, Khmers in Cochinchina, Tay Son, Gia Long and the Nguyễn dynasty, European missionaries, traders, and explorers, and French occupation. In-

cludes illustrations, books, statutes, official documents--letters, treaties, orders of Vietnamese emperors--and 8 photographs.
MH

DH13   Masson, André. Hanoï pendant la période héroïque (1873-1883). Paris: Guethner, 1929. 262 p.

    Unpublished documents (pp. 181-219) and Masson's interpretation (remainder of book) about early years of French intrusion in the North.
MH

DH14   Nguyễn Đông Khê [Also known as Nguyễn Văn Lý]. Bắc thành địa-dư chỉ [Geography of the Northern provinces]. 1845.

    Originally compiled under Lê Công Chất, governor general of the North. Translated into quốc-ngữ, with photographic reproduction of original Sino-Vietnamese text, by Đặng Chu Kỉnh (Saigon: Nha Văn-hóa, 1969), 4 vols. in 3. (Văn Hóa tùng-thư, 38c, 38d, 38e)

    Contents: Vols. I and II, Thăng Long city and Hai Dương province; vol. III, Northern Sơn Nam province; vol. IV, Southern Sơn Nam province. Comparison of geographical, political, historical, and social information about the northern province.
MH-V

DH15   Phan Huy Chú. "Dư-địa chỉ" [Geography]. Vol. 1, chapters 1-5 of Lịch-triều hiến-chương loại-chỉ [Monographs of the institutions of the dynasties].

    See AD1 for complete description of main work.

    Translated into quốc-ngữ by Nguyễn Thọ Dực: Lịch-triều hiến-chương loại-chỉ, do Nguyễn Thọ Dực dịch. [Saigon]: Phu Quốc Vụ Khanh Đặc Trách Văn-Hoá, 1972. 368, 295 p.

Text in quốc-ngữ, romanized transcription of original text, and photographic reproduction of the original text of 3064-MC and 5065-MC in the archives at Đà-Lạt. Historical geography of the provinces, names of districts in each province and number of villages, physical features, and writings about each province.
MH-V

DH16   Trịnh Hoài Đức [Vietnamese: Trang Hội Đức; Chinese: Chêng Huai-Te]. Gia-định thống chí [Description of Gia-định province]. ca. 1820.

History and description of the conquest and occupation of the southern provinces from about 1658 until about 1818, including customs, geography, natural resources, and government.

Translated into French by [L. G.] G. Aubaret, Gia-định thung-chi; histoire et description de la Basse Cochinchine. Paris: Impr. nationale, 1863. 359 p. Repr.: Farnborough, Eng.: Gregg, 1969.[1] Omitted the portion about towns; also, according to Lê Thành Khôi, Le Viet-Nam (DA7), p. 349, Aubaret consistently mistakenly converted the dates of the lunar calendar into the wrong dates on the Gregorian calendar.

Translated into quốc-ngữ by Nguyễn Tạo, Gia-định thành thống chí. [Saigon:] Nha Văn Hóa Phu Quốc Vụ Khanh đặc trách Văn Hóa, 1972. 4 vols. in 3. (Văn-hóa tùng-thư, 49-50-51). Text in Chinese characters and in quốc-ngữ.[2]
[1]MH [2]MH-V

DH17   *Vietnam (Republic). Directorate General of Reconstruction and Urban Planning. Đã phong (name of province or municipality). [Area handbook]. Saigon, 1966-1969. 35 vols.

Each vol. is written about a province or municipality. Length varies, from 15 pages on Đà-lạt to 130 pages on Ba Xuyên Province. Cited by Vũ Mạnh Phát in Urban Southeast Asia, ed. Gerald Breese (DH10).

ARCHAEOLOGY DI

MAJOR SOURCES

DI1   Cordier, Henri. Bibliotheca indosinica.
See AA23 for complete description. For publications on archaeology, see 3: 1875-1884 (in which are listed the contents of the Bulletin de la Commission Archéologique de l'Indochine, 1908-1913) and 4: 2935-2938, "Antiquités."

DI2   Boudet, Paul, and Rémy Bourgeois. Bibliographie de l'Indochine française.
See AA22 for complete description. For publications on archaeology, see "Archéologie" in each volume and "Préhistoire" in vol. 4, as well as subheading "Archéologie" under "Annam," "Cochinchine," and "Tonkin" in vol. 4. Vol. 4 has numerous references under "Archéologie sino-annamite."
MH

DI3   Bezacier, Louis. "L'archéologie au Viêt-Nam d'après les travaux de l'Ecole française d'Extrême-Orient." France-Asie, 15, no. 149-150 (1958), 513-534.
Bibliographic essay. Followed by his "Liste des travaux...," See AC11.
MH

DI4   _____. "Le Viêt-Nam." Vol. 2 of Manuel d'Archéologie d'Extrême-Orient, 1re ptie: Asie du Sud-Est. Paris: Picard, 1972. 343 p.
1er fascicle, by Bezacier: "De la préhistoire à la fin de l'occupation chinoise;" 2ème fascicle, to be written by

several Vietnamese archaeologists, will cover the period since A.D. 939. Published by J. Boisselier after the deaths of Bezacier in 1966 and G. Coedès in 1969.

Comprehensive and well-documented synthesis on art and archaeology in Vietnam, with over one-half of the work devoted to the Dongsonian excavations and the Bronze Age culture in Vietnam. Includes numerous drawings, plates, and photographs from previously published sources, collections of the Ecole française d'Extrême-Orient, and Bezacier's personal collection. Bibliography, pp. 297-307, mostly Western-language sources, with only a few publications reporting the research done in North Vietnam during the 1960's.
MH

DI5   Finot, Louis. "L'archéologie indochinoise (1917-1930)." Bulletin de la Commission Archéologique de l'Indochine, 1931, 1-77.

Lists about 100 books and articles in French, including legislation, administration, and publications.

Continued by Mme. G. de Coral-Remusat in "L'archéologie indochinoise en 1931 et 1932," ibid., 1931/34, 195-212, almost all of which cites research in Cambodia, Laos, and the Champa areas.
MH

DI6   Harvard University. Peabody Museum of Archaeology and Ethnology. Library. Author

and subject catalogues.
See CD4 for complete description.

DI7   *Lịch-sử Việt-Nam [History of Vietnam].
See DA8 for complete description.
Contains information on early Vietnamese history based on archaeological discoveries of past two decades.

DI8   *Vietnam (Democratic Republic). Viện Ngôn Ngữ Học. Thuật ngữ sử học, dân tộc học, khao cổ học, Nga-Việt có chú thêm tiếng Pháp [Terminology in history, ethnography, and archaeology. Russian-to-Vietnamese with French terms added]. Hanoi: Khoa học xã hội, 1970. 133 p. (Source: Châu.)

OTHER SOURCES

DI9   Annual bibliography of Indian archaeology. Leiden: Brill, 1925-

DI10   Bulletin signalétique section 525: Préhistoire. Paris: Centre national de la recherche scientifique, 1970- . Continuation of Bulletin signalétique (1940-1969) with various subtitles.

DI11   Répertoire d'art et d'archéologie. Paris: Morancé, 1910- . (Volumes before 1965 index books and periodical articles about art and archaeology in Vietnam.)

E Pure and Applied Sciences

SCIENCE EA

BIBLIOGRAPHIES

MAJOR SOURCES

EA1   Bulletin analytique des travaux scientifiques
       publiés au Viet-Nam. Saigon: Service de
       Documentation [1964-]. At head of title:
       République du Vietnam. Centre National de
       la Recherche Scientifique.

       Vol. 1, sec. 1, Médecine et sciences
       affiliées, 1942-1962, par Nguyễn Hữu et Vũ
       Văn Nguyên. [Saigon, 1964] 160 p. See
       EJ7 for annotation.

       Vol. 1, sec. 2, Autres sciences. Sai-
       gon, 1965. 59 p.

       Continuations of B. Noyer's Bibliogra-
       phie analytique des travaux scientifiques
       en Indochine, fasc. 1, 1942 (EJ9).
       Sec. 1: MBCo; sec. 2: TTAPC

EA2   Government reports index and Government re-
       ports announcements. Springfield, Va.:
       National Technical Information Service.

       See AH6 and AH7 for bibliographic
       description.

EA3   *Institut Scientifique de l'Indochine. Biblio-
       thèque. Catalogue de la bibliothèque. Ha-
       noi: IDEO, 1922. 433 p.

       Offered for sale by Thanh-long (Brus-
       sels), Nov. 1971. Comp. by Pierre Carton.

EA4   Science citation index; an international in-
       terdisciplinary index to the literature of
       science, medicine, agriculture, technology,
       and the behavioral and social sciences,
       1961- . Philadelphia: Institute for
       Scientific Information, 1963- . Quarter-
       ly, with annual and quinquennial cumula-
       tions.

       An index to source articles and to ar-
       ticles based on the ideas in those source
       articles. Physical arrangement is in five
       different indexes: "Citation index,"
       "Source index," "Permuterm subject index,"
       "Corporate index," and "Patent citation
       index." The "Citation index" is the usual
       index for beginning a literature search if
       one is interested in seeing what articles
       have been written based on a particular
       author's work. The "Source index" con-
       tains complete bibliographic information
       for the articles. The "Permuterm subject
       index" is a comprehensive subject index to
       literature in the Science citation index.

       The 1972 annual index contained
       3,645,017 citations to journal articles
       in 2,425 journals, most of which were pub-
       lished in the United States and Europe.
       Of these, the "Permuterm subject index"
       listed over 50 articles on Vietnam.
       MH-CSCL

EA5   U.S. Engineer Agency for Resources Invento-
       ries. Selected bibliography, Lower Mekong

SCIENCE EA

basin; bibliographie choisie, bassin infé-
rieur du Mékong.

See AA50 for complete description.

EA6 *Vietnam (Republic). Centre National de la
Recherche Scientifique. Bulletin mensuel
signalétique de documents scientifiques.
Saigon, 1963- .

Index of scientific and technical periodicals received by the libraries of Vietnam (Bibliographical services throughout
the world, 1965-69 [UNESCO]).

OTHER SOURCES

EA7 Academy of Natural Sciences, Philadelphia.
Library. Catalog. Boston: G. K. Hall,
1972. 16 vols.

EA8 Harvard University. Museum of Comparative
Zoology. Library. Catalogue. Boston:
G. K. Hall, 1967. 8 vols.

DICTIONARIES

EA9 *Đào Văn Tiến. Danh-từ khoa-học (vặn vật học)
[Scientific terms (natural sciences)].
1. éd. Paris: Minh-Tân, 1950, 104 p.;
2. éd. Ibid., 1955, 107 p.; In lần 3.
Ibid., 1955. (Source: NIC.)

EA10 Genibrel, J. F. M. Dictionnaire annamite-
français comprenant...3° la flore et la
faune de l'Indochine (1898). See AE19 for
complete description.

Names of plants and animals are defined
in the same alphabetical sequence as other
words, with the scientific name of plants
and animals included with the French name.

EA11 Nguyễn Khắc Kham et al. Thư-tịch tuyển-trạch
về danh-từ chuyên-môn; a selected bibliography on scientific and technical terminology in Vietnamese. Saigon: Nha Văn-
Khố và Thư-Viện Quốc-Gia, 1967. 21 p.

Lists 86 dictionaries--whether published in books or in periodicals--in many
subjects, including military science,
agriculture, religion, philosophy, physics, chemistry, medicine, economics, politics, and law. Also includes multilingual
dictionaries in those subjects.
mgc

EA12 *Nhiêm Thế Gi, and Nguyễn Đức Lưu. Danh-từ
kỹ-thuật Anh-Việt [English-Vietnamese
technical terms]. [Saigon: authors,
1972]. 285 p. (Source: TTQGVN 17-18
(1972).)

EA13 *Vietnam (Republic). Bộ Quốc-gia Giáo-dục.
Danh-từ kỹ-thuật [Technical terms]. Saigon, 1959. 278 p. (Source: TTAPC.)

EA14 *____. Ủy-ban Soạn-thảo Danh-từ Khoa-học.
Danh-từ khoa-học [Scientific glossary].
Saigon: Bộ Quốc-gia Giáo-dục, Trung-tâm
học-liệu, 1962- . (Tu-sách Khoa-học,
Giám-đốc Lê Văn Thới)

French-Vietnamese--Vietnamese-French
glossaries of terms in mathematics
(vol. 1), physics (vol. 2), chemistry
(vol. 3), zoology (vol. 4), botany
(vol. 5), geology, pharmacy, technology,
and atomic energy. Purpose is to provide
a scientific terminology for the various
scientific subjects and to systematize
Vietnamese terminology. Each volume is
described more completely in the appropriate section of this bibliography.

Also cited as: Saigon. Viện Đại-Học.
Danh-từ khoa-học. (Source: NIC.)

DESCRIPTIONS

EA15 Huard, Pierre, and Maurice Durand. "La science au Viêtnam." BSEI, n.s. 38 (1963),
533-555.

Historical survey from pre-Chinese
times to early 20th century. Observes in-

fluences from China, European missionaries,
and Western science upon the development
of science and technology in Vietnam. Includes names of missionaries who worked
with science. Notes the development of
science in certain areas as a response to
practical needs: geography (the use of
gazetteers in government and administration, especially in the 19th century);
mathematics (measurement of land, especially for rice fields); and medicine.

   Summaries of this article are included
in: Science in the nineteenth century,
ed. René Taton (New York: Basic Books,
1965) pp. 579-584, and Science in the
twentieth century, ed. René Taton (Ibid.,
1966), pp. 594-596.
MH

EA16   Saint-Arroman, R. de. "Les missions scientifiques dans l'Inde française, en Indo-chine
et en Malaisie." Bulletin de la Société
Académique Indo-chinoise de France, 2. sér.,
1 (1881), 1-19.

   Pp. 14-19, chronological listing of 77
scientific missions from 1680 (Pallu) to
1881 (Septans and Mondon). Each entry
gives the name of the leader of the mission, a sentence describing the purpose of
the mission, date, and source of published
or unpublished report. Does not include
explorations by missionaries (although
Paullu's is included), privately-funded
expeditions, contemporary diplomatic missions, purely military missions, and hydrographic and geodesic missions, of which he
lists about 50 in a footnote.
MH

ASTRONOMY AND NAVIGATION EB

EB1   Cordier, Henri. Bibliotheca indosinica.
   See AA22 for complete description. For
publications on astronomy and navigation,

see 3: 2275-2278 and 4: 2967-2970, "Art
militaire et navigation," 3: 1569-1620
and 4: 2922, "Géographie--Mer: Publications pour en faciliter la Navigation,
etc.," 3: 2149-2152, "Sciences mathéma-
tiques," and other references in this
bibliography under CK Geography.
MH

EB2   Boudet, Paul, and Rémy Bourgeois. Bibliographie de l'Indochine française.
   See AA21 for complete description. For
publications on astronomy and navigation,
see subject headings "Astronomie" and "Navigation," in each volume and "Ports" and
"Hydrographie" in vol. 4.
MH

EB3   Battelle Memorial Institute, Columbus, Ohio.
Remote Area Conflict Information Center.
Blue book of coastal vessels, South Viet-
nam; thanh-thư về tàu thuyền cận duyên,
Miền Nam Việt-Nam. [Columbus?], 1967.
556 p.

   "Blue Book project staff"--Advanced
Research Projects Agency, Office of the
Secretary of Defense, and the Combat De-
velopment and Test Center, Republic of
Vietnam Armed Forces [Trung-Tâm Phát-
Triển Kha-năng Tác-Chiến, Quân Lực Việt-
Nam Cộng-Hòa]

   Handbook for the use of naval personnel
in identifying different types of vessels:
contains pictures of every type of vessel
to be found in the area. Introductory
chapters on the origin and evolution of
Vietnamese boats, fishing techniques and
equipment, folklore, construction. Observations on the geographical areas in
which each type of vessel is found.

   Updated version of A handbook of junks
of South Vietnam (1962). Refers to Les
voiliers d'Indochine (Saigon, 1949) by
J.-B. Piétri, as the last view of Vietnamese boats in their native state--"before

they were altered by motorization or made
refugees by war."

MH

EB4   Ho, Peng-Yoke. "Natural phenomena recorded
      in the Dai Viet Su-ky Toan Thu, an early
      Annamese historical source." Journal of
      the American Oriental Society, 84 (1964),
      127-149.

      Lists observations of natural phenomena
      recorded in the Toàn Thư: comets (44 en-
      tries), meteors (17), planetary movements
      (27), solar eclipses (69), solar halos and
      parhelia (12), sunspots (2), lunar eclipses
      (34), earthquakes (40), epidemics and
      pestilences (11), and "miscellaneous," or
      auroa brontide, "rainbows" and other unde-
      fined phenomena (19). For each phenomena,
      lists the date (Vietnamese and western
      calendars), time of day, direction of
      comet, meteor, or planet. Compares this
      information with similar information from
      China, Japan, and Korea, and notes an in-
      consistency in some Vietnamese observa-
      tions: Records of comets seem to be reli-
      able; those of solar eclipses seem to be
      taken from Chinese sources and omit some
      eclipses which occurred over Thailand,
      South China, and Malaysia; and others ap-
      pear to be closely linked with astrology.
      Dates of observations cover 205 B.C. to
      A.D. 1674. Numerous footnotes provide sup-
      porting--or refuting--evidence from standard
      catalogs of phenomena.

      MH

EB5   *Hoằng Xuân Hãn. Danh-từ khoa-học (toán, lý,
      cơ, thiên văn) [Scientific terms (mathe-
      matics, physics, mechanics, astronomy)].
      See EG1 for complete description.

BIOLOGY EC

BOTANY

Except for Loureiro's Flora cochinchinensis,
the references in this section have been published
since the arrival of the French in the nineteenth
century. Although the French and Loureiro relied
upon Vietnamese for vernacular names of the plants,
there does not seem to have been many published descriptions of flora by Vietnamese before the present time. See the section of this chapter titled
"Special topics" and chapter EJ Medicine for publications on medical botany, some of which rely upon
pre-Western floras.

One problem encountered in compiling this
chapter was the lack of an index to current botanical literature corresponding to Zoological record
for zoology.

BIBLIOGRAPHIES

Major Sources

EC1   Cordier, Henri. Bibliotheca indosinica.
      See AA23 for complete description. For
      publications on botany, see 3: 1817-1824,
      "Botanique" which lists numerous publica-
      tions describing new species observed as
      the French explored the natural resources
      of Vietnam. Many of these articles ap-
      peared in scientific journals published
      in Europe and are also cited in the stand-
      ard reference sources.
      MH

EC2   Boudet, Paul, and Rémy Bourgeois. Biblio-
      graphie de l'Indochine française.
      See AA22 for complete description. For
      publications on botany, see "Botanique,"
      and the names of families in each volume.
      In vol. 4, the complete contents of FGI
      (EC24) as of 1935 are listed under "Bota-
      nique." In vol. 4, see also "Cryptogamie"
      and "Phytopathologie."
      MH

EC3   A bibliography of the botany of Southeast
      Asia. [n. p.] Washington, D.C.,
      August 1969. unpaged.

         Alphabetical listing, by author, of
      1,390 books, periodical articles, official
      publications, and learned society proceed-
      ings. Bibliographic information includes
      title, publication data, date and pagina-
      tion, does not always indicate a monograph
      in series. Index to botanical species.
      Indexes FGI under name of authors of indi-
      vidual articles. Less complete than
      Reed's bibliography (EC13).
      MH-G

EC4   *Duke, James A. Aquatic flora of the Mekong
      Delta and its relation to water traffic,
      a bibliographic survey. St. Louis, Mo.:
      Missouri Botanical Garden, 1961. (Source:
      Duke, Water weeds.)

EC5   Duke, James A., and Harry W. Mussell. Water
      weeds of the Mekong Delta, a bibliographic
      survey. Durham, No. Car.: [Duke Univ.,
      School of Forestry?], 1963. 70 p.

         Descriptions of aquatic flora--sea
      grasses, mangroves, palm swamps, marshes,
      rice paddies, water lilies, duckweeds,
      bladderworts. Recommendations for weed
      control and chemicals to be used. Bibli-
      ography of 140 references. Index to Eng-
      lish common names. Prepared for U.S. Army,
      to compare vegetation in United States and
      to study the controlling of weeds and the
      use of motor boats.
      MH-G

EC6   Flora Malesiana bulletin. Leyden: Rijks-
      herbarium, 1947- . Annual.

         News and bibliographical information
      about botany in Southeast Asia, South
      Asia, and Australasia. Useful as a cur-
      rent-awareness service, even though it is
      only issued annually. Since 1966, in-

cludes 10-20 references about Vietnam, including publications from Eastern Europe
and Russia.
MH-G

EC7   France. Office de la Recherche Scientifique
      et Technique d'Outre-Mer. Section de Bio-
      logie Végétale. Index bibliographique de
      botanique tropicale. Paris, 1964- .
      Frequency varies, quarterly beginning with
      vol. 5 (1968).

         Index to books, articles, symposia, and
      dissertations, mostly of publications from
      Europe and North America. Each issue has
      about 5 to 10 citations in the geographic
      index under "Vietnam" or "Indochine."
      MH-G

EC8   Gagnepain, F. "Contribution à l'étude géo-
      botanique de l'Indochine." Annales du
      Musée Colonial de Marseille, 4. sér.,
      vol. 4, no. 1 (1926), 5-40.

         Bibliographic essay on FGI and related
      works. Descriptions of the geographic
      distribution of the family of Composaceae
      (65 species) and of Euphorbiaceae (71
      genres) described in FGI.
      MH-EB

EC9   Pételot, Alfred. "Analyse des travaux de
      zoologie et de botanique concernant l'In-
      dochine...." and "Bibliographie des tra-
      vaux de botanique et de zoologie concer-
      nant l'Indochine...."
         See EC65 for annotation.

EC10   . Bibliographie botanique de l'Indo-
      chine. [Saigon] 1955. 98 p. (Archives
      des Recherches agronomiques et pastorales
      au Vietnam, 24) At head of title: Etat
      du Vietnam. Centre National de Recherches
      Scientifiques et Techniques.

         Alphabetical listing by author--divided
      into phanerograms, pteridophytes, bryo-
      phytes, mushrooms, algae, and lichens--of

books, periodical articles, and other reports. According to the author, it differs
from his 1929 bibliography (EC12) by including more references to botany of North
Vietnam.
MH-G

EC11 *____. "Bibliographie botanique de l'Indochine française." Notes et travaux, Ecole
Supérieure des Sciences de l'Université
indochinoise, 4 (1944). 57 p.
Cited in Pételot 1955 (EC10).

EC12 ____. "La botanique en Indochine; bibliographie." BEI no. 202 (1929), 587-632.
Lists about 400 bibliographies, books,
and articles of phanerogams, pteridophytes,
mosses, mushrooms, algae, and lichens. Includes numerous citations for the published
works of F. Gagnepain, C. Crevost, A. Guillaumin, H. Lecomte, A. Camus, and N. Pa-
touillard, all of whom have published extensive descriptions of species, but which
are not listed in the present Guide.
MH

EC13 Reed, Clyde Franklin. Bibliography to floras
of Southeast Asia; Burma, Laos, Thailand
(Siam), Cambodia, Viet Nam (Tonkin, Annam,
Cochinchina), Malay Peninsula, and Singapore. Baltimore, 1969. 191 p.
Author listing of about 3,800 publications. Includes works on floras in the
broad sense--vascular and non-vascular
plants, cultivated, agricultural, or medicinal plants, forestry, climatic and
edaphic phenomena, and fossil flora. Indexes articles in European periodicals--
mostly French and English languages--and
in European-language publications from
Southeast Asia. No indexes or annotations.
Entries are bibliographically complete.
Anonymous entries are listed under "Anonymous," then by date. Includes separate
references for FGI.
MH-G

EC14 Vidal, Jules E. "Bibliographie botanique
indochinoise." BSEI, n.s. 47 (1972),
655-749.
Author listing of books and periodicals written in Vietnamese, French, English, and Russian from 1955-1969, with
research being completed in 1971. Intended to update Bibliographie botanique de
l'Indochine, by A. Pételot (1955), and
format is similar, with indexes by subject and by species. Publications written
in Vietnamese are listed only under a
French title. Includes publications from
DRVN.
MH-HY

EC15 *Viện Khảo-cứu Cao-su Việt-Nam. Inventory of
publications. [Saigon?] 1968. various
pag.
Lists of publications of the Rubber
Research Institute of Viet-Nam, containing titles and document numbers, with entries in English and cover title in
French. (Source: EARI Natural Resources;
a selection of bibliographies, 2d ed.)

Other Sources

EC16 Harvard University. Arnold Arboretum. Library. Catalogue...by Ethelyn Maria
Tucker. Cambridge, Mass.: Cosmos Press,
1914-1933. 3 v. (Publications of the
Arnold Arboretum, 6)

EC17 Merrill, Elmer Drew, and Egbert H. Walker.
A bibliography of eastern Asiatic botany.
Jamaica Plain, Mass.: Arnold Arboretum
of Harvard University, 1938. 719 p.

EC18 Walker, Egbert H. A bibliography of Eastern
Asiatic botany, supplement 1. Washington,
D.C.: American Institute of Biological
Sciences, 1960. 552 p.

DICTIONARIES. SEE ALSO SCIENCE EA

EC19   Salomon, X., and Nguyễn Tường Du. "Lexique
         Latin-Annamite--Annamite-Latin des princi-
         pales plantes existant en Cochinchine pou-
         vant être demandées au Jardin Botanique de
         Saigon." Bulletin Agricole de l'Institut
         Scientifique de Saigon, 3 (1921), 116-123,
         154-161, 194-202, 225-232, 258-265,
         293-300, 335-336.
            Listing of about 1200 plants and their
         corresponding name in Latin or Vietnamese,
         with name of the family and the economic
         uses.
         MH-EB

EC20   Taberd, Jean Louis. Dictionarium Anamitico-
         Latinum (1838).
            See AE27 for complete description.
         Pp. 621-660 "Hortus Floridus Cocincinae,"
         names of botanical specimens, in Chinese,
         romanized Vietnamese, and Latin.

EC21   Vietnam (Republic). Ủy-ban Soạn-thảo Danh-từ
         Khoa-học. Danh-từ thực-vật-học Pháp-Việt,
         có phần đối-chiếu Việt-Pháp [French-Viet-
         namese--Vietnamese-French glossary of terms
         in botany]. Saigon: Bộ Quốc-gia Giáo-dục,
         1963. 275 p. (Its Danh-từ Khoa-học, 5)
         "Tủ sách Khoa-học"
            According to Vidal, "Bibl. bot. indo-
         chinoise" (EC14), the compilers were Lê
         Văn Thới and Phạm Hoàng Hộ. (Source:
         NIC.)

DESCRIPTIONS OF SEVERAL BOTANICAL DIVISIONS

EC22   *Cây cỏ thường thấy ở Việt-Nam [Common plants
         of Vietnam]. Hanoi: Khoa học và kỹ thuật.
            Tập 5: Võ Văn Chi, Vũ Văn Chuyển, Phan
         Nguyên Hồng, Cây hạt kín một lá mầm (Từ
         họ Agavaceae đến họ Zingiberaceae) [Vol. 5,
         Monocotyledons (From Agavaceae to Zingi-
         beraceae)]. 1975. 524 p. Chủ biên
         [Editor]: Lê Khả Kế. [Only volume locat-
         ed.] (Source: MLXBP, 11/75.)

EC23   Flore du Cambodge, du Laos, et du Vietnam,
         complément à la Flore générale de l'Indo-
         chine de H. Lecomte. Publ. sous la di-
         rection de A. Aubréville. Red. principal:
         Mme. Tardieu-Blot. Paris: Muséum Natio-
         nal d'Histoire Naturelle, 1960- . (In
         progress, fasc. 1-15 published as of
         1975)
            A complete revision--beginning with
         fasc. 2 (1962)--of FGI, as certain fas-
         cicles were out of print and out of date
         by 1960. Does not appear in the order of
         FGI, that is, according to Bentham and
         Hooker's Genera Plantarum, but without any
         particular order, as specialists are found
         to study the families. Coverage excludes
         Thailand and Hainan, as contrasted with
         coverage of FGI. Information includes,
         insofar as possible, habitat, ecology,
         phenology, economic uses, taxonomic com-
         mentaries, and vernacular names. Descrip-
         tions of individual families are preceded
         by short articles about the family in
         general and characteristics, locality,
         species, genera, and uses, as well as the
         name of the botanist who wrote the arti-
         cle. Bibliographical references are ex-
         tensive and include citations to FGI as
         well as to earlier botanical works. List
         of families described in FGI and its sup-
         pléments is printed in each fascicle.
         Index by vernacular name and by scientific
         name. Reviewed by M. Jacobs in Fl. Males.
         Bull., 3 (1961), 833-835, who compares
         this work with FGI.
         MH-G

EC24   Flore générale de l'Indochine, publ. sous la
         direction de H[enri] Lecomte [et de]
         H. Humbert. Réd. principal, F. Gagnepain.
         Paris: Masson, 1907-1951. 7 vols,
         60 fasc. Abbreviated as FGI.
            "A comprehensive flora of this area...,
         the various families treated by special-
         ists."--Merrill. Comprises descriptions

of the flora from Thailand through Indochina and to Hainan. Format is short, rather than extensive, descriptions of species
and sub-species. Arrangement follows the
Bentham and Hooker classification of Genera
Plantarum. Each fascicle lists, on the
inside cover, the fascicles published up
to date. Boudet 4, pp. 79-80, has a complete list of fascicles published as of
1935, with the notation that the work describes 135 of 170 families of Phanerogams
known at the time.

Flore générale de l'Indochine, tome
préliminaire. Introduction, Tables générales. Paris: Masson, 1944. 155 p.

Explains the geographical surroundings,
ecology, history of the writing of the FGI;
lists bibliographical sources; includes
photographs and biographical sketches of
the 88 collaborators; and outlines the arrangement of the FGI. Pp. 51-154, classification of families, structure of families, and indexes to the seven volumes,
by families, genera, and synonyms, and by
indigenous and common names. Outline map
shows itineraries of collectors and geological areas.

Gagnepain, F. "Clef des familles de la
Flore de l'Indo-Chine, supplément à la
Flore générale de l'Indochine. Clef analytique et synoptique des familles de plantes
vasculaires décrites dans la Flore de
l'Indochine." Revue Scientifique du Bour-
bonnais, 1922, 49-82. Cited in Boudet 4,
p. 80 as 2 vols., 34 pp.

Systematic index to vascular plants described in FGI undertaken in order to provide a guide to specimens listed throughout vols. 1-5. Described as a provisional
index by the author.

Flore générale de l'Indochine. Supplément [au Tome I], 1938-1950. Publ. sous
la direction de H. Humbert. Paris: Muséum National d'Histoire Naturelle, 1907-

1958. 63 parts, numbered fasc. 1-9,
1031 p. No more published.

Begun in order to update the information in FGI (1907-1934). Publication
ended with the appearance of tome 7,
fasc. 10 (1951), pp. 545-600, part 64,
titled "Fin de la Flore."

For corrections in the treatment of
Aleurites, see F. Gagnepain, "Deux espèces distinctes sous le nom d'Aleurites
cordata," Revue de botanique appliquée et
d'agriculture coloniale 14 (1934),
338-340.

For revision and updating of FGI, see
Flore du Cambodge, du Laos et du Vietnam
(1960-   ).
MH-G

EC25   *Lê Kha Kế, Vũ Văn Chuyên, and Thái Văn Trung.
Danh-lục thực-vật Bắc Việt-Nam [Prodome
of the flora of North Vietnam]. Hanoi:
[n. p.], 1961. 671 p., lithogr.
(Source: Pócs, "Analyse....")

EC26   Loureiro, João de. Flora Cochinchinensis;
sisten plantens in regno Cochinchina na-
scentes, quibus accedunt aliae observatae
in Sinensi Imperio, Africa orientali,
Indiaeque locis variis. Omnes dispositae
secundum systema sexulae Linnaeanum.
Ulyssipone, 1790. 2 vols. 2. ed. [by]
Carol Ludovici Willdenow. Berolini,
1793. 2 vols.

Scientific descriptions of about 1,000
botanical species. According to Elmer D.
Merrill, "A commentary on Loureiro's Flora
Cochinchinensis," Transactions of the
American Philosophical Society n.s. 24,
pt. 2 (1935), 1-445, this work lists 697
species from Cochinchina, 254 from China,
292 from China and Cochinchina, and about
27 from Mozambique, Zanzibar, India, Malaya, the Philippines, Madagascar, and
Sumatra. Merrill's article lists 60 ar-

ticles based on Loureiro's Flora and is also a biographical sketch of Loureiro and an extensive study of all of Loureiro's descriptions and notations of descriptions published by other botanists.

Loureiro (1710-1791) was a Portuguese Jesuit who lived in Vietnam from 1742 to 1777 and was mathematician and naturalist at the Nguyễn court. Self-taught for the most part, and unable to study fully Linnaeus' classification system which appeared in 1753, he described 185 new genera and 650 new species.--Merrill, in Proceedings of the American Philosophical Society, 73 (1933), 229-239.

Lists of Loureiro's publications are in Sommervogel, Bibliothèque de la Compagnie de Jésus, v. 5, cols. 35-36, and in Royal Society of London, Catalogue, v. 4. Merrill (1935) states that Loureiro also wrote a history of "Anam," 2 volumes of drawings of minerals, plants, and animals, 2 volumes of 397 colored drawings of plants, a "flora iconographica" of Cochinchina, and a Vietnamese-Portuguese dictionary. These were only in manuscript form, however, which he bequeathed to the Academia Real des Sciences de Lisboa and which do not seem to have been published.

Both editions have been made available on microfiche by the Inter-Documentation Company, Zug, Switzerland: the 1790 edition, on IDC number 6525, and the 1793 edition on IDC number 566.
MH-G

EC27   Phạm Hoàng Hộ, and Nguyễn Văn Dương. Cây-cỏ miền Nam Việt-Nam [Plants of the southern region of Vietnam]. Saigon: Bộ Quốc-gia Giáo-dục, 1960. 803 p.

Very brief (3-5 lines per plant) descriptions of about 1,600 plants with sketches of most species or sub-species. Names are given in scientific and Vietnamese terms. Preface discusses the problems of assigning Vietnamese names to many species and sub-species in view of past conflicts over terminology: The term xương-rồng, for example, is used to designate Euphorbiaceae, Cactaceae, Dideriaceae, Ampelidaceae, and Asclepiadaceae. In this book, the author has reduced terms to apply to one species [giống] or sub-species [loại]; if it has been necessary to formulate terms, he has used the name of the giống in conjunction with the name of the loại, for example, as in Acalypha (tai-tượng) and A. vilkesiana (tai-tượng nâu), etc. If one Vietnamese name has been used to refer to more than one species or sub-species, he has used the most commonly used term among Vietnamese. If no term exists, he has created a new word, either phonetically (Barringtonia becomes Bằng-linh-tôn), in translation (leonotis becomes sư-nhĩ), or according to characteristics (Colpomenia becomes rong bao-tử).

Descriptions include location of species throughout Vietnam or Cambodia, medicinal use, month in which flowers bloom, and economic use.

Authors have not been able to apply Vietnamese names to all plants described in books, but seem to have completed most of the terms; in order to identify all plants, it would have been a long task and would have required the assistance of a scholar who knew classical Vietnamese. Nguyễn Văn Dương contributed the information on medicinal plants; in his preface, he emphasizes the value of such plants over manufactured products and the need for more research and more use of medicinal plants. Pp. 12-45, discussion and definitions of botanical and medicinal terms and outline of classification, with nine detailed charts according to characteristics. Pp. 46-708, descriptions, illustrations, and systematic outline of species, again according to characteristics of individual species. Pp. 709-end, bibliography of 46 items, list of abbreviations, indexes by Vietnamese and scientific name, and errata.

Differs from FGI by being more restrictive in a geographic sense, but does include Rong (algae and seaweed), Rêu (moss), and Nấm (mushrooms) and adds to the information in FGI.

See EC28 for annotation of 2d edition, 1970-1972.

MH-G; MH-F

EC28   Phạm Hoàng Hộ. Cây-cỏ miền Nam Việt-Nam; an illustrated flora of South Viet-Nam. In lần thứ nhì, bổi-bỏ và sửa chửa [Second edition, enlarged and corrected]. Saigon: Bộ Giáo Dục, Trung Tâm Học-Liệu, 1970, 1972. 2 vols.

Revision of 1960 work, with omission of medical plants by Nguyễn Văn Dương (published separately in 1968--see EC55) and algae (rong biển), published separately in 1969 (see EC31). Format is similar--brief descriptions of plants, with sketches and bibliographical information. About 5,300 plants are described, divided into Fungi (48 species); Lichens (12); Bryophyta (22); Pteridophyta (122); Gymnosperms (35); and Angiosperms (5,135). Additions are on pp. 1104-1121 in vol. 2.

MH-V

EC29   Pierre, Jean Baptiste Louis. Flore forestière de la Cochinchine. Paris: Octave Doin, 1879-1899. 25 fasc., 400 plates; 1 fasc (register), issued in 1907. Folio size, bound in from 3-5 vols, depending upon the library. Repr., Amsterdam: Asher, 1966.

"A set of [black and white] plates, illustrating forest plants, the plates accompanied by descriptive letterpress."--Merrill. Descriptions stop unfortunately at Légumineuses, according to the classi-

fication of P. de Candolle. For additional information, see J. Léandri, "Louis Pierre, botaniste de terrain et systématicien français (1833-1905)," Adansonia n.s. 3 (1963), 207-220. Léandri observes that Pierre's attention to detail and failure to distinguish between essential and peripheral aspects of description delayed the completion of the work and resulted in the inclusion of some plants that were beyond the scope of the work. Léandri notes that Pierre also published his descriptions entirely in French rather than in Latin. Pierre published a few other works on plants of Indochina; he hoped to compile a Flore forestière de l'Indochine, but Léandri states that it was never achieved (although it was cited by Croizier.) Pierre spent the last decade of his life working on the flora of Gabon and the Middle Congo.

A related publication is by M. [Francis?] Evrard: Tables destinées à faciliter la consultation de la Flore forestière de la Cochinchine de J. B. L. Pierre (Saigon: Impr. de l'Union, 1922), 44-47 p.[1] Another source cites this work as being published in Saigon under the auspices of Institut scientifique de l'Indochine, Laboratoire de botanique; 47, 44 p.

MH-G   [1]Boudet 1

DESCRIPTIONS OF SEPARATE DIVISIONS OR CLASSES

Algae

EC30   Dawson, E. Yale. "Marine plants in the vicinity of the Institut Océanographique de Nhatrang." Pacific Science, 8 (1954), 373-469. Also issued as Contribution no. 12, Institut Océanographique de Nhatrang.

"The basic list" for the study of marine plants--Phạm Hoàng Hộ. List and descriptions of 209 species of algae, the first of its kind for the South China Sea region. Each species is illustrated, with notes on local distribution and typed locality. Comments intended to be used for identification purposes. Keys to genera and species. Extensive bibliography of about 200 publications, world-wide in scope.

The result of 3 months field surveys in 1953 by Dawson, who notes that the Vietnam coast is one of the most neglected regions in algology. Sets of specimens sent to 3 museums in U.S., 1 in Vietnam.
MH-Z

EC31   Phạm Hoàng Hộ. <u>Rong biển Việt-Nam; marine algae of South Vietnam</u>. Saigon: Trung-tâm học-liệu xuất bản, 1969. 560 p.

Extensive catalog of marine algae, arranged by type (<u>thanh-tao</u>, <u>hồng-tao</u>, <u>cát-tao</u>, and <u>lục-tao</u>, respectively blue, red, yellow, and green algae). Descriptions include scientific name, previously published descriptions, and short physical description. Text in Vietnamese. Bibliography of about 200 English and French publications on algae throughout the world. Profusely illustrated. Index to species, Vietnamese-French-English glossary of selected terms. Author had hoped to publish in a foreign language, but decided not to in order that all Vietnamese would be able to read the book.

EC32   * ____. <u>Tao-học</u> [algaology]. [Saigon] Bộ Giáo-dục, 1967. 274 p. (Tủ sách Khoa-học) (Source: NIC.)

Bryophyta

EC33   Pócs, Tamas. "Contribution à la Bryoflore du Nord Vietnam." <u>Revue Bryologique et Lichenologique</u>, n.s. 34 (1966), 799-806.

____, P. Tixier, and S. Jovet-Ast. "Seconde contribution à la Bryoflore du Nord Vietnam." <u>Botanikai Közlemények</u>, 54 (1967), 27-38.

Pócs, Tamas. "Troisième contribution à la Bryoflore du Nord Vietnam. Récoltes polonaises aux environs de Sapa [sic; Chapa?]" <u>Fragmenta floristia et geobotania</u> 14 (1968), 495-504.

____. "Studies on the mountain Bryoflora of the Ha-giang area, based on the collection of Prof. I. V. Grushvitzsky (Fourth contribution to the Bryoflora of North Vietnam.") <u>Botanicseskij Zhurnal</u>, 56 (1971), 845-853.

____. "Fifth contribution to the Bryoflora of North Vietnam." <u>Botanikai Közlemények</u>, 56 (1969), 139-147.

Enumeration of over 200 species, with name, location, and indication of new species. No physical descriptions or bibliographical information.
MH-G

EC34   Tixier, P. "Bryophytes du Vietnam. Récoltes de A. Pételot et V. Demange au Nord Vietnam (Relictae Henryanae)." <u>Revue Bryologique et Lichenologique</u>, n.s. 34 (1966), 127-181.

Enumeration, with geographic distribution and location of specimen, of 114 species, of which 21 are new to science, collected by Pételot and Demange in Chapa from 1919-1932 and studied in part by R. Henry. Henry did publish an article about the collection, in <u>Revue Bryologique et Lichenologique</u> (1928).
MH-F

EC35   ____. "Bryophytae indosinicae: reliquiae Pierreanae, bryophytes of L. Pierre's herbarium." <u>Natural History Bulletin of the Siam Society</u>, 22 (1968), 283-287.

A listing of the 170 specimens in Pierre's cryptogamic collection which has remained, according to Tixier, neglected until now. Information comprises only the scientific name, and in a few instances, the locality, date, or other collector (usually Harmand).

MH-Z

Pteridophyta

EC36   Bonaparte, R. N. Notes Ptéridologiques. Paris, 1914-1925. 16 fasc., fasc. 6 not published.

"Liste provisoire des Ptéridophytes croissant en Indo-Chine." Notes Ptérido-logiques, 7 (1918), 79-134.

"Synonymie des Ptéridophytes décrites par J. de Loureiro, 1793." Ibid., 135-140.

"Récoltes du Père Cadière, de Monsieur Ch. d'Alleizette, de Monsieur Eberhardt et de quelques autres collecteurs. 1re ptie." Ibid., 141-200.

Classified listings of species and sub-species.

"Les Ptéridophytes de l'Indochine. Première partie." Ibid., 8 (1919), 1-190.

Listing and brief bibliographical ref-erences to species and sub-species.

"Indochine. Récoltes de MM. Auguste Chevalier et F. Fleury. Herbiers de M. Auguste Chevalier et du Prince Bona-parte." Ibid., 13 (1920), 111-144.

"Indochine, plusieurs collecteurs. Herbier du Prince Bonaparte." Ibid., 14 (1921), 89-195.

Pételot, in "La botanique en Indochine--bibliographie," (EC12), p. 588, notes that Bonaparte only finished describing three families before he died, but that enough of his work was left unpublished so that Notes Ptéridologiques appeared for three or more years after his death. Numerous corrections and additions to Bonaparte's lists were published by various scientists in Bulletin du Muséum National d'Histoire Naturelle.

MH-G

EC36a   Christensen, C., and M. L. Tardieu-Blot. "Les fougères d'Indo-Chine." Bulletin du Muséum National d'Histoire Naturelle, 2. sér., 6 (1934), 287-290, 383-386, 445-451; Notulae systematicae, 5 (1935-36), 2-13, 165-173, 260-267; 6 (1937-38), 1-11, 129-134, 135-149, 161-176; 7 (1938), 65-104; 8 (1939), 175-210.

Additions and corrections to Bona-parte's Notes Ptéridologiques, esp. fasc. 8, 13 and 14 (see above).

MH-G

Gymnosperms.   See also FORESTRY EK

EC37   Flore générale de l'Indochine, publ. sous la direction de H[enri] Lecomte [et de] H. Humbert.

See EC24 for bibliographical descrip-tion and annotation. For references to Gymnosperms, see Tome V, pp. 1052-1092. The following families are described: Ceratophyllaceae, Taxaceae, Gnetaceae, Cupressaceae, Podocarpaceae, Araucariaceae, Abieteneae, and Cycadaceae.

MH-G

EC38   *Nguyen Kha. "Les forêts de 'Pinus khasya' et de 'Pinus merkusii' du Centre Vietnam." Annales de sciences forestières (Nancy), 23 (1966), 221-372.

Cited in: U.S. Engineer Agency for Re-sources Inventories, Selected bibliogra-phy, Lower Mekong basin (AA50)

Angiosperms.   See also EK FORESTRY.

EC39   Los Banos, Philippines. International Rice Research Institute. International bibli-ography of rice research. New York: Scarecrow Press, 1963.

Detailed subject listing of 7,274 ref-erences to books, periodical articles, bulletins, and official publications on all aspects of rice growing, marketing,

diseases, and trade, published in 23 languages. Vol. 1 includes publications issued from 1951 to 1961. Indexes are by
author, subject, and geographic area; 16
references are listed for Vietnam, but do
not include any in the Vietnamese language.

_____. _____. Supplement. Comp. by Milagros
Zamora. Los Banos: International Rice
Research Institute, 1964- . Annual.

Arrangement follows the 1963 volume,
but the indexes include a keyword-in-
title index instead of a subject and geographic index. Keyword index therefore
does not include references to Vietnam that
do not include the word "Vietnam" in the
title, so the researcher should search
through the author index in addition to
searching the keyword index.

Cumulative index for 1961-1965 published in 1968.

MH-EB

EC40   Phạm Hoàng Hộ. Hiển-hoa bí-tử [Angiosperms].
[Saigon]: Bộ Văn-hóa Giáo-dục và Thanh-
niên, Trung-tâm Học-liệu, 1968. 492 p.
(Tu-sách Khoa-học, Giám đốc Lê Văn Thới)

A textbook and systematic outline of
angiosperms, with emphasis on specimens
found in Vietnam. Numerous illustrations,
including maps showing world distribution
of species. Not a flora of Vietnam; does
not give bibliographical information or
location of species.

MH-V

EC41   *Schmid, Maurice. "Flore agrostologique de
l'Indochine." Agronomie Tropicale [Nogent-
sur-Marne], 13 (1958), 7-51, 143-237,
300-359, 459-522, 631-669, 687-703. 100
figures.

"Essentially a taxonomic work with
keys" (Fl. Males. Bull., 3 (1960), 782).
Often cited as published in Agric. Trop.

EC42   Seidenfaden, Gunnar. Contributions to a revision of the Orchid flora of Cambodia,
Laos, and Vietnam. I. A preliminary enumeration of all orchids hitherto recorded.
Fredensborg, Denmark, c/o Botanical Museum, Copenhagen: [privately printed],
1975. 117 p.

Alphabetical listing of 758 taxa and
1228 entries (including cross-references),
updating and correcting the entries in the
Guillaumin and Gagnepain fascicle on
Orchids in the Flore générale de l'Indochine. Author notes that nearly half of
the names used in FGI have subsequently
been found to be incorrect and has as a
result published this compilation rather
than wait until the revisions appear in
Flore du Cambodge, du Laos, et du Vietnam
(EC23).

MH-O

SPECIAL TOPICS: MUSEUM COLLECTIONS; ECONOMIC
BOTANY; AND MEDICAL BOTANY. SEE ALSO MEDICINE EJ--
PHARMACOLOGY.

Museum Collections and Economic Botany

EC43   *Crevost, Charles. Catalogue-memento en vue
de la réunion des échantillons devant fi-
gurer au Palais Central des Produits et
au Pavillion forestier à l'Exposition
intercoloniale de Marseille.... Hanoi:
Schneider, 1905. 161 p. At head of
title, Gouvernement Général de l'Indo-
Chine. Direction de l'Agriculture, des
Forêts et du Commerce.

Important enumeration of the flora of
Vietnam, mentioning the Vietnamese names
of specimens.--Thanh-Long, second-hand
catalog, Nov. 1971. (Source: Cordier 3:
2203.)

EC44   Crevost, Charles; Charles Lemarie; and Alfred Pételot. Catalogue des produits de

l'Indochine. Hanoi: IDEO, 1917-1941.
6 vols., vols. 2-6 also published serially
in BEI.

Titles of volumes and publication pat-
tern is as follows:

Vol. 1, "Produits alimentaires et
plantes fourragères," 1917. 489 p.

Vol. 2, "Plantes et produits filamen-
teux et textiles," 1919. 297 p.
Published in BEI, v. 22, nos. 136-139
(1919), 365-401, 553-591, 675-709, 813-837;
v. 23, nos. 140-144 (1920), 43-71, 207-231,
406-433.

Vol. 3, "Matières grasses et végétales,"
1922. 177 p. BEI, v. 25, nos. 153-155
(1922), 141-150, 325-343, 387-430; v. 26,
no. 163 (1923), 515-545; v. 27, no. 164
(1924), 37-77.

Vol. 4, "Exsudats végétaux," 1927.
194 p. BEI, v. 28, nos. 170-172, 174
(1925), 1-57, 191-205, 283-317, 475-503;
v. 29, no. 180 (1926), 507-532.

Vol. 5, fasc. 1, "Plantes medicinales,"
1928. 335 p. BEI, v. 32, nos. 199-202
(1929), 1-35, 119-170, 277-367, 491-585.

Vol. 5, fasc. 2, "Plantes medicinales,"
1928. 322 p. BEI, v. 37 (1934), 267-311,
507-553, 730-776, 999-1034, 1259-1300;
v. 38 (1935), 115-146.

Vol. 6, "Tannins et tinctoriaux," 1941.
125 p. BEI, v. 44 (1941), 371-426,
594-630.

"Compléments et rectifications au
tome I," BEI, v. 24 (1921), 131-156.

Errata and indexes (by family, by species and subspecies, by Vietnamese or
other vernacular language and the corresponding scientific term, and by Sino-
Vietnamese term and the corresponding
Vietnamese and scientific term) are published only in vol. 5, fasc. 2,
pp. 249-322.

Encyclopedic dictionary of economic
products, giving their background, geographic distribution in Indochina, vari-

eties, economic utilization, preparation,
diseases, scientific description, and
production figures. Numerous drawings
and photographs of plants and of the
stages in their preparation for human and
animal consumption, including workshops
and harvesting. Bibliographic references
to FGI.
MH; MH-EB

EC45   Duke, James A. Survival manual II: South
Viet Nam. St. Louis: Missouri Botanical
Garden, reproduced by Mimeograph Business
Machines, Durham, N.C., 1963. 45 p.,
b. & w. illus. A-T

Discusses the use of plants as food or
medicine in instances where necessary for
survival in the tropical jungle; plant
families and their uses as well as danger-
ous plants; and methods of identifying
plants. Includes indexes to Vietnamese
names and English names in the text.
Bibliography of about 70 books and articles on tropical botany.
MH-G

EC46   Hanson, Herbert C. Diseases and pests of
economic plants of Vietnam, Laos and Cambodia. Washington, D.C.: American Institute of Crop Ecology, 1963. 155 p.

Descriptions of diseases and pests, the
ways in which they affect plants, methods
of control, and species affected by various diseases and pests. About 1/3 of
book is about rice diseases and pests.
Includes bibliographic references for
documentation on diseases. Sources include articles in BEI and Compte-rendus
des travaux de l'Institut des Recherches
Agronomiques et Forestières.
NIC

EC47   Jumelle, Henri. "Catalogue descriptif des
collections botaniques du Musée Colonial
de Marseille: Indochine." Annales du

Musée Colonial de Marseille, 4. sér.,
vol. 8, fasc. 4 (1930), 5-63; vol. 9,
fasc. 1 (1931), 5-59.

Brief descriptions of 444 types of
plants harvested or collected in Indochina
or imported from China; includes 69 rice
plants. Data includes vernacular names
and economic uses. No index or
bibliography.
MH-EB

EC48   Lan, J. Les plantes indochinoises de grande
culture. Hanoi: IDEO, 1928-30. 2 vols.
Vol. 1, Plantes alimentaires. Vol. 2,
Plantes industrielles et quelquefois alimentaires. At head of title: Bibliothèque agricole indochinoise.

History, botanical characteristics, conditions needed for growth, classification
of soils, humidity, reproduction, cultiva-
tions, diseases, harvest, and usages. Includes Vietnamese names. No footnotes or
bibliography, but does quote from other
sources such as Crevost and Lemarie.
MH-EB

EC49   Lanessan, J. L. de. Les plantes utiles des
colonies françaises. Paris: Impr. Nationale, 1886. 990 p. At head of title:
République française. Ministère de la Marine et des Colonies (Administration des
Colonies).

"Annexes aux Notices coloniales publiées
à l'occasion de l'Exposition Universelle
d'Anvers en 1885."

Chapters on plants with economic uses
including sugar, rice, and forest products
throughout the French colonies. Pp. 280-
334, "Bois," and 702-791, "Flore," contain
most of the information on Cochinchina,
with brief descriptions of species and
Vietnamese names according to Loureiro.
Index to Vietnamese and Latin names.
MH-EB

EC50   Maurand, Paul. "Guide botanique de la ville
de Saigon." BSEI, n.s. 43 (1968),
311-351.

Originally published in 1949 as tourist
brochure; updated by Lý Văn Hội.

Alphabetical listing, by scientific
name, of 415 species and sub-species.
Information includes vernacular names,
height, and location in Botanic and Zo-
ologic Garden, City Garden, or city
streets. Pp. 342-348, descriptions of
trees. P. 351, map of Botanic and Zoo-
logic Garden and location of species as
of 1949.
MH

EC51   *Saigon. Jardin Botanique. Catalogue général
des plantes classées au Jardin Botanique
[par E. Haffner]. Saigon: Impr. Coloniale, 1898. 20, 42 p. (Source: Cordier 3: 1820.)

EC52   *Schmid, Maurice. Contribution à la connaissance de la végétation du Vietnam: le
massif sud-annamitique et les régions
limitrophes. Paris: P. Lechevalier,
1968. 250 p.[1]

Presented as thesis, Faculté des
Sciences de l'Université de Paris, Centre
d'Orsay (Série A, No. Orsay nº d'ordre 6),
[1963?] 424 p.[2]

[1]Cited in Index bibl. de bot. trop. 7
(1970), 70: 2459 [2]EARI

EC53   Schroeder, Karl, and Albert Schroeder. "Enu-
mération des végétaux cultivés en Cochinchine, avec leurs dénominations française,
latine, annamite, mandarine et cambod-
gienne," BCAI, 2. sér., vol. 1, no. 5
(1876), 287-375.

Lists 272 vegetable products by the
French name, 421 by the Latin name, the
terms in other languages, the commercial
uses, the families to which they belong,
and descriptions of their physical
properties.
MH

BIOLOGY EC

Medical Botany

EC54 *Đỗ Tất Lợi. [Les plantes médicinales et les
        drogues médicinales du Vietnam.] Hanoi:
        Khoa Học, 1969- . Vol. 1, 847 p., 1969.
        (Source: Vidal, "Bibl. bot. indoch."--
        Vietnamese-language title not given.)

EC55 *Nguyễn Văn Dương. Dược thảo và dược liệu
        Việt-Nam [Medicinal plants and pharmaceu-
        tical products]. Saigon: Cổ kim y dược
        tùng-thư, 1968- . Vol. 1, 1968, 85 p.

        Not available for annotation, but con-
        sidered to be revision of his contribution
        to Cây-cỏ miền Nam Việt-Nam (1960) (see
        EC27). (Source: Thư-mục 1968.)

EC56 Oakes, Albert J. Some harmful plants of
        Southeast Asia. Bethesda, Md.: Naval
        Medical School, National Naval Medical
        Center, for sale by the Superintendent of
        Documents, U.S. Government Printing Of-
        fice, 1967. 50 p.

        An "abbreviated guide to the most com-
        mon injurious plants of the area." Pre-
        pared for the use of U.S. troops in Viet-
        nam. Information includes brief physical
        descriptions, habitat, and nature of in-
        jury, toxicity, and symptoms. Names in
        Latin, Vietnamese, and English.
        MH-G

EC57 Pételot, Alfred. Les plantes médicinales du
        Cambodge, du Laos et du Vietnam. Saigon:
        Centre National de Recherches Scienti-
        fiques et Techniques, 1952-54. (Archives
        des recherches agronomiques au Cambodge,
        au Laos et au Vietnam, 14, 18, 22, 23)

        Descriptions of plants found in Indo-
        china--physical characteristics, locality,
        and medicinal uses. Arrangement is syste-
        matic by type of plant. Preface in vol. 1
        discusses the importance of FGI and the
        supplement to vol. 1 as related to medici-
        nal plants; the increasing use of medicinal
plants among chemists, pharmacists, and
doctors; the difficulty of giving a modern
classification to local drugs because of
the lack of research into the properties
of such drugs; and the difficulty of assigning correct vernacular names because
of the lack of knowledge of the Vietnamese
language among collectors in earlier times
and because of the lack of knowledge of
botanic terms by Vietnamese inhabitants,
who at times ascribed "noms fantaisistes"
to plants collected by French botanists.

        Descriptive information includes sci-
entific name, vernacular name, including
Chinese characters if known, physical description of perhaps 5 to 10 lines, and
medicinal uses, of perhaps 15 to 20 lines.
No illustrations or outline of the classification. Vol. 4--indexes to therapeutic
properties, illnesses and their remedies,
scientific and Latin names, and names of
plants in French, Vietnamese, Cambodian,
Laotian, mountain languages, Chinese, and
Sino-Vietnamese. Pp. 329 to 347 of vol. 4
are supplement to vols. 1 and 2.
MH-G

EC58 *Pho Duc Thanh. [450 plantes médicinales du
        Sud [i.e. du Vietnam].] Hanoi. [n. p.],
        1963. (Source: Vidal, "Bibl. bot.
        indoch."--Vietnamese-language title not
        given.)

EC59 *Vũ Đức Hiện. Dược-thảo Việt-Nam [Medicinal
        plants in Vietnam]. Saigon: Bộ Canh-
        Nông, 1957-1961. 3 vols.

        Fasc. 1 (1957), 75 p., fasc. 2 (1959),
        118 p., fasc. 3 (1961), 105 p.

        Illustrated list of 115 species of
medicinal plants. Each part begins with
gamopetals and ends with monocotyledons or
gymnosperms. (Source: UNESCO.)

EC60 *Vũ Văn Chuyên. Tóm tắt đặc điểm các họ cây thuốc; có kèm theo bảng tra cứu tên họ của một số cây thông thường. [Summary of the characteristics of medicinal plants]. [Hanoi]: Nhà Xuất bản Y Học và Thể dục Thể thao, 1966. (Source: SOAS.)

ZOOLOGY

Publications listed in this chapter are those written after the beginning of French rule; no publications were located which were written about zoology in Vietnam before that time. The bibliographies by Cordier (EC61) and Pételot (EC65) and the zoological descriptions by members of the Pavie mission (EC64) provide information on zoology in Vietnam at least from the 1860's.

In many instances, knowledge about the zoology of Vietnam is still limited; this is particularly true of insects, where the diversity of the insect population has yet to be adequately described. On the other hand, the Oceanographic Institute (Hải-Học-Viện) of Nha-trang has worked extensively with marine resources, only a few citations of which are cited here.

The best sources for locating publications on zoology are Zoological record (London, 1865-) and Biological abstracts (Philadelphia, 1926-), the latter of which is now produced by computer, with "Vietnam" as one of the terms under which literature is indexed.

BIBLIOGRAPHIES AND DESCRIPTIONS OF SEVERAL PHYLA

EC61 Cordier, Henri. Bibliotheca indosinica. See AA22 for complete description. For publications on zoology, see 3: 1801-1816, "Zoologie," which lists numerous publications describing new species observed as the French explored the natural resources of Vietnam.
MH

EC62 Boudet, Paul, and Rémy Bourgeois. Bibliographie de l'Indochine française. See AA21 for complete description. For publications on zoology, see "Zoologie" in each volume as well as names of individual classes.
MH

EC63 Bourret, René. Inventaire général de l'Indochine. La faune de l'Indochine: vertébrés. Hanoi: Société de Géographie, 1927. 453 p. (Société de Géographie de Hanoi. Fasc. 3) Classified listing of vertebrates, with as many examples as could be located. Includes brief physical descriptions of each order, sub-order, family, and species; object is to list as completely as possible the vertebrates in Indochina. Includes some names in Vietnamese or other vernacular languages. Bibliographies at beginning of each chapter, with most references in the section about birds. Mammals (31 references in the bibliography), pp. 7-80; birds (81 references), pp. 81-203; reptiles (15), pp. 205-247, with 8 more references on the "sea serpent" of Ha Long Bay; amphibians (5), pp. 249-265; and fish (52), pp. 267-427. Indexes are by French name and by family and specie.
MH-Z

EC64 Pavie, Auguste. Mission Pavie, Indochine, 1879-1895. Etudes diverses. Paris: Leroux, 1901. 3 vols. Vol. 3 [Zoology, pp. 41-549.] Describes, with illustrations, the species seen during the extensive exploration through Indochina. Categories described in this volume are Articulates, pp. 41-331; Mollusks, pp. 332-450; Vertebrates, pp. 451-549. Descriptions of species include scientific name, first published description, location obtained,

geographical distribution, and scientific
descriptions of some species. Includes 22
plates, mostly colored, with several specimens per plate: plate 10, for example,
shows 89 beetles. Because of the extensive range of exploring and collecting accomplished by the Pavie expedition, a
search for literature on the zoology of
Indochina should include this volume.
Cordier 3:1809-1812 and 4:2675-2678 include
references to source materials published in
these volumes and elsewhere describing
specimens collected during the Pavie
mission.

MH

EC65   Pételot, A. "Complément au chapitre de la
Bibliotheca Indosinica relatif à la zoologie de l'Indochine française." BEFEO, 27
(1927), 239-282.

_____. "Analyse des travaux de zoologie et de
botanique concernant l'Indochine publiés en
1928." Bulletin général de l'Instruction
Publique, 8 (1928/29), ptie. scolaire,
567-574.

_____. "Analyse...1929." Ibid., 9 (1930),
299-320.

_____. "Bibliographie des travaux de bota-
nique et de zoologie concernant l'Indochine (années 1930, 1931 et 1932 et
compléments des années antérieures)."
Ibid., 10 (1931), 163-174; 11 (1932),
20-23; 12 (1933), 11-16.

_____. "Bibliographie des travaux de zoo-
logie et de botanique concernant l'Indochine (année 1932 et complément des années
antérieures)." Ibid., ptie. générale,
sept. 1933, 21-23. (Source: Boudet 4.)

Intended to fill the gap for bibliographies about zoology of Indochina, of
which only one major bibliography--by
Vitalis de Salvaza--had been published by
the time Cordier's Bibliographie appeared.[1]
This might be considered as a complement to
the "Zoologie" sections in Cordier: 3:
1801-1816 and 4: 2673-2678, 2797-2798.
Includes publications cited by Cordier,

indicated with an asterisk. Includes
references to species collected by the
Pavie mission.

MH (BEFEO)

[1]Bibliography by Vitalis de Salvaza cited
by Pételot was not located by the compiler in Cordier nor any other bibliography.

EC66   Segal, B. D. et al. "Parasites of man and
domestic animals in Vietnam, Thailand,
Laos and Cambodia, host list and bibliography." Experimental parasitology, 23
(1968), 412-464.

Bibliography of about 700 books, articles, reports, and government publications in virtually all languages, but not
meant to be exhaustive. Compiled mainly
from references in the Index-Catalogue of
Medical and Veterinary Zoology of the
Beltsville Parasitology Laboratory. Host
list, pp. 141-436, indicates types of
parasites which affect humans and eight
kinds of domestic animals, correlated to
geographic area. Bibliography includes
articles in medical journals published in
French Indochina as well as contemporary
Western and Eastern European periodicals.
Except for Annales de la Faculté des
Sciences (Université de Saigon) and publications of the Instituts Pasteur, Vietnam, no contemporary Vietnamese publications are listed.

MH-B

DICTIONARIES. SEE ALSO SCIENCE EA

EC67   *Vietnam (Republic). Ủy-ban Soạn-thảo Danh-từ
Khoa-học. Danh-từ động-vật-học Pháp-Việt,
có phần đối-chiếu Việt-Pháp [French-Viet-
namese--Vietnamese-French glossary of zo-
ological terms]. Saigon: Bộ Văn-hóa
Giáo-dục, 1965. 298 p. (Its Danh-từ
Khoa-học, 4) "Tủ sách Khoa-học."
(Source: NIC.)

DESCRIPTIONS OF SEPARATE PHYLA

Marine Invertebrates. See also EC Botany-Algae for
  marine algae.

EC68 Davydoff, Konstantin Nikolaevich. "Contribu-
      tion à l'étude des invertébrés de la faune
      marine benthique de l'Indochine." Bulle-
      tin Biologique de la France et de la Bel-
      gique, suppl. 37 (1952), 1-158. Also
      issued as Contribution no. 9, Institut
      Océanographique de Nhatrang.

        Recapitulation of research in Indochina
      by Davydoff in 1903, 1929-35, and 1938-39.
      Pp. 1-45, physical background, research
      methods, general remarks on the fauna of
      the South China Sea. Pp. 46-154, inven-
      tory of benthic fauna, with brief descrip-
      tions of phylum, class, and order. Author
      observes that, except for the inventories
      of Fischer, Dautzenberg, and Morlet, our
      knowledge of marine invertebrate fauna of
      Indochina is limited to fragmentary indica-
      tions from occasional naturalists. States
      that the "DeLanessan" expedition (EC92)
      brought back an extremely weak collection
      of mollusks, its mission being to contrib-
      ute to ichthyology and practical fishing.
        Bibliography of 63 publications.
      MH-Z

EC69 Hoàng Quốc Trương. "Phiêu sinh vật trong
      Vịnh Nha Trang." [Marine plankton in Nha
      Trang Bay]. No. 1: Khuê tảo: Bacillari-
      ales. In Annales de la Faculté de Saigon,
      1962, 121-214. Also in Contribution
      no. 59, Institut Océanographique de Nha
      Trang, 1962.

        Description of the physical factors,
      list of planktonic organisms studied and
      identified, and short descriptions of 154
      species. Intended to be a working tool
      for students; systematic and descriptive
      characteristics reduced to a minimum. No
      bibliography. Text in Vietnamese.
      MH-Z

EC70 Ranson, Gilbert, and R. Serène. "New knowl-
      edge of the marine invertebrate fauna of
      Vietnam." Proceedings of the 9th Pacific
      Science Congress, 10 (1961), 40-42.

        Survey of new information and bibliog-
      raphy of 16 publications which have ap-
      peared since the article by Davydoff in
      1952 (EC68). References and lists of new
      species are primarily from Nha Trang Bay.
      MH-Z

EC71 Serène, R. Inventaire des invertébrés marins
      de l'Indochine (1re liste). Station Ma-
      ritime de Cauda [1937] 85 p. (Institut
      Océanographique de l'Indochine. 30e Note)

        List of about 1,000 species and sub-
      species of Crustaceans and Coelenterata,
      with systematic classification, locations
      obtained, and some vernacular names and
      indications of uses by humans. Includes
      bibliography.
      MH-Z

EC72 *Shirota, A., and Hoàng Quốc Trương. "The
      fresh water plankton of South Vietnam."
      Khao cứu niên san Khoa-học Đại-Học-Đường
      Saigon; Annales de la Faculté des Sciences
      de l'Université de Saigon 1963, 177-236.
      (Source: Vidal, "Bibl. bot. indo.")

EC73 *Shirota, A. The plankton of South Vietnam.
      Tokyo: Overseas Technical Cooperation
      Agency, 1966. 462 p. (Source: Vidal,
      "Bibl. bot. indo.")

EC74 Tixier-Durivault, A. "Les octocorailliaires
      de Nha-Trang (Vietnam)." Cahiers du Pa-
      cifique, 14 (1970), 115-236.

        Brief descriptions of 670 specimens--
      92 species, 18 of which are new to
      science--collected since 1916 in the
      Bay of Nha Trang. Numerous drawings.
      MH-Z

BIOLOGY EC

Annelids

EC75   Fauvel, Pierre. "Annélides Polychètes de
l'Annam." Memoria della Pontificia Acca-
demia romana dei Lincei, sér. 3, vol. 2
(1935), 279-354.

Listing and descriptions of about 100
species of polychaetous annelids, collected during night fishing in coastal areas.
Includes bibliographic references, location of species, geographic distribution,
and physical descriptions. About 100 publications in the bibliography.
MH

EC76   _____. "Annélides Polychètes de l'Indochine,
recueillies par M. C. Dawydoff." Commen-
tationes, Pontificia Academia Scientiarum
3 (1939), 243-368.

List and physical descriptions of about
200 species and sub-species collected during the day or by moonlight, rich in small
pelagic species and larvae. Descriptions
include bibliographic references, location
where gathered, and geographic distribution throughout the world. About 60 publications in the bibliography, few on
Indochina.
MH

EC77   Gravier, Ch., and J. L. Dantan. "Annélides
Polychètes recueillies au cours de pêches
nocturnes à la lumière sur les côtes d'Annam." Annales de l'Institut Océanographique [Monaco], n.s. 14 (1934), 37-136.

The first "travail d'ensemble" of polychaetous annelids (Fauvel 1935). Extensive taxonomic descriptions of species
taken around Cầu-đá, near Nha-trang, from
1925-1930. Bibliography of 48 publications world-wide.
MH-Z

Myriapods

EC78   Attems, C. G. "Myriapoden von Indochina,
expedition von Dr. C. Dawydoff (1938-
1939)." Mémoires du Muséum national
d'Histoire naturelle, sér. A (Zoologie)
vol. 5, fasc. 3 (1953), 133-199.

List and descriptions of 184 species
and sub-species, including locations, 52
drawings, and classified listing.
MH-Z

Insects

As a tropical country with a variety of vegetation, Vietnam is considered to be rich in entomological species, but little comprehensive research
on insect life there has been undertaken or completed. Part of the reason is that entomologists
are interested in various species rather than the
insect life of a geographical area. As a result,
the major sources for literature on insects in Vietnam are the published catalogs of the organisms,
such as Genera insectorum, Macrolepidoptera of the
world, and General catalogue of Homoptera, as well
as standard indexes to zoological literature such as
Zoological record, Entomological abstracts, and
Biological abstracts.

Monographs on a few orders and families--
such as Scarabs (Paulian 1945, 1958-1961); Bupres-
tids (Descarpentries and Villiers 1963-1965); Elat-
erids (Fleutiaux 1927-1940); mosquitoes (Borel
1926-1929, 1930); termites (Barthellier 1927); and
Lepidoptera (Joannis 1928-1929 and Candèze 1926-
1927)--have been published and are cited in the
above sources, but these represent only a small and
incomplete portion of the available literature and
comprise a fraction of the insect life in Vietnam.

The publications listed below are the major
bibliographic sources specifically on Indochina or
Vietnam; the researcher should also check the bibliographies by Pételot (EC65) and Segal (EC66), and
the descriptions and illustrations from the Pavie
mission (EC64). The works cited by Vitalis de Salvaza et al are not comprehensive, but they are

broader in coverage than any other listing or inventory for this area.

EC79 Cordier, Henri. Bibliotheca indosinica.
        See AA22 for complete description. For
        publications on entomology, see 3: 2193-
        2196 "Parasitologie," and 3: 2263-2265,
        and 4: 2968, "Parasitologie."
        MH

EC80 Boudet, Paul, and Rémy Bourgeois. Biblio-
        graphie de l'Indochine française.
        See AA21 for complete description. For
        publications on entomology, see "Parasito-
        logie," "Phytopathologie," "Insectes," and
        Entomologie" in most volumes.
        MH

EC81 Vitalis de Salvaza, R. Essai d'un traité
        d'entomologie indochinoise. Hanoi: Impr.
        Munsang dit T. B. Cay, 1919. 308 p.
        Provisional inventory of insects col-
        lected in Indochina, 2/3 of which are
        Coleoptera.--Notice, in Bulletin Agricole
        de l'Institut Scientifique de Saigon, I
        (1918).
        _____. Faune entomologique de l'Indochine
        française. Saigon: Portail, 1921-23.
        Fasc. 1-5, continued as:
        Opuscules de l'Institut Scientifique de Sai-
        gon. Saigon, 1923-28 [?]
        To 1929, Fasc. 1-8 were published.--BM
        Nat. Hist. Suppl., vol. 3
        Contents listed in Pételot: Fasc. 1,
        Fam. Histeridae (Coléoptères), par
        H. Desbordes, 1921. 103 p. Fasc. 2, Fam.
        Brenthidae, par E. Calabresi. Fasc. 3,
        Fam. Papilionidae, Pieridae et Danaidae,
        par E. Dubois et R. Vitalis de Salvaza.
        Fasc. 4, Fam. Scarabaeidae Laparosticti
        (Coléoptères), par A. Boucomont et
        G. Gillet, 1921. Fasc. 5, Fam. Hydro-
        phylidae (Coléoptères), par M. d'Orchymont,
        1921. Fasc. 6, Fam. Malacodermes, par
        M. Pic; Fam. Anthribides, par Dr. Jourdan;

Fam. Scarbeides, par A. Boucomont; Fam.
Gyrimides, par R. Peschet, 1923. Fasc. 7,
Fam. Melasidae et Elateridae, par
E. Fleutiaux. Fasc. 8, Fam. Cicindelidae,
Satyridae, Amathusiidae, Nymphaeidae,
Chrysomelidae, Eumolpinae, Gyrinidae,
Ephemeridae, Formicidae, Dermapteridae,
Nevroptères, 1924 (?).

Mollusks

EC82 Brandt, Rolf A. M. "The non-marine aquatic
        Mollusca of Thailand." Archiv für Mol-
        luskenkunde, 105 (1974), 423 p.
        Systematic description of mollusks
        based upon field work in Southeast Asia
        from 1963 to 1970. Although no field
        work was done in Vietnam, descriptions
        and bibliography (pp. 334-344) include
        references to species found there. Bib-
        liography includes references to early
        published articles by P. Fischer, More-
        let, Morlet, Bavay, Dautzenberg, and
        H. Crosse.
        MH-Z

EC83 Dautzenberg, Ph., and Henri Fischer. "Con-
        tribution à la faune malacologique de
        l'Indochine." Journal de Conchyliologie,
        54 (1906), 145-226. "Additions et recti-
        fications." Ibid., 56 (1908), 252.
        Descriptions of "a series of small very
        interesting species, mostly new and be-
        longing to species not yet observed in the
        region." Specimens collected mostly by
        L. Boutan during the Mission Scientifique
        Permanente d'Exploration en Indochine.
        MH-Z

EC84 _____. "Liste des mollusques récoltés par
        M. le Capitaine de Frégate Blaise au Ton-
        kin, et description d'espèces nouvelles."
        Journal de Conchyliologie, 53 (1905),
        85-234.

BIOLOGY EC

Lists and short descriptions of an extensive collection of mollusks obtained in
Hạ Long Bay and its tributaries as well as
from the region east of the Red River and
the Clear River (Sông Nhị Hà). Descriptions include bibliographic references to
earlier descriptions and locations of
species.
MH-Z

EC85   _____. "Liste des mollusques récoltés par
M. H. Mansuy en Indo-Chine et au Yunnan et
description d'espèces nouvelles." Journal
de Conchyliologie, 53 (1905), 343-471; 56
(1908), 169-217. "Additions et rectifications." Ibid., 252.
Descriptions of specimens obtained by
Mansuy throughout Indochina.
Species and sub-species described in
this and the following articles, as well
as authors of articles are indexed in the
indexes to Journal de Conchyliologie published in 1878, 1897, and 1940.
MH-Z

EC86   _____. "Catalogue des mollusques terrestres
et fluviatiles de l'Indo-Chine." Mission
Pavie, Indochine 1879-1895. Etudes diverses. Paris: Leroux, 1901. Vol. 3,
390-451.
Extensive listing of mollusks, updated
by Fischer's and Dautzenberg's articles in
Journal de Conchyliologie. An edition was
also issued as Catalogue et distribution
géographique des mollusques terrestres,
fluviatiles et marins d'une partie de
l'Indo-Chine (Siam, Laos, Cambodge, Cochinchine, Annam, Tonkin) by Paul-Henri Fischer
(Autun, 1891). 192 p.
MH

Fish. SEE ALSO FISHERIES EK

Bibliographies

EC87   Hai-Học-Viện, Nha-trang. Thư-viện. Bản
tổng-kê tập-san; catalogue des périodiques;

catalog of periodic-books. Nha-trang,
1960. 94 p. Introduction in Vietnamese,
French, and English.
List of 548 periodicals, arranged by
continent, then alphabetically by country. Information includes location number
in the library, title and issuing body,
abbreviation, earliest and latest issue
received, whether received as a purchase
or on exchange, and address of publisher.
Scope is worldwide coverage of marine
science since the Institute began in 1928.
Purpose is not only internal (for locating
periodicals in the library) but also to
encourage other libraries to publish their
holdings.
MH-Z

EC88   Soulier, A. Preliminary bibliography of fish
and fisheries for Cambodia, Laos, and
Vietnam. Bangkok: Indo-Pacific Fisheries Council, 1963. 80 p. (Its Occasional paper, 63/11) At head of title:
Food and Agriculture Organization of the
United Nations.
Alphabetical listing, by author "as
comprehensive as possible within the
limits of the resources" of the Council.
Coverage seems to be extensive, even citing chapters of books such as Pavie's.
Includes legislation, books, articles,
maps, and newspapers giving information
on fish, whether published in Indochina
or in Europe. Pp. 71-80, chronological
list of publications, 1803-1963.
NIC

Lists and Descriptions

EC89   *Bui Huu Cui. Liste des poissons d'Indochine.
Nha-trang: Institut Océanographique de
l'Indochine. (Cited in Kuronuma.)

EC90   Chabanaud, Paul. "Poissons d'Indochine."
BEI 27, no. 169 (1924), 561-581. Also
published as Inventaire de la faune

ichtyologique de l'Indochine (première liste), Saigon: Portail, 1926, 26 p. (Service océanographique des pêches de l'Indochine, 1re note)

Lists 275 species and sub-species, giving Latin name, location, Vietnamese or Cambodian term, physical description, economic value, and abundance.
MH

EC91 Chevey, Pierre, and J. Lemasson. Contribution à l'étude des poissons des eaux douces tonkinoises. Hanoi: Gouvernement Général de l'Indochine, 1937. 183 p. (Institut Océanographique de l'Indochine. 33e note)

The first comprehensive work on fishes of Tongking, according to the authors, as most previous work had been on fishes in Cambodia and Cochinchina; only Pellegrin had studied fishes of Tongking and had published articles on individual species and sub-species.

Describes 98 species and sub-species with complete physical descriptions, names in vernacular and scientific terms, geographic distribution, and economic uses. Pp. 15-141, "tableau de détermination des familles, étude systématique." Appendix: "La pisciculture indigène au Tonkin." Indexes by scientific and vernacular names; bibliography contains about 170 books and articles, although few are on Tongking specifically; text includes 44 black and white plates and 98 figures.
MH-Z

EC92 Chevey, Pierre. Iconographie ichtyologique de l'Indochine. Poissons des campagnes du "de Lanessan" (1925-1929). Saigon: Gouvernement Général de l'Indochine, 1932- .

Vol. 1, 155 p., 50 plates. (Travaux de l'Institut Océanographique de l'Indochine, 4e Mémoire.) No subsequent volumes seem to have been published.

Results of four years of oceanographic surveys and museum studies at 577 oceanographic and fisheries stations. A total of 4,000 specimens collected. Supersedes the provisional Inventaire de la faune ichtyologique de l'Indochine by P. Chabanaud in 1926 (1re Note de l'Institut Océanographique) and by Chevey in 1931 (19e Note de l'Institut). Attempts to list all species in Indochina.

Vol. 1, Order of Teleosteans, excludes Pleuronectids, which were to be described by Chabanaud, but might not have been published. Description includes classification, location and distribution, synonomy, iconography, bibliography, physical description, vernacular names, and usage. Indexes are bibliographic, alphabetical by genre and species, and alphabetical by vernacular name. Vernacular names are in all Southeast Asian languages, Chinese, "Indian," French, and Vietnamese and Sino-Vietnamese.
MH-Z

EC93 _____. Inventaire de la faune ichtyologique de l'Indochine, 2e liste. Saigon: Gouvernement Général de l'Indochine, 1932. 31 p. (Institut Océanographique de l'Indochine, 19e note)

Similar in format to Chabanaud's Inventaire of 1926. Species and sub-species numbered from 276 to 650.
MH-Z

EC94 _____. Revision synonymique de l'Oeuvre ichtyologique de G. Tirant. Saigon: Gouvernement Général de l'Indochine, 1934. 291 p. (Institut Océanographique de l'Indochine, 7e note)

A companion work to Tirant's Oeuvre ichtyologique (réimpression) of 1929, necessitated because of the need to update the original data published as early as 1883. Using a columnar arrangement,

BIOLOGY EC

Chevey indicates Tirant's appellations and
synonymies, references and indigenous
names; bibliographic references; and names
used as of 1934. Indexes to genera and
species and to vernacular names. References in boldface throughout indicate the
page in Réimpression.
MH-Z

EC95   Fourmanoir, P., and Do Thi Nhu-Nhung. "Liste
        complémentaire des poissons marins de Nha-
        Trang." Cahiers O.R.S.T.O.M.--océanogra-
        phie, no. spécial, juillet 1965. 114 p.
            Identification for the first time of
        306 species of fish in Vietnam, bringing to
        1,060 the number known in Vietnam as of
        1965. Intended to complete the inventories
        by Chevey, Chabanaud, and J. Durand and
        Quang (not verified). Specimens mostly
        from markets and commercial fishing at
        Cou-lao [sic] from July to December, span-
        ning the change in monsoon seasons. Of the
        specimens listed, 22 are Subclass Elasmo-
        branchii and 183 are Subclass Actinoptery-
        gii.
            Identification comprises physical de-
        scription, measurements, and identification
        in museum collections. No locality or
        bibliographical references.
        MH-Z

EC96   Kuronuma, Katsuzo. A checklist of fishes of
        Vietnam. [n. p.] Prepared by United
        States Consultants, Inc. for Division of
        Agriculture and Natural Resources, USOM,
        Vietnam, [1961]. 66 p.
            Contains names of fishes in Vietnamese,
        Latin, English, and Japanese. Lists 807
        species in 411 genera and 139 families,
        resulting from research in 1960. No de-
        scriptions or illustrations.

EC97   *Lê Văn Đằng. List of freshwater and brackish
        water fishes of Vietnam. [Saigon?], 1958.
        21 p. (Source: Soulier.)

EC98   *____. Liste des poissons du Vietnam.
        [Saigon?]: Direction [des] Pêches, 1961.
        (Source: Soulier.)

EC99   Sauvage, Henri-Emile. "Recherches sur la
        faune ichtyologique de l'Asie et descrip-
        tion d'espèces nouvelles de l'Indo-Chine."
        Nouvelles archives du Muséum d'Histoire
        Naturelle, 2. sér., 4 (1881), 123-194.
            Pp. 123-164, summary of ichthyological
        research in Asia by Europeans and geo-
        graphical distribution of species.
        Pp. 165-194, description of 40 species
        in Indochina with scientific name, first
        description, physical description, and
        location; pp. 159-164, list of 139 species
        and sub-species known at the time.
        MH-Z

EC100   Tirant, Gilbert. Oeuvre ichtyologique (ré-
        impression). Saigon: Gouvernement Géné-
        ral de l'Indochine, 1929. 175 p. (Ser-
        vice Océanographique des Pêches de l'Indo-
        chine, 6e note)
            Reprint of various works by Tirant:
        "Mémoire sur les poissons de la rivière de
        Hué," BSEI (1883); "Note sur quelques es-
        pèces de poissons des montagnes de Sam-
        rong-Tong (Cambodge)," BSEI (1883);
        "Note sur les poissons de la Basse-Cochin-
        chine et du Cambodge," Excursions et Re-
        connaissances, 1885; "Liste des poissons
        de l'Indochine envoyés...au Muséum des
        Sciences Naturelles de Lyon," pp. 159-167,
        in La pêche et les poissons by Loÿs Pe-
        tillot (Paris, 1911.)
            A companion work is Chevey's Revision
        synonymique...(EC94) which updates Ti-
        rant's descriptions and classifications
        as of 1934.
        MH-Z

EC101   Trần Ngọc Lợi, and Nguyễn Châu. "Les pois-
        sons d'importance commerciale au Việt-
        Nam." BSEI, n.s. 39 (1964), 323-425.

Also as Contribution no. 79, Institut Océanographique de l'Indochine, 1964.

Distribution, fishing seasons, and commercial uses of 97 fish, with illustration of each. Arranged in systematic order. Index to species. Names in Vietnamese, French, English, Japanese, and other local names if known. Text in French (pp. 323-362) and in Vietnamese (pp. 365-395), with illustrations on the remaining pages.

MH

Amphibians and Reptiles

EC102 Bourret, René. Les batraciens de l'Indochine. Hanoi: Gouvernement Général de l'Indochine, 1942. 547 p. (Mémoires de l'Institut Océanographique de l'Indochine, 6e mémoire)

"The first comprehensive work on Batrachia in Indochina." Includes an historical introduction, bibliography of about 1,000 citations, geographical distribution, index of characteristics (tables de détermination), and descriptive catalog (pp. 130-529). Indexes to illustrations and to species, genres, and families. Does not list vernacular names of species. Includes species from mainland Southeast Asia and its territorial waters.

MH-Z

EC103 _____. Les serpents de l'Indochine. Toulouse: Basayau, 1936. 2 vols.

Vol. 1 also published in Bulletin de la Société d'Histoire Naturelle de Toulouse, 69 (71e année, 1936), 137-276.

Vol. 1, Etudes sur la faune. Vol. 2, Catalogue systématique descriptif, of 203 species and 49 sub-species or varieties found in nearby areas.

A catalog as complete as possible of snakes of Indochina. Distinctive characteristics of this and other work by Bour-

ret listed in this bibliography are a comprehensive bibliography, survey of the geographic distribution of the species, tables of characteristics to provide an index to species and sub-species listed, and extensive scientific descriptions of each species or sub-species. References in vol. 2, such as "Angel (5)" refer to the fifth numbered citation in the bibliographic listing for M. Angel in vol. 1.

The bibliography (vol. 1, pp. 36-74, about 900-1,000 works) is as complete a list as possible of works on snakes of Indochina since the publication of Boulenger's Catalogue of the snakes in the British Museum (1893-1896).

MH-Z

EC104 _____. Les serpents marins de l'Indochine française. [Hanoi]: Institut Océanographique de l'Indochine, [1935]. 69 p. (Publications de l'Institut Océanographique de l'Indochine, note 25)

The first comprehensive study of marine snakes of Indochina in French (Préf.). Lists about 30 species and sub-species. 10 black and white plates. Acknowledges the work, Monograph of the sea snakes, by Malcolm A. Smith (London, 1926). Format and purpose follows Bourret's other works.

MH-Z

EC105 _____. Les tortues de l'Indochine, avec une note sur la pêche et l'élevage des tortues de mer, par F. Le Poulain. [Hanoi?]: Institut Océanographique de l'Indochine, 1941. 235 p. Also published as Publications de l'Institut Océanographique de l'Indochine, note 38.

Follows the arrangement and purpose of his other works in its attempt to be as comprehensive as possible. Acknowledges the work of Malcolm A. Smith in Fauna of British India (1931) as a basis for information on turtles of Indochina. Bib-

liography, pp. 31-56, of about 650
publications.
MH-Z

EC106 _____. "Liste des reptiles et batraciens ac-
tuellement connus en Indochine française."
Bulletin général de l'Instruction Publique,
1939, 49-60. (Notes herpetologiques sur
l'Indochine française, 20)

Classified order, with listing and location of 294 reptiles and 80 amphibians.
Later information on reptiles may be found
in Bourret's "Liste des reptiles reçus en
[year]", in each volume of Bulletin général de l'Instruction Publique, 1937-1941,
and in Notes et travaux de l'Ecole Supérieure des Sciences de l'Université indochinoise, 1943-1944.
MH-Z

EC107 Campden-Main, Simon M. A field guide to the
snakes of South Vietnam. Washington, D.C.:
Division of Reptiles and Amphibians,
United States National Museum, Smithsonian
Institution, 1969 [i.e. 1970] 114 p.

A field guide, listing snakes that have
been captured or killed in RVN, for use of
medical or military personnel who might
come into contact with snakes. Lists species "recorded in the literature with an
adequate description or those personally
examined in museum collections." Descrip-
tions--brief description of morphology,
color, habits and habitat, South Vietnam
locality records, venom, and toxicity.
Gives common English name if known; no new
information or scientific names. Format
is similar to work by Van Peenen (EC123)--
reader must use key of physical characteristics for identification.
MH-Z

EC108 Tirant, G. "Notes sur les reptiles de la
Cochinchine et du Cambodge." Excursions
et Reconnaissances, vol. 8, no. 19 (1885),
148-168.

_____. "Notes sur les reptiles de la Cochin-
chine et du Cambodge, III. Les serpents."
Ibid., vol. 8, no. 20 (1885), 387-428.

General notes on turtles and snakes,
not systematic descriptions. Includes
short physical descriptions and scientific
and vernacular names. Comprises 24 species and sub-species of turtles and 85
species and sub-species of snakes.
MH-H

Birds

EC109 Bangs, Outram, and Josselyn Van Tyne. "Birds
of the Kelley-Roosevelts expedition to
French Indo-China." Field Museum of Natural History, Publication no. 272,
Zoological series, 18, no. 3 (1931),
31-119.

Lists about 350 species collected in
northern Tongking, Laos and near Quảng
Trị, central Vietnam. Description includes scientific name, English name, published description if available previously, locale. Two colored plates.
MH-Z

EC111 Delacour, Jean, and P. Jabouille. Les
oiseaux de l'Indochine française.
Aurillac: Impr. du Cantal républicain,
1931. 4 vols. At head of title: Exposition coloniale internationale, Paris,
1931. Indochine française.

_____. "Liste des oiseaux de l'Indochine
française, complétée et mise à jour (7e
Expédition Ornithologique en Indochine
française)." L'Oiseau et la revue française d'ornithologie, n.s. 10 (1940),
89-220.

Delacour, Jean, and J.-C. Greenway, Jr.
"Commentaires, additions et modifications
à la liste des oiseaux de l'Indochine
française." Ibid., n.s. 11 (nº spécial,
1941), I-XXI.

Delacour, Jean. "Commentaires, additions et
modifications à la liste des oiseaux de

l'Indochine française." Ibid., 21 (1951), 1-32, 81-119.

The first comprehensive work on birds of Indochina; intended to be a "useful résumé of previous work and a solid basis for future research" (Préf.). A descriptive and annotated list of about 1,000 species and sub-species. Bibliography of about 200 general and specialized books and 80 periodical articles, including several articles by Delacour from 1925 to 1930. The four volume Oiseaux is the result of 5 expeditions in Indochina over an eight-year period, during which he discovered 125 new birds, 205 others for the first time in Indochina, and collected 20,000 specimens. Arranged by order, family, genera, species, and sub-species. Descriptions of species and sub-species are extensive. Contains 67 plates. Appendix at end of vol. 4 lists a few additional species or sub-species.

The Delacour and Jabouille "Liste des oiseaux" contains 71 new species and sub-species found since 1931 and omits 15 which were originally included. The numbers in the "Liste" correspond to the names of species and sub-species in Oiseaux, a useful addition because of the large number of listings. This article was written, according to the authors, because of the newly described forms, and changes in nomenclature necessitated by recent discoveries.

The "Commentaires" articles list new species and sub-species discovered by other scientists, the 1941 article containing about 100 new species and sub-species and the 1951 article listing a few hundred more. All four publications are necessary for complete bibliographical and zoological records.
MH-Z

EC111 Jouan, Henri. "Note sur les oiseaux de la Basse-Cochinchine." Mémoires de la Société des Sciences Naturelles de Cherbourg, 2. sér., 6; 16 (1872), 257-322.

Description of 192 species in 107 genera collected by M. Pierre, Director of the Jardin Publique in Saigon. Brief physical description, scientific name; mention of habitats in some instances.
MH-Z

EC112 King, Ben F., and Edward C. Dickinson. A field guide to the birds of South-East Asia. Boston: Houghton Mifflin, 1975. 480 p.

Descriptions and pictures of 1,198 species found as of May 1971. Names of birds are only in English and Latin. Location and range of birds are listed, but there is no separate geographical index. Includes bibliography and index to species.
MH-Z

EC113 Oustalet, Emile, and Rodolphe Germain. "Catalogue des oiseaux de la Basse-Cochin-Chine." Bulletin de la Société Nationale d'Acclimatation de France, 51 (1905), 169-184, 54 (1907), 43-51, 83-86, 148-154. (Page 154 ends, "à suivre" but no more seems to have been published.)

Description of about 30 species and sub-species, many of which are also described in Oustalet's "Les oiseaux du Cambodge, du Laos, de l'Annam et du Tonkin." Descriptions are more complete than for the earlier work; references to the earlier work are included for species found in other areas of Indochina.

Oustalet died in 1905; the work was completed by Germain and E. Trouessart. Obituary in the Bulletin 54 (1907), 41-42.
MH-Z

BIOLOGY EC

EC114 Oustalet, Emile. "Les oiseaux du Cambodge,
du Laos, de l'Annam et du Tonkin." Nouvelles archives du Muséum d'Histoire Naturelle, 4. sér., 1 (1899), 221-296;
5 (1903), 1-94. (Page 94 ends "à suivre,"
but no more seemed to have been published.)

Brief descriptions of 185 species and
sub-species, planned to be a preliminary
catalog comprised only of species which
Oustalet was able to verify existed in
Indochina, except for Cochinchina and Siam.
He hoped eventually to compile a catalog
of birds of Indochina as complete as
Oiseaux de la Chine compiled by Armand
David and himself in 1897, it does not
seem to have been accomplished, for Oustalet died in 1905.

Descriptions include scientific name,
short synonomy and bibliography, vernacular names (from Tirant and Harmand), brief
physical description, short historical description of specimens obtained by previous scientists, and locations. No index.
Intended to include only birds within the
political boundaries of Cambodia, Laos,
Annam, and Tongking, not throughout the
natural habitats of the birds. Descriptions do include mention of the range of
species outside of Indochina if known.
MH-Z

EC115 Robinson, Herbert C., and C. Boden Kloss.
"On birds from South Annam and Cochinchina." The Ibis, 11th ser, 1 (1919),
392-458, 565-625. 9 plates of birds.

List and description of 234 species, 34
of which were newly discovered, representing 1,525 specimens taken during about a
three-month expedition to the Lang-bian
region and Saigon-Biên-Hòa in 1918 by two
ornithologists from India. The first major
expedition, later eclipsed by Delacour and
Jabouille (EC110) in importance and
completeness.
MH-Z

EC116 Tirant, Gilbert. "Les oiseaux de la Basse-
Cochinchine." BCAI, 3. sér., vol. 1,
no. 1 (1878), 73-166. "Table des noms
annamites des oiseaux...." pp. 167-171,
and "Table des noms cambodgiens des
oiseaux...." pp. 172-174.

Describes 166 birds found in an area
from Baphônm [sic] on the Mekong to Đồng-
lách, near Biên-Hòa, Saigon, and Trà-
vinh. Gives the Latin name, published
source where described elsewhere, Vietnamese name, physical description, and habitat. Based upon collections in the Muséum
de Lyon and upon a 3-year trip in Indochina where he obtained over 1,000 species. "The best avifunal list of an Indochinese region published in the 19th
century...so good that the Basse-Cochin-
chine has been since somewhat neglected by
modern collectors."--Delacour, in "The
contribution of Gilbert Tirant to Indochinese ornithology," Natural history bulletin of the Siam Society, 23 (1970)
Deignan memorial issue, 325-329. Delacour's article includes commentaries on 30
specimens listed by Tirant.
MH

EC117 Wildash, Philip. Birds of South Vietnam.
Rutland, Vt.: Tuttle, 1968. 234 p.
Foreword by Jean Delacour.

Describes 586 species and pictures 213
species in color. "Follows the Wetmore
order of families as modified by Delacour
and Charles Vaurie for the passerine birds
and lists the scientific and English names
suggested by H. Elliott McClure."--Intro.
Acknowledges the assistance of Delacour in
preparing the manuscript. Describes birds
of South Vietnam only--although species in
South Vietnam are also found throughout
the mainland and island Southeast Asia--
in an attempt to keep the size of the
volume from being too bulky. Description
includes English name, scientific name,

first description, habitat, distribution, and brief identification. No measurements or vernacular names.

MH-Z

Mammals

EC118 Bourret, René. Les mammifères de l'Indochine. [Hanoi?, 1946-]

"Préparé au Laboratoire des Sciences Naturelles de l'Université indochinoise." Vol. 1, Les gibbons. 1946. 41 p.

Bibliography of about 200 publications and descriptions of 11 species of gibbons, which comprise the only species of the family of Hylobatidae in Indochina. Originally planned to cover by order the mammals of Indochina, as had been done for reptiles and amphibians, but had to be abandoned because of the lack of bibliographic information. Present work differs from other works by Bourret in its omission of morphology which he considers unnecessary for the determination of species in a given group. Descriptions are brief and not as detailed as for Bourret's other works. Bibliographies are extensive.

MH-Z; ZR 1946

EC119 Delacour, Jean. "Liste provisoire des mammifères de l'Indochine française. Mammalia, 4 (1940), 20-29, 46-58.

List of 212 species of mammals captured by several expeditions in Indochina during the 1920's. Some mammals had been classified by Delacour and his associates; others had been described by Osgood after the Kelley-Roosevelts Asiatic Expedition, but, according to Delacour, the description was unknown to many Frenchmen because it had been published in English [in the Field Museum series].

Descriptive information is primarily scientific name and locale in which cap-

tured, but in a few instances also includes physical description.

MH-Z

EC120 Osgood, Wilfred H. "Mammals of the Kelley-Roosevelts and Delacour Asiatic expeditions." Field Museum of Natural History, Publication no. 312, Zoological series, 18, no. 10 (1932), 193-339.

The Kelley-Roosevelts Asiatic Expedition of 1928-29 was divided into three sections covering Burma, southwestern China, and northern French Indochina. The latter section traveled from Hai Phòng up the Black River to Lào Kay, across northern Tongking to Phong Saly, down the Mekong to Savannaket, and across to Hue. This article lists 243 specimens taken during the expedition and obtained from expeditions led by Jean Delacour and others and is collated with four other sources--the British Museum, United States National Museum, the Paris Museum, and previously obtained specimens in the Field Musueum. Description includes scientific name, English name, first description or previously published description, physical description, and location obtained. Two colored plates.

MH-Z

EC121 Thomas, Oldfield. "The mammals obtained by Mr. Herbert Stevens on the Sladen-Godman expedition to Tonkin." Proceedings of the Zoological Society, 1925, 495-506.

Listing only of 35 species obtained.

_____. "The Delacour exploration of Indo-China.--Mammals." Ibid., 1927, 41-58.

Listing of 72 species and sub-species, 400 specimens in Annam.

_____. "The Delacour exploration of Indo-China.--Mammals II. On mammals collected during the winter of 1926-1927." Ibid., 1928, 139-150.

Listing, with some brief descriptions, of 68 species and sub-species, 300 specimens, collected in Tongking (Tam Đảo, Bắc Kạn, Ngân Sơn, Lạng Sơn), Hue, and Djiring.

_____. "The Delacour exploration of Indo-China.--Mammals III. Mammals collected during the winter of 1927-28." Ibid., 1928, 831-841.

List of 62 species and sub-species, representing 200 specimens captured in Annam (Phú Quí), Laos (Nape), Cambodia (Siem Reap and Angkor), and Cochinchina (Tây Ninh).

All of Thomas' articles are based upon specimens received in the British Museum and other museums, not upon collecting done by himself.
MH-Z

EC122 *Ryan, P. F., and T. J. McIntyre. A nominal list of names for South Vietnamese mammals. [Bethesda, Md.. Zoonoses Section, Clinical Investigation Department, Naval Medical Research Institute, National Naval Medical Center], 1967. 19 p. (Cited by Van Peenen; Ryan; and Light.)

EC123 Van Peenen, P. F. D.; P. F. Ryan; and R. H. Light. Preliminary identification manual for mammals of South Vietnam. Washington, D.C.: Smithsonian Institution, United States National Museum, 1969. 310 p.
Available from NTIS: AD 698 196.

"Written so that field medical personnel might identify species of wild mammals occurring in South Vietnam" (Pref.). Considered a necessary publication because of the lack of reliable identification information. Does not include Vietnamese names for species: Authors state that Vietnamese recognize "groups of mammals rather than species." Descriptions include scientific name, first description, published source, common English name, physical description and measurement, illustrations of skull or

body, locality in RVN, habitat. Bibliography of about 100 books and articles.
MH-Z

CHEMISTRY ED

ED1 *Vietnam (Republic). Ủy-ban Soạn thảo Danh-từ Khoa-học. Danh-từ hóa-học Pháp-Việt, có phần đối-chiếu Việt-Pháp [French-Vietnamese--Vietnamese-French glossary of terms in chemistry]. Saigon: Bộ Quốc-gia Giáo-dục, 1963. 427 p. (Its Danh-từ Khoa-học, 3) "Tủ-sách Khoa-học" (Source: NIC.)
Cited in TTAPC as: Saigon. Viện Đại Học. Danh-từ....

GEOLOGY, PALENTOLOGY, AND METEROROLOGY EE

BIBLIOGRAPHIES

EE1 Cordier, Henri. Bibliotheca indosinica.
See AA23 for complete description. For publications on earth sciences, see 3: 1823-1842, Géologie et minéralogie," and 3: 1791-1802, and 4: 2929-2930, "Climat et météorologie." Paleontology is included with "Géologie."
MH

EE2 Boudet, Paul, and Rémy Bourgeois. Bibliographie de l'Indochine française.
See AA22 for complete description. For publications on earth sciences, see "Climat" or "Climatologie," "Géographie," "Géologie," "Météorologie," "Mines," and "Typhons" in each volume, as well as "Tonkin--Géologie" and "Annam--Géologie" in vol. 3. Publications on paleontology are included with "Géologie" and "Paléontologie."
MH

GEOLOGY AND PALEONTOLOGY

BIBLIOGRAPHIES

EE3 Blondel, Fernand. Bibliographie géologique
et minière de la France d'Outre-Mer.
Paris: Didot, 1941-1952. 2 vols. (Publications du Bureau d'Etudes Géologiques
et Minières Coloniales, 11 and 20)
        Vol. 2 includes Indochina, pp. 873-946:
about 90 publications from Indochina and
France, covering publications from the
19th century.
    MH-Z

EE4 _____. "Etat de nos connaissances en 1929
sur la géologie de l'Indochine française."
BSGI, 18, fasc. 6 (1929), 16 p. Also published as International Geological Congress, Compte rendu of the 15th session,
South Africa, 1929. Pretoria: Wallach's
Ltd., 1930. Vol. 2, Europe and Asia,
pp. 518-531. Bibliography of 22 items,
p. 531.
        _____. "Les connaissances géologiques en
1930 dans l'Extrême-Orient méridional."
BSGF, sér. 4, vol. 30, no. 5 (1930-1931),
323-432.
        _____. "La géologie et les mines de l'Indo-
chine française." Annales de l'Académie
des Sciences Coloniales, 6 (1933), 169-322.
Also published as La géologie et les mines
de la France d'Outre Mer (Paris, Société
d'Editions Maritimes et Coloniales, 1932.
148 p.) [Catalog entry: France. Bureau
d'Etudes Géologiques et Minières Colo-
niales].
        Rev. of 1933 article in Bibl. géogr.
int., 1932, no. 1924 by L. Raveneau: "Bel
exposé des travaux accomplis en Indochine."
Bibliography of 99 items (Raveneau).
    Boudet 4

EE5 Gt. Brit. Commonwealth Bureau of Soils.
Bibliography on soils and land-use in Viet-

nam and Cambodia (1966-1930). Harpenden,
England, [n. d.] 9 p.
        Chronological listing--beginning with
1966--of 46 articles, mostly in French.
Annotations vary in length, from none to
one-half a page. Does not include any
articles from BEI, but several other colonial publications are included.
    EARI

EE6 "Publications relating to offshore geology
and mineral resources of the Republic of
Viet-Nam." Technical bulletin, United
Nations Economic Commission for Asia and
the Far East, Committee for Coordination
of Joint Prospecting for Mineral Resources
in Asian Offshore Areas, I (1968), 155-158.
        List of 36 articles published in 5 pe-
riodicals from RVN and 5 from France and
Russia from 1953-1967. Article also notes
that the Geological Survey of Vietnam has
compiled a bibliographic list of about 800
references through 1963 relating to the
geology of Cambodia, Laos, and Vietnam.
    MH

DESCRIPTIONS AND MAPS

EE7 *Dussault, Léon. Inventaire général de l'Indochine: Structure et géographie physique.
Hanoi, 1926. 76 p. (Société de Géographie de Hanoi. 1er fasc.)
        "Full treatment of the physical fea-
tures of the country" (Gt. Brit., Naval
Intelligence Division, Indo-China).

EE8 Fromaget, J. "Observations et réflexions sur
la géologie stratigraphique et structu-
rale de l'Indochine." BSGF, 5. sér., 4
(1934), 101-164.
        "Recent synthesis" (Gt. Brit., Naval
Intelligence Division, Indo-China). No
bibliography.
    MH-Z

GEOLOGY, PALEONTOLOGY, AND METEOROLOGY EE

EE9   Furon, Raymond. "Histoire de la géologie de la France d'Outre Mer." Mémoires du Muséum National d'Histoire Naturelle, n.s., sér. C, vol. 5 (1955).

"Indochine (1858-1954)," pp. 169-182. Contains brief summary of geological studies and explorations of Mouhot, Garnier, Petiton, Pavie, Counillon, and Jourdy--none of which are listed in his bibliography--outline of the work of Deprat, Mansuy, Blondel, and Fromaget, brief biographies of Deprat and Mansuy, and summaries of recent geological discoveries, geological structure of Indochina, and applied geology of Tongking.
MH-Z

EE10 "Guide to soil maps of midlands and plains." JPRS, 53,300, translations on North Vietnam, no. 951. MC, 1971: 11311-23, card 25.

Refers to five series of soil maps of the DRVN: 1) 1:200,000-scale soil maps of the midland and plains--17 maps published from 1961-1969 by the Ministry of Agriculture, Department of Land Administration and Regional Agricultural Production Planning; 2) 1:100,000-scale "rough chart of the soils of North Vietnam," in 1958; 3) 1:100,000-scale soil maps of the mountain provinces, expected by the end of 1970; 4) 1:50,000-scale soil maps of midland and plains provinces begun in 1961; and 5) 1:10,000-scale soil maps of the state-owned farms.
MH

EE11 *Henry, Yves. Terres rouges et terres noires basaltiques d'Indochine. Hanoi: Gouvernement général de l'Indochine, 1931. 211 p.

"Detailed descriptions, based on field observations and laboratory investigations, of the soil characteristics, with an appraisal of their agricultural value."

(M. W. Sentius, Bibl. econ. geol. 4, pt. 2).

EE12 *Mansuy, Henri. "Catalogue général par terrains et par localités, des fossiles recueillis en Indochine et au Yunnan...au cours des années 1903-1918." BSGI, 6, fasc. 6 (1919). 226 p.

_____. "Supplément au Catalogue général par terrains et par localités des fossiles recueillis en Indochine et au Yunnan." BSGI, 7, fasc. 3 (1920). (Source: Boudet 1.)

EE13 _____. Contribution à la carte géologique de l'Indochine: paléontologie. Hanoi: IDEO, 1908. 73 p. At head of title: Gouvernement Général de l'Indo-Chine. Direction Général des Travaux Publics. Service des Mines.

"A summary exposition of principal characteristics of primary and secondary fauna of Indochina." Brief listing of species in the Ecole Supérieure des Mines in Paris sent from Tongking since 1904. Divided into fossils from Silurian, Devonian, Permo-Carboniferous, Triassic, and Liassic eras. Black and white plates of about 300 specimens. Descriptions include Latin name, geographical distribution, physical description of fossil, and bibliographical references by other scientists.
MH-Z

EE14 *Nguyễn Hoài Văn. Inventory and nomenclature of Vietnam soils. Saigon: Ministry of Rural Affairs, Bureau of Soil Survey, 1962. 141 p.

Attempts to classify and name Northern and Southern Vietnam soils into a common system; applies 1960 U.S. Soil Survey system to establish a single scheme (EARI).

EE15 *Patte, Etienne. "Description de fossiles
        paléozoïques et mésozoïques recueillis par
        MM. Dussault et Fromaget en Extrême-
        Orient." BSGI, 18, fasc. 1 (1929). 108 p.
        (Source: Boudet 4.)

EE16 *Petiton, A. Géologie de l'Indochine. Paris:
        Impr. Nationale, 1895. 253 p.
            Divided into five parts: a record of
        geological exploration, 1869-1870, de-
        scription of geological specimens, de-
        scription of specimens in Indochina, sum-
        mary of the geology of Cochinchina and
        Cambodia, and maps and drawings. (Source:
        Boudet 1.)

EE17 Saurin, E. "Indochine." In Lexique strati-
        graphique international, fasc. 6a of
        vol. 3, Asie. Paris: Centre National de
        la Recherche Scientifique, 1956. 140 p.
        At head of title: International Geologi-
        cal Congress, 20th, Mexico, 1956.
            Definitions of about 200 terms relating
        to geology in Indochina; includes geologi-
        cal structure, paleontology, geological
        age, and geographical terminology. Defi-
        nitions include bibliographical citations.
        Bibliography of about 200 publications,
        mostly in BSGI and MSGI.
        MH-Z

EE18 ____. "Les recherches géologiques récentes
        en Indochine." In Proceedings of the 7th
        Pacific Science Congress, New Zealand,
        1953, vol. 2, pp. 157-169.
            Summary of the main results of research
        during the decade on the stratigraphy and
        structure of Indochina.--Bibl. and Index
        of Geol. 19 (1954). Bibliography and
        footnote references to 36 publications,
        1939-1947, mostly by Saurin, J. Fromaget,
        and C. Hoffet. References are mostly to
        publications issued in Saigon or Hanoi and
        not widely distributed outside Indochina.
        MH-Z

EE19 *Vietnam (Democratic Republic). Carte géo-
        logique du Nord Viet-Nam au 500,000ᵉ; ban
        đồ địa chất nước Việt-Nam Dân Chu Cộng
        Hòa. Hanoi: Arch. Dép. Gén. Géol., 1962.
            Cited in Biuletyn of the Instytut Geo-
        logiczny, Warsaw 177 (1967). Reference
        also made to maps at 1:25,000 scale.

EE20 *Vietnam (Republic). Nha Địa-Dư Quốc-Gia.
        Carte géologique "Viet-Nam--Cambodge--
        Laos." Đà-lạt, 1962-1964. 14 pts. Con-
        tinues: Indochina. Service Géologique
        de l'Indochine, Carte géologique de l'In-
        dochine (Hanoi, 1928-1956), 11 pts.
        (Source: Anglemyer-Gee-Koll.)

                    METEOROLOGY

BIBLIOGRAPHIES

EE21 Grimes, Annie E. An annotated bibliography
        on the climate of the Republic of Viet-
        nam. Washington, D.C.: Environmental
        Sciences Services Administration, 1966.
        122 p.
            At head of title: U.S. Department of
        Commerce. (WB/BC-90) Available from
        NTIS: AD 664 703.
            Chronological list of 268 books and
        articles, 1884-1965, mostly in English
        and French. Includes general monographs
        (such as Bouinais and Paulus, 1884), nu-
        merous articles in BEI, military publica-
        tions, especially U.S. and United Kingdom
        publications during World War II and U.S.
        publications after 1962. Author and sub-
        ject indexes, with listing of stations.
        MH-BH

EE22 ____. Bibliography of climatic maps of
        Indochina. Washington, D.C.: U.S.
        Weather Bureau, 1960. 59 p. At head of
        title: U.S. Weather Bureau, Office of
        Climatology, Foreign Section. (WB/BM-18)

Earlier edition, 1957-58. 2 vols. Neither edition available for inspection. Probably revised and published as Grimes' annotated bibliographies of climatic maps of the Republic of Vietnam and of North Vietnam. Available from NTIS: AD 665 181 and AD 665 188.

EE23 _____. An annotated bibliography of climatic maps of North Vietnam. Silver Springs, Md.: U.S. Environmental Data Service, 1968. 43 p. (WB/BM-73).

Chronological listing of 125 books, articles, and maps printed in books and articles, 1901-1967. Annotations include map scale and features (precipitation, wind currents, isobars, etc.). Scope includes maps of Vietnam as well as of larger areas in Asia. Includes references to maps in Washington area libraries. Publications listed include present-day publications from RVN in Vietnamese. Author and subject indexes. Most references are also in Grimes's bibliography of climatic maps of the Republic of Vietnam.
MH-BH

EE24 _____. An annotated bibliography of climatic maps of the Republic of Vietnam. Silver Spring, Md.: Environmental Sciences Services Administration, 1969. 46 p. At head of title: U.S. Dept. of Commerce. (WB/BM-74) Available from NTIS: AD 685 725.

Chronological listing of 137 books, articles, and maps printed in books and articles, 1901-1937. Format, annotations, and scope are virtually identical as for Grimes's bibliography of climatic maps of North Vietnam.
MH-BH

DESCRIPTIONS

EE25 Bruzon, Etienne; P. Carton; and A. Romer. Le climat de l'Indochine et les typhons de la Mer de Chine. Hanoi: IDEO, 1940. 2 vols. At head of title: Gouvernement Général de l'Indochine, Direction des Services Economiques.

Numéro hors-série du Bulletin Economique de l'Indochine. "Troisième édition."

First edition, 1929, 141 p. Second edition, 1931, 310 p., appeared as n° spécial des Annales du Service Météorologique de l'Indochine; at head of title: Exposition coloniale internationale, Paris, 1931. Indochine française. Section des Sciences. Observations central de l'Indochine.

Vol. 1, climate: extensive tables on seasonal and regional temperatures, precipitation, and other data. Includes rainfall. Vol. 2, typhoons and factors affecting aerial navigation.
DAS

EE26 Đỗ Đình Cương. Khí-hậu Việt-Nam [Climate of Vietnam]. Saigon. Khai-Trí, [1968]. [Approx. 200 pp.]

Text, graphs, and maps of temperature, winds, precipitation, and other aspects of weather for all of Vietnam (including DRVN) and for various regions. Maps of typhoons, 1948-1957, although details do not indicate precise areas in Vietnam where they struck.
MH-V

EE27 *Indochina. Service Météorologique. Atlas. Hanoi, 1930. 42 p.

Maps showing climatological and meteorological network, 1926 and 1930, pluviometrical network, 1926 and 1932, networks for the transmission of meteorological information in Indochina and the Far East, monthly typhoon trajectories, 1911-1929, and rainfall, 1907-1929 (Grimes).

EE28 *____. ____. Bulletin pluviométrique, 1906-1930.

Monthly statistical report on climatology, its influence on agriculture, stations, instruments, and station reports on weather. Information also reported in Annuaire statistique de l'Indochine and in Bulletin économique de l'Indochine.

____. ____. Annales, 1928-1939.

Annual report on weather. (Source: Grimes.)

EE29 Nuttonson, Michael Y. Climatological data of Vietnam, Laos, and Cambodia; a supplement to the report on the physical environment and agriculture of Vietnam, Laos and Cambodia; a study based on field survey data and on pertinent records, material, and reports. Washington, D.C.: American Institute of Crop Ecology, 1963. 75 p.

Lists average temperature and precipitation, mean monthly and annual temperatures and precipitation, mean relative humidity and mean minimum temperatures. Map shows meteorological and climatological stations.
MH

EE30 U.S. Air Weather Service. First Weather Wing. Climate of North Vietnam, prepared by Technical Service, 20th Weather Squadron. [n. p., n. d.] 92 p. (Special study 105-4)

Summaries of climatological conditions by month. Maps show typhoon tracks, 1947-1963 by month, terrain of North Vietnam, and weather stations at 17 locations. Monthly data includes temperature, precipitation, and humidity. Supersedes a study of Sept. 1964.
DAS

EE31 ____. ____. Climate of Republic of Vietnam, prepared by Technical Services, 20th Weather Squadron. Springfield, Va.:

Clearinghouse, 1965. 138 p. (Special study 105-9 revised) Available from NTIS: AD 689 786.

Charts and maps on monthly weather conditions and seasonal changes in temperature, humidity, precipitation, turbulence, cloudiness, visibility, surface winds, and upper winds. Data for Đà-Nẵng, Pleiku, Nha Trang, Saigon, Sóc Trăng. Supersedes a 1965 study.
DAS

EE32 ____. ____. Climatic atlas of Indochina (excluding Malaya and Burma), prepared by Technical Service, 20th Weather Squadron. [n. p., n. d. 1965?] 265 p. (Special study, 105-6)

Series of maps, showing, on 22 maps per month, temperatures, precipitation, cloudiness, ceiling, and sea pressure.
DAS

EE33 *Vietnam (Republic). Nha Giám Đốc Khí-tượng. Đại lược thời-tiết năm [Annual weather summary]. Saigon, 1961-1963.

____. ____. Đại-lược thời-tiết tháng [Monthly weather bulletin]. Saigon, 1962- . Continuation of Bulletin mensuel du temps and Résumé mensuel du temps, issued by the Service Météorologique de l'Indochine in Hanoi, 1937-1946 and Saigon, 1949-1962.

____. ____. Carte générale 00 UT. Saigon, 1961- . Continuation of Bulletin météorologique journalier. Saigon, 1955-61.

Latter work consists of maps with temperatures, weather observations, wind direction, and wind speed. (Source: Grimes.)

EE34 *____. Nha Tổng Giám-Đốc Khí-tượng. Résumés climatologiques (modèles ABCDK). Climatological summaries. Station Saigon-Tân-Sơn-Nhứt. [Saigon? 1965?]. (Source: Thư-mục 1966; BGI 1966.)

EE35 *_____. Nha Giám-Đốc Khí-tượng. <u>Temperature, humidity, rainfall, evaporation, sunshine duration, nebulosity, fog, thunderstorm and surface wind at 13 main weather stations of Vietnam</u>. Prepared by George L. McColm, USAID Vietnam. [n.d. 1967?] unpaged.

Records of observations at stations in RVN, some dating from 1907, through 1962. Tables in Vietnamese and English (<u>Meteor. & geo-astro. abstr.</u>, 1969).

OTHER SOURCES

EE36 <u>Bibliographie des sciences géologiques</u>. Paris: Société Géologique de France, 1923-1961. From 1948 to 1960 published as <u>Bulletin analytique et bulletin signalétique</u> by the Centre National de la Recherche Scientifique. After 1960, see <u>Bulletin signalétique 216 Géologie--Paléontologie</u>, published by the Centre.

EE37 <u>Bibliography and index of geology</u>. Washington, D.C.: Geological Society of America, 1933- . From 1933-1969: <u>Bibliography and index of geology exclusive of North America</u>.

EE38 U.S. Environmental Sciences Services Administration. Environmental Data Service. <u>World weather records, 1953-1960</u>. Washington, D.C.: GPO, 1967. vol. 4, Asia, 576 p. Continues <u>World weather records</u> (Smithsonian Institution, 1927; <u>Ibid.</u>, 1934; and U.S. Weather Bureau, 1959).

MATHEMATICS EF

See PHYSICS EG

PHYSICS EG

EG1 *Hoàng Xuân Hãn. <u>Danh-từ khoa-học (toán, lý, cơ, thiên văn)</u> [Scientific terms (mathe-

matics, physics, mechanics, astronomy)]. Paris: Minh Tân, 1951. 198 p. (Source: Unesco.)

EG2 *Vietnam (Democratic Republic). Ủy Ban Khoa học Nhã Nước. Ban tóan lý. <u>Danh từ vật lý Nga Anh Việt</u> [Dictionary of terms in physics in Russian, English, and Vietnamese]. Hanoi: Nhã Xuất bản Khoa học, 1964. 588 p.

Includes an index of English terms. (Source: SOAS: entry as: Vietnam. Ban toán lý thuộc Ủy Ban Khoa Học Nhã Nước.)

EG3 *Vietnam (Republic). Ủy-ban Soạn-thảo Danh-từ Khoa-học. <u>Danh-từ toán-học Pháp-Việt, có phần đối chiếu Việt Pháp</u> [French-Vietnamese--Vietnamese-French glossary of mathematical terms]. Saigon: Bộ Văn-hóa Giáo-dục, 1964. 234 p. (<u>Its</u> Danh-từ khoa-học, 1) "Tủ sách Khoa-học." (Source: NIC.)

EG4 *_____. Ủy-ban Soạn-thảo Danh-từ Khoa-học. <u>Danh-từ vật-lý</u> [Glossary of physics terms (French-Vietnamese--Vietnamese-French?)] Saigon: [Bộ Quốc-gia Giáo-dục] 1962. 178 p. (<u>Its</u> Danh-từ Khoa-học, 2)

Entry inferred from others in series. This volume cited only in <u>TTAPC</u> with entry as: Saigon. Viện Đại Học. <u>Danh từ....</u>

EG5 _____. Ủy-ban Quốc-gia Soạn-thảo danh-từ chuyên-môn. Tiểu-ban Nguyên-tử-năng. <u>Ngữ-vựng nguyên-tử-năng Anh-Việt, có phần đối chiếu Việt-Anh</u> [English-Vietnamese--Vietnamese-English glossary of terms on atomic energy]. [Saigon?]: Trung-tâm học liệu, 1969. 194 p.

Defines 640 terms in English, with long explanations in Vietnamese. MH-V

EG6 *____. Bộ Giáo-Dục. Nguyên-tử-lực-cuộc.
Danh-từ nguyên-tử-năng Pháp-Việt (với bảng
đối chiếu Việt-Pháp) [Vietnamese-French/
French-Vietnamese glossary of terms in
atomic energy]. [Saigon]: Nguyên-tử-lực
cuộc, 1970. 200 p. (Source: TTQGVN,
13/14.)

PSYCHOLOGY AND PSYCHIATRY; OCCULT SCIENCES EH

Many books and articles have been written on
Vietnamese psychology and aspects of Vietnamese life
concerning the mind. In bibliographies, they are
often considered with literature, sociology, religion, philosophy, social sciences, and superstitions.
Little attempt has been made to separate them in
this Guide; the researcher should check the reference sources under as many headings as necessary to
assure a coverage of the literature. In addition to
the sources listed below, the following sources also·
contain information on these topics: Connaissance
du Việt-Nam, by Huard and Durand; Người Việt, đất
Việt, by Cửu Long Giang and Toan Ánh; Boudet 4 (under
subject headings "Sciences occultes," "Géomancie");
Thư tịch hồi-tố quốc-gia Việt-Nam, retrospective national bibliography of Vietnam; Thư-tịch quốc-gia
Việt-Nam, national bibliography of Vietnam; and the
indexes for Bulletin de l'Ecole française d'Extrême-
Orient and Bulletin de la Société des Etudes indochinoises.

EH1 Durand, Maurice. Technique et panthéon des
médiums vietnamiens (đồng). Paris: Ecole
française d'Extrême-Orient, 1959. 333 p.
(Publications de l'Ecole française d'Extrême-Orient, 45)
Pp. 1-66, description of Vietnamese
mediums, their rituals, historical observations, and position as survivors of pre-
Buddhist cults and ancient chamanism.
Pp. 69-217, photographs of séances;
pp. 221-327, text in quốc-ngữ and nôm of

24 hymns which are chanted during séances.
Examples are from the delta area in North
Vietnam.
MH

EH2 *Huyền Mặc Đạo Nhân. Tướng mạng mộng bốc; yếu
pháp lập thành [Physiognomy, fate, dreams
and divination, essential rules]. Saigon:
Tin Đức Thư-Xã, [1958]. 296 p. (Source:
NIC.)

EH3 *Nguyễn Phát Lộc. Tử vi hàm số [Mathematical
functions in astrology]. [Saigon]: Khoa
Học Nhân Văn, [1972]. 468 p. (Tủ sách
khoa học nhân văn) (Source: NIC.)
Also by the same author: Tử vi tổng
hợp [synthesis of astrology]. (unverified).

ENGINEERING EI

EI1 Lower Mekong hydrologic yearbook. Bangkok:
Committee for Co-ordination of Investigations of the Lower Mekong Basin, 1962- .
Yearbook under review, 1970, in two
vols. Vol. 1, hydrologic data; vol. 2,
meteorological data. Statistics on
stream flow, sediment sampling, daily,
annual, and monthly precipitation and rain
days, daily evaporation, daily wind movement, and seismology--no evidences of
earth movement in the Lower Mekong Basin.
MH

EI2 U.N. Economic Commission for Asia and the
Far East. Committee for Coordination of
Investigations of the Lower Mekong Basin.
Mekong Project documentation.
See CH4 and CH5 for complete descrip-
tion.

MEDICINE EJ

Vietnamese medicine consists of Vietnamese, Chinese, and Western elements. All three are included in references cited in the "Bibliography" and "Pharmacology" sections, while the Western influences are evident mostly in publications in the "Public health" section.

BIBLIOGRAPHIES

MAJOR SOURCES

EJ1   Cordier, Henri. _Bibliotheca indosinica_.
          See AA22 for complete description. For publications on medical sciences, see 3: 2151-2196 and 4: 2947-2956, "Sciences médicales."

EJ2   Boudet, Paul, and Rémy Bourgeois. _Bibliographie de l'Indochine française_.
          See AA21 for complete description. For publications on medical sciences, see "Médecine," "Pathologie," "Médicaments," the names of related topics mentioned under those headings, and the names of diseases, in each volume, as well as subheading "Médecine" under "Annam," "Cochinchine," and "Tonkin," in vols. 2-4. Volume 4 also has additional sections titled "Médecine sino-annamite," and "Pharmacopée sino-annamite."
          MH

EJ3   Dương Bá Bành. "Bibliographie européenne concernant l'ancienne médecine vietnamienne." _L'Extrême-Orient médicale; Viễn-Đông Y-Học Tạp-Chí_, 2, no. 3 (Jan.-Juin 1950), 39-53.
          Bibliography in Western languages (mostly French and English) of about 300 books and articles, of which about 200 are specifically on Vietnamese medicine. Largest single section is on materia medica (about 50 citations).
          MH-HS

EJ4   Durand, Maurice. "Médecine sino-viêtnamienne; bibliographie." _BEFEO_, 49 (1959), 671-674.
          Bibliographic essay listing about 35 manuals and dictionaries in Chinese or quốc-ngữ dating back to third century B.C. Bibliographic details are not always given.
          MH

EJ5   Huard, Pierre, and Maurice Durand. "Lãn-Ông et la médecine sino-vietnamienne." _BSEI_, n.s. 28 (1953), 221-294.
          A summary of the medical encyclopedia of Lê Hữu Chẩn (also known as Lê Hữu Trác and Lê Hữu Huân, pseud. Hai Thượng Lãn Ông, b. 1720), the "greatest medical doctor of Vietnam," and of Sino-Vietnamese medicine. Includes bibliography of 234 publications in quốc-ngữ, Chinese, and European languages.
          The medical encyclopedia of Lãn Ông is described at greater length in Huard and Durand's "Un traité de médecine sino-vietnamienne du XVIIIᵉ siècle: La compréhension intuitive des recettes médicales de Hai Thượng," _Revue d'Histoire des Sciences_, 9 (1956), 126-149, which includes references to portions of the encyclopedia which have been translated into French at the Faculté de Médecine in Hanoi.
          MH

EJ6   *Nguyễn Đức Nguyên. _Bibliographie des thèses de médecine_. Saigon: Bibliothèque de Médecine de l'Université de Saigon, 1972. 409 p.
          Reviewed by P. Huard in _BEFEO_, 62 (1975), 530-531: Chronological listing by author and subject of 1,645 Doctor of Medicine theses at the University of Hanoi (1935-1954) and the University of Saigon (1947-1970). Supplementary list by subject headings according to _Index medicus_, with indexes in alphabetical arrange-

ment by subject and author. Pp. 326-345,
other documentation such as medical vocabularies, translations into Vietnamese, and
bi-lingual or tri-lingual works. Successor
to bibliographies by Noyer in 1943 and
Nguyễn Hữu and Vũ Văn Nguyên in 1964 (see
below) and by Hoang Hai Nam in 1969 (unverified). "An excellent instrument de
travail for all who are interested in Vietnamese medicine and its scientific and social realization."

EJ7 Nguyễn Hữu, and Vũ Văn Nguyên. Bulletin ana-
lytique des travaux scientifiques publiés
au Viet-Nam, 1942-1962. Vol. 1, sec. 1,
Médecine et sciences affiliées. Saigon:
Service de Documentation, [1964]. 160 p.
At head of title: République du Vietnam.
Centre National de la Recherche Scienti-
fique.

Bibliography of 1,494 articles and dissertations published in Indochina until
1954 and in RVN until 1963. Subjects include anatomy and physical anthropology,
illnesses, chemistry and medicines, techniques and equipment, public health and
environment, and biographies. Omits
pharmacology. Brief annotations. Author
index.
MBCo

EJ8 Nguyễn Trần Huân. Review of Danh-từ y dược
Pháp-Việt, vol. 1 Médecine [French-Viet-
namese medical dictionary]. (Hanoi: Editions médicales, 1963, 915 p.), and Dược-
tính chỉ nam [Treatise on pharmacopoeia]
by Nguyễn Văn Minh (Saigon: Việt-Nam Kỳ-
Lão Ái-Hữu, 1964-1967, 2 vols.) In BEFEO,
57 (1970), 266-273.

Bibliographic essay of major medical
and pharmacological books published in
Vietnam in Sino-Vietnamese, quốc-ngữ, and
French.
MH

EJ9 Noyer, B. Bibliographie analytique des travaux scientifiques en Indochine, 1939-
1940-1941 (sciences médicales et vétéri-
naires). Hanoi: IDEO, 1943. 48 p. At
head of title: Gouvernement général de
l'Indochine. Conseil des Recherches
Scientifiques de l'Indochine. Direction
de l'Instruction Publique.

Subject arrangement of 800 books, articles, and theses (Thèse de Doctorat en
Médecine, Hanoi) on anatomy, physical
anthropology, bacteriology, biological
chemistry, pharmacology and toxicology,
surgery, health and epidemiology, medicine, legal medicine and history of medicine, parasitology and medical entomology,
and veterinary science and zoology.
Sources used are 9 periodicals published
in Indochina and 11 published in France,
all in the French language.

Continued by Bulletin analytique des
travaux scientifiques publiés au Viet-
Nam, 1942-1962, (Saigon, 1964) (EJ7).
DLC

EJ10 Trần Hàm Tấn. "Note bibliographique sur la
pharmacopée sino-vietnamienne." Dân Việt
Nam, no. 2 (Décembre 1948), 29-36. Tr.
by Maurice Durand.

Lists 90 manuscripts or books in Chinese or nôm in the EFEO library. Some
entries are annotated and include the date
of publication or of writing. Titles are
in French and Chinese. Subjects include
pharmacopoeia, names of medicines, manuals
for treatment of illnesses.
MH

OTHER SOURCES

EJ11 Index medicus. Washington, D.C.: National
Library of Medicine, 1960- . (Subject
terms may be searched by computers--
MEDLARS or MEDLINE system.)

MEDICINE EJ

EJ12   U.S. National Library of Medicine. <u>Index-catalogue of the Library of the Surgeon General's Office, United States Army (Army Medical Library)</u>. Washington, D.C.: GPO, 1880-1961. 61 vols.

DICTIONARIES

EJ13   *<u>Danh-từ y dược Pháp-Việt</u> [French-Vietnamese medical dictionary]. Hanoi: Editions médicales, 1963--   . Vol. 1, <u>Médecine</u>, 1963, 915 p.

   Vol. 2 to comprise pharmacy, biochemistry, and related sciences. Distributed in France by Comité Médical du Viet-Nam en France.

   Rev. in <u>BEFEO</u>, 57 (1970), by Nguyễn Trần Huân, pp. 266-269.

EJ14   *Gouzien, Paul. <u>Manuel Franco-Tonkinois de conversation spécialement à l'usage du médecin</u>. Paris: Challamel, 1897. 174 p.

   Pp. 1-46 pages--study of the Vietnamese language in general; rest of book--medical terms in French, with translation into Vietnamese (N. T. Huân, <u>BEFEO</u>).

EJ15   *Hoàng Đình Khâu, and Nguyễn Văn Cổng. <u>Russko-v'etnamskij medicinskij slovar'</u>. Moscow: Sovetskaia enciklopedii; Hanoi: Khoa-học, 1967. 514 p. (Source: <u>Bibliography of interlingual scientific and technical dictionaries</u>, 5th ed. (Paris: UNESCO, 1969).)

EJ16   Lê Khắc Quyến. <u>Danh-từ y-học Pháp-Việt; lexique des termes médicaux français-vietnamiens</u>. Saigon: Khai-Trí, 1966. 717 p. Reprinted in 1971 by Khai-trí, 941 p.

   Definitions of French terms in medicine (medicine, pharmacology, and dentistry). Introduction explains the principles for translating words into Vietnamese, especially those which had not been previously translated.

   Work as originally completed was published (roneotyped) in 1961, revised from 1962-1966, revised again in 1969, and published in 1971.
   <u>MH-V</u> (1971); <u>NIC</u> (1966)

EJ17   Nguyễn Hữu, et al. <u>Danh-từ cơ-thể-học; Nomina anatomica; Nomenclature anatomique</u>. Saigon: Trung-tâm Quốc-gia Khao-cứu Khoa-học, 1963--   . 5 vols. published as of 1968.

   Vol. 1, <u>Cốt học và khớp học; Osteologia syndesmologia; Ostéologie arthrologie</u>, 1963, 144 p. Vol. 2, <u>Huyết quản học; Angiologia; Angéiologie</u>, 1965, 210 p. Vol. 3, <u>Cơ và hệ thần kinh ngoại biên; Musculi, systema nervosum periphericum; Muscles et système nerveux périphérique</u>, 1965, 154 p. Vol. 4, <u>Nội quan học; Splanchnologia; Splanchnologie</u>, 1965, 204 p. Vol. 5, <u>Hệ thần kinh trung ương; Systema nervosum centrale; Système nerveux central</u>, 1968, 181 p.

   Latin, French, and Vietnamese glossaries.
   <u>MBCo</u> (1, 4); <u>TTAPC</u>

EJ18   *Phạm Khắc Quang, and Lê Khắc Thiền. <u>Danh từ y học</u> [Vocabulary of medical terms]. Paris: Minh Tân, 1951. 250 p. (Source: N. T. Huân, <u>BEFEO</u>, 1970.)

EJ19   *Phạm Phan Địch; Đỗ Kinh; and Nguyễn Văn Ngọc. <u>Từ điển tế bào học--mô học--phôi thai học</u> [Dictionary of cells, tissues, and embryos]. Hanoi: Y học, 1975. 384 p. (Bộ môn Mô học và phôi thai học Trường Đại học Y Khoa Hà-Nội [Tissue and Embryology Branch of the College of Medicine of Hanoi]. (Source: <u>MLXBP</u>, 10/75.)

ANATOMY

EJ20   Huard, Pierre, and A. Bigot. "Les caractéristiques anthropobiologiques des Indochinois...."

   <u>See</u> CD5 for complete description.

PUBLIC HEALTH

EJ21 *Autret, M. and Nguyễn Văn Mẫu. "Tables ali-
      mentaires indochinoises." Revue Médicale
      Française d'Extrême-Orient, 1 (1944),
      73-78.
          "By using the technique described in the
      booklet Treatise of food analyses, by Le-
      prince and Lecoq, the authors have set up
      a list of 200 kinds of foods in Indo-China
      with their chemical composition and ener-
      getic value" (Unesco).

EJ22 "Index bibliographique des principaux travaux
      publiés sur le paludisme en Indochine."
      Archives des Instituts Pasteur d'Indochine,
      Vol. 5, no. 12 (1930), 91-110.
          Chronological listing of about 320 books
      and articles, 1864-1930. Periodicals in-
      dexed include Bulletin médical de l'Indo-
      chine, Bulletin de la Société de Patholo-
      gie Exotique, Annales d'hygiène et de mé-
      decine coloniales, and Bulletin de la So-
      ciété Médicale et Chirurgicale de l'Indo-
      chine.
          Published as part of Le paludisme en
      Indochine, pp. 3-110.
      MBCo

EJ23 "Internal medicine source book." USARV
      [United States Army, Vietnam] medical bul-
      letin, Jan.-Feb. 1969 (whole issue).
          A "concise, up to date background on
      diseases in Vietnam which are of military
      importance." Includes references.
          See also the issue of USARV medical bul-
      letin for Jan.-Feb. 1971 for a similar
      work.
      MBCo

EJ24 Lysenko, A. Ya., and O. L. Lusev. "The medi-
      cal geography of North Vietnam." Soviet
      geography: review and translation, 7
      (March 1966), 3-56. Translated from Vo-
      prosy geografii, no. 68 (1965), 14-71.

Description of physical and social conditions related to medical and sanitary
situation, with emphasis upon insect and
other parasites and their effects upon
human settlements. Maps of the geography
of diseases. Bibliography of 68 publications in Vietnamese, French, English, and
Russian.
MH

EJ25 Saigon. Viện Pasteur. Ban báo cáo về hoạt-
      động kỹ thuật; rapport annuel sur le fonc-
      tionnement technique. Saigon.
          Annual reports for 1925-1938 published
      in Archives des Instituts Pasteur d'Indo-
      chine.[1] Later years not available for
      verification.
          Thư-mục 1965 cites 1963 report (1965,
      272 p.).
      [1]MBCo

EJ26 Toumanoff, C. L'anophélisme en Extrême-
      Orient (Contribution faunistique et biolo-
      gique). Laval: Impr. Barnéoud, 1936.
      434 p. Thèse-Univ. de Paris, Docteur ès
      Sciences Naturelles.
          Systematic and geographical study of
      sub-group Rossi-ludlowi of anopheles in
      Indochina and of transmission of malaria
      in Indochina. Bibliography of 164 publi-
      cations, world-wide in scope.
      MH-Z

EJ27 *Vietnam (Republic). Bộ Y-Tế. Niên giám y-
      tế, kỷ-niệm Tết Cộng-Hòa 26.10.1958 [Viet-
      nam health yearbook, anniversary of the
      Republic, 26.10.1958]. Saigon, 1958.
      52 p. (Source: TTAPC.)

EJ28 *____. ____. Phòng Thống-Kê. Health sta-
      tistical yearbook, Vietnam. Saigon,
      1967- . (Source: EARI.)

EJ29 *____. ____. ____. Monthly bulletin of
   health statistics. Saigon. Publication
   ended in 1965. (Source: EARI.)

EJ30 *____. ____. ____. Phân-tích thống-kê
   bệnh-viện, về việc xử dụng số giường tại
   các khu trại, 1971 [Analysis of hospital
   statistics, on the use of beds in aid stations, 1971]. Saigon, 1972. 157 p.
   (Source: TTTV, VQGTK, 10/72.)

EJ31 *____. Viện Quốc-Gia Thống-Kê. Thống-kê hộ
   tịch [Vital statistics]. Saigon, 1964.
   3 vols.
      Issues for 1960 (24 p.), 1962 (25 p.),
   and 1964 (32 p.). (Source: TTHTQG.)

PHARMACOLOGY

SEE ALSO EC BIOLOGY--BOTANY--SPECIAL TOPICS

EJ32 *Dumoutier, Gustave. Essai sur la pharmacie
   annamite, détermination de 300 plantes et
   produits indigènes avec leur nom en annamite, en français, en latin et en chinois
   et l'indication de leurs qualités théra-
   peutiques d'après les pharmacopées annamites et chinoises. Hanoi: Schneider,
   1887. 54 p. (Source: Cordier.)

EJ33 *Hồ Thị Xuân-Huệ. Tự-điển dược phẩm đặc chế
   Việt-Nam và Âu-Mỹ [Dictionary of Vietnamese and western phramaceuticals]. Saigon:
   [the author], 1968. 1239 p. Also 1970 ed.
   (Source: TTQGVN, 1; NIC (1970).)

EJ34 *[Nguyễn] Linh Ba, and Vũ Nguyên Hoàng. Dược-
   phẩm đặc-chế 69, đầy đủ những thuốc hiệu
   của các nhà bào-chế Việt-Nam và ngoại-quốc
   bày bán trên thị-trường từ 1968 đến nay
   [Pharmaceutical products of 1969; various
   medicines from Vietnam or foreign countries sold since 1968]. [Saigon?]: Tiến-
   Bộ, 1969. 440 p. (Source: NIC.)

EJ35 *Nguyễn Mạnh Bổng [pseud. Đông-y Học-sĩ].
   Bắc-Nam dược-điển; sách dạy tính dược thuốc
   Nam, thuốc Bắc sếp theo thứ-tự vần ABC
   [Catalog of Chinese and Vietnamese pharmaceutical products, arranged in alphabetical
   order]. Hanoi: Hương-sơn [1942-43?] 2 v.
   Vol. 1, A-K; vol. 2 has title: Bắc
   Nam dược điển (tửo la dược bản, thao tiêu
   tự vựng có phụ thêm các vị thuốc Nam [Cat-
   alog of Chinese and Vietnamese pharmaceutical products (with appendix with
   Vietnamese medicines)] Hanoi: Hương-Sơn,
   1943. (Source: Connaissance du Việt-Nam.)

EJ36 Nguyễn Văn Dương; Nguyễn Vĩnh Niên; and Đặng
   Vũ Biền. Danh-từ dược-học Pháp-Việt (có
   phần đối-chiếu Việt-Pháp [French-Vietnam-
   ese--Vietnamese-French pharmaceutical
   glossary. Saigon]. Bộ Giáo-Dục, Trung-
   tâm học-liệu, 1970. 556 p. (Tu-sách
   Khoa-học, Giám-đốc Lê Văn Thới)
      Glossary of terms, with explanations as
   to form of translation--literal or phonet-
   ic--in the introduction.
   MH-V

EJ37 *Nguyễn Văn Dương. Tự-điển dược-phẩm đặc-chế
   [Dictionary of pharmaceutical products].
   Saigon: Dược-sĩ đoàn Quốc-Gia, 1970.
   1382 p. (Source: TTQGVN 11-12.)

EJ38 *Nguyễn Văn Minh. Dược-tính chỉ nam [Trea-
   tise on pharmacopoeia]. Saigon:
   Việt-Nam Kỳ-lão Ái-hữu, 1964-1967. 2 v.
   (4 fasc.) Fasc. 3, 1964, 823 p.;
   fasc. 4, 1967, 1731 p. (Source: Huấn,
   BEFEO (EJ8); Thư-mục 1965, 1967 [fasc. 3
   & 4]; NIC.)

EJ39 *Nguyễn Xuân Dương [Văn Lăng, pseud.] Sách
   thuốc Việt-Nam. Tính các vị thuốc. Rev.
   et corr. par Nguyễn Văn Hữu et Phạm Dung
   Hanh. Nam-định: Impr. Nam Việt, 1932.
   264 p., in 4 fasc, numbered 1, 2, C, and

D. Fasc. A, 2. éd., Hanoi, Impr. Lạc-long.

Sino-Vietnamese medicine, with alphabetical list of products. (Source: Boudet 4.)

EJ40 *Nordemann, Edmond. Manuel versifié de médecine annamite, suivi d'une formulaire d'indications techniques et d'une liste de 245 substances pharmaceutiques. Paris: Challamel, 1897. (Source: Lorenz.)

EJ41 Perrot, Emile, and Paul Hurrier. Matière médicale et pharmacopée sino-annamites. Paris: Vigot Frères, 1907. 292 p.

Pp. 1-50, history of medicine in China and Vietnam, kinds of treatment; pp. 51-57, drugs common to Vietnamese and to European pharmacopoeia. Pp. 57-199, methodical and scientific inventory of a thousand odd drugs, with names in Latin, Chinese characters, Vietnamese, and romanized Chinese. Indexes by names in Latin, romanized Chinese, Vietnamese, Japanese, and Cambodian. Vietnamese words do not always include diacritical markings.

MH-EB

EJ42 Sallet, Albert. L'officine sino-annamite en Annam. Paris: Impr. Nationale, Editions G. Van Oest, 1931. Vol. 1, La médecine annamite et la préparation des remèdes. 153 p. At head of title, Exposition Coloniale Internationale, Paris, 1931, Indochine française, Section des Sciences. (No other volumes recorded.)

Discusses methods of preparation and apparatus used to prepare medicines from plants. Compares thuốc Bắc ("northern medicine"--prepared from dried or preserved plants) and thuốc Nam ("southern medicine"--medicinal plants gathered locally and used without preserving), discusses reciprocity of medicines and human reactions, and provides information about the origin of medicine and exotic remedies. Illustrations include photographs of Vietnamese pharmacies and drawings of apparatus.

MH-EB

EJ43 *Trương Kế An. Tự-điển dược-phẩm đặc-chế [Dictionary of pharmaceutical products]. Saigon: Trương-Việt [1970] 480 p.

Editions titled Tự-điển dược-phẩm đặc-chế Việt Nam và nhập cang. Địa chỉ bác-sĩ và nha-sĩ tại Saigon-Cholon và các tỉnh. [Dictionary of pharmaceutical products. Addresses of doctors and dentists in Saigon-Cholon and the provinces] (Saigon: Trương-Việt, 1968, 412, 448 p., and 1968, 463 p.) cited in NIC and TTQGVN 7/8 1969. (Source: TTQGVN, 11/12, 1970.)

EJ44 *Vialard-Goudou, A. Recherches sur la composition chimique, la valeur nutritive et l'emploi des plantes alimentaires du Sud-Vietnam et de l'Asie tropicale. Thèse, Docteur ès Sciences, Toulouse, 1959. 183 p. (Source: Vidal, BEFEO, 55 (1969), 231.)

EJ45 *["Vietnamese pharmacopoeia"] Hanoi: Materia Medica Institute [1971?]. 2 vols. planned.

Vol. 1, medicines in use within modern medical science, 577 discourses on medicines and ingredients, analysis, plants, chemicals, medications and vaccines. Vol. 2, on traditional Vietnamese medical science, planned about 1974 or 1975.

Cited in JPRS, 52,057 (23 Dec. 1970), translations on North Vietnam, no. 84, p. 95; MC, 1971: 5349-25, card 9, and in "Education and science in North Vietnam," by Arthur W. Galston and Ethan Signer, Science, no. 4007 (October 22, 1971), p. 381.

EJ46 *Vũ Nguyên Hoằng. Tự điển dược phẩm đặc chế
Việt-Nam và ngoại quốc [Pharmaceutical
dictionary of Vietnamese and foreign
products]. Saigon: Khai-Trí, 1967.
1,041 p. (Source: Thư mục 1967.)

AGRICULTURE, FISHERIES, AND FORESTRY   EK

Agriculture and fishing are the two most
important economic elements in Vietnamese society,
and many general bibliographies about Vietnam contain references to publications in those topics.
The references in this chapter may be supplemented
by the bibliographies in chapters AA Bibliography,
AF Periodicals, and most of the chapters in part C
The Social Sciences. Sources from statistics on
agriculture, fishing, and forestry are cited in this
chapter and in chapter CG Statistics.

AGRICULTURE

BIBLIOGRAPHIES

EK1   Cordier, Henri. Bibliotheca indosinica.
See AA23 for complete description. For
publications on agriculture, see 3:
2195-2268, and 4: 2955-2968, "Agriculture
et économie rurale."
MH

EK2   Boudet, Paul, and Rémy Bourgeois. Bibliographie de l'Indochine française.
See AA22 for complete description. For
publications on agriculture, see "Agriculture," the names of related topics mentioned under the heading "Agriculture,"
and the names of individual products in
each volume, as well as subheading "Agriculture" under "Annam," "Cochinchine," and
"Tonkin" in vols. 2-4.
MH

EK3   *Nông nghiệp Việt-Nam và các nước nhiệt đới
(Thư mục biên soạn phục vụ chỉ thị 200-
CT/TƯ của Ban Bí thư trung ương Đang).
Nguyễn Ngọc Mô chu biên [Agriculture in
Vietnam and tropical countries. Catalog
prepared as a result of directive 200-
CT/TU by the Central Party Secretariat.
Editor, Nguyễn Ngọc Mô]. Hanoi: Thư
Viện Quốc Gia, 1975. 562 p. (Source:
MLXBP, 10/75.)

EK4   *Vietnam (Republic). Bộ Cải-Cách Điền-Địa và
Phát-triển Nông-Ngư-Nghiệp. Viện Khao-
Cứu. Bang tổng-kê phân-loại sách thư-
viện, 1969; classified catalog of books
in the library. Saigon, 1970. 323 p.
(Source: Tin tức thư viện VQGTK 12/70.)

EK5   *_____. _____. Institut de Recherches Agronomiques. Liste des publications (1969).
Saigon, 1969.
Cited in Bibliography, documentation,
terminology (UNESCO), July 1971).

EK6   Vietnam agriculture, a selected annotated
bibliography. Prepared by U.S. Engineer
Agency for Resources Inventories in cooperation with Vietnam Research and Evaluation Information Center, Bureau for Vietnam, Agency for International Development.
Washington, D.C., 1970. 58 p.
Subject listing of over 200 books and
periodicals about RVN, including government publications. Duplicates most of the
entries in Vietnam subject index catalog
about agriculture and related subjects--
agricultural economics, rural sociology,
credit, human nutrition, land reform, foreign aid, fisheries, and forestry. Descriptive annotations.
MH

DICTIONARIES

EK7 *Tổ Tự điển Khoa học và Kỹ thuật. Tự điển
Nga-Việt nông-nghiệp [Russian-to-Vietnam-
ese dictionary of agriculture]. Hanoi:
Khoa học, 1970. 771 p.

Prepared by the Scientific and Techno-
logical Dictionary Group. (Source: Châu.)

OTHER TOPICS

EK8 "Agricultural production in North Vietnam during the last 15 years." JPRS, 8980,
Sept. 29, 1961. MC, 1961: 19625. 51 p.

Text and statistics, including on
pp. 32-39, statistical summaries of agricultural production for 1939, 1957, and
annually to 1960.
MH

EK9 Nuttonson, Michael Y. The physical environment and agriculture of Vietnam, Laos, and
Cambodia; a study based on field survey
data and on pertinent records, material,
and reports. Washington, D.C.: American
Institute of Crop Ecology, 1963. 137 p.

Summary of the results of investigations
made from 1955-1958. Includes geology,
climate, crops, land use, fishing, and
forestry. Pp. 29-85 discuss rice--culti-
vation, harvest, production statistics of
different varieties, and in various regions up to 1937. Pp. 117-122, changes in
agriculture in Vietnam after 1946.
Pp. 123-137, bibliography of about 225
citations of books, articles, and government publications in English and French.
MH

EK10 Vietnam (Republic). Bộ Cải-cách Điền-địa và
Phát-triển Nông-Ngư-Nghiệp.
Five-year rural economic development
plan (agriculture, fisheries, forestry,
and animal husbandry) 1971-1975. Saigon,
1970. 26 v.: 4 v. un-numbered; 11 v. num-

bered Project 1/CN-11/CN; 11 v. numbered
Project 1/YT-11/YT. Edition also in Vietnamese, unavailable for annotation: Kế-
hoạch 5 năm phát-triển kinh-tế nông-ngư-
nghiệp (nông, lâm, ngư, súc).

Outline and specifications of the plan,
with statistics on production in all areas
of rural economy for past years up to 1969
as well as estimates of future production.
MH; TTTV, VQGTK, 8/71

EK11 ____. ____. Kế-hoạch thi hành cho kế-
hoạch 5 năm phát triển kinh-tế nông-thôn
(Nông, Ngư, Lâm, Súc) 1971-1975 [Plan of
action for the 5-year development plan for
rural economy (agriculture, fisheries,
forestry, animal husbandry) 1971-1975].
Saigon, 1971. 2 v.
TTTV, VQGTK, 9/71

EK12 ____. Sở Thống-Kê và Kinh-Tế Nông-Nghiệp.
Niên-giám thống-kê nông-nghiệp; agricultural statistics yearbook. Saigon,
1958- .

Statistics on crop area and production,
prices, imports and exports, credit, and
land reform, detailed by province. Monthly statistics published in Nguyệt-san
thống-kê nông-nghiệp.
MH

EK13 ____. ____. Phúc trình về cuộc kiểm-tra
canh-nông tại Việt-Nam; report on the
agriculture census of Viet-Nam, 1960-1961.
[Saigon? 1962?]. 188 p. Edition in
French, Recensement de l'agriculture au
Viet-Nam (Saigon, 1961), 193 p., cited in
Thư-mục 1965, p. 38.

Statistics on area and production of
paddy and other crops, number of live-
stock and poultry as well as land use,
mechanization, irrigation, fertilizer use,
farm population and labor, and plantation
crops.
MH

AGRICULTURE, FISHERIES AND FORESTRY EK

FISHERIES

EK14   United States Consultants, Inc. <u>Marine fish-</u>
<u>eries statistics of Vietnam [1960-] 1962</u>,
comp. Z. Takagi and K. Torikai. Saigon:
USOM, Division of Agriculture and Natural
Resources, [1963?]. 42 p.

  Based on data from a census of
marine fisheries in Vietnam begun on
December 1, 1960 and from on-the-spot
surveys by K. Torikai in 1963. Contents:
Population of fishing areas, number of
fishing boats, size of fish catch.
MH

EK15   *Vietnam (Republic). Nha Ngư-Nghiệp. <u>Niên-</u>
<u>giám thống-kê ngư-nghiệp</u> [Fisheries sta-
tistics yearbook]. 1963- . Saigon,
[1966?-]. (Source: EARI.)

FORESTRY
<u>SEE ALSO</u> BOTANY EC

BIBLIOGRAPHIES

EK16   Cordier, Henri. <u>Bibliotheca indosinica.</u>
  <u>See</u> AA23 for complete description. For
publications on forestry, see 3: 2212-
2218 and 4: 2956-2959, "Forêts--Bois."
MH

EK17   Boudet, Paul, and Rémy Bourgeois. <u>Biblio-</u>
<u>graphie de l'Indochine française.</u>
  <u>See</u> AA22 for complete description. For
publications on forestry, see "Forêts" and
"Bois" in each volume as well as subheading "Forêts" under "Tonkin" in vol. 4.
See also names of species, such as "Hevea"
and the products made from them, e.g.
"Caoutchouc."
MH

EK18   *Lê Văn Ky. <u>Thư-tịch lâm học</u> [Forestry bib-
liography]. Saigon: Research Institute,
Ministry of Agriculture, 1967. 67 p.
(Reference 1-241)

Cited in Henry S. Kernan, <u>Preliminary</u>
<u>report on forestry in Vietnam.</u> (Saigon:
Joint Development Group, 1968, <u>Its</u> Working
paper no. 17)

OTHER TOPICS

EK19   *<u>Carte forestière de l'Indochine.</u> Saigon:
Institut des Recherches forestières,
1950. (Unverified.)

EK20   Chevalier, [Jean Baptiste] Auguste. "Premier
inventaire des bois et autres produits
forestiers du Tonkin." <u>BEI</u>, n.s. 21,
nos. 131-132 (1918), 497-524, 742-884;
n.s. 22, no. 137 (1919), 495-552. Also
published separately: Hanoi, Haiphong:
IDEO, 1919. 227 p.

  Discussion of the forestry situation
in Tongking, with a portion (pp. 788-884)
comprising a classified order of tree
species, including notes on the economic
uses to be made of each species. Index in
1919 issue, pp. 540-551, of scientific and
of vernacular names of trees cited on
pp. 788-884. P. 533, corrections and additions to information on pp. 785, 839,
846. Issue for 1919 includes discussion
of "secondary products"--bamboo, palms,
tannine, resins, etc. P. 552, table of
contents.
MH

EK21   Forbé, E., and F. Trojani. "Etude des principaux bois d'Indochine." <u>BEI</u>, 33,
Sér. B, pt. 8 (1930), 5-175. At head of
title, Gouvernement général de l'Indochine. Inspection générale de l'agriculture, de l'élévage et des forêts. <u>Compte-</u>
<u>rendu des travaux</u>, 1928-29: VI.

  Detailed study of 46 varieties of
trees, with information about their
growth, general characteristics, ecology,
and specific characteristics according to
the Monnin classification. Pp. 157-175,

charts of usage and geographic distribution. Préambule mentions a second fascicle, comprising an alphabetical listing of
varieties and a forestry map of Indochina,
which has not been verified by the
compiler.
MH

EK22   Forbé, E., and Ðồng Phúc Hồ. "Répertoire des
essences forestières indochinoises." BEI,
33, pt. 6B (1930), 5-147. At head of
title: Gouvernement Général de l'Indochine. Inspection générale de l'agriculture, de l'élevage et des forêts. Compte
rendu des travaux, 1928-29: V.

Lists of names of forest species, compiled in order to rectify misinformation
about vernacular names and the distribution of species of trees in Indochina
which have appeared in various publications
about the flora of Indochina. Authors sug-
gest using the commercial names of forest
products. Pp. 20-109, listing by vernacular name, with pronunciation, family,
scientific name, and commercial name most
frequently used in Indochina. Pp. 111-147,
listing by scientific name. Vernacular
terms are given in one or more of 12 languages or dialects. Column titled "Réfé-
rence scientifique" in the second listing
(by scientific name) refers to the
sources in chart on page 9 titled "Répertoire de la documentation scientifique."
MH

EK23   Lecomte, Henri. Les bois de l'Indochine,
avec un appendice sur les caractères généraux de la forêt indochinoise, par
H. Guibier. Paris: Agence économique de
l'Indochine, 1926. 305 p. (Publications
de l'Agence économique de l'Indochine, 13);
Atlas, 68 plates.

Pp. 1-250, general observations about
forests in Indochina, systematic study of
species, table of characteristics

(pp. 224-234), and economic uses.
Pp. 251-291, appendix, by H. Guibier.
Bibliography, pp. 293-298, of about 130
references, especially to FGI and to articles in BEI. Index by family, genera,
species, and alphabetical table of Vietnamese, Cambodian, or French names. Extensive descriptions of physical properties of species, including numerous
illustrations.
MH-G

EK24   Magalon, Marius. Contribution à l'étude des
palmiers de l'Indochine française. Paris:
Les Presses modernes, 1930. 247 p. Also
publ. as Thèse, Faculté des Sciences de
Montpellier, 1930.

Pp. 17-177, study, with extensive descriptions, of palms growing in Indochina.
Pp. 181-232, economic uses. Pp. 237-245,
bibliography.
MH-G

EK25   *Maurand, P. L'Indochine forestière, rapport
au VIIe Congrès international d'agriculture tropicale et subtropicale, Paris,
1937. Hanoi, 1938. 180 p.

Chapters on forest resources, exploita-
tion, and varieties. Tables on forestry
utilization, lists of vernacular names of
trees.

Variant or subsequent editions: in
BEI, 41 (1938), 801-829, 975-1061,
1350-1374; also: Hanoi: Institut des
Recherches Agricoles et Forestières de
l'Indochine, 1938, 150 p.; also: Ibid.,
1943, 252 p.
Williams

EK26   Poilane, Eugène. "Les arbres fruitiers
d'Indochine." Journal d'agriculture
tropicale et de botanique appliquée, 12
(1965), 235-252, 438-453, 527-549.

Brief, unscientific descriptions of
about 80 varieties of fruit trees and

plants, published posthumously. Bibliography of 69 publications. Scientific, French, and Vietnamese names--the latter without diacritics--are given.

Biographical sketch of Poilane (1888-1964) in Ibid., 11 (1964), 104-106, which cites him as one of the great collectors of plants of our times, having collected over 120,000 specimens which provided the basis for the specimens described in Flore générale de l'Indochine.

MH-EB

EK27   Richard, Émilien. Nomenclature des principales essences forestières de Cochinchine. Saigon: Impr. coloniale, 1898. 79 p.

Designed as a handy guide for forestry personnel and others interested in forests. Gives Vietnamese name and names in Cambodian, French, and scientific terms, as well as physical characteristics of trees.

MH-G

EK28   *Rollet, B. Etudes sur les forêts claires du Sud de l'Indochine. Saigon: Direction des Recherches Forestières, 1952. 2 vols.

Analysis of the open deciduous forest in seven distinct regions in southern Indochina. Physiognomy, floristics, dynamic statistics and economic factors. List of botanical names of plants with Vietnamese and Cambodian names (Williams).

EK29   Spire, Camille, and André Spire. Le caoutchouc en Indo-Chine, étude botanique, industrielle et commerciale. Paris: Challamel, 1906. 260 p.

Pp. 2-146, "étude morphologique et histologique des plantes à caoutchouc." Includes 35 drawings of rubber plants. Remainder of book is geographical and economic information about growing and marketing of rubber.

MH-EB

EK30   *Thái Văn Trung. "Classification écosystématique de la végétation forestière du Viet-Nam." Beiträge zur Tropischen und Subtropischen Landwirtschaft und Tropenveterinarmedizin, 5 (1968), 277-292.

Classification of the forest vegetation in Vietnam, types of vegetation differing in physiognomy, structure, and composition in their ecologic conditions. Provisional map of vegetation (Biological abstracts 1969: 531).

EK31   Williams, Llewelyn. Vegetation of Southeast Asia; studies of forest types: 1963-1965. (CR 49-65). Washington, D.C.: Agricultural Research Service, 1965. 30 p.

Available from NTIS: AD 629 181. Not in MC.

Pp. 1-98, study of forest types--types, locations, economic importance (Vietnam, pp. 71-81); pp. 101-174, maps and photographs of forest types; pp. 175-287, "Contribution toward a bibliography of Southeast Asia." Bibliography includes 768 titles of books and articles, with emphasis upon publications issued in Southeast Asia.

MH-EB

OTHER SOURCES

EK32   Bibliography of agriculture. New York: CCM Corporation, 1970- . Continuation of same title, published 1942-1969 by U.S. Dept. of Agriculture Library and National Agricultural Library.

EK33   International Institute of Agriculture. European Regional Office. Library. Classified catalogue. Rome: Villa Borghese, 1948. 2747 p. Supplements 1-4, 1949-1950.

EK34   International yearbook of agricultural legislation; annuaire international de législation agricole. Rome: Institut International d'Agriculture and FAO, 1911-1952.
(Not published for 1946-1951.)

EK35   International yearbook of agricultural statistics; annuaire international de statistique agricole. Rome: International Institute of Agriculture, 1912-1947[?].
Continued by the following publications
from FAO: Yearbook of food and agricultural statistics (to 1950); Trade yearbook (1951-   ); and Production yearbook
(1951-   ).

EK36   U.S. National Agricultural Library. Dictionary catalog of the National Agricultural Library, 1862-1965. New York:
Rowman and Littlefield, 1968-1969.
73 vols.

Appendix

Translations of names of Vietnamese government and non-government bodies

Nguyễn Dynasty (Nhà Nguyễn; Triều Nguyễn)

Quốc Sử Quán   Bureau of National History

Democratic Republic of Vietnam (Việt-Nam Dân-Chủ Cộng-Hòa)

Cục Thống-Kê Trung Ương	Central Office of Statistics
Đảng Lao Động Việt-Nam	Vietnam Workers' Party
Quốc Hội	National Assembly
Thư Viện Khoa Học Trung Ương	Central Science Library
Thư Viện Quốc Gia	National Library
Ủy Ban Khoa Học Nhà Nước	Government Science Committee
Ban Toán lý	Mathematics Board
Viện Ngôn Ngữ Học	Institute of Linguistics
Viện Luật Học	Institute of Law
Viện Sử Học Việt-Nam	Institute of Historical Research
Vụ Bảo Tồn Bảo Tàng	Institute for the Preservation of Museums

State of Vietnam (Quốc-Gia Việt-Nam)

Bộ Kinh-Tế Quốc-Gia	Department of National Economy
Sở Địa-Chính và Địa Hình Bắc-Việt	Cadastral and Topographic Service of North Vietnam

Republic of Vietnam (Việt-Nam Cộng-Hòa)

Ban Soạn-thảo Mục-Lục Thư-dịch	Translations Preparation Committee
Bộ Cải-Cách Điền-Địa và Phát-Triển Nông-Ngư-Nghiệp	Ministry of Land Reform and Development of Agriculture and Fisheries
Bộ Cải-Tiến Nông-Thôn	Ministry of Agricultural Development
Sở Thống-kê và Kinh-Tế Nông-Nghiệp	Agricultural Economics and Statistical Service
Bộ Canh Nông	Ministry of Agriculture
Bộ Giáo-Dục và Thanh-Niên	Ministry of Education and Youth
Ủy-Ban Quốc-Gia Soạn-thảo Danh-từ Chuyên-môn,	National Committee to Prepare Technical Terminology,
Tiểu-ban Nguyên-tử-năng	Subcommittee on Atomic Energy

Bộ Ngoại-Giao	Ministry of Foreign Affairs
Bộ Quốc-Gia Giáo-Dục	Ministry of National Education
Trung Tâm Học Liệu	Educational Materials Center
Bộ Quốc-Phòng	Ministry of National Defense
Bộ Thanh-Niên	Ministry of Youth
Bộ Thông-Tin	Ministry of Information
Nha Tổng Giám-Đốc Thông-Tin	Directorate General of Information
Trung Tâm Quốc-Gia Điện Ảnh	National Motion Picture Center
Bộ Thông-Tin Chiêu-Hồi,	Ministry of Information and Open Arms,
Nha Kế-Hoạch Tâm-Lý-Chiến	Directorate of Psychological Warfare Planning
Bộ Tổng Tham-Mưu,	General Staff,
Quân Lực Việt-Nam Cộng-Hòa,	Army of the Republic of Vietnam,
Phòng 2	Intelligence Branch
Bộ Tư-Pháp	Ministry of Justice
Bộ Y-Tế,	Ministry of Health,
Phòng Thống-Kê	Bureau of Statistics
Đại Học Viện Sài-gòn	University of Saigon
Trường Luật Khoa Đại Học	Faculty of Law
Hạ-Nghị-Viện	House of Representatives
Hải-Học-Viện Nha-Trang	Nha-Trang Oceanographic Institute
Học-Viện Quốc-Gia Hành-Chánh	National Institute of Administration
Ngân Hàng Quốc-Gia Việt-Nam	National Bank of Vietnam
Nha Địa-Dư Quốc-Gia	National Geographic Service
Nha Giám-Đốc Khí-Tượng	Weather Service
Nha Ngư Nghiệp	Directorate of Fisheries
Nha Tổng Giám-Đốc Công-Vụ	Directorate General of Civil Service
Nha Tổng Giám-Đốc Kế-Hoạch	Directorate General of Planning
Nha Tổng Giám-Đốc Khí-Tượng	Directorate General of Weather
Nha Tổng Giám-Đốc Ngân-Sách và	Directorate General of the Budget
Ngoại-Viện	and Foreign Aid
Nha Văn-Khố	Directorate of Archives
Nha Văn-Khố và Thư-Viện Quốc-Gia,	Directorate of National Archives
Phủ Quốc-Vụ-Khanh Đặc-Trách Văn-Hóa	and Libraries, Secretary of State for Culture
Quốc-Hội	National Assembly
Thượng-Nghị-Viện	Senate
Tổng Bộ Tư-Pháp	Ministry-General of Justice
Tổng Nha Quan-Thuế	Directorate General of Customs
Tổng Nha Thuế-Vụ	Directorate General of Taxation
Tổng Thư-Viện Quốc-Gia	National General Library
Tổng Thống	President
Ủy-ban Soạn-thảo Danh-từ Khoa-học	Committee for the Preparation of Scientific
	Terminology
Viện Đại Học Vạn Hạnh	Van Hanh University
Viện Khảo-Cổ	Institute of Historical Research or
	Institute of Archaeological Researches
Viện Khảo-Cứu Cao-su Việt-Nam	Vietnam Rubber Research Institute

Viện Pasteur	Pasteur Institute
Viện Quốc-Gia Thống-Kê	National Institute of Statistics
Viện Thống-Kê và Khảo-Cứu Kinh-Tế	Institute of Statistics and Economic Research
Việt-Nam Đại Học Viện	University of Vietnam

Index

This index comprises personal and corporate authors and titles when the title is the main entry or
is an historical work. It also includes names of
contributors, compilers, editors, translators, and re-
viewers, and corporate bodies when appearing at head
of title. The references in the index are to entry
numbers in the main work.

Separate sequences have been established for the
Vietnamese "D," the Vietnamese "Đ," and the Western
"D," respectively. The compiler of this Guide has
included the names of all Vietnamese authors in correct alphabetical sequence, even though he could not
always determine the correct diacritics for all other
elements of authors' names. Users of the index are
advised to bear this in mind, since citations to
Vietnamese authors in other works may lack essential
diacritics.

In the case of the major works by Cordier, Boudet and Bourgeois, and Phan Huy Chú, the multiple
references to those works have been further identi-
fied by their headings in the classification scheme
used in the Guide.

Công-thương Việt-Nam; industrial and commercial
    directory; annuaire industrielle et commerciale,
    CH20
Công-văn tập-san nam-phần Việt-Nam. See Vietnam
    (State). Công-văn tập-san Nam-Việt; bulletin
    officiel du Sud Viet Nam.
Constitutions of Asian countries, CJ33-CJ37, CJ41
Coole, Arthur Bradden, BF13
Cordier, Georges, AA43, AE58, BD13, DC3
Cordier, Henri, DE2-DE5
--Bibliotheca indosinica; dictionnaire bibliogra-
    phique des ouvrages relatifs à la péninsule
    indochinoise, AA23
    Agriculture, EK1
    Anthropology and ethnology, CD1
    Applied arts, BF1
    Archaeology, DI1
    Astronomy-Navigation, EB1
    Biography, AJ1
    Botany, EC1
    Economics, CH1
    Education, CB1
    Fine Arts, BE1
    Forestry, EK16
    Folklore and Popular Customs, CF1
    Geography, CK1
    Geology, Paleontology, and Meterology, EE1
    History, DB1
    Insects, EC79
    Language Dictionaries, AE1
    Law, CJ1
    Learned Societies, AC1
    Linguistics and Philology, BC1
    Literature, BD1
    Medicine, EJ1
    Music, BH1
    Periodicals, AF1
    Philosophy, BA1
    Political Science and Government, CI1
    Regional and Local History, DH1
    Religion, BB1
    Sociology, CC1
    Theater Arts, BG1
    Zoology, EC61
Cornell University. Libraries, AA24. See also
    Giok Po Oey. See also Ross, Marion W.
El correo sino-annamita, BB1

Courrier de Saigon, CJ72
Crayssac, M., CH32
Crevost, Charles, EC43, EC44
Croizier, Edmé Casimir de, Marquis, AA57
Cumulative bibliography of Asian studies, AA21,
    AA26
Cung Đình Thanh, CJ85
Cung oán ngâm khúc, AE9
Current digest of the Soviet press, AG19
Cương-mục. See Khâm-định Việt-sử thông-giảm cương
    mục.
Cửu Long Giang, pseud. See Nguyễn Bảo Trị.

Dã Lan, pseud. See Nguyễn Đức Thu.
Dã Lan Nguyễn Đức Dụ, pseud. See Nguyễn Đức Thu.
Danh bạ điện thoại tự động Hà-nội 1975, CK49
Danh-từ Phật-giáo (Việt-Pháp-Anh), BB10
Danh-từ y dược Pháp-Việt, EJ13
Dao Chong Tkhyong. See [Đào] Chong Tkhyong.
Diên Hương, BD8
Dương Bá Bành, EJ3
Dương Đình Khuê, BD15
Dương Hội, Louis, BF15
Dương Quang Hàm, BD14

Đại-Học-Viện Saigon. Trường Luật-Khoa Đại-Học,
    CH15, CI27, CJ21
Đại-Nam chính-biên liệt-truyện, BD30
Đại-Nam chính biên liệt truyện sơ tập, AJ8
Đại-Nam điển-lệ toát-yếu, CJ44
Đại-Nam Hoàng-Việt luật-lệ, CJ43
Đại-nam hội-điển sự-lệ, CJ44
Đại Nam liệt truyện, AJ8
Đại Nam liệt truyện chính biên nhị tập, AJ8
Đại-Nam liệt truyện tiền biên, AJ8
Đại-Nam nhất-thống-chỉ, DH9
Đại-Nam thật-lục, DA1
Đại-Nam thực-lục, DA1
Đại-Nam thực-lục chính-biên, DA1
Đại-Nam thực-lục tiền-biên, DA1
Đại Việt lịch triều đăng khoa lục, CI26
Đại Việt sử ký, AA15, DA2

Ichikawa, Kenjiro, AA94

"Index bibliographique des principaux travaux publiés
    sur le paludisme en Indochine," EJ22

Index medicus, EJ11

Index to foreign legal periodicals and collections
    of essays, CJ12

Index to legal periodicals, CJ13

Index to Readex Microprint edition of JPRS Reports
    (Joint Publications Research Service), AA86,
    CI56

Index to Survey of China mainland press, Selections
    from China mainland magazines, and Current
    background, AG21

Index to the Times of India, Bombay, AG23

India. Survey of India Department, CK33

Indicateur G. B. indochinois, DF9

Indochina

--Budget général, CH16

--Bulletin officiel de l'Indochine française, CJ67
    1889-1901, CJ75
    1902-[1950?], CJ71
    deuxième partie, Annam et Tonkin, CJ67
    première partie, Cochinchine et Cambodge, CJ71

--Journal officiel de l'Indo-Chine française, CJ76

--Rapports au Conseil de Gouvernement, CI35

--Conseil d'Etat, CJ101

--Conseil de Gouvernement, CI35, CI36

--Conseil Supérieur, CI37

--Direction de l'Agriculture, des Forêts, et du
    Commerce, EC43

--Direction des Affaires Economiques, CH13

--Direction des Affaires Politiques et de la Sûreté
    Générale, CI46, CI47

--Direction des Archives et des Bibliothèques, AA65,
    CJ63, DD9

--Direction des Douanes et Régies, CH31

--Direction des Services Economiques, CG10, CH21,
    EE25

--Direction Général des Travaux Publics. Service
    des Mines, EE13

--Gouverneur général, CI38

--Inspection générale de l'agriculture, de l'élévage
    et des forêts, EK21, EK22

--Laws, statutes, etc., CJ48-CJ51, CJ59-CJ63,
    CJ102, CJ103

(Indochina)

--Service de la Statistique Générale, CG11, CG12

--Service de Législation et d'Administration, CJ61

--Service Géographique de l'Indochine, CK9, CK20,
    CK21

--Service Géologique de l'Indochine, EE20

--Service Météorologique, EE27, EE28

Indochina (Federation)

--Journal officiel de la Fédération indochinoise,
    CJ82

--Administration des Douanes et Régies, CH31

Indochine adresses; annuaire complet de l'Indo-
    chine: officiel, commerce, industrie, planta-
    tions, mines, adresses particulières, CH22

"Indochine annamite," AA42

Industrial and commercial directory, CH20

Institut Colonial International, CB7, CJ24, CJ25

Institut d'Etude du Viet Nam contemporain, AC8,
    AF5, AJ13, DD16

Institut für Asienkunde, Hamburg, CJ123

Institut Scientifique de l'Indochine. Bibliothèque,
    EA3

"Internal medicine source book," EJ23

International bibliography of book reviews of
    scholarly literature, AA112

International bibliography of periodical literature
    covering all fields of knowledge, AF19

International biographical directory of Southeast
    Asia specialists, AJ14

International Commission for Supervision and Con-
    trol in Viet Nam, DE25

International Geological Congress, 20th, Mexico,
    1956, EE17

International index, AF23, AF26

International Institute of Agriculture. European
    Regional Office. Library, EK33

International yearbook of agricultural legislation;
    annuaire international de législation agricole,
    EK34

International yearbook of agricultural statistics;
    annuaire international de statistique agricole,
    EK35

Internationale Bibliographie der Rezensionen wis-
    senschaftlicher Literatur; international bibli-
    ography of book reviews of scholarly literature;
    bibliographie internationale des recensions de
    la littérature savante, AA112

INDEX